COMMON ERRORS IN

ENGLISH

AND HOW TO AVOID THEM

Alexander M. Witherspoon, PH.D.
ASSOCIATE PROFESSOR OF ENGLISH, YALE UNIVERSITY

BARNES & NOBLE, INC. • NEW YORK

PUBLISHERS • BOOKSELLERS • FOUNDED 1874

Preface

GOOD USAGE in speaking and writing English is a goal toward which all of us are constantly striving. Although some writers and speakers seem to have an extraordinary gift for using words correctly, for pronouncing words correctly, and for spelling words correctly, there are a great many men and women who find themselves quite uncertain as to the exact usage or exact form of a word or expression which they need at a given moment. One of the great difficulties is that the rules of good usage in English do not for the most part apply to a large number of instances; we find that there are a great many exceptions to rules. Consequently the most helpful method is to study the correct forms of individual words and expressions, and along with them such rules as do apply.

This book has therefore been organized in such a way as to make it possible for the reader to turn easily to the word or phrase concerning which he is in doubt. If the problem is one which involves the exact meaning of a word or phrase, the discussion will be found in Part I. If the question is one of correct pronunciation, Part II will give the answer. For settling a question in spelling and for acquiring a knowledge of the various aids for remembering correct spelling, the reader should turn to Part III. Since uncertainties concerning proper names often involve both pronunciation and spelling, a separate section devoted to proper names will be found in Part IV. Foreign words and expressions frequently introduced in writing and speaking English are given, with their accepted pronunciations and meanings, in Part V.

Part I, "A Guide to the Correct Meaning of Words Frequently Misused", commences with general rules and cautions for recognizing the exact meaning of words and using them correctly. In the list that follows, words and phrases which the reader is likely to want to look up are arranged in alphabetical order in bold-face type, with discussions, rules, and advice at the right immediately opposite each entry. This list occupies nearly 200 pages, and is in itself a practical handbook for ready reference.

Part II, "A Guide to the Correct Pronunciation of Words Frequently Mispronounced", starts with general advice concerning pronunciation, then presents a key to the exact sounds of vowels and consonants. The section calls attention to groups of words, with a rule applying to all the words in each group. Then there is the main list of

v

words with the exact pronunciation of each word indicated in parentheses, the sounds being shown by the key given at the beginning of
Part II.

Part III, "A Guide to the Correct Spelling of Words Frequently
Misspelled", begins with rules, cautions, and aids for spelling, and con-
tinues with special groups of words with a specific rule applying to each
group. Important groups are arranged according to the syllable which
may lead to an error in spelling. Other aids deal with the formation of
plurals, and words with hyphens. The major list, showing the correct
spelling of words frequently misspelled, is arranged in alphabetical
order, with parenthetical comments where needed.

Part IV, "A Guide to the Correct Pronunciation and Spelling of
Proper Names", consists of four important lists: Names of Persons,
Names of Places, Names from Literature, and Miscellaneous Names.
The exact pronunciation of each word is indicated in parentheses, using
the same method and key as in Part II.

Part V, "A Guide to the Pronunciation and Meaning of Familiar
Foreign Words and Phrases", lists the expressions from various foreign
languages which are quite commonly used in writing and speaking
English. The preferred pronunciation is indicated in parentheses, again
using the same method and key as in Part II.

The Table of Contents has been made very complete so that the
reader who wishes a *rule for a particular problem* may readily find the
entry dealing with his question. When the reader is not looking for a
rule, but for help concerning a *particular word or phrase,* he should
turn immediately to the important long alphabetical lists, in Part I for
usage, in Part II for pronunciation, and in Part III for spelling.

Throughout the book the rules and practices accepted by authorities
as standard English have been followed. In cases where there is no
standard practice, the author has tried to steer a middle course between
the very strict usage of some scholars and the extreme informality of
others, and has pointed out certain variations in usage and pronunciation. The book does not attempt to include every allowable form of the
words and phrases considered, but it does definitely give the reader
the authoritative and preferred form in every instance.

For assistance in the preparation of Part I, I wish to thank Mr.
Lester W. Winter, of New York City, and Dr. Robert E. Moore, Instructor in English at Yale University. For many helpful suggestions I
am indebted to my friend, Mr. Carl P. Mason.

ALEXANDER M. WITHERSPOON

Contents

vii

CONTENTS

CONTENTS

Introductory Note on Grammar
and Good Usage

GOOD USAGE in English is based on a mastery of the meaning, pronunciation, and spelling of words and phrases. The field of Grammar as such is separate from that of Good Usage, and those who take up the study of *Common Errors in English and How to Avoid Them* will be familiar with the basic rules of English grammar. However certain details of grammar, such as the definitions of the parts of speech, are necessarily referred to quite often in discussions of good usage. Consequently we shall give at this point a summary of these fundamental grammatical details.

THE PARTS OF SPEECH*

1. NOUNS.   A **noun** is a word used as the name of a person, place, or thing: *boy, city, mountain, George, Denver, Andes.* The name of any one of a class of persons, places, or things is called a **common noun,** and is spelled with a small letter. The name of a particular person, place, or thing is called a **proper noun,** and is spelled with a capital letter. When the form indicates only one of a kind, the noun is **singular** in number; if it denotes more than one, it is **plural** in number.

2. PRONOUNS.   A **pronoun** is a word used instead of a **noun.** It designates a person, place, or thing without naming it: *he, she, it, we, you, who, which, any, each, all,* etc. Pronouns, like nouns, have numbers and cases.

3. ADJECTIVES.   An **adjective** is a word used with a **noun** or **pronoun** to express a quality of the person, place, or thing named, or to limit or define in some way the **noun** or **pronoun:** THUS, *a* person, *the large* city, *many* books, you are *good.* The adjective is said to **modify** the noun or pronoun. Adjectives may be **compared** in three grades or

---

*When these parts of speech are referred to in the lists of words in this book, we have sometimes used the following abbreviations: *n.* for noun; *pron.* for pronoun; *adj.* for adjective; *v.* for verb; *adv.* for adverb; *prep.* for preposition; *conj.* for conjunction; *interj.* for interjection.

degrees: THUS, positive degree, *good;* comparative degree, *better;* superlative degree, *best*. The adjectives *a* and *an* are called **indefinite articles;** *the* is the **definite article.**

4. VERBS.   A **verb** is a word expressing action or mood of being: THUS, *do, go, talk, be, become*. The time, or **tense,** of a verb is ex‹ pressed by its form: THUS, present tense, *be* or *is;* past tense, *was;* future tense, *shall be* or *will be*. The form of the verb which simply names the action or state is called the **infinitive,** and is commonly used with *to* in English: THUS, *to go, to be, to talk*. The infinitive some- times ends in *ing,* and is then called the **gerund:** FOR EXAMPLE, the advantages of *studying* a new language.

The distinction of form in a verb to express the manner in which the action or state it denotes is conceived is called the **mood.** The form that expresses the action or state as an objective fact is said to be in the **indicative mood:** THUS, It *is* true that we won the game. The form ex- pressing the action or state as contingent or doubtful or contrary to fact is said to be in the **subjunctive mood:** THUS, If it *be* true that we won the game; if it *were* we that won the game; lest he *lose* the game, etc.

A **participle** is a word that partakes of the nature of both **verb** and **adjective.** There are two participles: (1) the **present participle,** ending in *ing,* and (2) the **past** or **passive participle,** ending usually in *ed, d, t, en* or *n,* as *informed, blamed, kept, spoken, torn*.

5. ADVERBS.   An **adverb** is a word used to qualify or modify **verbs, adjectives,** and other **adverbs:** THUS, he writes *neatly;* a *very* neat letter; a *very neatly* written letter.

6. PREPOSITIONS.   A **preposition** is a word placed before a **noun** or **pronoun** to show its position, direction, or other relation to some other word in the sentence: *at, in, on, into, up, for,* etc.

7. CONJUNCTIONS.   A **conjunction** is a word joining words or groups of words: *and, but, or, though, if, as, unless,* etc.

8. INTERJECTIONS.   An **interjection** is an exclamatory word or sound, usually without grammatical connection, expressing some emo- tion or feeling: *Oh! Alas! Hurrah!*

It is interesting to note that the same word may be at times one part of speech and at other times another. This is illustrated by the three different uses of the word *light* in the following examples: He put out the *light* (noun) ; a *light* rain (adjective) ; the airplane will *light* in the the field (verb).

PART I

A Guide to the
Correct Meaning of Words
Frequently Misused

GENERAL RULES, CAUTIONS, ADVICE, AND AIDS FOR RECOGNIZING THE EXACT MEANING OF WORDS, AND USING THEM CORRECTLY

Good speaking and good writing depend upon a knowledge of the meaning of words and the ways in which words are used. Good usage is not absolutely standardized; but we do have, as definite guides, rules based on the practice of the best writers and best speakers.

It should be borne in mind that certain usages which are not recognized as good written English are nevertheless entirely appropriate in *spoken* English. This is because speech is ordinarily less formal than writing. The term *colloquial* is applied to a large body of words and expressions which are quite acceptable in conversation, for example, "Don't bother with it", "lots of food", "hard up", "It's up to you", "I'm through with that job", and such contractions as "didn't" and "won't". These colloquialisms, however, should be avoided in *formal* speech or writing. In ordinary conversation, for example, the word "phone" is appropriate, but on more formal occasions one should use the word *telephone*. Some colloquialisms eventually become accepted even in formal writing. When you are in doubt, use the formal word or expression.

Words and expressions, which, though commonly used in certain localities and regions, differ from the standard or literary form of English, are called *dialect*. A *dialectal* or provincial form or expression is a special type of colloquialism. Dialectal forms, like other colloquial.

isms, though they add strength and vividness in conversation, should not be used in formal English.

WHEN AND WHEN NOT TO USE COLLOQUIALISMS AND SLANG

Among colloquialisms is the large group of expressions known as *slang*. Some slang is picturesque and effective and may be used to give variety and flexibility to language. Many slang expressions, however, are vulgar and slovenly, and, when resorted to, are inadequate substitutes for expressions recognized as good usage. The use of slang is more often than not the sign of a lazy mind that will not take pains to decide whether, for instance, the exact word required is *good,* or *very good,* or *beautiful,* or *satisfactory,* or *appropriate,* or *desirable,* or *excellent,* but falls back instead on the word "swell". Other words which are made to do much more than their share of work, and hence do not do it well, are "awful", "fierce", "fine", "grand", "great".

Slang should be avoided in written or formal discourse, and the indiscriminate use of slang should be guarded against on all occasions. This does not mean, however, that good usage demands formality. Some of the rules observed by formal speakers and formal writers are so rigid that they tend to exclude words, phrases, and expressions which are valuable because of their colorfulness or forcefulness.

CAUTIONS CONCERNING WORDS WHICH ARE SIMILAR IN SOME RESPECTS BUT DIFFERENT IN OTHERS

Among the most common pitfalls in English are the many groups of words which are more or less alike in form, sound, or meaning, but which have distinct differences in one or the other of these elements. Careful attention should be given to the following:

(1) *Words which are pronounced alike, but are different in spelling and meaning;* such as, **complement** and **compliment, coarse** and **course, lead** (the metal) and **led, pane** and **pain, pore** and **pour, stationary** and **stationery.**

(2) *Words which have similar pronunciation, but are different in meaning and spelling;* such as, **accept** and **except, allusion** and **illusion, council, counsel,** and **consul, ingenious** and **ingenuous, perspicuous** and **perspicacious, potion** and **portion, prescribe** and **proscribe.**

(3) *Words which come from the same root and have related meanings, but are used in different senses and connections;* such as, **credible** and **credulous, continual** and **continuous, disinterested** and **uninter-**

ested, **percent** and **percentage, observance** and **observation, specie** and **species.**

(4) *Synonyms, or words having similar meanings;* such as, **complete** and **finished, custom** and **habit, exceed** and **excel, impetuous** and **vehement, requirement** and **requisition.**

(5) *Words not directly related but confused through association with each other;* such as, **complex** and **compound, imply** and **infer, infectious** and **contagious, immunity** and **impunity, propose** and **purpose.**

Many hundreds of such troublesome pairs and groups of words are considered in this book, with definitions and explanations of their proper significance and use.

Cautions Concerning the Importance of Grammatical Relationships in Determining the Form and Choice of Words

Failure to understand or to remember the significance of certain parts of speech and of their grammatical relations to each other is a common source of error. Definitions of the various parts of speech and standard rules concerning their use will be found in the Introductory Note on Grammar and Good Usage, commencing on page xiii. The following cautions with respect to nouns, pronouns, and verbs should be noted:

Nouns. Do not use a plural noun as a singular. Remember that the commonly used words, *bacteria, data, memoranda,* and *phenomena,* are plural in meaning, and that plural verbs and the plural articles (*these, those*) should be used with them.

Certain nouns, though plural in form, are singular in meaning and should always be treated as singular. Of these some of the most common are *news, physics, measles, mumps.*

Do not, except when absolutely necessary, use one noun to modify another. Say, for example, *analysis of propaganda,* not "propaganda analysis".

Do not use nouns as verbs. Avoid such improper and barbarous constructions as "to suspicion", "to contact", "to alibi", "to suicide".

Use the possessive case of the noun when it modifies a gerund (verbal noun). thus: *We heard of the ship's sailing* (not "the ship sailing"). *John's having seen the captain was very fortunate.*

Pronouns. The reference of a pronoun must be unmistakable, else ambiguity arises. Several interpretations are possible in such a careless sentence as, "He told the grocer that since his son had interfered with his plans he would not be allowed to participate".

A pronoun should refer to a definite antecedent, and not to the general idea of a clause or phrase. For example, do not say, "The news from the office was good, which encouraged me very much". The sentence may easily be recast as follows: "The good news from the office encouraged me very much", or "The news from the office was good, and encouraged me very much".

Avoid using the pronouns *this* and *that* loosely, as in the following sentence: "He complained bitterly, and I objected to that". Say rather: "He complained bitterly, and I objected to his attitude".

Avoid the indefinite use of *you, they,* and *it. One should not smoke in a department store* is preferable to "You should not smoke", etc. Say, *There was a blizzard in Buffalo yesterday,* not "They had a blizzard", etc. *The paper says* (not "It says in the paper") *that the President will speak at 10:30.*

Do not shift from one pronoun to another when referring to the same person or thing. Avoid such a careless sentence as, "You dislike to criticize the Governor, but when one sees such careless management he can't keep quiet". In such a sentence as "One must remember in criticizing the President that he has not all the facts before him", the impression given is that it is the President who has not all the facts before him. The writer meant to say, "One must remember that one has not all the facts", or "The critic must remember that he does not have all the facts".

Such words as *each, everyone, anybody, somebody, either,* and *neither,* are singular, and should be referred to by a singular pronoun. THUS: *Each student must have his* (not "their") *pen and paper. Every one of the men had had his* (not "their") *examination by ten o'clock.*

Remember that forms of the verb *to be,* such as *is* and *are,* always require the nominative case of the pronoun in the predicate. THUS: *I am sure that it is he* (not "him"). *Perhaps it is they* (not "them"). *Let me know if that is she* (not "her").

As in the case of nouns, a pronoun modifying a gerund (verbal noun) should be in the possessive case. THUS: *We had not heard of his* (not "him") *being here. I cannot understand their* (not "them") *not wanting to hear the concert.*

Do not omit a pronoun when it is the subject of a verb. Say, *In reply we wish to say,* not "In reply would say".

VERBS. A verb must always agree in number and person with its subject. Do not allow words that come between the subject and the verb to cause you to forget which word is the subject. In the sentence, "The cause of the disputes among the various groups are easily explained", the writer has forgotten that the subject is the singular noun *cause,* not the plural noun *groups.* The verb should, of course, be *is,* not *are.* Note carefully the agreement of subject and verb in the following sentences: *The teacher, as well as the students, was taken by surprise. The chairman, together with the members of his committee, was on the platform. Each of us has his problems. Neither of the boys is to be blamed. Every man or woman must do his or her share of the work. Attached to the letter were several recommendations. There are five persons too few in the group.*

A collective noun such as *group, audience, committee, board, class, family,* takes a *singular* verb when it is thought of as a unit, and a *plural* verb when the individuals that compose the group in question are thought of. THUS: *The committee is unanimous in its approval of the proposed regulation. The committee are now scattered over several states.*

Remember that in constructions such as *one of the things which, one of the persons who, one of the questions that,* the pronoun *which, who,* or *that,* should take a *plural* verb since it refers to a *plural* noun. THUS: *This is one of the questions that are hardest to answer. He is one of those persons who are always welcome at a party.*

With certain verbs such as *appear, be, become, feel, look, remain, seem, smell, sound, taste,* an adjective should be used when the *subject* of the verb is being described; an adverb should be used when the manner of the action of the *verb* is being described. Note carefully the uses of adjectives and adverbs in the following sentences: *He felt good.* (Here the subject of the verb is described by the adjective *good.*) *He felt the surface of the table carefully.* (Here the manner of the verb *felt* is described by the adverb *carefully.*) The verbs listed above are usually followed by an adjective, since they almost always introduce a description of the *subject.* THUS: *I feel bad* (not "badly"). *The fruit smells good* (not "well"). *She looks pale* (not "palely"). *The music sounds good* (not "well").

The tendency in conversation and familiar writing to contract such verbal forms as *do not* and *does not* to *don't* and *doesn't* respectively often leads to errors. A person who would never say "he do not" or "it do not" may thoughtlessly say "he don't" or "it don't". Remember that the contraction of *does not* is *doesn't.* Do not use such contractions as *don't, doesn't, haven't, isn't* in formal composition.

A participle used to introduce a sentence or clause must modify the subject of the principal verb. Failure to remember this rule results in one of the most common errors in English composition, the dangling participle. In the carelessly written sentence, "Running down the street, the theater came into view", the participle *running* is made to modify *theater,* and the sentence becomes ridiculous. What the writer meant to say is *Running down the street, I came in sight of the theater.* Similarly, one should not write, "Encouraged by approval from every side, acceptance of the nomination seemed the natural decision", but rather, *Encouraged by approval from every side, he naturally decided upon acceptance of the nomination.*

Whenever possible, use the active voice rather than the passive voice of the verb. The active voice is much more direct, forceful, and vivid. The sentence, *We reached New York at noon,* is obviously preferable to the weak and awkward sentence, "New York was reached by us at noon". *We needed salt* is simpler and more forceful than "Salt was felt to be needed".

Do not put an adverb or an adverbial phrase between an infinitive and its sign "to". In the phrase *to behave frivolously,* the adverb *frivolously* describes the manner *how,* and the statement becomes a matter of *to behave how.* If we split the infinitive and write "to frivolously behave", the expression resolves itself into a matter of "to how behave", a construction which is ridiculous. There are certain cases in which, to avoid ambiguity, awkwardness, or artificiality of expression, the infinitive may be split, as in the sentence, *It is difficult to always tell the truth.* Similarly, the sentence, *The factory will be expected to greatly increase its output* is preferable to "The factory will be expected greatly to increase" or "The factory will be expected to increase greatly", etc. In the great majority of cases, however, the simpler, more natural, and hence proper expression is attained by keeping the infinitive and its sign together.

Do not use verbs as nouns. Avoid such improprieties as "an invite", "a remit", "good eats".

In addition to the above cautions concerning parts of speech and their effect upon the forms of words, many individual words and expressions have special problems related to the matter of parts of speech. The distinctions to be borne in mind with such individual words, when used as nouns, verbs, etc., will be mentioned in the discussion of such words in the alphabetical list of commonly misused words and phrases, which commences on page 9 and runs through page 198.

AN ALPHABETICAL LIST OF WORDS AND PHRASES FREQUENTLY MISUSED SHOWING CORRECT USAGE

a, an

The article **a** is used before a word beginning with a consonant sound, the article **an** before a word beginning with a vowel sound. Note that **a** is used before words beginning with long *u* (when pronounced as *yu*), *eu*, and *ew*, and before the word *one*. THUS: *a united country, a ukase, a usurper, a eulogy, a ewe, many a one.* The article **an** is used before a word beginning with a silent *h: an honorable man, an heiress.*

abbreviate, abridge

To **abbreviate** is *to shorten* by contraction or omission. THUS, *Tennessee* is abbreviated to *Tenn., secretary* to *sec'y.* To **abridge** is *to reduce in compass, to condense* without losing the sense of the original. One *abridges* or summarizes a report or a lecture.

ability, capacity

These words are synonymous except when they refer to intellectual power, in which case **ability** implies the presence of a *developed* power, **capacity** a potential but *undeveloped* power. In the singular, **ability** means power to *do*, **capacity** a receiving or containing power. THUS: *He has the ability to think because education developed his capacity for thinking. He has ability to work and a capacity for work which permits him to labor long hours.* (Note that we say **ability** *to*, **capacity** *for*.)

above

Above as an adjective or a noun should be avoided except in business letters where it may be used to refer to a preceding portion of the text of the letter. THUS: *the above price-list, the above statement, the above is subject to change without notice.* By more careful speakers, **before-mentioned, foregoing,** or **preceding** is preferred to *above.*

Above as a noun is crude and vague. *The above is a good idea* is best changed to *This is a good idea,* or *Your idea is good.*

absolve from, absolve of

Nowadays we say **absolve from** plus a noun expressing guilt, obligation, duty. THUS: *The client was absolved from guilt.*

accede, concede

Accede implies actual agreement; **concede** implies yielding without necessarily agreeing. You may *concede* for the sake of argument, without changing your mind. When that which is *acceded to* follows **accede,** the preposition is *to.* THUS: *He acceded to the demands. To avoid useless debate, he conceded that his opponent's premise was correct.*

accept, except

Accept means *to receive,* **except** *to omit* or *to exempt.* The spellings rather than the meanings are sometimes confused.

accept of

This expression, though found occasionally in modern style (especially in *to accept of one's hospitality*) is old-fashioned and redundant. Use *accept* plus an object. THUS: *I gratefully accept your generous offer.*

acceptance, acceptation

Acceptance means the *act of receiving* or *taking.* **Acceptation** means general acceptance of a word, a usage. THUS: *Common acceptation permits us to say "auto" and "plane".*

accident, injury

An **accident** is an *unforeseen occurrence* or a *mishap* which may or may not result in injury, since **injury** means *damage* or *hurt.* THUS: *We crashed into the wall, but fortunately this accident caused injury to no one.*

accidentally

The word is always **accidentally,** pronounced in five syllables ac-ci-den'-tal-ly. "Accidently" is never correct.

accompanied by, with

With a personal or active agent, use **accompanied by.** Use **accompanied with** when the agency is secondary. THUS: *The singer was accompanied by a flutist. The singer was accompanied with a flute.*

accord, award, grant, give

To **accord** is to grant as suitable and proper; to **award** is to give or assign after careful consideration of the merits of the case; to **grant** is merely to bestow, usually in response to a request. THUS: *The diplomat was accorded great honor. The judges awarded the prize to the best student. In answer to my letter, he granted me an interview.* Do not use **accord, award,** or **grant** loosely as synonyms of **give.**

accord with

Use this to mean *in agreement and harmony,* especially *harmony.* The expression *to be in accord with* always implies emotional and spiritual harmony.

accordance with

Use this to mean *in agreement with,* as *in accordance with your instructions, in accordance with the terms of the contract.*

acme

See **climax.**

acoustics

Acoustics as denoting the science of sound is used as a singular noun. THUS: *Acoustics is a branch of the science of physics.* As denoting the qualities of an auditorium that determine its value as to distinct hearing, **acoustics** is used as a plural. THUS: *The acoustics of this theater are excellent.*

acquiesce

Means to accept or give consent by voicing no objection. In effect it is to agree to something by not disagreeing. THUS: *He did not approve of the plan, but, in order to be coöperative, he decided to acquiesce in its adoption.* Do not use *with* after **acquiesce.**

acquit of Do not use *from* after **acquit.** SAY: *He was acquitted of the charge.*

across **Across** is the only correct form, both in pronunciation and spelling. "Acrosst" is an incorrect spelling and pronunciation.

act,
action The chief distinction to make between these words is the *time* element implied. **Act** refers to something momentary, spontaneous; **action** to something occupying a period of time and several steps. THUS: *He smothered the bomb, and by this heroic act saved the lives of his comrades. The crew was applauded for its heroic action in saving the passengers of the sinking ship.*

A.D. Since the letters *A.D.* are the initials of the Latin *Anno Domini,* meaning *in the year of our Lord,* they should be used *before,* not after, a given year: A.D. 1942. Do not say, "In the year A.D. 1942."

adapted to,
for, from Though **adapted to** and **adapted for** may be used interchangeably, this distinction should be noted: the first implies *natural suitability to a purpose,* the second a *suitability brought about by design.* THUS: *The giraffe's neck is adapted to its food-gathering needs. The steam engine is constantly being adapted for new uses.*

  Adapted from means *altered or made suitable from.* THUS: *Many of his plays were adapted from plays of unknown authorship.*

addicted to,
subject to **Addicted to** means *habituated* or *accustomed to,* and is employed in a personal and bad sense; *addicted to drugs, addicted to drink.* **Subject to** means *exposed to* or *liable to.* THUS: *This coast is subject to heavy rainstorms. He is subject to melancholic moods.*

adequate

See **sufficient.**

adherence,
adhesion,
cohesion,
coherence,
attachment

Adherence is used of persons in the sense of *giving belief and support to,* as *adherence to Christianity.* **Adhesion** is reserved in its use to describing a physical phenomenon, the sticking together of two *dissimilar* substances. *A stamp sticks to the envelope by adhesion.* **Cohesion** also describes a physical phenomenon, but describes the sticking together of *similar particles; molecules of iron are held together by cohesion.* **Coherence,** which also means literally "sticking together" is now used chiefly in a figurative sense. THUS: *His remarks were without coherence.* The verb **adhere** is used with reference to both **adherence** and **adhesion. Cohere** similarly refers to both **coherence** and **cohesion.**

Attachment is the most general term of the four. It means the *state of being attached.* Therefore it covers cases of the other three terms, each of which expresses a specific kind of attachment.

admit,
admit of

To **admit** is *to give entrance to,* or, in a figurative sense, *to grant as true.* To **admit of** is *to allow or permit.* THUS: *The ticket admits one person to the concert. The size of the auditorium will admit of not more than a hundred persons' hearing the concert.*

admit,
confess

Admit is used of less serious or intimate matters; **confess** usually implies a personal fault or misdemeanor. THUS: *He admitted that he was mistaken. He confessed that he had been guilty of hoarding supplies.*

admittance,
admission

Admittance is limited to *letting in to a particular place or locality.* **Admission** is used in several senses: *act of letting in; granting privileges in membership.* Whenever *privilege* is involved use **admission**. THUS: *No admittance was permitted to the factory. Admission to the army was denied to him. Aliens may gain admission to this country.* (A privilege is here involved.)

advantage, benefit

An **advantage** is a *condition* favorable to success; a **benefit** is a *favor conferred, a profit.* THUS: *He sought advantages which would bring him benefits. Without benefit of a college education, he nevertheless had the advantage over the young man.*

advantage of, advantage over

The first implies *use with profit;* the second, *possession of a situation which can be used with profit.* **Advantage of** is used with a verb meaning *to take;* **advantage over** is used with the verb *to have.* THUS: *He took advantage of the fall in price, and stocked his warehouse. He had a considerable advantage over his opponent because he was much heavier.*

adversary, opponent

An **adversary** is one who is *actively hostile;* an **opponent** is one who *takes the other side.* THUS: *Adversaries meet on the field of battle; opponents meet on the debating platform or in the sports arena.*

affect, effect

Though the spellings rather than the meanings are usually confused, when the confusion occurs there is no certain way of telling whether spellings or meanings have been confused. Remember that **affect** can be only a *verb* meaning *to influence* (as *to affect his future*) or *to assume* (as *to affect a British accent*) or *to soften* (as *to affect her so deeply as to move her to tears*). **Effect** may be a *verb* or a *noun.* As a verb it means *to bring about;* as a noun it means *the result of a cause.* THUS: *We effected changes in our plant: the effect was to increase production.*

**affecting,
affection,
affectation**

Affecting is used as an adjective to describe that which *affects the emotions*. **Affection** is used as a noun to mean *a feeling, emotion,* or the *state of being affected*. **Affectation** is a noun derived from one meaning of affect, *to assume*. (See **affect.**) THUS: *It was an affecting sight to see the wife parted from her husband. We have an affection for our homes. His British accent is an affectation.*

afraid

See **frightened.**

**after,
afterward,
afterwards**

After implies movement or order in *time* or *place*. Both **afterward** and **afterwards** mean *later in time, subsequently.*

**after,
out for
(seeking)**

After and **out for,** in the sense of seeking, are permissible only in *informal* usage. Say: *He sought (searched for,* or *was trying to get) a job.* It should be noted that the circumstances determine whether *formal* or *informal* usage should be employed. When in doubt, use the *formal.*

**aggravate,
exasperate,
irritate,
provoke**

Aggravate means *to make a bad situation worse; it does not mean to make angry.* **Exasperate** is a synonym of **aggravate,** but it also has a second meaning which is synonymous with **irritate** and **provoke.** The last two do mean *to annoy, to anger.* **Exasperate** implies strong and bitter annoyance; **irritate,** mild and momentary annoyance; **provoke,** vexation in response to teasing or tantalizing. THUS: *His illness was aggravated by poor nursing.* A *condition* or *circumstance* may be **aggravated,** but not a *person.*

ago

See **since.**

**agree,
concur**

Agree is a broad term implying accord with regard to something (see **accord with**); concur implies a specific agreement in opinion or action. THUS: *We agree with our allies that production must be increased. The judges concurred in the verdict.*

agree with, agree to

Use **agree with** when a *person* follows the preposition; use **agree to** when an *idea* follows the preposition. THUS: *I agree with Mr. Churchill, but I cannot agree to this plan.*

"ain't"

In spite of its wide use, "ain't" is still regarded as illiterate usage in written or spoken English. "Aren't I" is used, although ungrammatical, in informal speech. It is an unsuccessful attempt to avoid "ain't" as too vulgar and "am I not" as too stiff. Fortunately or unfortunately, neither "ain't I" nor "aren't I" is accepted as good usage.

alibi

Alibi means *in another place*. It should not be used loosely to mean *any excuse*. Properly speaking, it is the plea that when the alleged act took place the accused was elsewhere than at the alleged place.

alien, foreigner, stranger

An **alien** is a foreign-born resident who is not a citizen; a **foreigner** is one who belongs to another nation; a **stranger** is merely one who is unknown or without acquaintances in a given place.

alimentary, elementary

These words are sometimes confused in pronunciation and spelling. The first vowel of **alimentary** is the same as the *a* in *fat*. The first vowel of **elementary** is the same as the *e* in *get*.

a line

See **line**.

all

See **not**.

all,
all of

In colloquial usage **all of** is frequently used where the *of* is unnecessary. The correct usage is *all his money, all the men, all these things, all our yesterdays. He met them all* is preferable to *"he met all of them."*

all, each,
every

All is used to refer to a collective whole; **each** refers to all the separate individuals that make up the whole; **every** refers to the individuals that make up the whole, but does not consider them as separate individuals. THUS: *All the men were wealthy. Each man had a fortune. Every man wants a home.*

all ready,
already

All ready refers to *state of readiness.* **Already** means prior to some specified time. THUS: *They were all ready to go when I arrived.* Do not use the expression "already did". Say, *I have already done the work.* Note that when a participle follows **already,** the auxiliary verb *must* precede it. THUS: *The school has already announced the opening of an evening session.*

all right

Write as two words; nothing else is accepted as correct.

all-round,
all around

All-round is used to mean *versatile* or *general;* as an *all-round mechanic.*
All around (two words) has the meaning of *all over a given area.* THUS: *The soldiers were entrenched for miles all around.*

all the farther,
all the higher

Do not use such expressions as *all the farther, all the higher,* in the sense of *as far as, as high as.* Instead say, *This is as far as I can go, this is as high as I can reach.* The following sentences illustrate the correct usage: *He will go all the farther because of his training. The dinner will taste all the better for our having been delayed.*

all together,
altogether

> All together means *in concert,* as *They sang all together.* Altogether means *wholly,* as *This is altogether strange.*

all ways,
always

> All ways means *every manner possible;* always means *at all times.* THUS: *He was always* (at all times) *kind and generous. He was in all ways* (every manner possible) *kind and generous.*

allay, alley,
ally

> The spellings, not the meanings, may give difficulty. For pronunciation the three words rhyme in order with *today, valley, supply.* The plural of **alley** is *alleys;* the plural of **ally** is *allies.*

allege

> See **claim.**

alleviate,
relieve

> Alleviate means to render more tolerable and is exactly opposite in meaning to aggravate. (See **aggravate.**) Alleviate and relieve are synonyms, but the second is much broader in meaning including the easing of almost any burden, trial, imposition.

allow

> Do not use **allow** in the sense of *suppose* or *think likely,* or *to express intention,* as in the colloquial expressions, "He allowed he would pay the bill," "She allowed he was a good man." It should be used only to express *approval* or *permission,* or when referring to something *granted.* THUS: *He allows his students a good deal of freedom. The company allows money for expenses.*

allude,
elude

> Allude is *to make an indirect or passing reference to;* elude is *to escape adroitly from, evade.*

allusion,
illusion

> Allusion is the noun derived from *allude.* (See **allude.**) Illusion is the action of deceiving the eye or mind by what is unreal or

false. THUS: *He made allusions* (passing references) *to his colleagues. As we grow older we regard many of the hopes of youth as mere illusions.*

alongside (of)

Alongside means *paralled to the side,* as in *Bring the ship alongside* (parallel to a pier or another ship). **Alongside of** means *side by side with,* as in *He stood alongside of James.*

a lot

A lot is a *measure* of land or a *quantity.* It is *always* two words.

**alternate,
alternative**

An **alternate** is a *substitute or second;* an **alternative** is a *statement or offer of two things of which either may be agreed to, but not both.* THUS: *He acted as an alternate to the delegate elected. Since you give me no alternative, I shall accept.*

**although,
though,
while**

Although means *even though;* **though** means *in spite of the fact that;* **while** in this connection means *it being granted that.* The first is really a variant of the second, but it is more emphatic. THUS: *Although he was warned, he persisted in his evil ways. We lost the game, though we tried in every way to win. While I cannot call him a liar, I have not found him completely candid.*

am

See **since**.

**amateur,
novice,
tyro**

An **amateur** is one who cultivates anything as a pastime; *it is the opposite of professional.* A **novice** is a beginner. A **tyro** is also a novice, but one who is exceedingly awkward and imperfect through lack of training.

**amendment,
emendation**

An **amendment** is a removal of faults or errors in the sense of *reforming.* An **emendation** is a critical improvement by alteration of a text, especially of literary and artistic work. THUS: *Every American should know the Constitution and its amendments. The author read his manuscript, and with careful emendations brought his work to perfection.*

among,
amongst,
between

Among and **amongst** are interchangeable, but **amongst** is less usual. They are used in connection with more than two persons or things. **Between** is used in connection with two persons or things. THUS: *The fortune was equally divided among* (or *amongst*) *the five sons. The estate was divided between the two sisters.*

amount,
number

Amount applies to quantities that are measured; **number** applies to quantities that are counted. **Amount** refers to the *sum* or *aggregate;* **number** refers to *units.* 500 is a **number;** $500 is an **amount.** THUS: *A large amount of flour; a number of pounds of flour; the amount of lead in this compound; the number of grams of lead,* etc.

ancient,
aged,
antique,
antiquated,
old,
venerable

Ancient refers to times long past, as **ancient** history, or to things that have existed long, as an **ancient** custom. **Aged** is used chiefly of old persons. **Antique** is used of *things* belonging to or coming from a period long past. **Antiquated** is used in the sense of *out of date;* as, an *antiquated theory.* **Old** is the most general of these terms. It includes part of the meaning of each of the others. **Venerable** means *respected for great age.*

and (for **to**)
and (before **also,**
therefore,
consequently)

Avoid the excessive colloquial use of **and** for **to** after the verb *try.* SAY, *Try to get there on time.* **And** may be used after **come** and **go** in informal remarks like *Come and see me; go and get the book.*

Before *also, therefore, consequently* the word **and** should not be used, since *also* carries the meaning of **and,** *therefore* expresses causal relation, and *consequently* expresses causal relation. THUS: *He was tall and strong,* or, *he was tall, also strong. He is righteous; therefore he shall be rewarded. I lost my money; consequently I sought a loan.*

and or etc.

And used before **etc.** is incorrect. **Etc.** stands for the Latin words *et cetera,* literally *and other things,* but usually read *and so forth.* Never use **and** with **etc.**

and which, but which

And which or **but which** should not be used unless the coming **which**-clause has been preceded by a clause or expression of the same grammatical value as itself. THUS: *The reviewer made statements which he thought were interesting but which he knew to be false.* (Note the grammatical equivalence of the two *which*-clauses.) Avoid such constructions as "I read a new novel yesterday, and which was very interesting."

anent

Anent means *about* or *concerning.* THUS: *The lawyer said very little anent this case.* **Anent** is seldom used in ordinary speech.

angel, angle

Confusion sometimes results from a failure to note carefully where the *e* is placed in each of these words. **Angel** is a heavenly creature; **angle** a geometric figure.

angry at, with

Angry at (or *annoyed*) applies to a situation or thing. **Angry with** is used of a person. THUS: *He was angry at the confusion resulting from the carelessness of his subordinate. He was angry with his subordinate because of the latter's carelessness.*

annotation

See **notation.**

another such

The correct expression is **another such,** not "such another". THUS: *Another such misdemeanor will land him in jail.*

another than

Another should be followed by *than*, nor *from*. THUS: *He seems quite another person than what he was.*

answer, reply

Reply is somewhat more formal than answer. THUS: *The answer to the question was quickly stated. The reply to the charge was carefully thought out.*

antagonize

In the sense of *to make an opponent of*, this word is colloquial, as: *Try not to antagonize him.* In formal usage, antagonize means *to contend with; to act in opposition to.*

ante-, anti-

These are both prefixes. Ante- means *before*. Anti- means *against*. Anteroom means *a room at the entrance to another room.* Anti-fascist means *opposed to fascists.*

anticipate, expect, hope

Anticipate means to look forward to, especially in such fashion as to realize to oneself what is to come. Expect is the strongest of the three words, and implies some ground or reason in the mind for considering the event as likely to happen. Hope adds to expectation the implication of desire. THUS: *We anticipate the pleasure of a long vacation. We expect our customers to pay their debts. We hope our friends will have happy lives.*

anxious, eager

Anxious means *worried*. Eager means *keenly desirous*. THUS: *He is anxious about his son. He is eager to complete his training.*

any, at all

Do not use any in the sense of at all, as in the expression, "I didn't swim any while at the beach." SAY, *I didn't swim at all, I didn't sleep at all*, etc.

any, either

Any is properly applied only to one of *three* or more; either refers to one of *two*.

any,
every

Any means *one chosen indifferently* out of a group; every is used when *all the individuals* of a group are referred to. Do not use the two words indiscriminately. The statement, *This job is not for any person in the battery,* implies that *no* soldier in the battery is capable of doing, or will be given, the job. *This job is not for every person in the battery* implies that certain qualified men, but not just *any* men in the company, are referred to.

any day,
any place,
any time

Note that each of these expressions is spelled as two words. The same is true of *every place, no place, some place.* The adverbs *sometime* and *sometimes* are spelled as one word.

Do not use such expressions as "I don't want to go any place", "He went some place". SAY, *I don't want to go anywhere, He went somewhere.*

anywhere,
everywhere,
somewhere

Avoid the incorrect expressions, "anywheres", "everywheres", "somewheres", etc.

apparent,
evident,
manifest

Apparent means *appearing to be.* Evident means *clear to the understanding and satisfactory to the judgment.* Manifest means *clear to the senses, especially to the sight.* THUS: *His apparent anger proved to be only a joke. If we attack in the west, it is evident that the enemy must send troops to meet the attack. By his wrinkled brow, it was manifest that he was thinking deeply.*

appear,
seem

That appears which is thought of as presenting itself to view. Seem is more general. It means *to look to be* with the implication that looks are deceiving. FOR EXAMPLE: *He appears to be wealthy. He seems to be honest.* See seem.

**appraise,
assess,
evaluate**

Appraise means *to estimate the worth of,* especially by persons appointed for the purpose. **Assess** means *to make a valuation or official estimate of (property) for the purpose of taxation.* **Evaluate** means *to ascertain the value or amount of.*

appreciate

To esteem something, or to recognize its worth is to **appreciate** it. This word does *not* mean "to be grateful for". *I appreciate your gift* means that I recognize your gift as having worth. It is not necessary to add *greatly* or *fully.*

**apprehend,
comprehend**

To apprehend is to lay hold of or catch the meaning of something. **To comprehend** is to embrace or understand a thing in all its compass and extent. THUS: *I apprehend the meaning of what you say, but I cannot comprehend the principles which have guided you.*

**approach
(for petition)**

Do not use **approach** in the sense of *address, petition,* or *request,* as in the expression, "The workers approached the company for higher wages". SAY, *The workers petitioned (or requested),* etc.

**apt,
likely,
liable**

Apt suggests habitual, often *inherent,* predisposition; **likely** stresses the idea of probability, which may either arise from the nature of things, or depend upon a given contingency. But **apt** and **likely** are often interchanged. **Liable,** as properly used, implies openness or exposure to something burdensome or disadvantageous. THUS: *He is apt to be lazy. They are not likely to return after the beating we gave them. You are liable to be sued for breach of contract.*

aren't I

See "ain't".

argue, quarrel

Argue is frequently misused as a synonym for **quarrel**. To **argue** is to establish the truth of a proposition by means of logic. To **quarrel** is to dispute, to enter into hostilities. The first implies the use of reason, the second the refusal to use reason.

arise

See **rise**.

art, dost, doth, wast, etc.

These older forms are used chiefly in the Bible and in poetry. Note that the form ending in -*t* is the second person singular (*thou* **art**, *thou* **dost**, *thou* **wast**); the form ending in -*th* is the third person singular (*he* **doth**, *he* **giveth**).

artisan, artist

An **artisan** is a *handicraftsman, a mechanic*. An **artist** is a *person who practices one of the fine arts*. THUS: *The artisan built a fine model of the machine. Rembrandt was a great artist.*

as, like

As may be used to introduce a clause. **Like,** in this connection, is a preposition and may never be so used. THUS: *Do as I do. He behaved like a fool.* Never use **like** as a conjunction, as in the incorrect expression, "He talks like he does". Do not omit the word *such* in an expression like the following: *commodities, such as sugar, coffee, and tea.*

as far as, so far as

As far as expresses distance; so far as implies a limitation, as of one's knowledge. THUS: *He walked as far as the postoffice. So far as I know, he is honest.*

as good as (for practically)

As good as should be reserved for comparing the *goodness* of two things: *This is as good as that.* It is incorrect to say, *He as good as promised me* when you mean, *He practically promised me.*

**as if,
like**

Do not use **like** for **as if**. SAY, *He walked as if his leg hurt him* (not "like his leg hurt him").

**as much
(for so, this)**

Avoid the use of **as much** in the sense of sc or **this**, as in the expressions, "I thought as much", "He said as much", "He admitted as much". SAY, *I thought so, he said so, he admitted this.*

as, so

As is used in comparing persons or things of equal or approximate size or quality; **so** when the comparison is unequal. FOR EXAMPLE: *He is as tall as his brother; he is not so tall as his father.* Note also the expressions, *hardly so well, rarely so numerous, scarcely so vigorous.*

as . . . than

Avoid careless contractions like "as good if not better than". The first member of the expression should be completed before the second is begun: *as good as if not better than, as large as if not larger than.* Such expressions are, however, wordy, and the idea is better conveyed in such a statement as *This weighs approximately as much as that.*

as (for that)

Do not use **as** for **that**, as in the expressions, "not as I know of", "He did not say as he would", "I don't know as I shall see him". SAY, *not that I know of, he did not say that he would, I don't know that I shall see him.*

as to

As to should not be used to introduce words which could stand without it. Change *As to what train he will take I don't know* to *What train he will take I don't know.*

Do not use **as to** in place of the preposition *of.* Change *What do you think as to this?* to *What do you think of this?*

as to whether

As to is never needed before **whether.**

ascent, assent	Do not confuse the spelling of the two words. Ascent is the *act of rising;* assent is *concurrence with approval.*
assay, essay	Assay is *to make a trial or an experiment.* Essay is *to make an intellectual or bodily effort.* The noun assay means an *evaluation* in metallurgy; the noun essay means a *literary composition.*
assert	See claim.
assess	See appraise.
assume, perform, discharge	With respect to tasks or duties, assume means *to take on;* perform, *to do* or *fulfill;* discharge, *to do and finish successfully.* Discharge implies that, having been fulfilled, an obligation has been thrown off: *the duty was discharged; the debt was discharged.*
astonish, surprise	Astonish refers to the *state of shock* brought about by *surprise.* It is the stronger of the two terms, since one may be surprised without experiencing shock. Astonish implies inability to explain or account for that which surprises.
at	Never use at with where. SAY, *Where were you?* not "Where were you at?"
at, in	When a place is regarded as a geographical point, use at. When the interior of a place is meant, use in. THUS: *We met at the library. We met in the library* (meaning *not outside*). At or in should be used in referring to a city or village, in when referring to a state or country. THUS: *at Dayton, at* (or *in*) *Liverpool, in Ohio, in England.*
attacked	Attacked is pronounced with two syllables. Avoid the incorrect pronunciation, "at-tack-ted".

attend   See **tend**.

**audience,
  spectators**

An **audience** is an assembly that *listens;* **spectators** are people who are *watching.* THUS: *A concert is performed for an audi- ence; a baseball game is played for spec- tators.* If an assembly both *watches and listens* it is usually called an **audience.**

**aught,
  ought,
  naught**

The figure o (zero) is called **naught** or **aught. Ought** is a variant spelling of **aught,** the preferred spelling. **Naught** is a synonym of *nothing.*

The use of *had* with the verb *ought* ("had ought") is incorrect, and should be carefully avoided.

**authentic,
  authoritative,
  genuine**

Authentic should be used as the *opposite of false, fictitious, counterfeit.* **Authoritative** means proceeding from authority. **Genuine** has a meaning very close to **authentic,** and the distinction between the two is that **genuine** usually implies native quality, or descent from or correspondence to an original stock, as in *genuine piety, genuine leather.* THUS: *This is an authentic Rembrandt painting. My information is authoritative, since it comes from an expert. A genuine silk muffler is worth a high price.*

authoress

Women who are authors should be called *authors.* The only justification for using **authoress** is in finding it absolutely essential to make the gender clear where doubt would otherwise exist.

auto

Auto is an acceptable colloquialism, but in formal usage only *automobile* is correct.

**average
  (for ordinary)**

Average is a term borrowed from mathe- matics to mean "generally conforming to pre- vailing standards" as, *average man, average* *book.* In such phrases it is much better to say *ordinary man, ordinary book.* **Average** should be reserved to its precise meaning: a *medial* or *mean* quantity.

avocation, vocation

That which calls us away from our regular employment (**vocation**) is called an **avocation.** THUS, a man whose **vocation** is medicine may have fishing for his **avocation.**

award, reward

The distinction between these terms is that an **award** is the result of a considered decision, as *judges award damages;* **reward** is *recompense* or pay for good or evil done. See **accord.**

aware

See **conscious.**

awful, awfully

Do *not* use these words loosely to mean *bad* or *very.* **Awful** means *inspiring awe;* **awfully** is the adverbial form. Other uses are slang, pardonable in very informal speech, but unpardonable in formal, everyday usage. Change *awfully good* to *very good* or *exceedingly good.*

a while, awhile

A while is a period of time, usually short. THUS: *He seemed powerful, but he failed after a while.* Note that the expression **a while** is two words. *Awhile* is an adverb, used chiefly in poetry, meaning *for a time.* THUS: *"which I have loved long since, and lost awhile."*

awkward at, in

Awkward means *unhandy, bungling, blundering.* One is **awkward** at a process, **awkward** in an attribute. THUS: *He is awkward at tennis. He is awkward in his gait.*

axis *(pl.* **axes**)

Note that **axis** forms its plural by changing the *i* to *e.*

ay,
  aye

When pronounced to rhyme with *hay*, **ay** and **aye** mean *always* or *ever*. When pronounced to rhyme with *my*, both mean *yes*. Compare *forever and aye* with *aye, aye sir*.

back

Since the prefix *re-* means *back* or *again*, it is not necessary to use **back** with such words as *rebound, recede, refer, return,* etc.

Such expressions as "He will be back soon" are colloquial, and should not be used in formal English.

back of,
  in front of

Careful speakers do not use "in back" or "in back of" to mean *behind, at the back of,* or as a variant of the informal *back of.* The correct form is *behind the house* or *at the back of the house,* not "in back of the house". The expression, *in front of,* is, however, correct.

backward,
  backwards

In the adverbial use, **backward** and **backwards** are interchangeable. THUS: *He tried to walk backward or backwards.* In the adjective use, the only form is **backward. Backward,** as an adjective, means *slow in learning.* THUS: *He is a backward pupil.*

bacteria
  (*pl.*)

This is the plural form. The singular is *bacterium.*

bad,
  badly,
  ill

Bad may mean *sick* or *in pain.* In *I feel bad* or *He looks bad,* the word **bad** is an adjective modifying *I* or *He.* **Badly** is an adverb and should not be used as an adjective. It is incorrect, therefore, to say, "I feel badly", or "He looks badly". The same rule applies, of course, to **ill.**

Avoid the colloquial use of **badly** in the sense of *much* or *very much.* SAY, *He wanted very much to go to the game,* not "He wanted badly to go". SAY, *He will miss you very much* (or *greatly*) instead of "He will miss you badly".

**balance,
remainder,
rest**

Balance may not be used to mean rest or remainder. Your **balance** in a bank is so called because it *off-sets* future withdrawals. If you spend half of a thousand dollars, you have five hundred dollars as a **remainder.** If you put it in a bank and draw checks against it, it becomes a *balance against the checks you draw.* SAY, *the rest* or *the remainder* (not the "balance") *of the money,* or *the day,* etc.

**bank on,
take stock in**

These expressions when used to mean *to depend on, to put faith in,* are colloquial, and should not be employed in formal English.

**barbarous,
barbaric**

Barbarous means *uncivilized, cruel.* **Barbaric** means *barbarian or uncivilized in style or taste.* THUS: *The custom which forces the widow to throw herself into the flames is barbarous. A cultivated person may occasionally enjoy barbaric music.*

**baring,
barring,
bearing**

Note the spelling. These are, of course, the present participles of *to bare, to bar,* and *to bear.*

**be able,
can,
could**

Although the meanings are synonymous, the various forms of the verbs **be able** and **can** may not always be used interchangeably. Avoid especially the incorrect expression "might could," for *might be able.*

beat

Beat is used in many colloquial expressions which should be *recognized as colloquial.* These are: "to beat down the price" (to haggle); "to beat the Dutch" (to be surprising); "which team beat?" (won); "I'm dead beat" (very weary), etc. **Beat** may be used figuratively, but care should be taken to avoid colloquial uses in formal circumstances.

The past tense of **beat** is **beat;** the past participle is **beaten.** THUS: *In ancient times the master beat his slaves. Our football team was beaten last week.*

because

Because means *for the reason*. It is therefore unnecessary and incorrect to say "the reason is because". SAY, *The reason I was not there is that I was out of town.* Avoid also the combination "because why?"

**because,
on account**

Because may be used to introduce a clause. THUS: *I did not answer because I could not.* On account may be used only before a phrase. THUS: *We had to stay home on account of the rain.*

**because of,
due to**

Because of means *by reason of*. Due to means *owing* or *attributable to*. THUS: *Because of these things, citizenship is denied. His absence was due to illness.* See **due to**.

become

See **come to be**.

**before . . .
first**

Before includes the idea of first. First should not be used with it. THUS: *Before you can go, you must meet certain requirements.*

**begin,
commence,
inaugurate,
initiate**

Begin and commence are interchangeable. Begin is more general and less formal than commence. Inaugurate and initiate mean to begin in the sense of setting into action a considerable project, or starting off a person on the duties of office or membership. Inaugurate strongly implies formality and ceremony. It should be applied only to things of great importance and dignity, as *to inaugurate a president, to inaugurate a new fiscal policy.*

benefit (*noun*)

See **advantage**.

benefit (*verb*)

The participles are benefiting, benefited; the past tense, benefited. To benefit, meaning *to profit* should be followed by the word *by*. THUS: *He will benefit by the change.*

beside,
besides

Beside is usually a preposition, and means *by the side of.* THUS: *He sat beside his brother.* **Besides** is usually an adverb, meaning *over and above.* FOR EXAMPLE: *He found the material he wanted, and much more besides.* Occasionally **besides** may be used as a preposition (meaning *in addition to*), as in the sentence: *Besides giving us directions, he went with us.*

besought

Besought is the past tense of *beseech,* meaning *to entreat, implore.*

bestow

The preposition *on* or *upon* should follow the verb bestow. THUS: *The king bestowed wealth and honors upon his faithful knight.*

better
(for well)

Do not use **better** to mean *well,* as in the expression, "I am all better now". One who is not yet recovered from an illness may say that he is **better,** meaning better than he was at his worst. *One who has recovered* is *well.*

better part of

Better part of implies *quality* and not *quantity.* Do not confuse it with *greater part of,* as *He squandered the greater part of his wealth. The better part of the performance* would mean *the superior part,* not the greater part in length of time.

between,
among

Between refers to *two;* **among** to *more than two.* THUS: *The child stood between the door and the table. Between you and me there is a deep understanding. We could not see our friends among the three hundred persons in the room.* See **among.**

Between must not be followed by *each* or *every,* since these words are singular in meaning. Do not say, "The difference in ability between each student varies greatly". SAY, *The difference in ability among our students,*

etc. or *The difference in ability between one
student and another*, etc.

Be careful not to say "Between you and I".
The pronouns should be in the objective case;
THUS: *Between you and me.*

blame on

This is not good usage for **blame**, or **blame
for**, except when **blame** is used as a *noun*.
THUS: *Place the blame on the man who is
guilty. Blame him. Don't blame him for it.*

**born,
   borne**

The adjective is **born**, not "borned".
THUS: *Lincoln was born in Kentucky.* **Borne,**
pronounced *bōrn*, is the past participle of
bear. THUS: *Lincoln's body was borne by
train to Springfield.*

**both,
   each**

Both means *two considered together.* **Each**
means *one of two or more.* THUS: *Both of
the children succeeded, and each received a
prize.* It is obviously incorrect to say "Both
children had on a new suit". SAY, *Each child
had on a new suit.* SIMILARLY, *Each child* (not
"both children") *tried to outdo the other.*
The expression "their both" is incorrect. SAY,
Both of their parents, etc.

Avoid the expression "both alike". *Alike*
means *having resemblance to one or more.* If
two are alike, it is sufficient to say *they are
alike.* The word **both** is superfluous here.

**breath,
   breathe**

Breath is the noun, pronounced so as to
rhyme with *death.* **Breathe** is the verb, pronounced so as to rhyme with *sheathe.*

**bring,
   carry,
   fetch,
   take**

Bring implies the conveying of something
from a distant person or place to a nearer.
Carry implies *bearing from one place to another*, without necessarily referring to a person or place. **Fetch** implies a two-way trip,
that is, *to go for something and to bring it*

back. **Take** implies motion *away from* the speaker or from some other person or place. EXAMPLES: *Bring me my coat. Is that too heavy to carry? Fetch a bucket of water from the well. Take the samples with you when you go out.*

broach,
brooch

Broach is the name of certain kinds of pointed tools. As a verb, **broach** means (1) to tap a cask or other container in order to draw the liquor; (2) to introduce as a topic for conversation.

A **brooch** (identical in pronunciation with **broach**) is a breastpin or similar article of jewelry.

broadcast

The past tense and the past particle are both **broadcast.** THUS: *The station broadcast the President's speech yesterday. That program was broadcast last week.*

broke,
broken

The past tense of *break* is **broke.** The past participle is **broken.** THUS: *He broke the chair. The chair was broken.* The expression "broke", meaning *without money* is slang.

brothers,
brethren

Brothers is used of sons in a family, **brethren** of members of a fraternal organization. None that **brethren** has only two syllables.

bound

The use of **bound** for *determined* is colloquial but not objectionable.

bunch,
crowd

A **bunch** is a collection of *things of the same kind.* It is used of *inanimate objects.* A **crowd** is a number of *persons collected closely together.*

Bunch and **crowd** in the sense of *group, set, coterie,* are slang.

burglar

The noun **burglar** has no accepted verb form. "Burglarize" is colloquial. "Burgle" is used only humorously. Use *robbed, broke in, entered*. THUS: *Thieves robbed the store of valuable silks.*

burst

Burst is the past tense and past participle of the verb *to burst*. The words "bust" and "busted" are slang.

but,
   however

When reference is made to an event, these words may not be used together; use one or the other. THUS: (1) *We were prepared for the storm, but, fortunately, it did not rain.* (2) *We have lost the first round. We shall, however, win the final one.* See **however**.

but that,
   but what

But that or **but what** in expressions where only *that* is required is permissible only in informal usage. It is better and simpler to omit *but*. THUS: *We don't doubt that the truth will out* is preferable to "We don't doubt but that (or but what) the truth will out".

But that is correctly used in the sense of *except that* or *were it not that*. THUS: *He would have been severely punished but that he had previously borne a good character.*

but which

But which requires that another *which*-clause precede it. THUS: *The overcoats, which were made of fine wool, but which were poorly tailored, had to be sent to the tailor for refinishing.* Avoid such slovenly usage as "A new film, but which I didn't like, was shown last night".

by and by,
   by the bye,
   by the way

Note the *spellings*. **By and by** means *before long;* **by the bye** means *incidentally;* **by the way** (close in meaning to **by the bye**) emphasizes the idea that what follows it is a digression. THUS: *We shall see each other by and by. First you should leave here; and, by the bye, take this with you. Tell me, by the way, have you seen him lately?*

by dint of

Dint must be followed by **of.** The expression means *by force or power of.* THUS: *By dint of hard work he managed to pull through.*

byword,
pass-word,
catch-word

A **byword** is a word, a phrase, or an expression used proverbially. A **pass-word** is a secret word or phrase which must be given to gain entry to an otherwise prohibited place. A **catch-word** means a *guide-word,* since it was once used by printers at the bottom of each sheet as a guide to the correct ordering of the sheets that made up a book. It is used frequently now to mean a word or phrase repeated for effect. THUS: *Equality and justice have frequently been used as mere political catch-words.*

calculate

Calculate means *to compute,* NOT to plan, think, expect, etc.

calculated

Calculated is now acceptable in the sense of *apt, fit, likely to,* as in the expression, *a condition calculated to insure success.*

calendar,
calender,
colander

These words are not confused in meaning, but they are frequently spelled incorrectly. A **calendar** is a system of time. A **calender** is a glazing machine. A **colander** is a vessel with a perforated bottom.

Calvary,
cavalry

Be careful not to confuse the pronunciation of these two words. **Calvary** is the name of the place of the Crucifixion. **Cavalry** is a military force serving on horseback.

can,
may

Can implies ability to do. **May** implies volition or permission. THUS: *I can steal, but I may not.* See **be able.**

can but,
cannot but

The two phrases have somewhat different meanings. **Can but think** is the equivalent of *can only think;* **cannot but think** means *cannot help thinking.* The latter is the more forceful of the two. FOR EXAMPLE: *I can but think him careless, since he loses so many things. I cannot but think he is dishonest.*

canine

Canine is an *adjective, not a noun,* and should not be used for *dog.* It is used to mean dog-like, as, *canine features, canine teeth.*

cannot help

Do not use *but* after **cannot help.** Once the *but* is used, the grammar of the rest of the sentence is ruined. CORRECT: *I cannot help saying that this is bad.*

canst,
dost,
wast

These are archaic forms that go with the second person pronoun *thou.* They may not be used with other pronouns. Aside from poetic or Biblical usage, they are not employed in modern English. See **art.**

can hardly

Hardly is negative in meaning and should not be coupled with another negative, as in the expression "can't hardly". The only correct form is **can hardly.** THUS: *He can hardly walk.*

capacity

See **ability.**

caption

In the United States, **caption,** which means literally *seizure,* has, by force of custom, come to mean the heading or title of a chapter, section, or page. It is also frequently used to mean the title of a cartoon, though this use is not sanctioned by the best writers.

carry	See **bring.**
case, **instance**	Do not use **case** loosely to mean *place, person, situation,* **instance,** etc. A **case** is, properly speaking, a *happening,* an *occurrence.* It should not be used therefore, as in the following: "He is a case." "In Ohio that custom holds; in other cases it is not found." An **instance** is a **case** offered as an illustrative example. THUS: *The case of Burke's speech is a good example of the failure of logic to change circumstances.*
casket, **coffin**	By the best writers and speakers, **casket** is not used as a euphemism for **coffin.** A **casket** is a small, elegant box, used chiefly for keeping jewels.
casualty	A **casualty** is an *unfortunate occurrence, a mishap.* In the military sense, *casualties* are the losses of soldiers' services by any means, whether through death, slight wounds, disappearance, etc. Note that it is used, in this sense, in the *plural.*
catalogue, **category**	The distinction between these terms is that a **catalogue** is a list arranged according to some scheme, whereas a **category** is a *class* of things.
cause for, of	**Cause for** should be followed by the thing for which there is a cause. *He had cause for complaint, she had cause for her refusal.* **Cause of** should be followed by the thing for which there is a cause *and the cause must be stated.* THUS: *The cause of his bad behavior was the sharp criticism of the teacher,* or *The death of his mother was the cause of his deep melancholy.*
caused by	This expression should always be followed by a noun, a noun phrase, or clause. THUS:

Malaria is caused by a tropical mosquito. The accident was caused by his careless delay in closing the fire-door.

cautious,
   cautiously

Cautious is an *adjective,* **cautiously** an *adverb.* THUS: *Smith is a cautious man. He cautiously opened the door. Cross crossings cautiously.*

censor,
   censure

Do not confuse the meaning or the pronunciation of these two words. A **censor** is an examiner or official licenser. **Censure** as a noun means adverse criticism; as a verb it means to offer such criticism. FOR EXAMPLE: *The government censors of news have been censured by some newspapers.*

cent,
   penny,
   copper

Cent is the official name of the coin of lowest value in the monetary system of the United States. **Penny** and **copper** are colloquialisms. **Copper** is not in reputable use.

center in,
   center on,
   center around

Center in or **on** are correct. It is impossible to *center around* anything since *a center* is equidistant from all points on a perimeter, and is, therefore, a single point.

certainly,
   surely,
   sure

Certainly and **surely** are adverbs. They may not be replaced by the adjective, **sure.** THUS: *He was certainly* (or *surely*) *traveling at a high speed.* Avoid such expressions as "He sure was".

cession,
   session

Cession is related to *cede;* therefore it means a yielding to a demand. **Session** is an assemblage or a meeting, usually of some official body or the period of such a meeting. One speaks of the *cession of territorial rights,* or of a *court session.*

change,
   exchange

In general, one **exchanges** (not **changes**) one object for another. **Exchange for** is equivalent to *replace by*. THUS: *Mr. Marshall exchanged his old coat for a new one.* Notice that *for* not *with* is used after **exchange**. In a few common expressions, **change** is used instead of **exchange**. THUS, one **changes** a bill; two persons **change** places, or seats.

change for, change with

Change for is used with reference to *things* or *conditions*. You may *change for the better,* or *change for a crosstown trolley.* **Change with** applies to persons. FOR EXAMPLE: *I wish to change seats with him. I would not change with a king, now that I own my own house.*

character, reputation

Character means the sum total of *distinctive qualities* or *moral excellence*. **Reputation** means *generally known or supposed* distinctive qualities. Used without qualifications both words imply *excellence,* **character** implying *moral* excellence, **reputation** implying *known* or *supposed* excellence in character *or* in a particular field. THUS: *He has a reputation as a man of character.* (His generally known distinctive qualities are those of moral excellence.)

Note that when an abstract noun or its equivalent follows **reputation** the preposition **for** must be used. THUS: *He has a reputation for his skill in debate.*

characteristics

The individual distinctive qualities which make up the sum total (called **character**) are **characteristics**. This word may be applied to physical, mental, or moral qualities.

chassis

The French origin of this word has kept the singular and plural **chassis**. In the singular the pronunciation is *shăs'-ĭ*, in the plural *shăs'-ĭz*.

**cherubim,
seraphim**

The plural of *cherub* is **cherubim;** that of *seraph* is **seraphim.** The **-im** is a plural ending of Hebrew origin. Certain terms of Hebrew origin have, like these two, retained their Hebrew plurals in English: *Chasidim, Sephardim.*

**childish,
childlike**

The two words are not synonymous. **Childish** is a derogatory term, meaning *puerile, silly.* **Childlike** refers to the admirable qualities of a child, such as *innocence, trustfulness.*

chorister

A **chorister,** strictly speaking, is a choirboy or any singer in a choir, not the choirmaster.

chuck-full

Colloquial usage admits **chuck-full** for *chock-full.* It is close to slang, however, and should not be used in formal speech or writing.

**citizen,
native,
inhabitant**

See **alien.** A **citizen** is one who *holds rights* from a government in return for his implied or sworn allegiance to it. A **native** is one who was *born in* a country. *He is a native of France* is equivalent to *He was born in France. He is a native* means *He was born here.* An **inhabitant** is *one who resides in a place.* The inhabitant may be a native, or a citizen, or both, or neither.

**circumstances,
conditions**

Careful speakers say *in these* **circumstances,** *under these* **conditions.**

**claim,
allege,
assert,
maintain**

Do not use **claim** loosely to mean **allege,** or **assert,** or **maintain.** The word **claim** implies the right or title to the thing claimed. THUS: *He claimed the reward that had been offered by the police.* One does not **claim** a fact or a theory or a proposition.

To **allege** is to state or declare without proof. FOR EXAMPLE: *He alleged that the* *prisoner had committed the murder. The alleged murderer claimed the right to be tried.*

To **assert** is to declare in a positive fashion, that is, with assurance. THUS: *The man stoutly asserted his innocence.*

To **maintain** is to declare as true or capable of proof. THUS: *The President maintained* (not *claimed*) *that the government's policy was wise.*

clerk

It is improper to use **clerk** as a verb. Use instead the word or words which describe the functions of the clerk. THUS: *He is selling in a retail shop,* or *He is a sales-clerk.*

clever

Clever properly means *deft, resourceful, ingenious.* It does *not* mean to be educated, wise, attractive, pretty, etc. **Clever** is a word which careless people frequently use as if it were a verbal blanket to cover a multitude of words which they are too lazy to use. These examples may help: *She is clever at sewing and stitching. Fred is a clever man, but he is uninformed. This design is clever, but the execution is very poor.*

climax, acme, epitome

A **climax** is the high point of interest in a *continuous series* of events. **Acme** means the *highest point,* usually in the sense of perfection, and no continuity is implied. An **epitome** is that which contains the essence of something, a *summary.* THUS: *The story reached a climax when Helen married her former husband. The acme of English style is to be found in the writings of Addison. The musical work of Sor is an epitome of eighteenth-century delicacy.* (Note that **epitome** does *not* mean *acme, copy, replica, the best,* etc.)

climb down

Climb means to ascend. It is impossible to ascend down. The error arises from the fact that many remember that *climb* describes a *manner of ascending,* and forget that it *includes* direction.

close   See **conclude**.

coincidence   **Coincidence,** from *coincide,* to happen at the same time, implies the simultaneous occurrence of two or more events. It does not refer to a single event. THUS: *That the two should meet in the park was a coincidence.*

come to be   Note that the phrase is **come to be,** not "become to be". *Become* itself means **come to be.**

comely   **Comely** means handsome, and it is pronounced like the word *come* plus the suffix *-ly.*

comic,
  comical   What is intended to be funny may be described as **comic.** If something or someone is unintentionally funny, the word **comical** applies. Only in colloquial usage or dialect do these words mean *odd* or *strange.* THUS: *The clown amused the children with comic gestures. Her manner of applying cosmetics gave her face a comical appearance.*

commence   See **begin**.

commodious   See **convenient**.

common   The first meaning of **common** is *belonging to the community.* THUS: *In the middle ages common land was used for grazing cattle and sheep.*

common,
  mutual,
  reciprocal   **Common** may mean shared equally; as *our common friend.* **Mutual** means *interchanged;* as *their mutual profit.* **Reciprocal** and **mutual** are often used interchangeably. **Reciprocal**

often has, however, the meaning of *in return for something previously done.* THUS: *We made a reciprocal agreement whereby he taught me French and I taught him English. It was a reciprocal favor.*

**commonly,
frequently,
generally,
usually**

Commonly should not be loosely used to mean **frequently, generally,** or **usually.** What is **commonly** understood is understood by *all.* What is **generally** understood is understood by the *larger number.* **Frequently** means *often.* **Usually** means *customarily.*

**company
(for guest)**

Company may be used to mean a group of visitors. It does not apply to one guest.

**compare to,
compare with**

To **compare to** means, in general, to *liken to.* THUS, a prominent citizen may be **compared to** a pillar; a protecting group of airplanes may be **compared to** an umbrella; the rainfall in New Mexico cannot be **compared to** (likened to) that of Oregon.

We often compare persons or objects **to** each other when they are different in kind but have some fancied resemblance. THUS, a minister or priest is often **compared to** a shepherd; an attractive person may be **compared to** a magnet; Shakespeare **compares** a beautiful woman **to** a summer's day.

We **compare** persons or things **with** each other when they are of the same kind or nature, in order to note points of agreement or difference. THUS: The president's conduct of the present situation is often **compared with** his predecessor's conduct of a similar problem. Byron's poems are **compared with** those of Keats. The government of Cincinnati is **compared with** that of Milwaukee.

**complement,
compliment**

Complement means *that which completes;* as, *a predicate complement, the complement* *of a ship.* **Compliment** means *an expression of admiration or approval;* as, *a sincere compliment.*

**complexion,
complexioned**

Avoid "complected" when speaking of a person's complexion. SAY, *He is of dark complexion,* or *He is dark complexioned.*

comply with

Comply with means *to consent to.* THUS: *They will comply with our wishes. Comply to* is no longer used.

comprehend

See **apprehend.**

**comprehensible,
comprehensive**

Comprehensible means *understandable.* **Comprehensive** means *including a great deal.* THUS: *His anxiety is comprehensible. This comprehensive work covers the entire history of the country.*

**comprise,
compose**

Comprise means to *include.* THUS: *This encyclopedia comprises ten volumes.* **Compose** means *to form the substance of,* and implies an intimate relationship among the parts. THUS: *The human body is composed chiefly of carbon, hydrogen, and oxygen.*

**compute,
plan,
devise**

Do not confuse the meaning of the word **compute** with that of **plan** or **devise.** Compute means *to determine by calculation, to reckon.* THUS: *They computed the cost of the proposed bridge. They planned how they would build it. They devised means of defraying the cost.* Avoid the incorrect expression, "compute as to how".

concede

See **accede.**

**conclude,
close**

Conclude means *to arrive at an opinion or belief as a result of reasoning.* THUS: *Having considered your arguments, I conclude that you are right.* Do not use **conclude** for **close.** To **close** is a *physical* not a mental process.

concur   See **agree.**

concur in, with

> **Concur in** should be *followed by an action;* **concur with** should be *followed by a person.* THUS: *I concur in the decision to place the matter before the president. Professor Lang concurred with his colleague in the opinion that Bacon never wrote plays.* See **agree to, agree with.**

condign

> **Condign** means *deserved,* and does *not* mean severe. It is pronounced with a stress on the first syllable, and the word rhymes with *sign.* THUS: *For his crime the prisoner received condign punishment.*

confer on
(give to)

> **Confer** has the meaning of *granting as a possession or privilege* and is used of abstract things; as, *to confer a favor on a friend; to confer a degree on a candidate.* **Confer on,** therefore, should not be used as a simple equivalent of *give to.*

confer with
(talk with)

> **Confer with** should not be used as an equivalent of *talk with,* since **confer with** means *to exchange views with.* THUS: *The chairman conferred with the committee on the proposed budget.* Mere talk and an exchange of views are different things.

confess   See **admit.**

confide in, to

> **Confide in** means to *have faith in.* THUS: *One must be able to confide in one's friends.* **Confide to** means *to give to with a feeling of trust.* THUS: *They confided their possessions to their friends' care.*

conform to, with

> **Conform to** means *adapt one's self to.* THUS: *All the inmates of the institution conformed to a pattern.* **Conform with** means *in*

harmony with. THUS: *If you enter, your conduct must conform with our ideas.* The expressions are often interchangeable, but the
distinction here pointed out should be borne
in mind.

congenial   See **genial.**

conjecture   See **guess.**

**conscience,
conscientiousness,
conscious,
consciousness**

Conscience means one's sense of what is
right. THUS: *His conscience prevents him
from stealing.* **Conscientiousness** means *faith-
fulness,* especially to duty or principles. THUS:
*He depended on the conscientiousness of his
caretaker.*

Conscious refers to knowledge of or within
one's self. THUS: *We were relieved to see
that the injured man was still conscious.*
Consciousness is the noun derived from
conscious. THUS: *The injured man soon re-
gained consciousness.*

**conscious,
aware**

Do not confuse the two words. We are
conscious of what we perceive or feel within
ourselves; we are **aware** of what goes on
about us. One may be **conscious** of fear, but
not altogether **aware** of the dangers about
one.

consequently   See **and.**

**consider,
consider as**

Do not use *as* with **consider** when it is used
in the sense of *think.* THUS: *I consider it my
duty to tell you all the facts. I consider the
report adequate.*

Consider in the sense of *look upon* or *regard* may be followed by **as.** THUS: *I considered his action as an effort to be helpful.
The committee considered his plan as having
possibilities.*

considerable

Considerable should not be used to mean *very, difficult, much, many,* or *plentiful.* It is properly used in such expressions as *considerable time, considerable delay, a considerable expenditure,* or *sum.* Do not use it in connection with groups of persons or objects, as in "considerable books", or "considerable purchases". It is incorrect, likewise, to say "considerable money", or "considerable frost", or "considerable goods". Do not use it as a noun, in the sense of *much.* SAY, *Much* (not "considerable") *remains in spite of our losses.*

**consistently,
constantly**

Consistently means *in a manner that is not contradictory.* It should not be used loosely as a synonym of **constantly,** which means *regularly, steadily, persistently.* THUS: *If you take it upon yourself to tell others what to do, you must act consistently with your own statements. He constantly (but not always consistently) warned against over-eating.* See **continually.**

**consul,
council,
counsel**

Consul means *a representative of one country in another.* The first syllable rhymes with *John.* THUS: *When there was trouble, they sought the protection of their consul.*

Council is *an assembly which meets for deliberation.* The first syllable rhymes with *down.* THUS: *A council of his teachers considered his case.*

Counsel means *advice.* THUS: *He accepted the counsel of his elders.*

contact

To contact with the meaning of *to communicate with (a person)* is not good usage although it has wide colloquial use in business.

**contagious,
contiguous**

Note the spelling of these words. **Contagious** means *catching; as, a contagious disease.* **Contiguous** means *adjacent* or *touching; as, contiguous countries.*

**contagious,
infectious**

Contagious means *communicable by contact.* **Infectious** means *communicable by infection.* As applied to diseases: *a contagious disease* is one which may be caught by direct or indirect contact with the patient; *an infectious disease* is one which may be contracted through germs carried by the air or water.

contemplate

Contemplate means *to look forward to* and implies a serious act. For instance, one would not say that one contemplates going to the circus.

**contemptible,
contemptuous**

Contemptible means *worthy of contempt or scorn;* as, *a contemptible act.* **Contemptuous** means feeling contempt or scorn. THUS: *His stinginess is contemptible. A brave man is contemptuous of a coward.*

**contemptibly,
contemptuously**

These are the adverbial forms of **contemptible** and **contemptuous**.

**continual,
continuous,
consecutive**

Continual means *happening again and again at short intervals;* as, *continual reminders.* **Continuous** means *uninterrupted,* whether of time or space; as, *a continuous misery, continuous rain, a continuous range of mountains.* THUS: *The continual noise gave me a continuous headache.*

Since continuous means *uninterrupted,* the phrase should be *the 150th year of continuous publication,* not "the 150th continuous year". The publication is continuous, *not the year.*

Consecutive means *occurring one after the other;* as, *consecutive days of the week.*

contract (verb)

Note that the stress is on the second syllable. To **contract** implies that at least two persons have entered into an agreement, each of them undertaking certain obligations towards the other. Do not use **contract** loosely in the sense of *agree*. THUS: *I agreed* (not "contracted") *to meet him for supper.*

contrast to,
contrast with

When **contrast** is a verb, it is followed by with. THUS: *The lecturer contrasted the Arctic with the Antarctic region. The Texan dialect contrasts strangely with that of Maine.* With the noun **contrast**, either **to** or **with** may be used. THUS: *Present conditions provide a strong contrast to* (or *with*) *those of five years ago. His situation is in strong contrast to* (or *with*) *that of his brother.*

Do not use *from* with **contrast**, whether noun or verb. SAY, *This contrasts with* (not *from*) *that. This is in contrast to* or *with* (not *from*) *that.*

convenient to,
convenient for

Convenient to should be followed by a person; **convenient for** should be followed by a purpose. THUS: *This arrangement will be convenient to you. This book is convenient for reference.*

convenient,
commodious

Convenient means *suitable, appropriate.* **Commodious** means *ample, spacious.* The two words are thus not synonymous. FOR INSTANCE, a house or an automobile may be **convenient** in size or arrangement without being **commodious**.

converse

See **reverse.**

convince

See **persuade.**

copy

See **replica.**

corporeal,
corporal (adj.)

Note the difference in spelling and pronunciation. **Corporeal** means *bodily, physical,* as the opposite of *spiritual;* as, *our corporeal existence.* **Corporal** means *bodily* in the sense of *personal,* or *relating to the individual body;* as *corporal punishment,* meaning *beating, flogging,* etc.

correspond to, with

Correspond to means *to be like,* or *to be in harmony with.* THUS: *His idea corresponds to mine.* Correspond has a completely different meaning in the next case. Correspond with means *to exchange letters with.* THUS: *They corresponded with each other during their long separation.*

could

See be able.

could have

Avoid the expression "could of" for could have. In speech, the expression "could've" is permissible. It must, however, be written could have. Similar care must be taken with *may have, must have, would have,* etc.

councilor, counselor

See consul, council, counsel.

couple, pair, two

Couple refers to two things that are *united.* THUS: *A married couple, a couple of links.* Do not say "a couple of dollars", or "a couple of apples". Pair refers to two things which must be taken together to be useful. THUS: *A pair of gloves,* or *a pair of cuff-buttons.*

credible, creditable, credulous

Credible means *worthy of belief;* as, *a credible explanation.* Creditable means *worthy of receiving esteem;* as, *a creditable act.* Credulous means *believing too easily;* as, *credulous as a child.*

crowd

Crowd means *a great number of persons.* To use crowd to mean a circle of friends is at best colloquial, at worst slang. See bunch.

cunning

Cunning means *clever, crafty,* or *sly.* It is frequently used colloquially in the U. S. in describing small children. In this use, it means *attractive.*

cupfuls, teaspoonfuls

Note the formation of the plural by adding *s* to the *end* of such compounds as these.

custom	See **habit.**
'cute	An abbreviation of *acute.* Colloquially, it is often used to mean attractive. The word is overworked and should be avoided.
dairy, diary	Our eyes are likely to play tricks on us with these words. Note the spelling.
damage	**Damage,** when used to mean *the price* or *the cost of something* is slang. It is properly used only with reference to injury or harm done to a person or estate.
damp, dampen	As transitive verbs, these have about the same meaning, though as a verb, **dampen** is preferred.
dare	See **need.**
data	Remember that **data** is the plural of *datum,* hence one should say *these data are,* not "this data is".
date	**Date,** meaning *an appointment,* is colloquial. **Date,** meaning *to make an appointment,* or *the person with whom the appointment is made,* is slang.
days, nights	The use of **days** or **nights** as an adverb to mean *during the day* or *during the night* is incorrect. Do not say, "He stays there nights", or "We live there summers". *At night,* or *during the day,* or *in summer* is the correct usage.
dead, deceased	**Dead** is the general term. **Deceased** is used of persons, but not of animals. Many speakers and writers overuse **deceased** in order to avoid using **dead.** As a noun, **deceased** is used only in the singular. Do not use **deceased** as a verb.

deal

Deal means *an undefined quantity*. Used to mean *a good deal* or *a great deal* it is colloquial. Avoid the slangy use of **deal** to mean a *business transaction*.

Dear,
  My dear

Dear is now the more usual salutation in formal and informal letters. My dear is the most formal of salutations when used with a title plus a name. THUS: *My dear Dr. Thornton, My dear Mr. Clark*. Note that when *dear* is preceded by *My* it is spelled with a small *d*.

decent,
  descent,
  dissent

Decent means *suitable, proper, good.* Descent means *going down,* the opposite of *ascent.* Dissent means *disagreement,* the opposite of *assent.* Note spelling.

decided
  decisive

Decided is used of persons or things. Decisive is used especially of things. Decided, when used of things, means *unmistakable;* as, *a decided color.* Decided, when used of persons, means *showing determination.* THUS: *You seem to be a decided supporter of this candidate.*

Decisive means *bringing things to a conclusion.* THUS: *These arrangements must be decisive as we can no longer make changes.*

deduction,
  induction

Deduction is that form of reasoning which goes from general laws or principles to particular facts. THUS: *Since all human beings are mortal, and since I am a human being, I am mortal.* Induction is that form of reasoning which goes from particular facts to general truths. For instance, a scientist observes the ways of many primitive tribes and writes a book of general truths about the behavior of primitive peoples.

definite,
  definitive

Definite means *clear, explicit, having set limits.* Definitive means *decisive, final.* THUS:

A definite answer is always appreciated by a questioner. The dictionary gives definitive meanings of words.

delighted at, in, with, by

Delighted at should be followed by an abstract term or phrase. You may be *delighted at the prospect* but not *at* a dress or a coat. **Delighted in** should be followed by a term or phrase expressing *an activity;* you may say that *he delighted in acting, singing, speaking.* **Delighted with** should be followed by a term or phrase describing or naming a *material object.* You may be *delighted with a dress, a coat, a new piano.* **Delighted by** may be followed by an abstract or concrete term, but the emphasis will then be on the thing that gives the delight rather than on the state of delight.

These may best be made clear by example. THUS: *The old soldier was delighted at the news of the victory of his regiment. The musician delighted in playing his excellent instrument. "I am delighted with your progress," the teacher told his pupil. The prisoner was delighted by the news that he would be released.*

delusion, illusion

Delusion and **illusion** both involve thinking something is so when it is not. **Delusion** is stronger. It often includes the idea that someone is deliberately fooling someone else. Often, **delusion** means a wrong idea about real things. **Illusion** means strictly *a deceptive appearance,* as a mirage. THUS: *The child in the den of thieves was under the delusion that he was among kindly and honest people. The desperately sick man had an illusion of great strength and power.*

demand

When you **demand** a thing, you ask for what you believe to be your right. THUS: *As a citizen of the United States, I demand to* *know why I am being held by foreign authorities.*

demean, **debase**	**Demean,** used to mean *degrade,* is colloquial. **Debase** means *degrade.* **Demean** is synonymous with *behave.* THUS: *Demean yourself as a gentleman.*
denominate	See **nominate.**
dependent on, **independent of**	Note the prepositions. THUS: *A child is dependent on his parents. An adolescent likes to make himself independent of his parents.*
depositary, **depository**	The words are now interchangeable. The second is the commonly accepted form in the U. S.
depot, **station,** **terminal**	In the U. S., **depot** often means *a railroad station.* Properly, however, it is used of *a storehouse;* as *a freight depot.* **Terminal** means *the end of a railroad line.*
depravity, **depravation**	**Depravity** means *the state of being depraved or degenerate.* **Depravation** means *the act of making or becoming degenerate.* **Depravity** implies that which deserves strong blame or censure. **Depravation** may simply mean *becoming worse.*
deprecate, **depreciate,**	**Deprecate** means *to express disapproval of.* THUS: *His colleagues deprecated his action.* **Depreciate** means *to lower the value.* THUS: *The factory depreciated the property.*
derogatory	**Derogatory** means *disparaging, making lower in value.* THUS: *What he said was derogatory to his associates.*
desirable, **desirous**	**Desirable** is applied to that which one may well desire. **Desirous** is applied to the person who feels desire. THUS: *She was a desirable woman,* and *he was desirous of marrying her.*

desire,
want,
need

In formal speaking or writing, **desire** is often used instead of **want**. Desire implies less pressure than **want**. **Need** means to *require*. THUS: *Most men desire riches. All men need food.*

despite,
in spite of

Note that **despite** is one word, **in spite** two words. **Despite** should not be followed by *of*. THUS: *Despite his illness, he went to the theater. In spite of the weather, he went for a walk.*

detail,
detailed

Detail is a noun or verb. **Detailed** is the adjective. SAY, *a detailed description,* not "a detail description".

device,
devise,

Device is the noun. **Devise** is the verb. Compare *advice* (noun) and *advise* (verb); *prophecy* (noun) and *prophesy* (verb). [In legal terminology **devise** is also a noun signifying the act of disposing of property by a will.]

devise

See **compute**.

dice,
die

Dice (small cubes used in gaming) is the plural of **die**.

did

Avoid the use of *already* and *yet* when the auxiliary of the verb is **did**. CORRECT: *Did you finish the work?* INCORRECT: "Did you finish the work yet?" "Did you finish the work already?"

die, dye,
dying, dyeing

The present participle of **die** (to cease to live) is *dying*. The present participle of **dye** (to color) is *dyeing*.

differ from, with

Differ from points out a contrast: *this differs from that, a cap differs from a hat.* **Differ with** points out a state of disagreement in opinion: *they differ with me.*

different from,
  dissimilar to

Note that **different** should always be followed by **from,** not by *to* or *than.* FOR INSTANCE, a house may be *larger than,* or **dissimilar to,** but can only be **different from** another house.

diner

See **sleeper.**

dint

See **by dint of.**

directly
  (for **as soon as**)

It is best to reserve **directly** in this sense to colloquial usage. It should be noted that **directly** means strictly *in a direct or straight manner.*

disappointed,
  in, of

Disappointed in is followed by a thing obtained or an event that took place. THUS: *He was disappointed in his position at the bank. She was disappointed in her marriage.*

Disappointed of is followed by a thing not obtained. THUS: *The turncoat was disappointed of his reward.*

discern,
  discriminate,
  distinguish

Discern is the most general of these three terms. It usually means *to see and recognize* apart from other persons or things. (It may mean *to hear and recognize.*) THUS: *He discerned his friend's sailboat far from shore.* Of the other two terms, **distinguish** is the more general as applied to making distinctions, and has reference usually to external qualities. **Discriminate** refers to distinction influenced by intellectual or emotional judgment. THUS: *He could distinguish red from green, but he could not discriminate between bad designs and good ones.*

discharge

See **assume.**

discommode,
  incommode

Both words mean *to inconvenience,* but **incommode** is often used to mean inconvenience brought about by lack of space. THUS:

The host discommoded his guests by over-turning the coffee-cups, and incommoded them by seating twenty at the table.

**discover,
invent**

Discover means to find something that had been there all the time, but had not been found before. THUS: *The explorer discovered a lake.* Invent means to put together something new. THUS: *The Wright brothers invented the airplane.*

**discreet,
discrete**

Discreet means *judicious, not rash.* Discrete means *separate, distinct.* THUS: *The employee was discreet in his conversation with his employer. These two questions are discrete; if you have the answer to one, it will not help in finding the answer to the other.*

**disinterested,
uninterested**

Disinterested means *impartial, not seeking benefit for one's self.* Uninterested means *bored.* THUS: *I am a disinterested observer in these negotiations. I am uninterested by his speech.*

disremember

Dialect for *forget,* which is a more forceful word.

dissent from

Dissent from means *to differ in opinion or faith from.* THUS: *He dissented from the religion to which he had been born. The judge dissented from the opinion of his colleagues.*

dissimilar to

See **different from.**

**dissociate,
dissassociate**

Dissociate is the simpler and better of the two words. Dissociate means *to separate one's self from fellowship or union.* THUS: *He dissociated himself from his old club.* Dissociate also has a technical meaning in chemistry: *to divide into component parts; as, sodium chloride dissociates into sodium and chlorine ions.*

distinguish

See **discern.**

dived

Dived is the correct form of the past tense of *dive.* "Dove" is colloquial.

**divers,
  diverse**

Divers means *several, various, more than one.* Its use is limited to the plural. **Diverse** means *different in character, unlike.* (Note spelling.) THUS: *There were divers articles offered for sale in the bazaar. Their opinions were completely diverse.*

done

Done is the past participle of *to do.* It must have an auxiliary, such as *have* or *had.* THUS: *I have done the work. They have done him wrong.* (Note: He *did the work.*)

don't

Don't is the contraction of the plural form *do not.* It must be used only with a plural subject, and is not to be used as a contraction of *does not.* THUS: *They don't come here. We don't see them.*

doth

The old form of the third person singular, present tense, of *do.* It is now used only in poetry.

**doubt
  (doubtful),
  that**

Use **that** (not *whether*) with **doubt** or **doubtful,** when making mention of the exact thing doubted. THUS: *It is doubtful that* (or *I doubt that*) *he will arrive today.*

Do not use *but* with **doubt.** SAY, *I do not doubt that he is ill.* It is obvious that "but" is unnecessary in such a sentence. See **but.**

doubtless

Avoid the use of "doubtlessly". **Doubtless** is itself an adverb, and does not require the suffix *-ly.*

down (*verb*)

The use of **down** in the sense of *overthrow* is colloquial.

dozen,
dozens

Use **dozen** if a number precedes the word, otherwise **dozens**. THUS: *twelve dozen eggs, several dozens of bananas, many dozens of lemons.* Note that *of* is always used after **dozens**. Do not say, "Several dozens worshipers were in church".

draft,
draught

Note that the form **draft** may now mean either *a current of air* or *an order drawn by a person or firm for the payment of money.* **Draught,** the older spelling of the word, means only the *current of air.*

drank,
drunk

Drank is in modern usage the past tense of *drink.* **Drunk** is now confined to the past participle. THUS: *He drank the water. He has drunk all the milk.* Do not say, "I drunk" or "I have drank".

drop,
particle

Drop should be used with reference to *liquids;* **particle** with reference to *solids.* THUS: *There was not a particle of meat in the refrigerator. There was not a drop of paint in the can.*

drowned

Drowned is the only correct form. "Drownded" is never correct.

drought,
drouth

These are two forms of the same word. The first is preferred in modern usage.

dual,
duel

Note the spelling. **Dual,** an adjective, means *relating to two.* **Duel,** a noun, means *a combat between two persons.*

due to

Due to is one of the most commonly misused expressions in the language. *Due,* an adjective here, is used properly only when it modifies some noun. Some form of the verb *to be* should always be expressed or understood before it. **Due to** should never be used as a preposition in the sense of *because of, on account of, as the result of, owing to, through.* The correct use is illustrated in the following sentences and clauses: *The explosion was due to carelessness. The explosion, due to carelessness, might have been avoided. His not coming was due to a misunderstanding. The respect due to his rank; death due to accident.* For practical purposes it may be said that *no sentence should ever begin with* **due to.**

due to,
  owing to

The two phrases are now commonly considered interchangeable in the sense of *attributable to.*

each,
  all,
  both

Each refers to individuals separately; **all** refers to them together. THUS: *Each man must live his own life. All men must have food.* **Both** means *the two.* THUS: *Both parents approved.* See **all** and **both.**

each,
  every

Every refers to individuals, but not to separate individuals. It is a more general word than **each.** THUS: *Every passenger on the ship heard the explosion. After the explosion, each passenger aboard the ship was examined by the captain.* Remember that both **each** and **every** are singular. THUS: *Each of us paid his fare. Every man has his responsibilities.*

each other,
  one another

Each other should be used when the reference is to two; **one another** when the reference is to more than two. THUS: *The two brothers were devoted to each other. All the members of the family were devoted to one another.*

Avoid such expressions as "between each" and "behind each other". SAY, *between the two, the one behind the other.*

economic,
economical

Economic refers to economics, the study of the material needs of man, or to the needs themselves. **Economical** means *thrifty.* THUS: *Economic necessity makes men work. The economical housewife is a useful citizen.*

effect,
affect

Effect, as a noun, means *result.* **Affect** means *to have an effect on.* THUS: *What is the effect of this treatment? How will this treatment affect the patient?* See **affect.**

egoism,
egotism

Both mean substantially *paying great attention to one's self.* **Egoism** implies the philosophy of self-interest, which is likely to lead to **egotism,** a too high opinion of one's self, conceit.

either,
neither

Either means *one or the other of two.* **Neither** is the negative. THUS: *Either of you may leave. Neither of us may leave.* In the first example, one of two persons may leave. In the second, no one may leave.

Note that both **either** and **neither** are singular. THUS: *Either of us is ready to go. Neither of us has had any experience. Has either of you the key? Was neither of you here when he came?*

either . . . or,
neither . . . nor

Remember that or is used with **either, nor** with **neither.** FOR EXAMPLE: *Either John or Henry; neither John nor Henry.*

either you or I
neither he nor we

Complications arise in combinations like **either you or I** (*am, are, is*) *right,* **neither he nor we** (*were, was*) *willing,* etc. The difficulty, of course, is that the same verb-form does not fit both members of the combination. There is no unanimity of opinion among either authorities or laymen concerning which verb-form shall follow the second member. In all such difficulties the only safe and wise thing to do is to recast the statement so as to avoid the complication. Instead of saying "Either you or I (am, are, is) right", say simply, *Either you are right or I am.* Instead of beginning a sentence, "Neither the state nor its citizens (has, have) the right", say, *To neither the state nor its citizens belongs the right,* etc.

Avoid such obviously incorrect expressions as "Neither saving money nor buying bonds are going to help". Since each of the subjects is singular, SAY, *Neither saving money nor buying bonds is going to help.*

**elder, eldest
older, oldest**

Elder and **eldest** are used only of persons, and usually of persons in the same family; as, *the elder daughter.* **Older** and **oldest** may be used of either persons or things.

elegant

Elegant should never be used to mean *excellent.* Remember that it properly means *refined, fastidious.*

**element,
factor,
feature,
phase**

Element means *a component part.* **Factor** means *one of a number of elements or conditions that make up a whole thing.* **Feature** means *a particular and very evident characteristic.* **Phase** means *one aspect of a situation or set of conditions.* THUS: *Honesty was an element of his character. An important factor in determining the point of attack was the supply of materials. The outstanding feature of this landscape is the tall mountain in the background. The second phase of the disease leads us to believe that it can be controlled with sulfa drugs.*

else

Avoid the superfluous use of **else** in such expressions as "Nobody else but you". SAY, *No one but you.* The usual possessive form is else's; *somebody else's, everyone else's,* etc.

emendation	See amendment.
emigrate, immigrate	Note carefully the distinctions between these two words. To emigrate is to leave one's country for residence in another. To immigrate is to come into a country of which one is not a native. FOR EXAMPLE: *A Portuguese emigrates from Portugal; he immigrates to Brazil.* Similarly, an *emigrant* is one who *emigrates from* one country to another; he arrives as an *immigrant* in the country of his choice.
eminence, eminent; imminence, imminent; immanence, immanent	Discriminate carefully between these words, with respect to spelling, meaning, and pronunciation. In each of these pairs, the first is the noun, the second the adjective form. **Eminence** means a *high place or rank*. THUS: *His deed received wide publicity because of his eminence.* **Imminence** means a *state of threatening*. THUS: *They sensed the imminence of danger.* **Immanence** means a *being part of, an indwelling*. THUS: *According to the doctrine of immanence, God is the essence of the universe.*
emphatically, undoubtedly, decidedly	**Emphatically** means *forcefully*. **Undoubtedly** means *unquestionably*. **Decidedly** means *clearly*. THUS: *He emphatically denied the charge although he was undoubtedly guilty. The trial was a decidedly fair one.*
en- and in-	Both prefixes mean *in* or *into* and form verbs. En- will be found chiefly in words derived from the French. Some words are written with en- or in- interchangeably. Both *en*close and *in*close, for example, are acceptable.
enclosed	Avoid the stock expression, "Enclosed please find". *You will find enclosed* is better.

Enclosed should not be followed by *herewith,* since the latter is superfluous.

end,
conclusion

End (not conclusion) must be used for the termination of anything which occupies space, as, *the end of the road.* **Conclusion** means *summing up.* THUS: *In conclusion, let me say.* . . .

endorse
(indorse),
approve

Endorse means to support in the sense of lending one's name. **Approve** conveys the idea of supporting with enthusiasm.

Since **endorse** means literally *to write on the back of,* do not say "endorse on the back of".

enjoy

Enjoy means *to find satisfaction in experiencing;* therefore the expression "to enjoy poor health" is incorrect, and "to enjoy good health" is unnecessary. **Enjoy** is always transitive. THUS: *Did you enjoy the excursion?*

enormity,
enormousness

Enormity is used of viciousness that is unnatural. **Enormousness** is used of that which is vast. THUS: *The mind grasps with difficulty the enormity of criminal activity. The enormousness of unused land in Africa exceeds that of any other continent.*

enough

See **sufficient**.

en route

En route means *on the way.* According to the best usage, **route** should rhyme with *boot.* The words are taken directly from the French. THUS: *We motored to California and saw many sights en route.*

"enthuse"

This is a coined verb, colloquial in the U. S. It is never used in formal English. SAY, *I was enthusiastic over the report,* not "I enthused over it".

enthusiastic, fanatic

Enthusiastic means *showing great liking and interest*. **Fanatic** means *enthusiastic to a point where wisdom and poise are lost*. It is used especially with reference to religion. THUS: *He is an enthusiastic painter. His fanatic attempts to convert everyone to his beliefs made him wearisome company.*

epitome

See **climax.**

equally

Do not say "equally as good", "equally as capable", etc. **Equally** is sufficient. Or, still better, say, *This wine is just as good as that. The boy is quite* (or *fully*) *as capable as his father.*

-er, -or

Both these suffixes indicate a *doer*. The suffix **-er** is usually added to words of English origin, **-or** to words of Latin origin; THUS: *borrower, maker, speaker; auditor, surveyor, vendor.*

eruption, irruption

Eruption means *a breaking out*. THUS: *The eruption of the volcano brought destruction for miles around.* **Irruption** means *a breaking in*. THUS: *The irruption of the waters destroyed the village on the coast.*

etc.

Etc. stands for two Latin words. They are *et*, which means *and*, plus *cetera*, which means *other things*. It is usually preferable, however, to list the things referred to rather than merely to indicate that there are other things, unless the list is completely obvious. **Etc.** is unnecessary after a list of words introduced by *such as* or similar phrases.

Avoid the use of *and* before **etc.**

eternal, everlasting

Eternal means *existing always without beginning or end*. **Everlasting** usually means going on without end. The words are often used interchangeably, however.

**euphemism,
euphuism**

Euphemism means *calling an unpleasant thing by a pleasant name.* There are many euphemisms for the stark word *death;* as, *passing away, passing on.* **Euphuism** means *an affected form of speech or writing.* The term is derived from the title of Lyly's "Euphues", which is written in a highly affected style.

**evacuate,
vacate**

Evacuate means *to send the inhabitants out of.* THUS: *The civilian population was evacuated because of grave danger of air raids.* Note that it is incorrect to use **evacuate** to apply to a few persons casually leaving a place.

Vacate means merely *to give up the occupancy of.* THUS: *The battalion vacated the barracks.*

**evaluate,
assess,
appraise**

See **appraise, assess, evaluate.**

even

The placing of this adverb is important to the sense. THUS: *By that time, even the casual reader knew the truth. Even by that time, the casual reader knew the truth.* In the first sentence, the reference is to *reader,* in the second to *time.*

ever

Such expressions as "who **ever**", in the sense of *who in the world,* "what **ever**", in the sense of *what in the world,* are examples of colloquial emphasis, never employed in formal English. To be correct, omit **ever.**

every

See **each, every.**

**every bit,
every place**

For **every bit,** it would be better to say *just as.* THUS: *She is just as clever as he is.* **Every place** is incorrectly used for *everywhere,* which means *in every place.* There is no such word as "everyplace".

every day
This should be written as one word, *every-day*, if it is to be employed as a modifier. THUS: *This is my everyday suit.* (Note: *He came every day in the week.*)

every one,
everyone
These are interchangeable.

every once
in a while
Every once in a while and *every now and then* are colloquial.

every so
often
This is a colloquial expression for *once in a while*.

every time
Every time, with the meaning of *always*, is not good usage. "Everytime" is a non-existent form.

"every which way"
This expression borders on slang. Use *in all directions, scattered*.

everyone
Since **everyone** is singular in form, it must be used with the singular verb. It may *not* be followed by the plural pronoun *they* or *their*. THUS: *Everyone here in the village says that the taxes are high. Everyone complains that his* (not *their*) *taxes are the highest.*

evidence,
testimony,
proof
If you have **evidence,** you have a better reason for believing a thing than if you merely have **testimony.** THUS: *We are inclined to believe the evidence of our senses.* Testimony is less direct, for it involves what other persons say. THUS: *The jury tried to arrive at the truth through the testimony of the witnesses. The fingerprints on the pistol were evidence of the truth of the witness's testimony.* We arrive at **proof** by means of *evidence.* **Proof** implies that a fact has been established. THUS: *When all the evidence had been presented, we believed that we had proof of his guilt.*

evident	See **apparent**.
exasperate	See **aggravate**.
exceed, excel	**Exceed** means *going beyond a boundary or limit*. **Excel** refers to *better quality*. THUS: *They have exceeded their quota in the selling of bonds. They excel in the ability to sell bonds.*
except	See **accept**.
except, unless, without	**Except** has the meaning of *omitting* and it should not be used for **unless**, which always introduces a conditional clause. Similarly, **without** means *not with*, or *outside*. It is not good usage to employ **without** when **unless** is meant. FOR EXAMPLE: *I was here every day except Monday. I shall be here every day unless* (not *except*, or *without*) *I am ill.*
exceptional, exceptionable	**Exceptional** means *out of the ordinary*. **Exceptionable** refers to *that to which exception may be taken, hence objectionable*. THUS: *This child's reasoning power at the age of six is exceptional. I find your very frequent lateness exceptionable.*
excessively, exceedingly	**Excessively** has the meaning of *to too great a degree, beyond the proper extent*. THUS: *He was excessively cordial.* **Exceedingly** simply means *to a very great degree*. THUS: *I am exceedingly glad to see you. The weather was exceedingly* (not *excessively*) *hot.*
exchange	See **change**.
excite, incite	**To excite** means *to produce agitation*. It is usually used of arousing the feelings. THUS: *The book excited interest in a national problem.* **Incite** means *to drive on to a particular end*. THUS: *The speaker incited the mob to set fire to the building.*

excuse,
pardon,
forgive

Excuse is used of small faults, **pardon** of grave faults or crimes, except in the expression "Pardon me". **Pardon** usually implies generosity towards a wrongdoer. One **forgives** an injury done to one's self, or **forgives** (remits) a debt. THUS: *Please excuse my absence. The governor pardoned the convict. The saint forgave his enemies. Forgive us our debts, as we forgive our debtors.*

executer,
executor

Note spelling and pronunciation. An **executer** is a performer of some act; an **executor** is a legal administrator.

ex officio

The adjective form requires a hyphen. THUS: *We are ex-officio members of the club. Mr. Gordon is chairman ex officio.*

expect

See **anticipate.**

expect,
suspect

The two words are not interchangeable, and neither should be used loosely in the general sense of *suppose* or *believe.* One **expects** future events, particularly if they are considered likely to occur. One **suspects** events or conditions, past, present, or future, but the word implies doubt or lack of evidence. **Suspect** often implies suspicion or a belief in something undesirable or discreditable. EXAMPLES: *I expect that the boys will come home for Christmas. I suspect that their letters may have miscarried. He suspected that there was sabotage in connection with the fire.*

extra

When **extra** is combined with an adjective, a hyphen should be used: *extra-fine wire, extra-thin cord.*

facsimile

See **replica.**

factor

See **element.**

fail

Fail, in the sense of *to fall short,* is an intransitive verb. THUS: *He failed in two subjects at school.* Such expressions as "He failed me in history", and "She failed her English course" are campus slang.

faint,
feint,
feign

Faint and **feint** are pronounced the same way, but have entirely different meanings. To **faint** is *to lose consciousness.* To **feint** means *to make a pretended attack.* **Feint** may also be a noun. It is then the noun form of **feign**, meaning *to counterfeit.* THUS: *The boxer raised his guard when his opponent feinted, whereupon his opponent struck at his body. He lay in bed feigning illness to evade work.*

falls,
ways,
woods

These nouns are plurals and should be so used.

family

Treat as a collective noun when thought of as a unit. THUS: *My family is spending the winter in Florida.* BUT NOTE: *My family are always quarreling with one another.*

farther,
further

Often used interchangeably. In correct usage, **farther** usually implies the idea of *distance;* **further** is used figuratively. THUS: *We walked farther into the wood. He developed the argument further.*

Farther is usually reserved for reference to physical distance, **further** for abstract degrees. THUS: *If you go much farther you will arrive at New York. A man who uses English correctly will go further in his profession.* See **all the farther.**

fascinated,
fascination

Fascinated and **fascination** are two of the most frequently misused words in the language. **Fascinate** means *to charm, to bewitch.* The misinformed person who says, "I have a fascination for Miss X", is saying, unintentionally, "I fascinate (bewitch) Miss X". Since the two words are greatly over-used, it is better to say *pleased with* or *attracted to*. The following examples illustrate the proper use of the words: *She fascinates me*, or *I am fascinated by her. She exercises a fascination on* (or *over*) *me*, or *She has a fascination for me.*

fast

Fast is the form for both adjective and adverb. Do not add -*ly* to form the adverb. THUS: *They drove fast in order to get home by dinner time.*

at fault
in fault

At fault is often incorrectly used for **in fault**, which means *having done something wrong*. At fault means *unable to go on, to be puzzled*, as when a hound has lost the scent.

faun,
fawn

Note the difference in spelling. **Faun** is a term from mythology and means *a god of the fields*. **Fawn** (noun) means *a young deer*. The verb, **to fawn**, means *to court favor by cringing and subserviency*.

favor
(for letter)

The use of **favor** to mean *letter* is incorrect.

favor
(for resemble)

The use of **favor** for *resemble* is a colloqui-alism which should be avoided.

faze

This word (also spelled *feaze* and *feeze*), meaning *to disturb* or *worry*, is colloquial in the U. S. and is not recommended.

feature

See **character, circumstance,** and **element.**

feel bad,
badly

See **bad, badly, ill.** To feel bad is to feel ill or depressed, but to **feel badly** is to have a *bad sense of touch.*

feel good,
well

To **feel good** means *to feel happy, to be in good spirits.* To **feel well** means *to be in good health.*

fellow	The use of **fellow** in the sense of *man, person,* is accepted in colloquial speech. In formal usage it implies contempt.
female, woman	Do not use **female** as a synonym for **woman,** or as an adjective to mean *feminine.* It is used properly only when distinction of sex is to be emphasized. SAY, *A woman of importance, an arrangement for women's voices, the female of the species.*
fetch	**Fetch** means to go to a place and get a thing with the intention of returning with it to the place from which you started. THUS: *He asked the servant to fetch his purse.* See **carry, bring.**
few, a few	Notice the difference between the two. *Few persons will venture out on a night like this* means that scarcely any will. *A few persons may always be seen on the streets* means that there are some, though perhaps not many, who are to be seen.
few, little	Use **few** to refer to that which can be counted, **little** to refer to that which can be measured, but not counted. THUS: *I have few free hours. I have little free time.*
fewer, less	These are the comparatives of *few* and *little* respectively. **Fewer** is used of persons or articles that can be counted; **less** refers to quality, quantity, or degree. THUS: *fewer men, fewer dollars, fewer errors; less sugar, less money, less strength.*
final	Since **final** means *pertaining to the end,* do not use it to modify such words as *completion, conclusion, end, finish.*
finance (*verb*)	Note that the accent is on the second syllable. The meaning is *to provide capital for.* It should be used only when relatively large sums are referred to.

financial,
fiscal,
monetary,
pecuniary

Financial is the most general term of the four, and may refer to *money matters in any sense,* but *particularly to large sums.* **Fiscal** refers to *public revenue.* **Monetary** is closest in meaning to the word *money* itself or *coinage.* **Pecuniary** is used of *money in connection with the transactions or affairs of individuals.* THUS: *Britain's financial condition, the government's expenditures during the fiscal year, the monetary system of the U. S., the pecuniary difficulties of Mr. Smith.*

fine

As applied to one's spirits or health, the word **fine** is colloquial.

finely

This is the adverb of *fine.* It is correctly used in such expressions as *finely ground, finely attuned.*

fire (*verb*)

In the sense of *discharge from employment,* the word **fire** is slang.

firsthand,
at first hand

Firsthand, at first hand, at second hand, etc., are adverbial phrases. The adjectives are written *firsthand, second-hand, third-hand,* etc.

first-rate

First-rate as an adverb is an undesirable colloquialism. The expression, *He shoots well,* or *excellently,* is preferable to "He shoots first rate".

It is correct to use the adjective **first-rate** before a noun. THUS: *He is a first-rate shot.* The use of the adjective after a noun is colloquial, as in the expression, "I feel first-rate".

first two,
last two

The first two, not "the two first" is the correct expression. Similarly, **the last two,** not "the two last", etc.

fix

The proper meaning of the verb **fix** is *to make firm, stable, permanent.* THUS: *The clock was fixed on the wall. His heart was fixed on going to Europe.* "Fix" or "fix up" in the sense of *adjust, arrange, mend, repair,* etc., is a familiar colloquialism, but must be considered inaccurate. One gains definiteness and variety by using the appropriate verb— *adjust, repair,* etc.

The use of **fix** as a noun to denote an awkward or embarrassing condition, as in "I'm in a terrible fix", is slang.

flair,
 flare

Note the difference in spelling and meaning. **Flair** is *an instinctive liking or aptitude;* **flare** is *an outburst of flame or light.*

fled,
 flew

Do not confuse the two words. **Fled** is the past tense of *flee;* **flew** the past tense of *fly.*

flout,
 flaunt

Flout means *to insult.* **Flaunt** means *to make a show of.* THUS: *He flouted the authority of the court. He flaunted his new title constantly.*

flowed,
 flown

Flowed, the past participle of *flow,* is often confused with **flown,** the past participle of *fly.* CORRECT: *Much water has flowed over the dam since then. Many wild geese have flown over today.* Note also that the past participle of *overflow* is *overflowed.*

folk,
 folks

Folk means *people* in the sense of a group, tribe, or nation. It is now usually used of a people in a social organization that is not very far advanced in the scale of civilization. It is often used as an adjective in this sense; as, *folk music, folk literature.* "Folks" is dialect or slang for *relatives, friends, neighbors,* etc.

fondling, **foundling**	Fondling is the present participle of the verb *to fondle* or *caress*. Fondling (noun) is *a person fondled or caressed*. **Foundling** means *a child who is found* by others after it has been deserted by its parents.
forbear, **forebear**	Forbear is a verb. The stress is on the second syllable. It means *to refrain from doing a thing*. THUS: *Forbear to strike when angry.* Forebear is a noun, meaning *ancestor*. The stress is on the first syllable. THUS: *Their forebears came from Holland.*
forbid to	Forbid should be followed by **to,** not *from*. THUS: *I forbid you to enter the house.*
foreigner	See **alien.**
forgive	See **excuse.**
formally, **formerly**	Note spelling. **Formally** means *in a formal or set manner*. THUS: *We were formally introduced.* **Formerly** means *at an earlier time*. THUS: *Formerly voters were not granted a secret ballot.*
former, **latter**	Former means *the first of two persons, things, or parts*. It should never be used to refer to the first of three or more. Similarly, **latter** means *the second of two*. THUS: *John and James were mentioned. The former is the father; the latter is the son. The latter half of the book was more exciting.*
fort, **forte**	The two words, pronounced alike, have different meanings. A **fort,** is *a fortified place*. Forte means *one's strong point*. THUS: *Playing baseball was his forte.*
forth, **fourth**	Note the spelling. The words are pronounced alike. **Forth** means *forward*. **Fourth** comes after *third*.

ᶜreeze,
frieze

Do not confuse the two words, which are pronounced alike. **Freeze** means *to become so cold as to form ice.* **Frieze** is a term in architecture. It means *a decorated band in a building.*

frequently

See **commonly.**

freshman,
freshmen

Singular and plural respectively. Compare *man* and *men.*

frightened,
scared,
afraid

Frightened and **scared** imply a *sudden* or *temporary* condition of alarm, and are to be distinguished from **afraid,** which signifies a *habitual* state of fear or apprehension. FOR EXAMPLE: *The child is afraid of the dark. She was frightened* (or *scared*) *by the sudden blowing of the siren.* **Scared** is less formal than **frighten.**

Do not use *of* after **frightened** or **scared.** One is **frightened** (or **scared**) *by* something. Avoid the slang expression, "He frightens (or scares). . . . " SAY, *He is frightened,* etc.

from,
of

Avoid the use of **from** for **of** in such statements as: *She is ill of diphtheria. He died of starvation.*

froze,
frozen

Do not confuse **froze,** the past tense of *freeze,* with **frozen,** the past participial adjective. CORRECT: *The lake froze yesterday. My feet are frozen* (not *froze*).

-ful,
-fuls

Note that the suffix **-ful** has only one *l*: *cupful, spoonful, helpful, harmful.*

The plural of nouns ending in **-ful** is formed by adding a final *s*: *cupfuls, spoonfuls.* Be careful not to say "spoons full" when you mean *spoonfuls.* CORRECT: *The prescription calls for three spoonfuls* (not "spoons full") *of the medicine a day.*

funny

Funny, meaning *odd, queer,* is colloquial. The word properly means *amusing, comical.*

further

See **farther.**

gambling,
  gamboling

Note spelling. **Gambling** has two syllables. **Gamboling** has three. **Gambling** is the present participle of the verb *to gamble.* **Gamboling** is the present participle of the verb *to gambol,* meaning *to frolic.* It is not much used in ordinary speech.

generally

See **commonly.**

genial,
  congenial

Genial means *jovial.* **Congenial** means *kindred.* THUS: *The genial host welcomed his guests. Their natures are congenial.*

genius,
  genus

Note spelling. **Genius** means *extraordinary ability* or *one who has such ability.* **Genus** means *class* or *kind,* as *a genus of a family of bulbous herbs.* The *e* is pronounced to rhyme with *key.*

gentleman,
  lady

Do not use **gentleman** and **lady** as general terms for *man* and *woman.* The terms "gentleman friend" and "lady friend", are not good usage. Use instead *friend, fiancée, sweetheart, a woman (a man) of my acquaintance,* according to the meaning intended. The use of the word "gent" is inexcusable.

genuine

See **authentic.**

gesture (*verb*),
  gesticulate

Note that the *g* is pronounced like the *j* in *just.* If lively motions are meant, **gesticulate** is preferred, especially if the motions are made instead of speech.

get

Get is used in many colloquial or provincial expressions, as in the following: "get him", in the sense of *wreak vengeance on him;* "get even with him", meaning *to get revenge;* "get to see", meaning *be able to see;* "get to be", meaning *become;* "get together on", meaning *agree on.* The expressions, "get across with", "get away with", "get by with", are slang.

"get-up"   "Get-up", meaning *costume,* is colloquial.

gibe,   Gibe and jibe are interchangeable. They
   jibe   mean *to scoff,* and rhyme with *tribe.* The participles are *gibing* and *jibing,* respectively.

give   See accord.

give to,   Confusion sometimes arises in the use of
  give for   these phrases. With **give to,** the object of *to* is the receiver of what is given. THUS: *He gave money to a hospital.* With **give for,** the object of *for* is the purpose of the giving. THUS: *He gave fifty dollars for the establishment of a hospital.*

give way to,   **Give way to** means *to yield place to an-*
  give away   *other person.* THUS: *He gave way to his superior. To* is not used with **give away** except colloquially. **Give away** means *to make a gift of a thing to another person.* THUS: *He gave his fortune away.* Colloquially, *away* is sometimes used after *give* in order to emphasize the completeness or generosity of the giving.

glad at,   **Glad at** means that joy is occasioned by a
  glad of   thing. THUS: *I was glad at the news.* **Glad of** is equivalent to *thankful for.* THUS: *I was glad of the chance to serve, so I joined the club.*

going to   **Going to** is often used colloquially to mean *just about.* It is better to say, *I was just about* *to mention it,* or *I was on the point of leaving,* than "I was just going to", etc. Avoid especially the awkward expression, "I was just going to go".

good   See **bad.**

good,
  well   Do not use the adjective **good** for the adverb **well.** CORRECT: *I feel very well* (not *very good*). *To feel good* means *to feel virtuous. He plays the piano pretty well* (not *pretty good*).

got   **Got** (past participle of *get*) is preferred to the older form *gotten.*

"Got to" is used colloquially to mean *must,* as in "He can win the race; he's got to win". "Has got" is a colloquialism for *has*: "The boy's got horse sense."

gourmand,
  gourmet   **Gourmand** and **gourmet** both mean *a person who knows good food and very much enjoys eating it.* A **gourmand,** however, eats large quantities of food. A **gourmet** is more fastidious. Both words come from the French. In **gourmet** the final *t* is silent, and the *e* is pronounced *ay* as in *say.*

grand   **Grand** means *magnificent.* In the sense of *excellent,* it is colloquial.

grant   See **accord.**

grateful to,
  grateful for   One is **grateful to** a person, **grateful for** an act or favor. THUS: *I am grateful to you for your help. He is grateful for the kindness shown to him.*

gratis   Since **gratis** means *free,* it is incorrect and unnecessary to say "free gratis". The first syllable of **gratis** is pronounced as "gray".

grip

Grip, in the sense of *valise* or *traveling bag,* is colloquial in the U. S.

groom

The use of **groom** for *bridegroom* is colloquial.

guard,
  regard

Note spelling.

guess,
  suppose,
  think,
  conjecture

Guess means *to hazard an opinion.* In the sense of **think,** it is colloquial. If no doubt is involved, the use of **guess** is incorrect. **Suppose** means *to assume as true.* **Conjecture** means *to form an opinion which is short of absolute conviction.* THUS: *I cannot guess at the answer. Let us suppose that angle A equals angle B. Since I have not all the data, I can only offer a conjecture with respect to the outcome.*

habit,
  custom,
  usage

Habit refers to the tendency to repeat a thing. It refers especially to the individual. **Custom** refers to what one sees done as the result of **habit.** It pertains to groups rather than to individuals. **Usage** means habitual practice in large groups. It implies official sanction.

had better,
  had best,
  had rather

Had better and **had best** indicate *advisability.* **Had rather** indicates *preference.* THUS: *You had better stay. I had rather stay than go.*

had

Avoid the use of such combinations as "had have", "had of", and "had ought" or "hadn't ought". SAY, *Had I known it,* or *If I had known it,* not "Had I have known it"; *I wish I had been there,* not "I wish I had of been there"; *You ought not to go out,* not "You hadn't ought to go out". See **could have.**

half hour

The correct expression is a **half hour** not "half an hour".

handful

Note that the plural is *handfuls*. Compare *cupfuls, spoonfuls,* etc.

hanged,
hung

Note that the past participle of *hang* is **hanged** when the reference is to a person, **hung** when the reference is to a thing. THUS: *The criminal was hanged. The picture was hung from the molding.*

happen,
occur,
transpire

Happen and **occur** are used almost interchangeably. **Happen** is more general, **occur** more formal. **Transpire** does not mean *to happen;* it does mean *to pass from secret to general knowledge.* THUS: *The events at that session did not transpire until five years later.* See **occur.**

hard (*adverb*)

The common adverb is **hard** not *hardly,* except in the sense of *with difficulty, barely.* THUS: *We worked hard, were hard pressed,* etc.

hard put to it

Hard put to it means *in difficulties.* THUS: *He was hard put to it to make ends meet.*

hardly,
scarcely

Hardly implies that a thing is done with difficulty. **Scarcely** suggests that there is no quantitative margin. THUS: *He could hardly breathe in the coal-pit. There is scarcely food enough for three.*

hate,
love

Avoid the use of **hate** and **love,** which are properly expressive of strong emotions, when only *like* and *dislike* are meant.

have

Observe carefully the proper use of the auxiliary **have** in expressions referring to desires or intentions at a given time in the past. SAY, *I meant to speak to you about it,* not "I meant to have spoken. . .". SAY, *I should have liked to see him,* not "I should like to have seen him", or "I should have liked to have seen him". Similarly, SAY, *I intended to give you the key,* not "I intended to have given you . . . ". *I had intended to be present at the wedding* is correct, not "I had intended to have been present". If the intention referred to was to have been carried out *before* the time or the event in question, the past infinitive should be doubled. THUS: *I meant to have done my Christmas shopping, and to have mailed the parcels, before the first of December,* not "I meant to do . . . and to mail", etc.

**have . . . do,
have . . . will**

Avoid such telescoped expressions as "never have nor never will fight", "have not and do not propose". SAY RATHER, *I have never fought and I never will. They have not proposed and do not propose that . . .*

**have given (gave)
have seen (saw)**

Do not confuse the use of the perfect (or present perfect) tense forms, **have given, have seen,** etc., with those of the past tense forms, **gave, saw,** etc. Past tense forms should be used when referring to an act completed at a given time in the past. THUS: *I gave* (not "have given") *it to him yesterday. I saw* (not "have seen") *him yesterday.*

**he, she,
her, him,
they, them**

Use the nominative forms, **he, she,** and **they,** as subjects of verbs and as predicate nominative complements; **her, him,** and **them** as objects. THUS: *It was he (she). Give it to him (her). If I were he; if you were she; if we were they.*

Note that the subject of an infinitive is in the objective case. THUS: *The lieutenant ordered them to charge. I believe her to be loyal. The judge declared them to be saboteurs.*

healthful,
  healthy

Healthful means *good for the health.* Healthy means *in good health.* THUS: *These children are healthy because they eat healthful foods.*

heap,
  heaps

Heap means *a pile.* The plural is **heaps.** THUS: *Heaps of stones lay in the field.* The use of **heap** to mean *a great number of persons or things* is colloquial or provincial. The use of **heaps** as in the expression "Thanks heaps" is slang. See **lots.**

hear,
  listen to

Hear takes a direct object. THUS: *I hear the bell.* It is the verb **listen** which is followed by **to.** THUS: *Listen to the bell.* See **listen.**

heartily,
  whole-heartedly

Note spelling. **Heartily** is the adverb of *hearty.* It means *zealously* or *spiritedly.* **Whole-heartedly** is the adverb of *whole-hearted,* which means *single-hearted,* hence *sincere.* THUS: *It was good to be so heartily welcomed. Mr. Smith whole-heartedly supports our efforts.*

help,
  (for employee)

Help, used as a collective plural, means *the whole force of those who are hired to help or assist.* In the sense of *a domestic servant* or *a farm hand* it is used locally in the U. S. It is not acceptable in formal usage.

help,
  (to express
  necessity)

Help is sometimes used idiomatically to express necessity. THUS: *He spends no more than he can help.*

help but,
  choose but

Help but and **choose but** mean *avoid.* THUS: *I could not help (choose) but hear,* is equivalent to *I could not avoid hearing.*

help in

In not *at* should follow the verb **help** in such expressions as, *We must all help in winning the country's support of this measure.*

hence,
thence,
whence

In meaning, these three words include the idea of *from*. It is incorrect, therefore, to use the word *from* with any of them. CORRECT: *They went hence* (that is, *from here*) *; a week hence* (*from now*). *They proceeded thence* (*from that place*). *Whence* (*from what place, or person*) *had you this news?*

him going,
his going

Him going is correct when the word **him** is an object and **going** is a participle modifying it. THUS: *I saw him going down the street.* **His going** should be used when **going** is a gerund, or verbal noun. THUS: *We regret his going so soon.* Note that in this construction the possessive case of the pronoun is always used: *her going, their going, our going,* etc. The same is true, of course, of other gerunds, *leaving, working,* etc.

hire,
hired,
lease,
let

The use of **hire** for **lease** or **let** is not correct. THUS: *He let* (or *leased*) *me an apartment;* not, "He hired me an apartment". **Hire** means securing for temporary services or use by payment of a fee or wage. SAY, *lease an apartment, hire a hall, lease a building, hire a typist.*

The use of the term "hired girl" for *domestic servant* is provincial in the U. S. It is not good usage.

holocaust

Holocaust may be used figuratively to refer to *the destroying of a large number of human beings by fire.* It should not be used to refer to disasters of all kinds.

holy,
holey,
holly,
wholly

Note spelling. **Holy, holey,** and **wholly** rhyme with the proper name *Foley.* **Holy** means *sacred.* **Holey** means *having a hole or holes.* **Wholly** means *completely.* **Holly** (a tree) rhymes with *jolly.*

home

Home should be preceded by *at* not *to.* THUS: *She is at home.* The use of **home** as an adverb to mean *at home* is a localism, and should be avoided. With such verbs as *coming* or *going,* no preposition is necessary. THUS: *The boys are coming* (or *going*) *home.* To *be home,* meaning to *come home,* as in "I'll be home next week", is an acceptable colloquialism.

Honorable, Reverend

Note that these words, when used as parts of titles, should always be capitalized, preceded by *the,* and followed immediately by the *given name,* or the *initials,* or the *rest of the title.* They should *never* be followed immediately by the surname. CORRECT: *The Honorable George L.* (or *G. L.,* or *Mr.*) *Adams. The Reverend John E.* (or *J. E.,* or *Dr.,* or *Mr.*) *Hale.* (*Honorable* and *Reverend* are not abbreviated in formal usage.) **It is incorrect to say "the Honorable Adams" or "the Reverend Hale".**

hope, wish

If one **hopes** for a thing, one also **wishes** it to happen. One may **wish** for a thing without grounds for **hoping** that it will happen. **Hope** implies anticipation with desire; **wish** implies desire, not necessarily anticipation. Use *will* with **hope**; *would* in the clause with **wish**. THUS: *I hope it will rain. I wish it would rain.* Note the following uses of **hope** and **wish**: *I hope you will have good luck. I wish you good luck.* See **anticipate**.

The phrase, **in hopes,** may be used for *hopeful.* THUS: *I am in hopes that this will not be necessary.*

hoping, hopping

Hoping is the present participle of *hope;* **hopping,** the present participle of *hop.*

hover

Hover rhymes with *cover.*

how

Do not use **how** or "as how" in the sense of the conjunction *that* or in combination with *that*. Do not say: "He wrote me how he had built a house", or, "He said as how he was coming", or, "He told how that they had been adrift for several days". The exclamations "And how!" and "But how!" are slang.

however,
but,
nevertheless,
notwithstanding

Note carefully the distinctions among the conjunctions **however, but, nevertheless, notwithstanding.** When simple antithesis is to be indicated, use **but** rather than **however.** THUS: *He is a well-to-do man, but not so rich as you seem to think.* Do not say, "He is a well-to-do man; not, however, so rich", etc. CORRECT: *The audience was warned not to run to the exits. Nevertheless* (or *Notwithstanding,* or *In spite of the warning*), *several hundred persons rushed to the main entrance.* Do not say, "Several hundred persons, however", etc.

However as a conjunction is properly used when the relation of a second statement to a preceding one is that of *concession* or *qualification* or *simple transition.* THUS: *He has not written to me yet. I thank him, however, for his good intentions. She said she would not write; however, I expect a letter soon.* Avoid the excessive use of the conjunction **however** at the beginning of sentences. BEGIN, *There is, however,* or *In many cases, however,* rather than, "However, there is" or "However, in many cases".

however,
how ever

Do not use the word **however** as the equivalent of the two words **how ever.** CORRECT: *How ever* (not "however") *could he have so misunderstood me?* or, *How could he ever have so misunderstood me?*

human,
human being

Human is an adjective, and is not by the best writers and speakers used as a noun for **human being.**

hung	See hanged.
hustle	Hustle, meaning *to move quickly, to work hard,* is colloquial. In formal usage the word should be reserved to its meaning: *to jostle* or *push unceremoniously.*
I, me	I is used as subject. Me is used as object. THUS: *Who is there? I (am here)* or *It is I. Do you want a man like me? Give it to me. They employed my brother and me.*
ice cream, ice water	Ice cream and ice water (without hyphens) are now the commonly preferred forms. Note, however, that it is *iced tea* and *iced milk.*
idea, opinion	These two words are not interchangeable. An idea is a *concept.* An opinion is a *belief, view,* or *judgment.* THUS: *He gave us an idea of what the future world would be like. The general expressed his opinions on the progress of the fighting.*
identical with	Identical with is correct. THUS: *My plan is identical with yours.* Note that one plan may be *similar to* another, but not "identical to" it.
i.e., e.g.	I.e. stands for the Latin words *id est.* The meaning is *that is.* It should not be confused with e.g. (*exempli gratia*) which means *for the sake of example.*
if, whether	If is not correct in such expressions as, *I do not know if I can go or not.* Use whether instead. THUS: *Do you know whether or not he paid? I cannot say whether he will go or not.* If may be used to mean whether in dependent or indirect questions. THUS: *He asked if you were in.* Whether is commoner in modern speech.

**if it was,
if it were**

If it was means that something may have been true in the past. THUS: *If it was there this morning, it is there now*. **If it were** implies doubt or indicates a circumstance contrary to fact. THUS: *If it were there this morning (but it was not) it would be there now*.

ilk

Ilk is incorrectly used to mean kind or group. In the expression *of that ilk* it means *of the same name, surname, or place*. THUS: *They are Macgregors of that ilk*. (That is, *Macgregors of Macgregor*.)

ill

Ill in the sense of *sick* or *ailing* is now used chiefly as a predicate adjective, and not before a noun. THUS: *His grandfather, an old man who was ill*, not "an ill old man". Use *of* not *with* after **ill**. THUS: *He is ill of* (not *with*) *bronchitis*.

Ill not "illy" is the adverb. THUS: *He spoke ill of you; he behaved ill; ill-disposed*, etc. See **bad**.

illusion

See **allusion** and **delusion.**

immigrate

See **emigrate.**

**immunity,
impunity**

Immunity usually refers to resistance to a disease. **Impunity** means exemption from punishment. THUS: *Vaccination develops an immunity to smallpox. The child misbehaved with impunity.*

**imperative,
imperious**

Imperative refers to that which is commanding, authoritative, urgent. **Imperious** refers to that which is domineering. THUS: *He received an imperative summons. It is imperative that you come at once. She was a woman of imperious mind.*

**implacable,
  impregnable**

Do not confuse **implacable** with **impregnable** (or *impenetrable*). **Implacable** means *inexorable, unappeasable.* THUS: *the impregnable* (or *impenetrable;* not *implacable*) *defenses of the region; the implacable wrath of Achilles.*

**implicate,
  involve**

These terms are not exactly synonymous. **Implicate** means *to entwine* or *entangle.* **Involve** means *to enfold* or *envelop.* To say that a person is *implicated in a crime* is to suggest that he is guilty. One who is *involved in a crime* certainly has some connection with it, although he may have been entangled in it against his will or judgment.

**imply,
  infer**

The author or speaker **implies** (that is, *expresses indirectly,* or *hints at*) a meaning; the reader or hearer **infers** (that is, *deduces, derives,* or *concludes*) a meaning from the statement made. THUS: *He implied that I had been negligent. I infer from your remarks that you think me negligent. Do you mean to imply that I am negligent?*

**in,
  into**

In expresses rest, not motion. THUS: *I shall remain in the room.* **Into** expresses motion from one place to another. THUS: *He walked into the room.* See **at.**

**inasmuch,
  in so far**

Inasmuch is one word. The expression **in so far** is written as three words. The word *in* is not needed, and should be omitted. SAY, *so far as I know; so far as he is able.*

**in front of,
  before**

In front of is good usage but it refers only to physical position. **Before** may have the same meaning but it is also used to describe relative position in time, place, position in a series, etc. THUS: *A comes before B.*

in regard to

Do not say "in (or with) regards to". See **regard.**

in search of　　Say **in search of**, not "in search for".

in the future　　Use **in the future,** not "in future".

in the midst of　　**In the midst of,** not "in midst of", is the correct expression.

in our midst　　**In our midst,** strictly speaking, should be *in the midst of us.* **In our midst** is an expression that is widely used but that has never been completely established as good usage.

incidentally,
**　accidentally**　　Be careful not to pronounce **incidentally** as "incidently". Likewise, avoid the pronunciation of **accidentally** as "accidently".

inclosed　　See **enclosed.**

incommode　　See **discommode.**

incredible,
**　incredulous**　　(See **credible, creditable, credulous.**) Such expressions as "facts, however incredulous" are incorrect. **Incredible** and **incredulous** are the opposites of *credible* and *credulous.* These words are not interchangeable.

indexes,
**　indices**　　Variant plural forms of *index.* **Indexes** is the English plural. **Indices** is the Latin plural. The latter form is used chiefly in mathematics and other sciences.

indict,
**　indite**　　These words are pronounced alike but have different meanings. **Indict** means *to charge with a crime.* **Indite** means *to compose,* or *to write.* It is not used in everyday speech.

individual,
**　party,**
**　person**　　The noun, **individual,** should not be used loosely in the sense of **party** or **person.** **Individual** is properly used only when it is necessary to distinguish the *particular* from the

general. THUS: *The benefits will accrue to the whole group as well as to each individual in it.* **Party,** likewise, is not interchangeable with **individual** or **person.** It is used properly of a single person only when that person is represented as *taking part in* or *consenting to* an action. THUS: *each of the two parties to the lawsuit; he will never be a party to such a disgraceful surrender.* **Individual** and **party** are often used jocosely for **person,** as "the meddlesome individual (or party) in Apartment C". **Person** is the proper and sufficient word in quite all circumstances. CORRECT: *A pleasant-voiced person* (not *individual* or *party*) *called this morning to ask for John's address. I have several persons in mind who may be able to help you.*

induction   See **deduction.**

infect,
 infest   **Infect** means *to contaminate with germs.* **Infest** means *to be present in great numbers and thus to cause difficulty.* THUS: *Because the wound had not been properly cleaned, the hand became infected. The house was infested with mice.*

infectious   See **contagious.**

infer   See **imply.**

ingenious,
 ingenuous   An **ingenious** man means one who is *skilful, clever at invention.* **Ingenuous** means *frank, open, candid.*

injury   See **accident.**

innumerable   **Innumerable** means *too many to be numbered,* or *counted.* It is not interchangeable with *many.* Since the idea of *number* is embraced in the word, do not say "an innumerable number". See **number.**

initiate	See **begin**.
insanitary, **unsanitary**	**Insanitary** is the established form when the meaning intended is *contrary to sanitary principles, injurious to health;* as *insanitary housing*. **Unsanitary** is used properly to mean *lacking sanitation, not planned to promote or safeguard health*. THUS: *The health of the community seemed to be good in spite of the unsanitary conditions of daily life.*
inside, **inside of**	**Inside** is preferable to **inside of,** though the latter is colloquially permissible. THUS: *During his illness he was careful to stay inside* (rather than *inside of*) *the house.*
in so far	See **inasmuch**.
in spite of	See **despite**.
instance	See **case**.
instill	**Instill** means *to pour in slowly,* hence *to impart gradually*. Do not use it in the passive with the preposition *with*. CORRECT: *The idea was instilled in the boy by constant repetition*. One may be *inspired with,* but not "instilled with" an idea.
in the light of, **in view of**	**In the light of** implies that what follows is the result of information. **In view of** means *in consideration of, with regard to*. THUS: *In the light of recent discoveries, the books must be changed. In view of their needs, we shall increase the allowance*. Note that the phrase is **in the light of,** not "in light of".
invent	See **discover**.
invite, **invitation**	**Invite** is a *verb*. Do not use the word as a noun to mean **invitation**.

involve   See **implicate**.

irresponsible,   **Irresponsible** means *having no sense of re-*
   not responsible for   *sponsibility.* **Not responsible for** means *not*
                                  accountable or *liable for some particular*
                                  thing or things. THUS: *He was irresponsible*
                                  in that he left his debts unpaid. I am not re-
                                  sponsible for debts contracted by you.

irritate   See **aggravate**.

irruption   See **eruption**.

is, are   When the subject is third person singular,
                                  use **is**. When the subject is third person
                                  plural, use **are**. Care must be taken when a
                                  phrase or clause comes between the subject
                                  and the verb. THUS: *One of the two is here.*
                                  None of the men is to be employed. There
                                  are two reasons, neither of which is (not *are*)
                                  mentioned.

                                  English usage permits, in certain cases, the
                                  employment of **is** or any other singular verb
                                  with two (or more) subjects *if these are*
                                  thought of as in reality constituting the same
                                  thing. The most familiar example of this use
                                  is in the Lord's Prayer: *Thine is the kingdom,*
                                  and the power, and the glory. Another
                                  familiar example is Kipling's line, *The tumult*
                                  and the shouting dies. Here *tumult* and *shout-*
                                  ing are thought of as identical. Similarly in
                                  such expressions as, *The sum and substance*
                                  of his remarks was . . . , and *The fount and*
                                  origin of the movement was. . . . Care
                                  should be taken, however, to avoid the ex-
                                  cessive use of this construction.

it   Avoid the loose and ambiguous use of **it**
                                  and other pronouns illustrated in such sen-
                                  tences as the following: "It was a five-dollar
                                  gold piece, and it was in Washington that I

had last seen one." "A book dealing with this subject ought to be published if it is possible to find a person sufficiently expert to write it." The latter sentence could be more simply and clearly re-written as, *A book dealing with this subject ought to be written, if a person sufficiently expert could be found to write it.*

The use of **it** to refer to a preceding statement is permitted only in informal English. THUS: *We had long ago changed our minds. It* (meaning *this*) *did not affect the others, however.*

its,
it's,
'tis

The possessive of **it** has no apostrophe; *its kennel, its puppies.* **It's** means *it is.* The apostrophe indicates the omission of the letter *i.* THUS: *It's late.* **'Tis** means *it is.* **'Tis** is not often used in modern American speech, except in dialect.

jewels,
jewelry

Note that **jewels** has two syllables, **jewelry** three. **Jewelry** refers to *jewels taken collectively,* as *a jeweler's stock in trade.* One speaks of a lady's **jewels** (not *jewelry.*)

journal

Journal comes from the French *jour* (day). A **journal,** thus, is, primarily, *an account of daily events or daily transactions,* or *a newspaper published daily.* By extension, however, it is now used to mean *any periodical publication.*

judicial,
judicious

Judicial means *pertaining to courts of law, or to judges.* **Judicious** means *showing good judgment; wise.* THUS: *There was a judicial calm in his delivery. The decision was judicious in that all the evils were remedied.*

jump at,
to

To **jump at** means *to accept eagerly;* as *to jump at an opportunity.* To **jump to** means *to spring to;* as, *to jump to safety, to jump to attention.*

just

Just, in the intensive sense of *simply, quite* (as "just terrible"), is colloquial.

keep from

Keep from in the sense of *refrain from, help,* is colloquial. Formal usage prefers *I could not refrain from* (or *help*) *speaking to you about it* to "I couldn't keep from speaking to you . . ."

kin,
akin

These two adjectives, both meaning *related,* are not always interchangeable. Of persons one may say either *She is kin to him* or *She is akin to him.* Similarly, *They are kin,* or *They are akin.* With abstractions **akin** is the proper word. THUS: *These two problems are closely akin; an admiration akin to idolatry.*

kind,
sort

Remember that **kind** and **sort** are singular, and as such require a singular demonstrative adjective, *this* or *that,* not *these* or *those.* CORRECT: *this kind of carton* (not "these kinds of cartons"); *that sort of spray* (not "those sorts of sprays"). In certain cases, if the speaker is thinking of the *individual members* of a class, he may say *this kind of chocolates, that kind of tubes,* etc., but never "these kinds".

Avoid the use of *a* or *an* after **kind** and **sort.** CORRECT: *What kind* (or *sort*) *of man do you want?* Do not say "What kind of a man . . .?" etc.

"kind of",
"sort of"
(for rather)

These expressions are undesirable colloquialisms for *rather, somewhat,* before adjectives. PREFERABLE: *He is rather tired; he is somewhat discouraged.* These expressions must not be used before *verbs.* CORRECT: *I rather* (not "kind of" or "sort of") *thought he would put in an appearance.* Avoid the expression, "kind of a", for *rather,* as in "He had kind of a hard time making ends meet".

"Kinder" and "sorter" are, of course, incorrect forms of **kind of** and **sort of.**

kindly

Do not use **kindly** as a variant of "kind of" in the sense of *rather* or *somewhat.* COR-RECT: *He feels somewhat discouraged,* not "kindly discouraged".

kinsfolk

This is the proper form. Avoid the provincialism, "kinfolks".

Knight Templar

The plural is *Knights Templars* when members of the medieval religious and military order are referred to. The plural is *Knights Templar* when the reference is to members of a certain order of Freemasonry.

lady

See **gentleman.**

laid, lain

Laid and **lain,** the past participles respectively of the verbs, *lay* and *lie,* are often confused. **Laid** in tense-combinations is always followed by an object. **Lain** is never followed by an object. CORRECT: *She laid her sewing on the table. He has lain* (not *laid*) *unconscious for two hours. He laid the parcels on the floor an hour ago, and has lain asleep on the bench since. He has laid away his civilian clothes for a naval uniform.* See **lay, lie.**

last, latest

Last refers to the final member in a series. **Latest** refers to the most recent in time. THUS: *Here is the latest bulletin. It will not be the last.*

last, latter

Last properly refers to a series of more than two. See **last,** above. **Latter** refers to the second of two. See **former.**

lay,
lie

Avoid the incorrect use of lay for lie. Lay (*to put down*) is a transitive verb and always takes an object. Lie (*to be at rest, to rest*) is an intransitive verb, and thus takes no object. CORRECT: *Lay the parcels on the table. The dog lies in the sun.*

Confusion is likely to occur in the use of the past tenses of the two verbs. Lay is the past tense of lie; laid is the past tense of lay. THUS: *The hen lay in the nest this morning and laid an egg. He laid aside his overcoat and lay down. I lie tonight where he lay last night. The book still lay where I had laid it a week before.*

In poetry the pronouns *me, him, her,* etc., are often used as objects with lay. THUS: *I lay me* (meaning *I lie*) *down to sleep. He laid him* (*himself*) *down to rest. They laid them* (*themselves*) *down in peace.* See laid, lain.

lead,
led

Do not confuse the spelling of lead (the metal) with that of led (the past tense of the verb, lead). CORRECT: *The melted lead ran from the roof of the church. The sergeant led his men back to the barracks.*

learn,
teach

Learn is not good English for teach. To learn is *to get knowledge;* to teach is *to give knowledge.* CORRECT: *The old sailor will teach* (not *learn*) *you how to tie knots. He taught* (not *learned*) *me how to tie a slide knot.*

lease

See hire.

least,
less

Be careful not to use least (the superlative) when you mean less (the comparative). Of *two* unequal things, one is less, not least. CORRECT: *The less* (not *least*) *dangerous of the two courses; the least desirable of the three houses.* See more, most.

leave,
let

Do not use **leave** for **let**. **Leave** means *to allow or cause to remain*. THUS: *I shall leave my raincoat at home. Leave the children where they are.* **Let** means *to permit,* or *to allow;* as, *Let him go.* If the meaning intended is "Don't disturb (or bother) him", the correct expressions are: *Let* (not *leave*) *him be. Let* (not *leave*) *him alone. Leave him alone* means properly, *Allow him to remain by himself.* Note also the following: *Let* (not *leave*) *him see it. Let* (not *leave*) *them go,* if you mean "Don't hinder them from going". "Let (not leave) me off" is colloquial for *Allow me to get off.*

leave,
depart

Leave may be used without an expressed object to mean **depart**. THUS: *He leaves to-morrow; she has just left.*

legible,
readable

Legible means *able to be read* in the sense of *written or printed clearly.* **Readable** means *able to be read with pleasure.* It refers to the content of what is read. THUS: *His manuscript is legible. This is a very readable novel.*

lengthened,
lengthy

Do not confuse the two words. **Lengthen** means *to make or become longer.* **Lengthy** means *of unusual or undue length.* A gown or an essay may be **lengthened** without being made long enough. A **lengthy** discourse means an *unduly long* (and usually tiresome) speech.

lengthways,
sideways,
endways

Interchangeable with *lengthwise, sidewise, endwise.* The forms ending in *-wise* are often preferred in formal usage, and are considered by some to have a less literal significance.

lens

Note that the plural is *lenses.*

less,
fewer

See **few** and **fewer**.

lessen   See **reduce.**

lesser,   Do not use **lesser** when merely **less** is meant.
less   **Lesser** is an attributive adjective in the *positive* degree meaning *minor, inferior*. THUS,
one speaks of the Great Bear and the Lesser
Bear. CORRECT: *Of two dangerous courses,
choose the less. He was a person of less importance than she. The lesser powers of a
country are perforce influenced by the greater
powers. The lesser discomforts of army life
are forgotten when times of danger come
along.*

let   See **hire.**

let's   **Let's** means *let us*. Therefore *you and me*
should be omitted. THUS: *Let's celebrate. Do
let's go,* not "Let's do go".

levy,   The words are pronounced alike in the
levee   U.S. They rhyme with *heavy*. **Levy** means *a
levying*. **Levee** means either *a large gather-
ing,* or *an embankment to prevent floods.*

liable,   See **apt, likely, liable.**
likely

libel,   A **libel** is a *written and published* state-
slander   ment damaging to the character and reputation of a person. A **slander** is a false and
malicious statement *spoken* to injure another.

lick   The verb **lick** in the sense of *defeat, thrash,*
is colloquial; as in, "Our team got licked
yesterday", or "He got a licking for being
late". It is likewise colloquial when used to
mean *stroke of work* or *burst of energy;* as in,
"He put in several licks on his essay".

lie   See **laid, lay.**

lie,
** lying**

Lying is the present participle of **lie,** in all senses of the word.

lief

Avoid the pronunciation "liv". **Lief** is pronounced as *leaf*. It means *gladly, willingly,* and is used chiefly in the expressions, *had as lief, would as lief, had liefer, would liefer.* THUS: *I had as lief give you the books as lend them to you. I would liefer resign than agree to your proposal.*

lightening,
** lightning**

Lightening is the present participle of the verb *to lighten;* as, *lightening the load.* **Lightning** is a noun, and means *the flashes of light in a thunder storm.*

like

Do not use **like** as a conjunction in the sense of *as, as if.* CORRECT: *B as in Boston* (not "like in Boston"). *Speak as if* (not "like") *you mean what you say. It looks as if* (not "like") *it would rain.*

Avoid the improper use of **like** for *rather* or *somewhat.* Say, *He looked rather* (or *somewhat*) *frightened,* not "He looked frightened like".

Like and **unlike** may be treated as prepositions in such constructions as: *It flew like a bird. He was of medium stature like his father. The shape of the earth is not unlike that of an orange.* See **as.**

like,
** liking**

Like, as a noun, is used chiefly in the plural; as, *likes and dislikes.* **Liking,** meaning *fondness, preference,* is used only in the singular. THUS: *He had a great liking for* (not a "great like for") *tennis.*

like,
** love**

Avoid the use of the word **love** when the meaning of *to find agreeable* is intended. THUS: *I like* (not "love") *Morrison's drawings.* See **hate.**

**like,
liked**   See **have**.

likely   See **apt**.

limited   **Limited** means *confined within limits,* hence, *narrow, circumscribed.* It should not be used as a synonym for *scanty, slight,* or *little.* SAY, *a little time,* or *a short time,* not "a limited time"; *a slight acquaintance,* not "a limited acquaintance". The opposite of **limited** is *unlimited.* It is permissible to say, *His opportunities* (or *means*) *were limited* (or *unlimited*).

The word *Limited,* commonly abbreviated as *Ltd.,* is, roughly speaking, the British equivalent of the American *Incorporated,* abbreviated as *Inc.*

line   A greatly overworked word, borrowed from the world of trade, and used colloquially in such expressions as: "Her line was to agree with everything the instructor said." "What's his line?"

Avoid the excessive use of the phrase, "along that line", in such expressions as, "They raised beans, carrots, squash, and other things along that line."

"To get a line on", meaning to find out something (usually unfavorable) about a person, or to get a clue to his motives, etc., is slang.

**lineament,
liniment**   **Lineament** means *feature, outline, contour,* especially of the face. It is used chiefly in the plural. THUS: *Her face had the lineaments of that of a Greek statue.* **Liniment** is *a medicated liquid* applied to the skin by rubbing.

**listen,
hear**   **Listen** implies paying close attention to words or music. **Hear** does not necessarily imply attention or application. **Listen** is followed by *to,* never by *at.* THUS: *We listened*

to the symphony over the radio. We heard voices within as we walked by the house.

literature

The word **literature** is applied properly to writing notable for literary form or expression. It should not be used loosely to refer to any printed matter such as catalogues, circulars, or pamphlets.

little,
  a little

Little, or **a little,** as an adverb means *slightly, in a small degree.* THUS: *The change mattered little to him. He decreased his speed a little.* When **little** precedes a verb, it often has the meaning of *not at all.* THUS: *The dead little heed your words of praise.* See **few.**

live,
  alive

The two words are not to be used interchangeably. **Alive** is never placed before a noun. CORRECT: *There were three live* (not "alive") *men in the wreck when he got there. He sells live* (not "alive") *lobsters. He was still alive at five o'clock.*

loan,
  lend

Loan should not be loosely used for **lend. Loan,** as a verb, is common in financial and commercial transactions, but is not otherwise approved by the best writers. CORRECT: *Lend* (not "loan") *me your fountain pen. He lent* (not "loaned") *me the fare for the trip. The paintings were lent* (not "loaned") *to the art gallery.*

locate,
  settle,
  discover

The use of **locate** for settle is colloquial. PREFERABLE: *His family settled* (not "located") *in Pennsylvania. The new state government established itself* (not "located") *at Frankfort.*

The use of **locate** in the sense of **discover** is not sanctioned by the best writers. CORRECT: *The patrols discovered* (not "located") *two suspicious characters.*

lonely, solitary	**Lonely** implies *a longing for congenial companionship*. **Solitary** implies nothing more than *absence of companions, isolation*. One may be **lonely**, though surrounded by uncongenial persons. One may live a **solitary** life without being **lonely**. THUS: *The lonely old man lived with two unsympathetic daughters. Busy with his sketching, the artist forgot his solitary surroundings.* By extension, **lonely** may be used of inanimate objects; as *a lonely house, a lonely road*.
look	When used in the sense of *seem,* the verb **look** should be followed by an adjective. THUS: *He looks sympathetic*. When used to mean *exercising the visual sense,* **look** is followed by an adverb. THUS: *He looked sympathetically at the refugees. She looked carefully about her.*
lose out, win out	**Lose out** is an unapproved colloquialism. **Win out,** though colloquial, has support among the best writers and speakers.
lots, a lot, a whole lot	The use of **lot** in any of these expressions to mean *a great deal, much,* is colloquial. Note that there is no such word as "alot". See **heap**.
love	See **hate, like.**
lovely	A greatly abused word. Properly used, it means *delicately or exquisitely beautiful.* THUS: *a lovely girl, a lovely flower, a lovely bracelet.* It should not be used loosely to refer to anything or everything that is pleasing, delightful, or amusing; as, "a lovely luncheon", "a lovely hat", "a lovely typewriter", "a lovely play".
luxuriant, luxurious	**Luxuriant** means *profuse of growth*. It should not be confused with **luxurious,** which

implies *luxury*. THUS: *luxuriant foliage; a luxurious house.*

mad

Mad properly means *insane*. Its use to mean *angry* is colloquial.

madam,
Madame

Madam is the English form of polite address to a lady. It is commonly shortened to *ma'am*. **Madame** is a French title given to all married women. In English usage, it is commonly prefixed like *Mrs.* to a foreign lady's name. The abbreviation is *Mme.*

maintain,
maintenance

Maintain is accented on the second syllable. **Maintenance** is accented on the first syllable. Note the spelling of the second syllable in each case. **Maintain,** in this connection, means paying the cost of upkeep. **Maintenance** is the noun derived from **maintain.**

majority,
plurality,
most

Majority means a number which is *more than half of the total* of a set or series. In elections it is used to refer to the excess of this number of votes over the remainder. THUS: *Of the two candidates for selectman, Mr. Mason received a majority of 460 votes over those cast for Mr. Jackson.* **Majority** should be distinguished from **plurality** which, in an election, refers to the leading candidate's excess of votes over those cast for his nearest competitor, or for any other candidate for the same office. THUS: *Mr. Wilson in 1912 received a plurality of more than 2,000,000 votes over those cast for Mr. Roosevelt. He did not, however, receive a majority of the total number of votes cast.*

Majority should be used only when an *exact* count has been made. **Most** or **the greater part** should be used when only a rough estimate is given. CORRECT: *A majority of the members of the club voted to admit* *him. Most* (not "the majority") *of the members of the club are out of town just now. Most* (not "the majority") *of my friends think otherwise. The greater part* (not "the majority") *of the city was destroyed.*

manual, Manuel

Manual is a handbook. **Manuel** is a man's name.

many, much

Many means *a great number.* **Much** means *a great quantity.* THUS: *Many drops of water go to make up the stream. Much water has flowed under the bridge since then.*

marine, maritime, naval, nautical

Marine pertains especially to that which is produced by the sea; as, *marine life.* **Maritime** refers especially to that which borders on the sea; as, *the maritime provinces.* **Naval** means that which pertains to ships, or to the navy; as, *a naval battle.* **Nautical** refers to seamen, navigation, or ships; as *a nautical mile.*

material, matériel

Material means *of or pertaining to matter, physical.* **Matériel** is a French noun meaning the *material equipment, apparatus, etc., of an organization* (usually military).

matricide, parricide

Matricide means *the murder of a mother by a son or daughter.* **Parricide** means *the murder of a parent or near relative, or of a ruler or any person entitled to veneration. Patricide* is a less common form of **parricide.**

may

See **can.**

may be, maybe

Note that the verbal phrase **may be** is written as two words. THUS: *You may be right.* The adverb, **maybe,** meaning *perhaps,* is written as one word. THUS: *Maybe you will be chosen.*

me,
  my

The correct expression is *It is I,* not "It is me", since the verb *to be* is always followed by the same case as that which precedes it. Note also, *He is taller than I* (not "me"), since the completed statement would be *He is taller than I am* (tall).

In such a construction as *Would you object to my going?,* note that **my** (not "me") precedes the gerund (verbal noun) *going.* CORRECT: *He had not heard of my* (not "me") *being here. What do you think of my* (not "me") *being elected?* See **he, her.**

mean

The use of **mean** in the sense of *ill-tempered, disagreeable,* or *ashamed of one's self,* is colloquial.

measles,
  mumps

Both nouns, though plural in form, are singular in meaning, and take a singular verb. THUS: *Measles is a contagious disease. Mumps is an affection of the salivary glands.* The pronoun *it* (not "them") should be used in referring to either ailment. THUS: *Have you had mumps? Yes, I had it when I was four years old.*

medieval,
  Middle Ages,
  middle-aged

Note that **medieval** has *four* syllables. It means of or pertaining to the **Middle Ages,** commonly reckoned as about A.D. 1000–1400. SAY, the **Middle Ages** rather than "the medieval era", as the idea of *era* is included in the term **medieval.** Do not refer to "a Middle Age man", as the term **middle-aged** is applied to persons in the middle period of life.

memorandum,
  memoranda

Memorandum is the singular, **memoranda** the plural. THUS: *Please send me a memorandum of the purchase. These memoranda are to be filed with the vouchers.*

Messrs., **Mesdames**	The French terms, **Messrs.** (abbreviation of *messieurs,* plural of *monsieur*) and **Mesdames** (plural of *Madame*), are used in English as the plurals of *Mr.* and *Mrs.* respectively. THUS: *The Messrs. Howe, Stimson, and Lyons; Mesdames Howe, Stimson and Lyons.* **Messrs.** is also prefixed to the name of a firm; as, *Messrs. Wallace, Marshall & Company.*
midst	See **in the midst of.**
mighty	**Mighty,** as an adverb, in the sense of *very, exceedingly,* is colloquial, and should be avoided in formal usage.
minutiae	**Minutiae** is the plural of *minutia,* and means *minor details.* THUS: *These minutiae are not worth so much time and trouble.* Note that the last syllable of *minutiae* is pronounced as *ē,* not *ah.*
mistaken	Avoid the incorrect form "mistakened".
moment, **minute**	A **moment** is a brief space of time, the duration of which is not exactly designated. It should not be used as synonymous with **minute,** the more precise term, which means the sixtieth part of an hour.
monetary	See **financial.**
moneys	The plural of words ending in *-ey* is formed by adding *s* to the singular. The plural of *money,* therefore, is **moneys.**
more, **most**	Be careful to use **more** when only *two* persons or things are being compared. Use **most** only when *more than two* are being compared. THUS: *Of the two metals, tin is the more useful. This is the most expensive of the three coats.*

**more,
rather**

Do not use both **more** and **rather** in the same connection. CORRECT: *They considered it more practicable to remain where they were than* (not "rather than") *to push on across the river. He depends more on you than* (not "rather than") *on me. He depends on you rather than on me.*

most

See **majority, more.**

most

Avoid the use of "most" as an abbreviation or equivalent of *almost.* CORRECT: *The orchestra had almost* (not "most") *finished the overture when we arrived. It's almost* (not "most") *time to be going.*

movies

Movies, the colloquial term for *moving pictures,* should not be used in formal conversation or writing.

much

The expression "muchly" is slang, and should be avoided. See **many.**

mumps

See **measles.**

mutual

See **common.**

my

See **me.**

**myself,
I,
me**

Do not use the reflexive pronoun **myself** for **I.** CORRECT: *My wife and I* (not "myself") *are going. She is a more faithful attendant than I* (not "myself"). **Myself,** likewise, should not be used for **me** as the object of a verb unless the subject of the verb is **I.** CORRECT: *They gave my wife and me* (not "myself") *their tickets. I fancy myself to be a good judge of music. I always give myself the benefit of the doubt. I know myself. He knows my brother and me.*

Certain colloquial expressions are exceptions to the rule; as, *I gazed about me, I bought me a flashlight, I never looked behind me.*

The same practice is to be followed with the other reflexive pronouns, *himself, themselves,* etc. See **himself.**

naught, nought

These terms are interchangeable. The meaning may be *nothing* or *zero.* See **aught.**

nautical, naval

See **marine.**

near

Near as an adjective in the sense of *narrow,* as in "a near escape", is colloquial. It is also colloquial in the sense of *almost, closely resembling or approximating the genuine,* as in *a near accident, a near tragedy, near beer, near silk,* etc.

near, nearly

Do not use the adjective **near** for the adverb **nearly.** CORRECT: *It is nearly* (not "near") *a year since we met.*

near by

Near by (near-by) is colloquial whether as an adjective or adverb. The words *near, close, neighboring* are preferred by more careful writers. THUS: *The post office and the bank are both near* (not "near by"). *His pipe and tobacco were close at hand* (not "near by"). *Near* (not "near by") *the house stood a clump of trees. He moved from Concord to a neighboring* (not "near-by") *village.*

necessaries, necessities

These two words are frequently confused. The **necessaries** of life are *those things, such as food and water, without which life cannot be maintained.* **Necessities** is used to mean *pressing needs, poverty, want.* CORRECT: *Their necessities drove the refugees to seek help from the Red Cross, which provided them with the necessaries of life.*

need   See **desire.**

need,
needs,
dare,
dares

Need is often used as an auxiliary before an infinitive without *to* in certain negative and interrogative constructions. THUS: *He need not go. He need not have troubled himself. Why need he spend so much time there? Need it be finished this week?* But when the statement is affirmative, the form **needs** is used. THUS: *It needs to be done at once. He needs to see a doctor.* The same practice holds, in general, for the verb **dare,** the form **dare** being used in negative and interrogative constructions, and the form **dares** in affirmative expressions. THUS: *He dare not go. Dare he say that? He dares to do what he thinks right.*

needs

Needs as an adverb means *of necessity,* and is used chiefly with *must.* THUS: *He needs must go. He went as needs he must.*

neglect,
negligence

The distinction to be noted in the use of these words is that **neglect** refers to the actual and specific failure or omission; **negligence** to the trait of character, habit, or tendency which results in the specific act. THUS: *His negligence has caused his family much distress. His neglect of the notice will cost him dearly.*

neither,
none

Neither should not be used for **none** or **not one.** Neither means *not either of two.* CORRECT: *Neither of his two plays has been performed recently. Of all the half-dozen plays examined not one* (not "neither") *will suit our purposes. Not one* (not "neither") *of the three boys has come up to our expectations.* See **either.**

neither . . . nor

Neither should be followed by **nor,** not by *or.* This is easy to remember, since they are both negatives, and both begin with *n*, as does *negative* itself. THUS: *Neither the Senate nor the House will agree to this proposal. I could neither believe him nor discover when he was lying.* See **either . . . or.**

never,
not

Do not use **never** as the equivalent of **not.** CORRECT: *He did not tell me his name* (not "he never told me his name"). *Mr. Adams did not say that* (not "never said that"). *Woodrow Wilson was not a candidate* (not "never was a candidate") *for President in 1908.*

Never means *at no time,* that is, *not ever,* and is correctly used as follows: *Chaucer was never in Greece. Never had he seen such a sight as now confronted him. Realizations never quite fulfill anticipations.*

Since **never** gives a sentence a negative meaning, do not use **no** or **not** with it. THUS: *He never pays attention to any one* (not "to no one"). *He is never* (not "isn't never") *pleased.*

nevertheless,
none the less

These two terms are frequently confused and misused. Note that **nevertheless** is one word, and that the expression **none the less** is written as three words. **Nevertheless** is a conjunction meaning *notwithstanding, yet.* **None the less** means *not any the less.* It is always followed by an adjective. CORRECT: *She is not altogether dependable. She is, nevertheless, a good cook. I warned him about the danger; nevertheless, he would go. He is none the less willing to work, but his health will not permit. For all her years and infirmities, she is none the less eager to keep up with things.*

news

The word **news** is *singular,* and therefore takes a singular verb. THUS: *The news is good.*

newsy A colloquialism for *abounding in news.*

nice In formal English **nice** means *discriminating* or *precise;* as, *a nice ear for music, a nice distinction.* In colloquial English it is established as a synonym for *kind, good-tempered, pleasing, agreeable,* etc. Care should be taken, however, to keep in mind the accurate use of the word, and to avoid overworking it in its colloquial sense.

nicely The use of **nicely** to mean *in good health* or *improving in health,* as *he is doing nicely,* is colloquial. See **nice.**

nineteenth, ninetieth, ninth Note that in **nineteenth** and **ninetieth,** the word *nine* is included. In **ninth** the *e* is dropped.

no Since **no** means *not any,* do not use another negative with it. CORRECT: *He had no reason* (not "he didn't have no reason") *to be angry. I don't want to hear that any more* (not "no more").

"no account," "no good," "no use" Such expressions as, "he is no account", "a no-account musician", "he's no good", "it's no use", are colloquialisms to be avoided. "Of no account", meaning *worthless,* and "of no use", meaning *useless,* are reputable phrases.

no better, no worse, no more The use of **no** with certain comparatives, such as **better, worse, more, farther, higher,** is colloquially admissible. THUS: *He is no better than he should be. She is no more interested in it than I am.*
Avoid, however, the use of "no different". SAY, *This plan is essentially not different from mine,* or *does not differ from mine,* or *differs not at all from mine;* not "is no different from mine".

no one,
no-one

To aid the reader's eye, write the expression as two separate words, or as a hyphenated word. Do not write "noone".

no place,
nowhere

Note that the phrase **no place** is written as two words. "Noplace" and "nohow" are incorrect forms. The adverb **nowhere** is preferable to "no place". SAY, *He had nowhere* (not "no place") *to go. He could find her nowhere* (not "no place"). See **anywhere, nowhere.**

nominate,
denominate

To **nominate** is *to propose as a candidate for election.* To **denominate** is *to describe as so-and-so, to apply an epithet to.* THUS: *Harrison was nominated for President in 1840. He was denominated "Tippecanoe" by his followers.*

none

None is, strictly speaking, the equivalent of *not one,* but it may be used as either singular or plural. The intention of the speaker decides whether **none** shall take a singular or a plural verb. The following sentences illustrate some of its uses: *Does none* (not one) *of you trust me? There is none* (not one) *so stupid as to believe that the enemy's retreat was voluntary. Did you gather any blueberries? There were none to be found when we got to the field. I looked in to see if any of our friends had arrived, but none were there.*

none the less

See **nevertheless.**

nor, or

To prevent misunderstanding on the part of the reader, care must be exercised in using **nor** and **or** after the words *no* and *not.* In statements expressing a *single* negative idea, use **or** after *no* or *not.* FOR EXAMPLE: *He has no pen or pencil.* (Here "pen or pencil" expresses the single idea of *implement for writ-*

ing.) SIMILARLY: *There was no malice or ill-will in his remarks. He did not hesitate or falter. He does not either write to or visit me.* In statements expressing *two* different negative ideas, use **nor** after *no* or *not.* FOR EXAMPLE: *He is not a Spaniard nor an Italian. He knows not nor cares where we live. The committee has no funds nor any plans for raising funds.*

Particular attention must be paid to the use of **nor** and **or** after *no* or *not* in more complicated sentences, especially those in which the verb has an auxiliary such as *does, have,* or *was being.* If a *single* negative idea is expressed in both members of the sentence, the auxiliary should *not* be repeated, and **or** should be used. THUS: *I was delighted to see that you had not forgotten me or failed to send me a card. He was not being flattered or deluded into supposing that he could win against such experts.* If *two different* ideas are expressed in the two members of the sentence, *repeat* the auxiliary and use **nor** after *no* or *not.* THUS: *The witness said that he had not seen the defendant on the night of June 1, nor had been in communication with him since the first of May. The colonel had not given orders that the soldiers should be confined to their barracks, nor had had any intention of doing so.*

not

Be careful to place **not** before the word or phrase it is meant to qualify. THUS: *Not all the boys will be going home for Christmas.* (Note that this sentence expresses an idea different from that of the statement, "All the boys will not be going home for Christmas.") SIMILARLY: *Not every man that registers will be accepted.* (Compare, "Every man that registers will not be accepted.") *Not to respond when you are called on indicates a lack* *of civility.* (Note, *not to respond.* Do not say "To not respond".)

not so . . . as

See **as . . . as.**

**notable,
    noted,
    notorious,
    notoriety**

Notable and **noted** are used chiefly of persons or things that are remarkable or distinguished for *favorable* reasons. **Notorious** is now almost always used to mean *of ill repute.* **Notoriety,** likewise, means *unfavorable* publicity or distinction. THUS: *that notable day, November 11, 1918; the noted orator, Edward Everett; the notorious Boss Tweed; the notoriety achieved by certain criminals.*

**notation,
    annotation**

These two words are very commonly confused. **Notation** is a *method of representation* by a system of marks, signs, or symbols, as in mathematics or music. The word is also used to refer to any one of the marks. An **annotation** is a *note* added to a text by way of explanation or comment. CORRECT: *The musical notation to signify "staccato" is a dot or an apostrophe placed over or under a note. Emerson had the habit of making annotations on the margins of his books.*

"nothing like"

Do not use "nothing like" in the sense of *not nearly* or *not comparable to.* CORRECT: *He is not nearly* (not "nothing like") *so spry as he was. She is not comparable to* (not "nothing like") *Adelina Patti.*

novice

See **amateur.**

nowhere

Nowhere (not "nowheres") is the correct form. See **anywhere.** Avoid the use of "nowhere near" for *not nearly* or *far from.* CORRECT: *He was not nearly* (not "nowhere near") *so rich as he was supposed to be. She was far from* (not "nowhere near") *ready when I called.*

nth degree

The mathematical symbol *n* does not signify necessarily an *infinite* or *very large* number. It is used properly to represent an *unspecified* or *indefinite* number, which may be any from 1 up. The common use of the expression **to the nth degree** to mean "to the greatest possible extent" is, therefore, technically incorrect. The following sentences illustrate the correct use of **nth**: *Our specifications provide for enlarging the army to the nth degree* (that is, *to any required size*). *This calculation may be carried out to the nth degree* (that is, *to any required power*).

number

Number may take either a singular or a plural verb, according to the sense intended. When the *total* is meant, **number** is treated as singular. When the individual units are referred to, **number** takes a plural verb. THUS: *The number of pages in the book is two hundred. A number of the pages are illustrated.*

Since the words *innumerable* and *numerous* contain the idea of number, do not use them as adjectives with the noun number. CORRECT: *A countless* (not "innumerable") *number; numerous groups* (not "numerous numbers") *of specimens.*

numerous, many

Numerous means *containing a great number of units*. It is not used interchangeably with **many**. Do not say "numerous of". Note the correct uses of **numerous** and **many** in the following sentences: *His library consists of numerous collections of books on railroads. Numerous species of birds are to be seen in the zoo. Many* (not "numerous") *wild geese have been flying over today. Many of* (not "numerous of") *his stamps have brought high prices. Many persons of* (not "numerous of") *the crowd came forward. Many* (not "numerous") *sheep were grazing in the field.* See **number.**

O, oh

O is used (1) before the name of a person or thing directly addressed; (2) as part of a longer exclamation, or with the word *for* in expressing a wish. It is *never* followed by a mark of punctuation. THUS: *O Lord, make haste to help me! O George, come here! O dear! there it goes again! O for a breath of fresh air! O be joyful in the Lord!*

Oh is used in all other cases, and is *always* followed by either a comma or an exclamation mark. THUS: *Oh, say, can you see, by the dawn's early light, . . . ? Oh, no! you are quite wrong. Oh! did you see that? Oh, see who's coming! Oh, but I couldn't think of it. Oh, for Heaven's sake, stop it!*

O.K.

An expressive, but greatly overworked colloquialism, meaning in general "All right", or "All correct". It is used as an adjective ("This is O.K."), as a noun ("Will you give this statement your O.K.?"), and as a verb ("He O.K.'d the bill").

obligate, oblige

Obligate implies a moral or legal duty or constraint. **Oblige** is a less formal word, and is used to express constraint or obligation in general. Hence, it has come to mean *to do a favor to, to accommodate.* FOR EXAMPLE: *As guardian of the child, he was obligated to provide for her education. Because of his business connection with the plaintiff, the judge felt obligated to disqualify himself. He was obliged to remain overnight because of the bad weather. You will oblige me by calling at the office tomorrow morning.*

observance, observation

Observance means *compliance with,* as in *observance of the law;* or *conformity to,* as in *observance of old customs;* or *celebration of,* as in *observance of a holiday.* **Observation** means *taking note of,* as in *observation of his neighbors;* or *the information gained or conclusions reached as the result of taking note,* as in *he published his scientific observations.*

occupancy, occupation

Occupancy refers more particularly to the mere act or state of occupying on the part of a tenant. **Occupation** refers to the taking over, or possession of, a place by legal right or physical force. THUS: *During their occupancy of the house, they had it redecorated and refurnished. The occupation of the country by the opposing forces began during the winter.*

occur, happen, take place

Occur and **happen** are properly applied to circumstances which are not the result of planning. **Occur** is the more formal word, and applies specially to a definite event. **Happen** involves more of the element of chance. THUS: *His death occurred at five in the evening. How did you happen to be there at the time?* **Take place** should be used of events that are planned or arranged. THUS: *The wedding took place in the chapel at high noon.*

Do not use **occur** loosely in the sense of *appear, present itself,* etc. CORRECT: *Many fresh springs are to be found* (not "occur") *near the village. Several species of conifers grow* (not "occur") *in the northern counties.* See **happen.**

ocher (ochre), okra

Ocher is a red or yellow pigment used in making paints. **Okra** is a vegetable.

oculist, optometrist, optician

An **oculist** is a physician who is skilled in treating diseases of the eye. An **optometrist** is one who is skilled in finding and measuring errors in vision for the purpose of determining the kind of lens which will correct the error. An **optician** is one who makes lenses and fits them to frames according to the specifications provided by an optometrist. An **oculist** is usually able to perform the work of an **optometrist**. An **optometrist** is *not* a physician and may not perform the work of an **oculist**.

of

See from, have, inside, outside.

of all,
"of any",
"of anyone"

Do not say "of any" or "of anyone" when you mean of all. CORRECT: *His was the largest collection of all* (not "the largest of any"). *He is the oldest man* (not "the oldest man of anyone") *I know. We had more men in Class A than any other regiment* (not "the most . . . of any regiment").

of his,
of John's

The double possessive, as in *that picture of his, a friend of John's,* is correct and fitting in familiar conversation, but is not appropriate in formal English or when applied to a great man or to a person of prominence. CORRECT: *a friend of Washington* (not "of Washington's"); *an acquaintance of Secretary Hull* (not "of Secretary Hull's"); *a cousin of the Prime Minister* (not "of the Prime Minister's"). To avoid misunderstanding, however, one says *a saying of Goethe's, a book of Shelley's, a habit of Darwin's.*

of which,
whose

Of which is commonly applied to things; **whose** to persons. THUS: *my farm, the acreage of which,* etc.; *Tenth Street, at the end of which I live.* **Whose** may be used of any object that has life; as, *my dog, whose name is Terry; a tree whose leaves were withered.* **Whose** may also be used of objects in personification; as, *the old town, whose age was one of her chief attractions.* To avoid awkward constructions, **whose** may be used for **of which** in speaking of inanimate objects. THUS: *a city, whose builder and maker is God; a cube whose sides are made of metal.*

off

Avoid adding *of* or *from* to the preposition **off**. CORRECT: *Keep off* (not "off of") *the grass. He fell off* (not "off of" or "off from") *the ladder. They took their coats off* (not "off of" or "off from") *the hooks. We ate off* (not "off of") *wooden trenchers.* Colloquial: *off* (not "off of") *his food; off* (not "off of") *his game.*

"Off of" in the sense of *from* is bad usage. CORRECT: *He stole the knife from* (not "off of") *the boy next him. The policeman took it from* (not "off of") *him. We got our vegetables from* (not "off of") *a neighbor.*

**official,
officer**

An **official** is one who holds public office, especially one who exercises subordinate executive powers; as *customs official.* An **officer** is one who holds office in any organization. In the service of the state, the word **officer** is usually restricted to those in positions of command in *uniformed* services.

**often,
at times,
sometimes**

These words refer properly to periods or intervals of *time,* and should not be used loosely to refer to *place* or *number.* CORRECT: *In some sections* (not "sometimes") *we found that the drought had ruined the pastures. Here and there* (not "at times") *we saw herds of cattle trying to find a bit of green. Many of* (not "often") *the poor things looked as if they had not strength enough to continue their search much longer.*

old   See **ancient.**

older   See **elder.**

on account of

Avoid the use of **on account of** for *because*. CORRECT: *I did not come, because* (not "on account of") *I did not get your invitation.*

on to,
onto

Until recently the preposition **onto** was not recognized by the best writers, but the popular demand for a word corresponding to *into* which would express motion **on to** or *against* an object may be said to have established **onto** in the language. THUS: *He held onto the window ledge. They climbed out of the attic window onto the roof. He stepped out of the boat onto the shore.*

Do not, however, use the preposition **onto** when the meaning requires the two words **on** and **to,** as in the following sentences: *Send the goods on to* (not "onto") *me. He passed the ball on to* (not "onto") *the player at his right.*

one, one's,
oneself

To avoid confusing the reader, the indefinite pronoun **one** should be followed by **one, one's, oneself,** etc. THUS: *The more one thinks of Lincoln, the more one* (not "he", since the reader will think that "he" refers to Lincoln) *wonders how he accomplished what he did. One asks oneself what one would have done in his place.* Do not allow the sentence to become awkward or ridiculous through the too frequent use of **one.** Begin the sentence with *A person, A man, The reader, Anybody,* or some other appropriate word instead of **one.**

one another,
each other

One another is used of *more than two.* **Each other** is used of *two.* See **each other.**

one of the . . . that,
one of those . . .
that

In using such expressions as *That is one of those things that annoy me most,* or *She is one of those women who are always on time,* the common tendency is to lose sight of the fact that in the first sentence *things* (not *that* or *one*) is the word that determines whether the verb shall be *annoy* or *annoys,* and that in the second sentence *women* (not *she* or *one*) is the word that determines whether the verb shall be *are* or *is*. One may say either *She is a woman who is always on time,* or *She is one of those women who are always on time*. The predicate clause in the first sentence is *a woman who is*. The predicate clause in the second is *those women who are*. Note carefully the following sentences: *His is not* a mind that jumps *from subject to subject. His is not one of* those minds that jump *from subject to subject. This is* an issue that is *being hotly debated. This is one of* the issues that are *being hotly debated*.

only

Be careful to place **only** before the word or phrase it modifies. Note how the statement, "He mentioned this subject to me", can be altered in four different ways by placing **only** at four different positions in it. THUS: *Only he mentioned,* etc.; *he only mentioned,* etc.; *he mentioned only this subject,* etc.; *he mentioned this subject only to me*.

Avoid the use of "only but" for *but* or *only*. SAY, *There is only one day more,* or *There is but one day more;* not "There is only but one day more."

or

Remember that the expression is *seldom if ever,* not "seldom or ever." The phrase *seldom or never* is, of course, correct.

or, nor

See **either . . . or, neither . . . nor,** and **nor.**

oral, verbal

The *o* in **oral** is pronounced like that in *oval*. Avoid the common confusion of **oral** and **verbal**. **Oral** means, in this connection, spoken. **Verbal** means expressed in words. A verbal communication may, therefore, be either *spoken* or *written*. CORRECT: *To prevent a copy of the instructions from falling into enemy hands, his superior officer gave them to him orally* (that is, *by word of mouth*). *The secretary made a verbal transcript of the cipher code.*

**ordinance,
ordnance**

The two words, though similar in appearance, are spelled differently and have entirely different meanings. An **ordinance** is a *decree,* or a *prescribed practice.* **Ordnance** is a military term meaning *mounted guns, cannon,* etc.

ordinary

The dialectal variant of **ordinary**, "ornery", is incorrect and should be avoided. See **average.**

**ostensible,
ostentatious**

Ostensible and **ostentatious** both come from the Latin word meaning *to show.* **Ostensible** means *shown for the purpose of deceiving others.* **Ostentatious** means *showy.* THUS: *His ostensible motive was patriotism. Actually, he was a spy. Therefore his gestures of devotion to the country were ostentatious.*

other

Be careful to use the word **other** in making comparisons between two persons or things belonging to the same class. THUS: *Leonard is a better student than the other boys in his fraternity* (not "than the boys in his fraternity"). **Other** should, of course, not be used when the comparison is between two persons or things which belong to different classes. THUS: *Ellen is a better artist than the boys of the family.* If the *superlative* is employed in a comparison, **other** is not used. THUS: *The Americans have developed the highest technical proficiency that has yet been seen in any nation.*

other than

Notice that **other** is followed by **than,** not by *but* or *except.* CORRECT: *I have no other samples than* (not "but" or "except") *these to show you. The "stranger" was no other than* (not "but" or "except") *my brother.*

other,
otherwise

Careful writers and speakers discriminate between these two words, using **other** as the *adjective,* and **otherwise** as the *adverb.* **Other,** in this connection means *different.* **Otherwise** means *in a different manner, in different circumstances, in other respects.* FOR EXAMPLE: *The quality is other than* (that is, *different from) that originally promised. The facts appear to be other* (not "otherwise") *than as stated in your report. His income, earned or other* (not "otherwise"), *did not amount to more than $5,000. All taxpayers—merchants, industrialists, farmers, or other* (not "otherwise")—*will be affected by the new law. I could not speak otherwise* (not "other") *than frankly to so good a friend. He could not look otherwise than with* (not "with other than") *sorrow at the condition the home was in. Whether he spoke facetiously or otherwise, he always held his audience.*

Do not use "other than" or "otherwise than" if the simpler words *except* and *unless* express the meaning adequately. THUS: *All men, except* (not "other than") *those registered, should apply. The students, unless they have been* (not "other than those who have been") *specially excused, will remain after the faculty has left the room. I always forgot that he was a judge except when he spoke in terms of court procedure* (preferable to "when he spoke otherwise than in terms of court procedure").

other times

Use *at* with the expression **other times** when it is employed to modify a verb. THUS: *At other times, he seemed very glad to see me.*

ought,
  nought

. See **aught**.

ought,
  should

Ought and **should** both express obligation, and are used more or less interchangeably. **Ought** implies more particularly *moral* obligation. **Should** is used particularly with respect to *appropriateness* or *fitness*. THUS: *We ought to refrain from censure when we do not know all the circumstances. A man ought, if necessary, to support his aged parents. A boy should remove his hat on entering the house.*

Avoid the incorrect use of *had* with **ought**. See **had**.

out of

Out is followed by **of**, not *from*. THUS: *He came out of the house. He took the hat out of the box.*

"out for",
  "out to"

"Out for", in the sense of *looking for, seeking for,* is slang, as is also "out to" in the expression "out to get him", etc. See **after**.

out loud

A colloquialism for *aloud*.

outdoor,
  out-of-door,
  outdoors,
  out-of-doors

Outdoor, **out-of-door**, and **out-of-doors** are adjectives; **outdoors** and **out-of-doors** are adverbs. THUS: *She spent the winter in an outdoor* (or *out-of-door,* or *out-of-doors*) *hospital. He spent most of his time outdoors* (or *out-of-doors*).

outside

The use of the preposition *of* with **outside** is colloquial. PREFERABLE: *He was outside* (not "outside of") *the group.* Avoid the slang use of **outside** or "outside of" for *besides*. SAY, *Besides us* (not "outside of us") *there were seven in the group.* See **inside**.

over

Do not use "overly" for **over**. SAY, *overanxious, over-eager,* etc., not "overly anxious", "overly eager", etc.

overflowed

Be careful not to say "overflown" when you mean **overflowed**. *Flowed* is the past participle of *flow;* **overflowed** the past participle of *overflow*. *Flown* is the past participle of *fly*. There is no verb "to overfly". CORRECT: *The water has overflowed* (not "overflown") *the fields on both sides of the river.*

"over with"

"Over with" in the sense of *completed* is slang; as in the expression, "There! That job is over with!"

owing to

See **due to**.

pain,
  pane

Do not confuse the spellings of the two words. **Pain** means *suffering*. **Pane** is the *glass part of a window*.

pair,
  pare

Note carefully the spellings of the two words. **Pair** means *a set of two;* as, *a pair of shoes*. **Pare** means *to trim,* or *to cut away the surface;* as, *to pare one's nails, to pare an apple.*

pair,
  couple,
  set

For the distinction between **pair** and **couple**, see **couple**. **Set** means *a number of articles which belong together;* as, *a coffee set, a toilet set*. **Set** usually refers to more than two articles.

The plural of **pair** is *pair* when a specific number precedes the word; otherwise it is *pairs*. THUS: *four pair of shoes; several pairs of boots; many pairs of gloves.*

pants

A colloquialism for *trousers.*

pardon

See **excuse**.

parricide

See **matricide**.

part,
  portion

Part and **portion** are commonly used interchangeably, but are not exactly so. **Part** is the more general word, and means *a fraction* *of a whole;* as *part of a story.* **Portion** means strictly *a part allotted or assigned to a particular person or purpose;* as, *your portion of the pie,* or *the university's portion of the estate.*

**part from,
part with**

To part from means *to go away from* (a person). To part with means *to give up* (a thing). THUS: *He parted from his wife. He parted with some of his most cherished possessions.*

partake of

Partake of, meaning *to have a share in,* should not be used as a refined synonym of the ordinary words *eat* or *drink.* A person may **partake of,** that is *participate in,* a meal or anything else with others, but he does not **partake of** a meal or of anything else by himself.

**partial,
partially,
partly**

Since the word **partial** has two quite different meanings, (1) *biased in favor of one side,* and (2) *not total or complete,* care should be taken not to use **partial** in the second sense in constructions which might be ambiguous and cause misunderstanding. THUS: *a partial history, a partial report,* etc., might mean either a *biased* or an *incomplete* history, report, etc. In such constructions use *incomplete* or *unfinished* instead of **partial,** and **partly** instead of **partially.** CORRECT: *Because of the pressure of work, I must present an incomplete* (not "partial") *report of what we have been doing. Only incomplete* (not "partial") *records of his business dealings have been found. His account of the trial was based partly* (not "partially") *on what he had heard at the club.*

partial to

Partial to in the sense of *fond of* is colloquial; as in, "She is partial to the color blue."

particle   See **drop.**

party   See **individual.**

passed,   Passed is the past tense of the verb, *to pass.*
past   THUS: *They passed by the house.* **Past,** also
                            derived from the verb *to pass,* may be a noun,
                            an adjective, an adverb, or a preposition.
                            THUS: *shades of the past* (noun); *the past
                            week* (adjective); *he walked past* (adverb);
                            it is now past two o'clock (preposition).

patron,   **Patron** and **patronize** are greatly over-
patronize   worked words in the colloquial sense of *cus-
                            tomer* and *to trade with,* respectively. **Patron**
                            properly means a person of wealth or im-
                            portance who *fosters* or *protects* a person,
                            institution, or cause. **Patronize,** correspond-
                            ingly, means *to act as patron to.* It is used
                            also in the unfavorable sense of *to condescend
                            to.* The following sentences illustrate the cor-
                            rect uses of the words: *Mr. Mason had for
                            over thirty years been a patron of the Chil-
                            dren's Welfare Society. The artist, in his
                            youthful struggles, had been patronized by
                            Mr. Stransky, the conductor of the orchestra.
                            She never failed to patronize (act con-
                            descendingly towards) the grocer when she
                            appeared at his shop.* NOTE: Either **patron** or
                            patroness may be used of a woman. **Patron**
                            is now more commonly used. THUS: *Lady
                            Donaldson was an enthusiastic patron of
                            music.*

pecuniary   See **financial.**

peel,   Note the differences in spelling. **Peel**
peal   means *rind;* **peal** means *a loud ringing of
                            bells.* Both words are used also as verbs.

penny,   The plural of **penny** (the British coin) is
pennies,   **pennies,** when the individual coins are
pence   thought of as objects. THUS: *The child had*

saved three pennies. In computing sums and values, the plural is **pence.** From *twopence* through *tenpence,* and in *twentypence,* the word **pence** is written together with the number (as here illustrated). Otherwise **pence** is written separately; as *eleven pence.*

people, persons

People, which means persons in a *collective* sense, *a body of persons united in some way or other,* should not be used when *individual persons* are referred to. CORRECT: *There were only two or three, or at most half a dozen, persons* (not "people") *in the room. A few persons* (not "people") *have called this morning. We, the people* (not "persons") *of Cincinnati, will have something to say about this. Will the peoples* (that is, *the different races, nations, etc.) of Europe learn to get on with one another?*

per

The Latin preposition **per** was formerly restricted to use with Latin terms, as *per annum, per centum, per diem,* etc. It is now used more or less generally with English terms as well. Its use should, however, be restricted to technical terms; as *ten revolutions per minute, two grams per cubic centimeter.* The use of **per** is common and appropriate in commercial locutions; as in *ten dollars per dozen, as per invoice, per inclosed account.* For general use, the simple English word *a* is better. THUS: *four times a year, ten dollars a day, two dollars a person,* etc.

per cent, percentage

Per cent (formerly always written with a period, as *per cent.,* and as two words) is often written as one word. It is from the Latin *per centum,* meaning *by the hundred,* or *in the hundred.* It is properly an adverbial phrase, not a noun. Its use should be distinguished from that of the noun **percentage,** which means *rate per cent,* that is, *rate in* or *on a hundred.* **Percentage** is used loosely, but improperly, to mean *a proportion or part of the whole;* as "A small percentage of the men were disqualified." CORRECT: *The rate of interest on United States Savings Bonds is 2.9 per cent a year. The percentage* (not "per cent", nor "percentage per hundred") *of adult illiteracy in the United States is constantly decreasing.* The expression, "There's no percentage in that", is slang.

perform   See **assume.**

permit   See **allow.**

persecute,   The two words are sometimes confused.
prosecute   **Persecute** means *to subject to persistent ill-treatment.* **Prosecute** means *to pursue or carry on,* or *to bring a lawsuit against.* CORRECT: *This group has for many years persecuted* (not "prosecuted") *helpless minorities. The candidates for officers' commissions must prosecute* (not "persecute") *their studies day in and day out. We hope to prosecute* (not "persecute") *tc a successful completion our plan to rid the city of the smoke nuisance. The government will prosecute* (not "persecute") *in a Federal Court the directors of the company.* The noun *persecution* is followed by the preposition *of,* not *against.* THUS: *His prosecution of the suit against his wife was part of his persecution of her.*

person   See **individual.**

personal,   Note the spellings. **Personal** is an adjective,
personnel   meaning *pertaining to a person.* **Personnel** is a noun taken directly from the French. It means *a body of persons engaged in public service,* or *the personal staff of an organization.*

personalty,
realty

Personalty means personal property of *any kind whatever* that may be moved, as distinguished from **realty**, which means *real estate, landed property in any form.* Compare the legal expression, "property personal or real".

persons

See **people.**

perspicacity,
perspicuity

Perspicacity means *keenness in seeing or understanding* a thing, especially in the sense of having *foresight.* THUS: *The president showed perspicacity in respect to the needs of the people.* **Perspicuity** means *clearness to the understanding,* and is applied chiefly to speech and writing. THUS: *There was great perspicuity in his explanation of the causes of the catastrophe. Perspicuity is one of the prime qualities of good prose.*

persuade,
convince

Persuade emphasizes the idea of *winning over.* **Convince** emphasizes the idea of *proof by argument.* THUS: *They persuaded me to go home with them. They convinced me that their candidate was best by showing me his record, and persuaded me to vote for him.*

perturb,
unperturbed

Perturb means *to disturb greatly; to agitate.* THUS: *He was perturbed by his family's financial distress.* **Unperturbed,** which is the opposite of *perturbed,* is often incorrectly used in a trivial sense, with the meaning of *calm.*

petition,
partition

A **petition** is a *plea;* a **partition,** *a dividing wall.* Avoid confusion of spelling and pronunciation.

peruse,
read

Do not use **peruse** when you mean merely **read. Peruse** means *to read carefully and critically, to examine a text in detail.*

phase

Phase means *aspect,* or *side;* as, *a phase of history that should be emphasized.* Phase also has technical meanings in various sciences. In popular use the word is much overworked. See **element.**

phenomenon,
phenomena

Phenomenon, from the Latin, is the singular; phenomena, the plural. Be careful not to say "a phenomena".

phone

Phone is the shortened form of *telephone.* It is acceptable in informal usage, and may be used as a noun or a verb.

photo

Colloquial for *photograph,* but not approved by the best speakers.

piece

Piece, used to mean *distance,* as in "He lives a short piece down the road", is a provincialism.

pillar,
pillow

A pillar is a *supporting column;* as, *Greek pillars.* A pillow is a *cushion.* Note carefully the differences in spelling and pronunciation. Pillow rhymes with *willow.*

pity,
sympathy

Pity implies feeling for the sufferings of one who is regarded as weak or inferior. Sympathy refers to the sharing of feelings between persons of similar qualities. THUS: *The President expressed pity for the homeless children of Europe. We extend sympathy to our friends in their bereavement.*

place,
places

Avoid the use of the words **place** and **places** without a preposition, as if they were adverbs. CORRECT: *I could find him nowhere* (not "no place"). *I went everywhere* (not "every place") *in search of him. He always wants to go somewhere* (not "to go places"). *He is likely to be found anywhere* (not "any place"). See **anyhow, any place.**

plan	See **compute.**
plan to	**Plan to** is the correct expression. Avoid "plan on." CORRECT: *They planned to stay* (not "on staying") *a week.*
plead, pleaded	**Pleaded** is the approved past tense of **plead.** THUS: *He pleaded* (not "pled" or "plĕad") *not guilty.*
plenty, plentiful, plentifully	**Plenty** is properly a noun, meaning *abundance;* as, *plenty of food.* In correct usage it is followed always by *of.* It is used provincially as an adjective, "plenty room", and as an adverb, "plenty large". These expressions should be avoided, as should also the provincialism, "he ate plenty", and "plenty big enough". Use the words **plentiful** and **plentifully** to express ideas of this nature. THUS: *Fresh vegetables are plentiful. The larder was plentifully supplied* (not "there was plenty enough in the larder").
plurality	See **majority.**
politics	**Politics** may be used as either a singular or a plural noun. Do not, however, change from one to the other number after you have begun a discussion. See **acoustics.**
poorly	**Poorly,** in the sense of *not in good health* is an unacceptable provincialism; as, "She is feeling poorly today."
popular	A greatly overworked word, used improperly to refer to persons or things that are attractive, lively, well liked, congenial, sympathetic, etc. **Popular** should be reserved for use in its proper sense—*of, or pertaining to, or suitable to, the whole body of the people;* hence, *generally understood, liked, and ad-*

mired. Avoid the construction "popular with". CORRECT: *The captain was well liked by,* or *was greatly admired by* (not "was popular with") *his men. We like Mr. Johnson* (not "Mr. Johnson is popular with us"). *The new plan is very popular,* or *is exciting popular enthusiasm* (not "is popular with the public").

pore,
pour

Note the differences in spelling and meaning. To **pore** over means *to look at,* or *read, intently.* To **pour** is *to cause to flow in a continuous stream.*

portion,
potion

Do not pronounce **portion** as **potion.** Potion is *a dose, usually of liquid medicine.* For **portion** see **part.**

postal

Colloquial for *postal card* in the U. S.

posted

Posted for *informed* is an unacceptable colloquialism. CORRECT: *He is a very well informed* (not "well posted") *man. I'll keep you informed* (not "posted").

practicable,
practical

Discriminate carefully between the two words. **Practical** is the more general of the two, and means *usable, useful, having to do with action,* as opposed to *theoretical, ideal, speculative.* Thus, one speaks of *a practical mind, a practical man, practical science, practical knowledge, practical considerations, practical agriculture.* **Practicable** is used only of *objects, plans,* etc., and is never applied to persons. THUS: *Of all the plans submitted by the committee of practical men, only one proved to be really practicable* (that is, *able to be put into practice*). *Practical minds are engaged in trying to invent a practicable method of combating the submarine.*

**practice,
practise**

The noun should always be spelled **prac-tice**. The verb may be spelled either **practice** or **practise**.

**pray,
prey**

These words are pronounced alike. Note the differences in spelling and meaning. **To pray** is *to offer prayers*. **To prey upon** means *to take violently as food*, or *to plunder*. THUS: *Cats prey upon birds. The barbarians preyed upon the little country.*

**precede,
proceed,
procedure,
supersede**

Observe carefully the spellings of these often misspelled words. Note specially that the second syllable of **procedure**, although derived from the verb **proceed**, has only one *e*.

**predominate,
predominant,
predominantly**

Predominate is a verb, and means *to have the chief power, to prevail over*. THUS: *Democratic theories of government have always predominated in that country.* **Predominant** is an adjective; **predominantly**, an adverb. Avoid the incorrect form "predominately". Since **predominant** implies the superlative degree, do not use *more* or *most* with it. CORRECT: *The predominant* (not "more" or "most" *predominant*) *aim of his life was to get rich.*

prefer

Prefer should be followed by *to*, not by *than* or *rather than*. CORRECT: *He preferred reading to studying* (not "preferred reading rather than studying"). *I prefer to sit down; I do not care to dance* (not "I prefer to sit than dance").

preferable

The stress is on the first syllable, *pref-*, which rhymes with *clef*. **Preferable**, like *prefer*, is followed by *to*, never by *than*. THUS: *Work is preferable to* (not "preferable than") *idleness.* Since **preferable** implies the comparative degree, do not use *more* with it.

CORRECT: *Which of the two houses is preferable* (not "more preferable")?

prejudice

Notice the spelling. Do not put a *d* before the *j*. **Prejudice** comes from the same Latin root as *judicial*, and means a *preconceived judgment, opinion,* or *bias*. Note that the proper usage is *prejudice against* a person or thing, but prejudice *in favor of* (not "for", or "on behalf of", or "towards") a person or thing. THUS: *a prejudice against being seen at the theater; a prejudice in favor of Oriental paintings.*

prescribe,
proscribe

The two words, often confused, have almost opposite meanings. **To prescribe** is *to lay down as a guide or course of action.* THUS: *The doctor prescribed a series of exercises for the boy.* **To proscribe** is *to outlaw, to banish, to forbid.* THUS: *The practice of smoking in department stores has been proscribed in many cities.* The nouns, *prescription* and *proscription* have similar distinctions.

prevent

Prevent is followed by *from*, not by *to*. CORRECT: *His cold will prevent him from doing* (not "to do") *his work.*

preventive

Preventive means *that which prevents.* Note that **preventive**, not "preventative", is the correct form.

previous,
previously

Previous, meaning *foregoing, prior to,* is both an adjective and an adverb. There is also the adverb **previously**. THUS: *The previous day had been stormy. He arrived two days previous to his wedding. He had telegraphed previous to his coming. They are now friendly, but were previously bitter enemies.*

prey   See **pray.**

principal,   These are among the words most com-
  principle   monly confused. Observe the difference in
    spelling. **Principal** as an adjective means
    chief, main, leading. THUS: *Mr. Cox's prin-*
    cipal supporters; the principal food; the prin-
    cipal reason. As a noun, **principal** means *a*
    leader, a head; or *a sum placed at interest.*
    THUS: *Dr. Jacobs has been appointed prin-*
    cipal of the school. The principal at interest
    this year is $1,500. **Principle** means *a rule of*
    action, or *a fundamental truth.* THUS: *Hon-*
    esty was the guiding principle of his life. He
    demonstrated the principle of the new engine.
    He acted always on principle, not on impulse.

proof   See **evidence.**

prophecy,   **Prophecy** is the noun. The last syllable,
  prophesy   *-cy,* is pronounced like the last syllable in
    policy. **Prophesy** is the verb. The last syllable,
    -sy, rhymes with *why.*

proposal,   A **proposal** is *a plan or scheme proposed,*
  proposition   *an offer;* as, *a proposal of marriage.* A
    proposition is *a statement or assertion, a prin-*
    ciple, a suggestion of terms, or, in mathe-
    matics or logic, *a problem formally stated.*
    A **proposal** may usually be accepted or re-
    jected without prolonged consideration. A
    proposition usually invites discussion and
    debate. In many cases the simpler word
    proposal is meant when the word **proposition**
    is used. FOR EXAMPLE: *His proposal* (not
    "proposition") *that both the operators and*
    the miners submit their dispute to arbitra-
    tion was accepted. They rejected our pro-
    posal of coöperation in distributing the ques-
    tionnaires. Our government, Lincoln asserted,
    is "dedicated to the proposition that all men

are created free and equal". How are we to reconcile the two propositions, that all things are done by Fate, and yet that some things lie within our own power?

Proposition is used also in the sense of *a project, a business undertaking*. The expressions, "It's not a paying proposition", "He's a tough proposition", etc., are slang.

propose, purpose

The two words are often confused. To **propose** is *to offer, to put forward as a plan or candidate*. To **purpose** is *to have as a purpose, to resolve, to intend*. Use **propose** if you are *proposing* or *offering something;* use **purpose** if you are *expressing an intention*. FOR EXAMPLE: *I propose this subject for debate. The speaker proposed Mr. Miller for secretary. I propose a toast to the retiring chairman. I propose (announce my intention) to publish the complete records of the investigation. I purpose (intend) to give the committee all the details. We purpose that such disaster shall not occur again. I purpose to devote myself to the cause from now on.*

proscribe See **prescribe**.

prosecute See **persecute**.

proved, proven

Proved is the accepted form, although **proven** seems to be the more commonly used.

provided, providing

The preferred form is **provided** or **provided that**. THUS: *You will receive your degree provided* (rather than *providing*) *you have completed your prescribed work satisfactorily.*

provoke See **aggravate**.

"pull" "Pull" in the sense of *influence, backing*, is slang.

pupil,
student,
scholar

Pupil is used of younger persons, and especially in relation to a teacher's personal care. **Student** is the general term for one in attendance at a higher institution of learning. **Scholar** is now applied chiefly to one who has engaged in advanced study, and acquired knowledge in some special field.

quantity,
number

Quantity is a general word, and may be applied to an amount that may be either counted or measured; as, *a large quantity of oranges, an equal quantity of water.* **Number** should be applied only to a total that can be counted; as, *a number of persons, large numbers of ships.* See **amount.**

quay

Quay (a landing place) is pronounced like *key* (an instrument for turning the bolt of a lock).

quite

The proper meaning of **quite** is *completely, wholly, perfectly.* It is much overworked colloquially in the sense of *considerably, very, rather,* etc. Special care should be taken to avoid the use of **quite** in the colloquial sense whenever ambiguity may result. Thus, in the sentence, *The present methods of computing the assessments are quite unsatisfactory,* the word **quite,** if used precisely means *altogether, wholly.* If used in the loose colloquial sense, it might mean merely *rather* or *very.* **Quite** is allowable in informal English in such expressions as, "It is quite early", "The weather has been quite cold", "He is quite ill". The colloquialisms, "quite a good many" and "quite a good deal", are acceptable. Avoid the provincialisms, "quite a number" (for *many*), "quite a little" (for *much*), "quite a few" (for *several,* or *many*), "quite the artist" (for *artistic*), "quite the thing" (for *fashionable*), "quite so" (for "I agree with you").

"quotes" — The abbreviation "quotes" for *quotation marks* is not acceptable in good English usage. Similarly, the expressions "quote" and "unquote", meaning respectively to begin and to end a quotation, are colloquial.

rabbit,
rarebit — The term in cookery is properly **Welsh rabbit,** but "rarebit", the product of false etymology, is now much used.

radical,
extremist — **Radical** comes from the Latin word that means *root*. Hence, a **radical** is a person who wishes to get to the root or fundamentals of a thing, or to make fundamental changes in a government or other institution. In popular speech, **radical** and **extremist** are often used interchangeably, but, strictly regarded, such interchange is incorrect. An **extremist** is one who *goes to extremes in anything.*

The adjective **radical** means *original, fundamental, affecting the vital principle.* The adverb **radically** means *in a radical or thoroughgoing manner,* and should not be used loosely in the sense of *greatly, considerably.* CORRECT: *The engineers are making radical changes in the design of the engine. The voters will be called upon to alter radically the constitution of the state. He has changed greatly* (not "radically") *in appearance since he came.*

rain,
reign,
rein — All three are pronounced alike. Notice the spellings. **Rain** is *condensed moisture falling in drops.* **To reign** means *to rule.* **Rein** is *the strap used to guide or check a horse.*

raise (*noun*) — In the sense of *increase in salary or wages,* the word **raise** is colloquial.

raise (*verb*) — **Raise** in the sense of *bring up* or *rear* is unacceptable as applied to children. In this sense it is properly used only of animals.

raise, **raze**	The two words are pronounced alike. **Raze** means *to destroy utterly, to make level with the ground.*
rang, **wrung**	The pronunciation, the spelling, and the meaning of the two words are often confused. **Rang** is the past tense of *ring* (*to give forth a sound as of a bell*); **wrung** is the past tense of *wring* (*to squeeze tightly*). Avoid the incorrect form "wrang".
rarely if ever, **seldom if ever,** **seldom or never**	These are the approved expressions. The expressions, "rarely ever", "rarely or ever", "seldom ever", "seldom or ever", are unaccepted colloquialisms.
rather	See **more, prefer.**
react, **respond**	**React** in the sense of **respond** is greatly overworked in current usage. Try to express the exact kind of response in each case. **React** is a technical term meaning *to display some form of energy in response to a stimulus.* THUS: *In administering ether, the anaesthetist observes carefully how his patient reacts. How did he respond* (not "react") *to your efforts to be friendly?*
real, **really**	**Real** is an adjective; as, *real money.* Avoid the vulgar use of **real** as an adverb, in the sense of *very,* or instead of the adverb **really.** CORRECT: *She's a very* (not "real") *pretty girl. This is very,* or *really* (not "real") *important. That was a really,* or *very* (not "real") *admirable effort on their part.* See **regular.**
realize	The word has three syllables. Do not say "re-lize".
realty	See **personalty.**

reason

Do not say "The reason is because . . .", or "The reason is due to . . .", or "The reason is on account of . . .". The **reason** is *the fact given as the motive or cause or justification of an act, or condition.* CORRECT: *The reason for my saying this is that* (not "because") *I firmly believe it. The reason he did not receive the letter this morning is that* (not "on account of the fact that") *the mails have been delayed.* The expression, "The reason why . . .", is an accepted colloquialism.

rebellion, revolt, revolution

A **rebellion** is *an open, organized, and armed resistance to established government.* A **revolt** is *an armed uprising on a smaller scale.* A **revolution** involves *the overthrowing of one government and the setting up of another.*

receipt, recipe

Receipt and **recipe** are now used interchangeably in cookery. **Recipe** is used more particularly to refer to a formula for compounding a *medicine.*

reciprocal

See **common.**

reckon

A provincialism for *suppose* or *think.*

recollect, remember

Recollect and **remember** are not interchangeable. **To recollect** means *to make an effort to remember.* One may **remember** without trying to or wishing to. THUS: *I remember with chagrin this morning that I did not recollect the tickets when I went to the theater last evening.*

reconciled to, reconciled with

One is **reconciled with** or **to** a person; that is, becomes friendly with him after an estrangement. One **reconciles** one set of facts or figures **with** another; that is, brings them into harmony or compatibility one with another. One becomes **reconciled to,** that is, *resigned to* or *adjusted to,* circumstances or conditions, such as poverty or illness.

recur

See **reopen.**

reduce, lessen

The two words are in many cases, but not in all, interchangeable. **Reduce** refers chiefly to diminishing in *bulk, amount,* or *extent.* THUS: one's *income,* or *weight,* or the *acreage of one's farm* is **reduced.** One's *pain,* or *the number of trips to the dentist,* or *one's desire to go to the dentist* is **lessened.** Note that it is the *number* of trips or the *number* of accidents, etc., that is **lessened,** not the *trips* nor the *accidents,* etc.

refer, reply

Since the prefix **re-** means *back,* do not use the word *back* with such words as **refer, reply, return, rebound, regain, revert.**

refill

See **reopen.**

regain

See **refer.**

regard, regards

Regard means *esteem* or *admiration.* THUS: *We have a great regard for him.* The plural, **regards,** means *compliments, good wishes, greetings.* THUS: *Please give our kind regards to your mother.*

regard to

Notice that only the singular form, **regard,** is used in such expressions as *with regard to, in regard to, without regard to, pay no regard to.* Avoid the incorrect expressions, "in regards to", "with regards to", etc. CORRECT: *With regard to your question, you may dispose of the house if you wish. With regard to this,* etc., is preferable to *as regards this,* etc.

**regardless,
irrespective**

Be careful to avoid the incorrect form "irregardless" through confusion of these two words. **Regardless** and **irrespective** are usually followed by *of*. CORRECT: *The arrangements must be made regardless of* (or *irrespective of*) *his personal feelings in the matter;* not "must be made regardless". Since **regardless** and **doubtless** are adverbs as used in such expressions, do not add the suffix -*ly* to either word.

**regular,
real**

Regular in the sense of **real** or **true** is colloquial; as, "a regular tyrant". PREFERRED: *He was a real, or true* (not "regular") *pioneer.*

**relation,
relative**

Relation and **relative,** for *kinsman,* are now established in current usage, and are interchangeable. *Kinsman* properly means *a person related by blood.*

relieve

See **alleviate.**

remainder

See **balance.**

remember

Do not use *of* after **remember.** CORRECT: *I remember* (not "remember of") *seeing you last year.* See **recollect.**

**remit,
remittance**

Do not use the verb **remit** as a substitute for the noun **remittance.** CORRECT: *He received regular remittances* (not "remits") *from his banker.*

**reopen,
replace**

Since the prefix *re-* means *again,* do not use *again* with such words as **reopen, replace, rebuild, recur, refill.**

**repel,
repulse**

Repel and **repulse** are in most respects interchangeable. **Repulse** is the more forceful word, and it commonly implies the use of *physical force,* or the presence of something *shocking* or *extremely distasteful*. **Repel** may imply the unconscious or unwilling effect of driving others away. THUS: *The coldness of his manner repelled me. The defenders of the city repulsed* (or *repelled*) *the attackers with great slaughter.* The corresponding adjectives, *repellent* and *repulsive,* have respectively somewhat the same distinctions in their meanings.

replica,
copy,
facsimile

A **replica** is properly a *duplicate* of a work of art made by the original artist. A **copy** is an *imitation* of an original work. A **facsimile** is an *exact copy* of a manuscript or a printed page or a picture.

reply

See **answer, refer.**

repulse

See **repel.**

reputation

See **character.**

requirement,
requisite,
requisition

Requirement and **requisite** are often used interchangeably. Strictly speaking, a **requirement** is a *thing required;* a **requisite** is *a thing needed.* One's **requirements** may be many, therefore, although one's **requisites** may be few. THUS: *A strong constitution was one of the requirements for admission to the athletic club. Eagerness to learn and willingness to study are prime requisites for any genuine education. The only requirements he made of us were the requisites of good taste.* **Requisition** is the *formal act of requiring on the part of authority;* as, *the requisition of automobiles for purposes of defense.*

resemble

Note that there is only one *s* in the word. See **favor.**

reside,
residence

The verb **reside** is a formal or legal word for *live.* **Residence** is a formal or legal word for *home* or *house*. Both words connote, apart from legal expressions, elegance or importance, and should not be used in general for *live, home* or *house*, respectively.

respectably,
respectfully,
respectively

Respectably means *in a manner deserving respect*, or *with decent behavior*. THUS: *He conducted himself respectably at all times.* **Respectfully** means *with respect*. THUS: *The men bowed respectfully to the old lady.* **Respectively** means *as relating to each, in the order given.* THUS: *Tim and Ellen are the son and daughter respectively of Mr. Clark and Mr. Jones.* One ends a letter or a petition, *Yours respectfully* (not "respectively").

respond

See **react.**

rest

See **balance.**

rest you merry

Rest you merry is an old expression most frequently met in the famous carol, "God rest you merry, gentlemen". The expression means "God keep you in good health and spirits". Observe the punctuation. **Merry** goes with the verb **rest,** and is not an adjective modifying *gentlemen.*

restive,
restless

Restive and **restless** are not altogether synonymous. **Restive** is most commonly applied to a horse, and means *balky.* As applied to persons, it means *fretting under restraint;* as, *a restive audience, the pupils were becoming restive.* **Restless** means *unrestful,* or *disinclined to rest; fidgety.*

return

See **refer.**

reverend,
reverent

Reverend means *worthy of reverence or of great respect;* as *the reverend master.* **Reverend** (commonly abbreviated *Rev.*) is used as a prefix to a clergyman's name. (For its use as a prefix see **honorable**.) **Reverent** means *feeling or showing reverence or great respect;* as *a reverent attitude.*

reverse,
converse

Reverse means *opposite, inverted, the contrary.* THUS: *The names John, George, Henry, James, are, in reverse order, James, Henry, George, John.* **Converse** is used of a statement or proposition when the different terms of it are turned round, as in putting the subject in the place of the predicate, and the predicate in the place of the subject. THUS: *If you knew John* is a converse statement of *If John knew you.*

revert

See **refer.**

revolt,
revolution

See **rebellion.**

reward

See **award.**

ride,
drive

Ride and **drive** in the general sense of *travel* are interchangeable in many cases. In current usage **ride** only is applied to *travel on horseback,* or *in any public conveyance,* or *in any conveyance not drawn by an animal* (as an airplane or motor vehicle).

right

As an adverb **right** is used properly to mean *straight* or *directly,* as in the expressions, *right behind you, right before you, go right on, right to the bottom.* **Right** is used colloquially (as in older English) in the sense of *quite, very,* or *in a great degree;* as in the expressions, "right well", "right glad", "right angry". This older use survives in the prefixes *Right Reverend* and *Right Honorable.* **Right** in the sense of *exactly* or *immediately* is colloquial; as in "right now", "right here and now", "right away", "right off", "right along". The expression "a right smart of", meaning *a large amount of* is provincial. "To get in right with" is slang.

**rinse,
wrench**

Be careful not to confuse the pronunciation of **rinse** and **wrench**. **To rinse** means *to wash lightly with water*. **To wrench** means to *twist violently*. The noun **wrench** means either *a violent twisting* or *an instrument for exerting a twisting strain*.

rise

Rise, both as noun and verb, is pronounced so as to rhyme with *prize*.

**rise,
arise**

Rise is the form now commonly used in the sense of *to get up from lying or sitting*. **Arise**, an older form of the verb, is now used chiefly in poetry, or in the sense of *to originate, spring up,* or *come into being*. THUS: *The audience will rise when the colors are presented. Many difficulties arise. This question has often arisen. A storm arose last night.*

**rise,
raise**

The words are sometimes confused. **Rise** does not take an object. **Raise** always takes an object. THUS: *The audience rose when the color guard raised the flag. He raised his head. Will you rise from your seat?* Avoid "Raise up", for *Rise,* or *Rise up*. See **raise**.

**round,
around**

The uses of **round** and **around** should be carefully discriminated. **Around** is often used colloquially when the proper usage requires **round**. **Round** is not merely an abbreviated form of **around,** and should not be written with an apostrophe, unless in *direct* quotation a writer wishes to indicate the incorrect pronunciation of **around**. The following distinctions should be studied carefully:

The adverb **round** means *circularly, in succession, in circumference*. THUS: *the sun goes* *round; all the year round; the hall was hung round with flags.* The preposition **round** means *so as to encircle,* or *enclose on all sides.* THUS: *An airplane goes round the world. We looked round us.* SIMILARLY, *round the meadows, round the table, round the center, round its axis, a cloak wrapped round him.*

Around as an adverb means *on all sides, here and there on every side.* THUS: *The soldiers' tents were pitched for miles around. Relics of old battles were scattered around.* **Around** as a preposition means *along the circumference or circuit.* THUS: *The globe had small dials placed around the line of the equator to indicate the time throughout the world. Lights were placed around the circumference of the dome.*

There are many colloquial uses of **around,** as in the phrases, "to hang around", "around six o'clock".

run

Run, in the sense of *conduct, manage,* is acceptable in informal usage. THUS: *He runs a restaurant. He is able to run a car.*

's

The apostrophe is used with *s* to indicate the possessive case; as, *John's home.* The apostrophe is also used before *s,* as before other letters, to indicate the omission of one or more letters. THUS: *He's* (he has) *gone. It's* (it is) *good.* Notice that the possessive form of *it* is *its,* not *it's.* See **its.** For rules for spelling the possessive cases of nouns and pronouns see Page 297.

sacrilegious

Sacrilegious is often spelled and pronounced as if the last three syllables of the word constituted the word *religious.* **Sacrilegious** is an adjective formed from the noun *sacrilege,* not from the word *religion.* The *e* in **sacrilegious** is pronounced as the *e* in *collegiate*. Observe carefully the correct spelling.

said

The term **said,** or **the said,** in the sense of *before-mentioned,* should be restricted to legal phraseology. CORRECT: *The student will be punished, because he* (not "said student") *was disobeying the rules.*

salary, wages

Salary, in current usage, denotes a fixed periodical payment, made usually by the month or half-month, to persons employed in other than manual or mechanical work. **Wages** denotes the price paid, usually by the day or week, to a laborer. THUS: *the mayor's monthly salary; the day-laborer's wages.* See **wages.**

same

The term **same** or **the same,** meaning *he, him, it, them,* etc., borrowed from legal terminology, is greatly overworked in colloquial speech, especially in the business world. Careful writers and speakers, in business or in other fields, avoid it. CORRECT: *If the envelopes are available, please send them* (not "same") *by parcel post.* See **similar.**

sameness, similarity

Sameness means the state of being *exactly the same,* or *identical.* Hence, *tedious monotony* or *lack of variety* is implied. **Similarity** means simply *likeness* or *resemblance.* See **similar.**

sanatorium, sanitarium

The two words are often used interchangeably to mean *a health resort,* or *an institution for the treatment of invalids.* **Sanatorium** is applied specifically to an establishment that uses *natural* curative agents. The forms "sanitorium" and "sanatarium" are misspellings.

**sanatory,
  sanitary**

Sanatory means *conducive to health, curative;* as *sanatory exercises.* **Sanitary** means *pertaining to health* in the sense of *hygienic;* as *sanitary regulations, sanitary drinking-cups.* See **insanitary.**

**sank,
  sunk**

These two forms of the verb *sink* are sometimes confused. **Sank** is the *past tense;* as, *the torpedoed vessel sank rapidly.* **Sunk** is the *past participial form;* as, *the ship was sunk by a torpedo.*

**satire,
  satyr**

Observe the differences in spelling, pronunciation, and meaning. A **satire** is a literary form in which persons or things are held up to ridicule; or the ridicule or sarcasm used to expose persons or conditions. The first syllable of **satire** is pronounced as *sat,* the second as *ire.* A **satyr** is a mythological divinity, half man and half beast. The first syllable of **satyr** may be pronounced as *sat,* or may be pronounced to rhyme with *fate.* The second syllable is pronounced like the *er* in *crater.*

**saw,
  seen**

The past tense **saw** and the participial form **seen** are sometimes carelessly interchanged. CORRECT: *I saw today what I have never seen before.*

**say,
  says**

Avoid the inappropriate use of "Say!" as an exclamation to draw attention, or to introduce a remark. The third person singular, **says,** should not be used with the first person singular pronoun I, as in the incorrect expressions, "I says", or "says I". The expression, "It says in the Bible (or in the paper)" is also bad usage.

scarcely

Since the word **scarcely** is negative in its implications, do not use *not* before it. CORRECT: *It is* (not "is not" or "isn't") *scarcely a month since I last saw him.* See **hardly.**

scare (*noun*)

The noun **scare** is properly used in the sense of *baseless general apprehension* of war or of a commercial panic. THUS: *A war scare spread over the country. The market was upset by the scare in Wall Street.* Good usage does not sanction the colloquialism, "The news gave me quite a scare".

scared

See **frightened**.

scarify

The word **scarify** has no connection whatever with *scar* or *scare*. **Scarify**, as a surgical term, means *to scratch the skin,* or *to make small incisions in the skin.* As an agricultural term, it refers to the *scratching of hard-coated seeds* to aid germination. *Figuratively,* **scarify** means *to criticize mercilessly, to wound the feelings.*

schedule

Do not make three syllables of **schedule**. In the U.S. the preferred pronunciation is skĕd'-yul.

scholar

See **pupil**.

see

Avoid the bad habit of injecting "See?" or "See what I mean?" in conversation. "I see by the paper" is an unapproved colloquialism.

**see,
witness**

Do not use the more specific term **witness** in the general sense of **see**. **Witness** means *to observe with one's own eyes or ears,* and thus to have direct knowledge of an event. THUS: *He saw the admiral leave the building, but did not witness his assassination a few minutes later.*

seem

The expressions, "I couldn't seem to" and "I don't seem to" in the sense of *be unable to* are unacceptable colloquialisms. CORRECT: *I* can't find (not "I can't seem to find") *the article I referred to.* "It should seem" and "it would seem" are acceptable as less positive forms of *it seems.* See **appear.**

seem to have been, seemed to be, seemed to have been

Uncertainty over the use of these phrases usually results from failure to consider carefully what idea one wishes to express. Note the following uses: *He seems to have been wealthy* (that is, *he now gives the impression of having at a past time been wealthy*). *He seemed to be wealthy* (that is, *at a given time in the past he gave the impression of being wealthy*). *He seemed to have been wealthy* (that is, *at a given time in the past he gave the impression of once having been wealthy*).

seldom if ever

See **rarely if ever.**

sensation

Avoid the colloquial expression, "He's a sensation".

sensible of, sensibility, sensitive to, sensitiveness, sensitivity

Sensible of means *aware of* or *mindful of.* THUS: *He is very sensible of his defects.* **Sensibility,** in this connection, means *capacity to feel, susceptibility to external impressions.* THUS: *His sensibility to human suffering, and his susceptibilities in general, often caused him unhappiness.* **Sensitive** means *acutely affected by external impressions, quick to take offense.* THUS: *He was morbidly sensitive to any unfavorable criticism of his book.* **Sensitiveness** is used of acute sensibility in a person. THUS: *His sensitiveness to public criticism ruined his career as a politician.* **Sensitivity** refers chiefly to the degree of sensitiveness of paper, instruments, etc.; as, *the sensitivity of a radio to incoming waves.*

sensual, sensuous

Sensual and **sensuous** should never be used as synonymous. **Sensual** means *given to the* *pursuit of the baser pleasures of the senses;* hence, *self-indulgent, fleshly, licentious.* **Sensuous** means *of or pertaining to the senses in general, or addressed to the senses;* hence, *highly susceptible to influence through the senses, aesthetic.* **Sensual** is, therefore, derogatory in its connotations; **sensuous** may be either favorable or neutral. FOR EXAMPLE: *The sensual man knows nothing of the pleasures of the intellect or the spirit. Keats's sensuous descriptions of delicacies in his poem, "The Eve of St. Agnes", are among the most famous of the sort in English literature.*

separate

Separate is one of the most commonly misspelled words in English. A convenient trick for remembering the proper spelling is to bear in mind that the two *a*'s in the word are *separated* by an *r*.

seraphim

Seraphim is the plural of *seraph.* Do not, therefore, say "seraphims". See **cherubim.**

sergeant

Notice that **sergeant,** the title of the highest non-commissioned officer in the army, is spelled with *g* not with *j.*

series, species

Series and **species** have the same form, respectively, for both singular and plural. THUS: *one series, five series; one species, several species.*

session

See **cession.**

set (*noun*)

See **bunch.**

set, sit

The principal parts of the verb **set** are: *set, set, have set.* **Set** is, in most ordinary uses, a transitive verb; that is, it takes an object. THUS: *to set a watch, to set a hen, to set a guard, to set a price on an article.* The principal parts of **sit** are: **sit, sat, have sat. Sit** is, in ordinary usage, intransitive. THUS: *he sits down, the clock sits on the shelf, the hen sits on the eggs, the crime sits heavy on his conscience.* **Sit** in a few cases is used as a transitive verb; as, for example, *he sits his horse well, he sat himself down.* Note that the sinking below the horizon of the heavenly bodies is referred to as *setting,* not as *sitting.* THUS: *The sun set yesterday at 5:36. The moon will set this morning at 5:21.*

settle

The expression, "to settle a bill", is colloquial. Properly one should say, *He paid the bill, and settled the account.* Such expressions as, "I'll settle you", or "I'll settle your hash", are, of course, colloquial.

severally

Severally means *separately, respectively.* See **respectively** under **respectably.**

sewage, sewerage

Do not confuse the two words. **Sewage** is *the contents of the sewer, the refuse matter.* **Sewerage** means *the system of sewers* by means of which the **sewage** is removed.

shall, will

Correct grammatical usage requires that simple futurity be expressed by **shall** in the first person and by **will** in the second and third; and that determination be expressed by **will** in the first person and by **shall** in the second and third. FOR EXAMPLE: [Simple futurity]—*I shall go to town tomorrow if the weather remains good. You will probably remain here while I am gone. The boys will also be here.* [Determination]—*I will go, whatever the weather. You shall stay here while I am gone. The boys shall stay here also.*

In questions involving the second and third persons, the rule is that the speaker use the auxiliary (**shall** or **will**) which he expects in the answer to the question. THUS: *Shall you go with me? I shall. Will you see that no one enters the room? I will.*

In constructions in the present tense when the first person with **shall** or **will** in *direct discourse* becomes the second or third person in *indirect discourse,* **shall** or **will** should be retained. FOR EXAMPLE: (*Direct*) *You say, "I shall see him".* (*Indirect*) *You say that you shall see him.* (*Direct*) *He says, "I shall see him".* (*Indirect*) *He says that he shall see him.* (*Direct*) *You say, "I will go".* (*Indirect*) *You say that you will go.* (*Direct*) *He says, "I will go".* (*Indirect*) *He says that he will go.*

In subordinate clauses, **shall** is used in all three persons except when the subject is thought of as wishing or consenting. FOR EXAMPLE: *Whenever I shall find an opportunity, I shall give him the message. He is to remain there until you shall dismiss him. Whatever student shall disobey the rules shall be punished.* **Will** is used in all three persons when the subject is thought of as wishing or consenting. FOR EXAMPLE: *He will come if I will let him. If you will only make the effort, you will win the prize. Whoever will join us will receive a hearty welcome.*

Informal usage is not always in strict accord with the rules of grammar. Colloquially, **will** is commonly used in all persons to express simple futurity. In expressing determination, wish, or consent, informal usage varies, since there is a tendency to express the meaning by the tone of voice or by placement of stress. In ordinary conversation **shall** is commonly employed to express determination. It is common practice in conversation to contract **I will, you shall,** etc., to "I'll", "you'll", etc., so that the distinctions are lost. See **should, would.**

shambles

Shambles has come recently to be one of the most frequently and most incorrectly used words in the language. It means properly *a place where butcher's meat is sold, or a place for slaughtering animals.* Figuratively, it may mean *a place or scene of slaughter.* It is used loosely to mean *a scene of disorder of any sort;* as, "The room was a shambles"; "The garden was a shambles after the hurricane". Care should be taken to avoid the erroneous and meaningless use of the word.

shan't

Shan't is a colloquial contraction of *shall not.*

shape

Shape, in the sense of *state* or *condition,* is an unapproved colloquialism. CORRECT: *He was in a serious condition* (not "in a bad shape") *when I arrived. The old car is still in good condition* (not "shape").

should

See **ought.**

should, would

Should and **would** in formal usage follow in general the rules for *shall* and *will.* See **shall** and **will.** Certain uses of **should** and **would** in indirect discourse and in subordinate clauses frequently cause difficulty.

When a statement made in the past is quoted indirectly, **should** is used in place of the *shall* of the original statement, and **would** in place of the *will* of the original statement. FOR EXAMPLE: (*Direct*) *He asked me, "Shall you see him?"* (*Indirect*) *He asked me if I should see him.* (*Direct*) *He said, "You will find him at his office."* (*Indirect*) *He said that I would find him at his office.* (*Direct*) *He asked, "Will you give him this message?"* (*Indirect*) *He asked me if I would give him this message.* Do not mix direct and indirect discourse in the same sentence. CORRECT: *He* *asked me if I should see him* (not "he asked me would I see him" or "should I see him").

In subordinate clauses, **should** is used in all three persons except when the subject is thought of as *wishing* or *consenting*. FOR EXAMPLE: *What would he say if I should not come? If you should see him, please give him my kind regards. I promised to assist him whenever he should need my help.* Use **would** in the subordinate clause in all three persons if the subject is thought of as wishing or consenting. FOR EXAMPLE: *He would tell me if I would promise not to reveal the secret. You would be successful if you would take pains with your work. He would assist them if they would let him.*

should seem, would seem

See **seem**.

show

Show is used properly of exhibitions, displays, and entertainments that are spectacular in nature; as, *the horse show, a vaudeville show, a moving picture show.* It is used colloquially for *play;* as, "The best show in New York is at the Empire Theatre". **Show** in the sense of *opportunity, chance,* is an unacceptable colloquialism; as "We haven't a show".

show up

Show up in the sense of *appear, arrive,* or *come,* is not good formal *usage.* CORRECT: *Did he arrive* (not "show up") *before the evening was over?* **Show up** is also an undesirable colloquialism for *expose.* CORRECT: *We intend to expose his false pretensions* (not "show him up") *at the next opportunity.*

shut

Avoid the dialectal expression "to be shut of" meaning *to be rid* or *free of.* CORRECT: *We finally got rid of* (not "shut of") *the pests.*

sideways

Sideways and *sidewise* are interchangeable.

sight
  (for **quantity**)

An undesirable colloquialism or dialectal term for *a great number or quantity;* as, "a sight of people", "a sight of money", "a sight of trouble".

similar,
  same

Use **same,** not **similar,** if you mean **same,** or **the same.** CORRECT: *His older brother was killed in battle, and he met the same* (not "a similar") *end. His grandfather lived to be seventy years old, and his father reached the same* (not "a similar") *age. I had two callers this morning and the same* (not "a similar") *number this afternoon.*

simply

Simply in the loose general sense of *absolutely, altogether, really,* etc., is slang. Avoid such expressions as "simply marvelous", "simply priceless".

since,
  ago

Since means *from a definite time in the past until now,* or *until the time indicated in the sentence.* Do not omit the auxiliary *have* or *had* with the verb used in constructions with **since.** CORRECT: *I have been* (not "am") *here since June. I had been* (not "was") *in Boston since I was five years old.* To prevent misunderstanding, use whatever verb is necessary in a clause following **since.** CORRECT: *It is twenty years since his reign began* (not "since his reign"). The adverb **ago** puts the entire action in the past. THUS: *He died twenty years ago.*

Sir

The title **Sir** is prefixed to the *given name,* or to the initials of the given name, of a knight or baronet, *never* to his surname. CORRECT: *Sir Stafford Cripps* (not "Sir Cripps") ; *Sir J. J. Thomson* (not "Sir Thomson"). See **Honorable.**

sit, sat   See **set.**

slander   See **libel.**

sleeper,
smoker,
diner   Colloquial in the U.S. for *sleeping car, smoking car, dining car,* respectively.

slick   **Slick** in the sense of *slippery* is a provincialism.

slow,
slowly   Both **slow** and **slowly** are adverbs. *Go slow* is preferable to "Proceed slowly" as a direction to motorists. Compare *slow-footed, slow-moving, slow-paced* for other uses of **slow** as an adverb. In most cases, however, except in poetry, **slowly** is used. THUS: *The procession moved slowly away. The sun sank slowly. Slowly and quietly he closed the door.*

smart   **Smart** is colloquial in the sense of *fashionable* and *clever;* as, "the smart set", "a smart boy". The expression, "a right smart", meaning *a large amount,* is provincial.

smoker   See **sleeper.**

so   See **as.**

so far as   See **as far as.**

so,
such   In formal English after a negative, **so** is preferable to **such** before an adjective. THUS: *I do not know where you would find so valuable a* (not "such a valuable") *collection. I never heard so strange a* (not "such a strange") *story.*

     So and **such** are greatly overworked colloquially in the sense of *very, great,* etc., as in the exclamations, "He's so handsome!" "They are such good friends!" The two words should be specially avoided in formal writing. COR-RECT: *Dr. Johnson was very* (not "so") *out-spoken in his manner. The queen devoted a great amount of* (not "such a great amount of") *time and energy to the establishment of municipal hospitals.*

sociable,
social

Sociable is used of individual persons, in the sense of *friendly, liking companions; as, a very sociable neighbor.* **Social,** as distin-guished from **sociable,** means *relating to orga-nized society; as, social welfare, the social contract.*

some,
somewhat

Do not use **some** for **somewhat.** CORRECT: *He is somewhat* (not "some") *better today. They have changed the arrangement some-what* (not "some"). See **any.**

The use of **some** as a word to give em-phasis is slang; as, "We had some narrow escape".

some day

Some day is written as two words. See **some time.**

some one,
someone

Some one means *some particular unnamed person or thing.* THUS: *Some one of his friends will help him. Choose some one of these pictures for your room.* **Someone** is interchangeable with *somebody.* THUS: *Some-one usually helps us in an emergency.*

someone else,
somebody else

See **else.**

some place,
somewhere

Some place is written as two words. **Some-where** is one word. See **any place.**

some things,
something

Some things is written as two words; **some-thing** as one word. THUS: *There are some* *things I must pick up at the grocery. There is something I wish to speak to you about.*

Something is often used colloquially in the sense of *somewhat;* as, "He is something like his father". "She is something under five feet tall". Correct usage, however, requires *somewhat* in such constructions.

Avoid the use of **something** as an adverb in such slang expressions as "something fierce", "something awful".

some time,
sometime,
sometimes

Some time indicates *an undefined period of time.* THUS: *He left some time ago. I waited some time for him. I was there for some time.* **Sometime** is an adverb meaning *at an undefined time in the future.* THUS: *I'll see you sometime. I shall arrive sometime after five.* **Sometimes** means *at times, now and then, occasionally.* THUS: *Sometimes I prefer to travel by train. I go there sometimes.*

some way

Some way and **some ways** are both written as two words. See **anyway,** under **anyhow.**

somewhat

See **kind of, some.**

somewhere

Avoid "somewheres". See **anywhere.**

sort of

See **kind of.**

specie,
species

Specie and **species** are not related to each other in current usage. **Specie** means *money in the shape of coin.* It is a collective noun and has no plural form. THUS, *He was paid in specie.* **Species** means *a class of things having some characteristics in common;* as, *a species of the crow-foot family of plants.* **Species** is the form in both the singular and the plural.

spectator

See **audience.**

spell

> **Spell,** in the sense of *a period of time* is colloquial; as, "I shall be here for a spell".

splendid

> See **elegant.**

spontaneity

> The third syllable of **spontaneity** is pronounced as *knee.*

spoonfuls, spoons full

> **Spoonfuls** is the plural of the term of measurement, a **spoonful.** THUS: *Use two spoonfuls of sugar.* The expression **spoons full** refers to two or more *spoons,* not to the measure. THUS: *He arranged several spoons full of sugar in order.* See **-ful.**

stake, steak

> Do not confuse the spellings of the two words, which are pronounced alike. A **stake** is a stout stick pointed for driving into the ground. A **steak** is a slice of meat.

stand

> **Stand** is used in several expressive colloquialisms. THUS: "I can't stand it." "I won't stand his coming late every morning." "I won't stand for it." These, of course, should not be used in formal English.

start

> The addition of *in* or *up* to the verb **start** is a common colloquial habit, which is contrary to good usage. CORRECT: *When do you start* (not "start in") *to work? He started* (not "started in") *shouting. They began* (or *started;* not "started up") *a quarrel as soon as they entered the room. They have started* (not "started up") *a factory to make the articles.*

state, say

> **State** should not be used loosely for **say.** It should be restricted to references to formal statements. CORRECT: *Secretary Hull stated that the treaty would be signed on June 15. She said* (not "stated") *that she would be unable to go to the meeting.*

station   See **depot.**

stationary,   **Stationary** means *fixed in one place;* as,
   stationery   *a stationary block, a stationary engine.*
           Stationery means *writing supplies;* as, *a sta-*
           tionery shop, legal and commercial stationery.

statue,   **Statuary** should not be used as the plural
   statuary   of **statue. Statuary** means *the branch of*
           sculpture that treats of figures in the round.
           It may be used also of *a collection of statues,*
           particularly if they are part of a general de-
           sign. CORRECT: *He is enrolled in a course in*
           statuary at the Conservatory. The statuary in
           the Court of Honor was designed by Lorado
           Taft. They are planning to place some new
           statues (not "statuary") *in the church.*

statue,   A **statue** is *a piece of sculpture;* as, *a statue*
   stature,   *of George Washington.* **Stature** means *height;*
   statute   as, *a man of great stature.* A **statute** is a *law;*
           as, *the General Statutes of the State of Con-*
           necticut.

stay,   Do not use the verb **stop** for **stay** in the
   stop   sense of *remaining for a time.* CORRECT: *We*
           stayed (not "stopped") *in Minneapolis for*
           the week end. We stayed (not "stopped") *at*
           the Madison Hotel. **Stop** properly means *to*
           cease, or *cause to cease; to arrest the progress*
           or action of; as, *to stop a clock, to stop quar-*
           reling, to stop someone from going. "To stop
           off", "to stop over" are colloquialisms. "To
           stay put", in the sense of *to remain in the*
           same place, is a colloquialism.

stile,   The spellings of the words are often con-
   style   fused. A **stile** is *a set of steps arranged to pro-*
           vide passage over a fence or wall. **Style** means
           manner; as, *a style of writing.*

stimulant, stimulus, stimulation	A **stimulant** is *that which stimulates or excites.* Coffee, tea, and alcohol are *stimulants.* A **stimulus** (plural, *stimuli*) *is a rousing inflence, something that incites to activity; an incentive.* THUS: *The stimulus of ambition kept him busy. He is studying the responses of the nerve cells to certain stimuli.* **Stimulation** is the result of the application of either a **stimulant** or a **stimulus**.
stole	Avoid the incorrect pronunciation, "stoled".
stop	See **stay**.
straight, strait	**Straight** means *not crooked;* as, *a straight road.* **Strait** is an old adjective meaning *narrow, restricted;* as in the Biblical statement, *Strait is the gate, and narrow is the path.* The popular expression, "the straight and narrow path", is a misquotation and misinterpretation of the Biblical text. **Strait** is used today chiefly in the compound words, *strait jacket* and *strait-laced,* and as a geographical term meaning *a narrow water passage between two large bodies of water.* In this sense it occurs chiefly in the plural; as, *the Straits of Gibraltar.* It is used also in the expression, *to be in great straits,* that is, *in difficult circumstances.*
straightened, straitened	**Straightened** means *made straight;* as, *he straightened the fence.* **Straitened** is an old adjective meaning *restricted, confined;* as, *in straitened circumstances.* See **straight**.
stranger	See **alien**.
stratagem, strategy	Observe the differences in spelling.

strategy, tactics

Strategy, in warfare, refers to the planning and conducting of *campaigns*. **Tactics** is the art of disposing troops or warships in single *battles*.

student

See **pupil.**

subtile, subtle

Subtile and **subtle** are interchangeable in most cases. **Subtile** is rather rare now, but is used occasionally to refer to an odor or perfume in the sense of *elusive, hard to analyze or define*. In **subtle** the *b* is silent; in **subtile** it may or may not be pronounced.

success

The use of **success** to mean the person or thing that is successful is colloquial; as, "He is a success", "Her novel was a success". In formal English this colloquial use should be avoided.

such

See **another, so.**

sufficient, adequate, enough

Sufficient means *completely fulfilling a proposed end or purpose.* THUS: *The evidence was sufficient to convince me of his guilt.* **Adequate** means *equal to a requirement.* THUS: *Our supply of fuel oil is adequate for heating the house this winter.* **Enough** means *satisfying a desire, or meeting a want.* THUS: *I have enough coal, thank you.*

summers

See **days.**

summons

The noun **summons** is singular. The plural is **summonses.** THUS: *He received a summons to appear in court. He has received several summonses in the past few months.* **Summons** is also a verb. THUS: *The officer will summons several persons to appear. We were summonsed yesterday.*

sung,
sang

Sang is the preferred form of the past tense of *sing*. Sung is used as a past tense in poetry. Sung is the past participle. THUS: *The choir sang at the wedding. The anthem was well sung.*

superior

Superior is followed by *to,* not by *than;* as, *powers superior to another's.* See **inferior**.

suppose

See **guess**.

sure,
surely

Sure, for **surely**, is colloquial, and is never used in formal English in this sense.

surprise

See **astonish**.

surround

Surround means *to inclose on all sides,* and should not be followed by the phrase "on all sides". THUS: *The house was surrounded by water.*

suspect,
suspicion

Suspect is the verb; **suspicion** the noun. Avoid the use of **suspicion** as a verb. CORRECT: *I suspected* (not "suspicioned") *that his claims were false.* See **expect**.

swam,
swum

Swam is the past tense of *swim;* **swum** is the past participle. "Swum" is a dialectal form of the past tense.

swell
(for **excellent**)

The use of **swell** in the sense of *excellent* (as, "a swell job") is slang.

symbol,
emblem

A symbol is something which stands as a visible sign for something else, usually for something which is invisible. THUS: *Lincoln is a symbol of American democracy. The cross is the symbol of Christianity. The letters x and y are used as symbols of unknown quantities.* An **emblem** is a visible object representing something else, usually because of association with it. THUS: *The flag is the emblem of our nation. Holly and mistletoe are emblems of Christmas festivity. The five-pointed star is the religious emblem of Christmas.*

sympathize

Sympathize is followed by *with*. **Sympathize** means to feel or express sympathy with another in *any* circumstances. THUS: *Friends sympathize with one another in their joys as well as in their sorrows.*

sympathy for, sympathy with

Sympathy for implies a feeling of grief for another who is in trouble or distress; as, *sympathy for a friend on the death of his father.* **Sympathy with** implies similarity or identity of circumstances between persons. THUS: *The refugees sympathized with each other in their plight.* See **pity.**

"take in"

The expression *take in* is used colloquially in several different senses, as in "I was taken in (that is, *deceived* or *misled*) by his suave manner." "We took in (that is, *attended*) several plays while in New York."

take place

See **occur.**

talk

Informal for *a short address.*

tasteful, tasty

Tasteful and **tasty** are often confused. **Tasteful** only is used of persons, and means *having good taste.* It may also be used of objects, to mean *done in good taste.* **Tasty** is a colloquial term, and means *pleasing to the palate, savory.* It should never be used of persons. CORRECT: *Miss Ellis is a tasteful* (not "tasty") *decorator. The flowers were tastefully* (not "tastily") *arranged. The hostess served a tasty luncheon before the game.*

teach

See **learn.**

telegraphist

Telegraphist (a telegraph operator) is accented on the second syllable *-leg.*

tend,
attend

Tend and **attend**, though synonymous in certain cases, are now used in different connections. The following sentences illustrate the proper uses of **attend:** *Please attend to this. I attended her to the door. We attended the theater. Dr. Morris attended the wounded man. The operation was attended by no ill effects.* **Tend** is now commonly restricted to such uses as the following: *tend the fire, tend the boiler, tend the machine, tend the cattle.*

tender,
give

Tender should not be used as a synonym of **give.** In legal usage, **tender** means *to offer money or services in satisfaction of a debt or other obligation.* THUS: *He tendered payment of his debt on the first of the year.* In formal English, **tender** is used in such expressions as: *The chairman tendered his resignation. The committee tendered a vote of thanks to the retiring chairman. The editor tendered an apology to the mayor for the error made in reporting his speech.*

terminal

See **depot.**

testament,
testimony

Do not confuse the meanings of the two words. **Testament** is a legal term meaning a *will, a document in which a person determines the disposition of his property after his death.* An older meaning of **testament,** *a covenant,* gave rise to the names of the two general divisions of the Bible, the *Old Testament* and the *New Testament.* **Testimony** means *a thing that testifies or bears witness to something; evidence.* THUS: *He made bequests to all his servants in his last will and testament. His public career was a constant testimony* (not "testament") *to his lack of prejudice.* See **evidence.**

than   See **more, prefer.**

that,
  this

That and **this** are accepted colloquially as adverbs meaning *thus, so;* as, *that much, that far, this high, this long.* Avoid, however, the incorrect use of **that** and **this** as adverbs in exclamations; as, "He was that angry!" See **as.**

Do not reinforce the adjectives **that** and **this** with the words *there* and *here* respectively. CORRECT: *That* (not "that there") *automobile has been worth twice the money I paid for it. This* (not "this here") *road gets worse the farther it goes.* The same rule applies, of course, to the plurals *those* and *these.*

that (*conj.*)

Avoid careless repetition of the conjunction **that** in introducing clauses, as in the sentence, "I know that, if he could come, that he would be here". Omit the second **that.** The error is more likely to occur in longer sentences, such as the following: *The cold fact remains that if one subtracts from the present situation the gains made during the winter, and then subtracts again the gains made during the summer months, there will be nothing left.* Be careful not to insert a second **that** before the final clause, *there will be nothing left.*

that,
  which

The relative pronouns **that** and **which** are now, and have always been, used more or less interchangeably in many cases. They are not, however, so akin as to be always interchangeable. No short and simple rule can be given that will settle the entire problem of the distinctive uses of the two pronouns, but the following suggestions will be of practical help in the use of them.

That is used of *persons, animals, or things;* **which** is used *only of animals or things.*

According to the best current usage, the distinctive purpose of **that** is to *restrict,* or *limit,* or *define* the meaning or application of the word or phrase preceding it. **Which** does not restrict or define, but, on the contrary, *expands* the meaning or application of the preceding word or phrase, usually by the addition of a new thought. Observe carefully the distinctive employments of the two words in the sentences that follow. *The house that my father built has been destroyed.* (Here the pronoun **that** restricts the meaning or application of the word *house* to *the house that my father built.* It does not add a new idea.) *The big white house on the hill, which you may have noticed, was built by my father.* (In this sentence, the word *house* has been sufficiently defined or limited by the adjectives *big* and *white,* and the pronoun **which** adds a new thought—*you may have noticed it.*) Note the uses of **that** and **which** in the sentences that follow: *The monument that you see was erected to the memory of Washington. The Washington Monument, which was begun in 1848, was completed in 1884. The book that he lent me was a detective story. This little book, which I hope you will read, is by the editor of the "Advertiser". The train that was due at six o'clock is now an hour late. The midnight express, which left Buffalo on time, has been delayed by a washout on the line.*

Note that relative clauses beginning with the restrictive pronoun **that** are not preceded by a comma, and that a comma is used before a relative clause beginning with the expansive pronoun **which.**

that, who

Both the relative pronouns **that** and **who** are used of persons; **that** only is used of things. **That** and **who** are used more or less indiscriminately of persons, and no definite rule can be given that will cover all circumstances. In certain cases, **that** may imply a *definition* or *restriction* not implied by **who**. FOR EXAMPLE: *He knows the architect that designed the postoffice.* (Here a particular architect, *the one that designed the postoffice,* is referred to.) In the sentence, *He knows the architect, who designed the postoffice,* there are two implications: *He knows the architect,* and *that architect designed the postoffice.* In the best current usage, **that** is commonly employed in informal expressions, and when the antecedent is less definite or particular. **Who** is more commonly used when the antecedent is a particular person or persons, and in more formal expressions. The following sentences illustrate current usage: *Which of us that is over thirty can forget November 11, 1918? It is he that must be held responsible. Everyone that comes will be admitted. Anyone that was there will tell you that my account of the proceedings is accurate. Who is this little man that would prescribe what the citizens of Philadelphia shall read? It was a wise man that said, "Make haste slowly". One of those who were prominent in the negotiations was the Secretary of the Interior. A man who has given much attention to this problem is Mr. Daley. We are combating an enemy who has for years been making preparations. We, who are now relinquishing the task, salute you. A man that never makes mistakes never makes anything else. Sgt. Washburn, who made several mistakes in his earlier computations, finally got the correct answer to the problem.*

the

Use the article **the** before each of two or more connected nouns or adjectives when clearness requires. Notice that *the orange and black pennants* implies a different idea from

that of *the orange and the black pennants.*
Compare the following pairs of phrases: *the
red, white, and blue cards* and *the red, the
white, and the blue cards; the Secretary and
Treasurer* and *the Secretary and the Treasurer; camps for boys and girls* and *camps for
the boys and for the girls.*

In formal style, **the** is used with the titles
Reverend and *Honorable;* as, *the Reverend
Mr. Martin, the Honorable John H. Weller.*

their	See **they.**
them	**Them** is a pronoun. Its use as a demonstra-tive adjective, as in the expression, "them papers", for *those papers,* is very bad usage.
themselves	Do not use the incorrect form "theirselves" for **themselves.**
thence	See **hence.**
there	See **that** (*adj.*).
therefor, therefore	Distinguish between the spelling and the meaning of the two words. **Therefor** means *for that* or *for it.* THUS: *Five years' imprison-ment is the punishment therefor.* **Therefore** means *for that reason* or *because of that.* THUS: *He was acquitted of the charge, and was, therefore, released.* See **and.**
there is, there are	Whether **is** or **are** shall follow an introduc-tory **there** depends upon what follows the **is** or the **are.** If a singular noun or pronoun fol-lows the verb, use **is** (or, in the past tense, **was**). If the verb is followed by a plural noun or pronoun, or by two or more singular nouns or pronouns, use **are** (or, in the past tense, **were**). FOR EXAMPLE: *There is a tavern in the town. There was a fire in the city last*

night. There were only three members of the group present. In that box there are several documents. There are a knife and fork on the table. In special cases, when the speaker is thinking of two or more persons or things individually, it is permissible to use a singular verb before two or more nouns or pronouns after the introductory **there.** FOR EXAMPLE: *There was a chair, and a table, and a bed in the room. There was a man with a wheelbarrow and a boy with a basket at the door.* See **is.**

these,
those

See **kind, that.**

they,
their,
them

Avoid the careless use of the plural pronouns **they, their, them,** to refer to singular nouns and pronouns. The error is most commonly made in connection with the indefinite pronouns, *each, one, anybody, everybody,* etc. CORRECT: *If anyone thinks we are not aware of this, he is* (not "they are") *mistaken. Each member of the sorority brought her own* (not "their own") *luncheon. Any one of us is* (not "are") *likely to be called on to express his* (not "their") *opinions on the subject. Only one boy in six had his* (not "their") *things in order. If anybody calls for the package, give it to him* (not "them").

think

Do not use *for* after **think** when expressing expectation or supposition. CORRECT: *It is later than you think* (not "think for"). *The income tax will be higher next year than most people suppose,* or *expect it to be* (not "think for").

this

See **that.**

though

See **although, while.**

**thousand,
thousands,
hundreds**

Do not use the preposition *of* when a noun follows the word **thousand** or **hundred**. CORRECT: *A thousand* (not "thousand of") *ships were in the convoy. A hundred* (not "hundred of") *ships have been launched since the first of May.*

Be careful to use *of* after the plural forms **thousands, hundreds,** etc., when they are used before nouns. CORRECT: *Thousands of* (not "thousands") *incendiary bombs and hundreds of* (not "hundreds") *high explosives were dropped.* See **dozen.**

through

Through, in the sense of *finished* or *completed,* is colloquial in the U.S.; as, "I'll be through by five", "I'm through eating", "I'm through with that". See **done.**

throughout

Since **throughout** means *from end to end of,* or *in every part of,* do not add "the whole" or "the entire" to phrases in which it is used. CORRECT: *He was with us throughout the week* (not "the whole week"). *She did not miss a day throughout the session* (not "the entire session").

thus

Avoid the slang term "thusly".

**till,
until**

These words are interchangeable. **Until** is more commonly preferred at the beginning of a sentence. Notice that **till** is a word in its own right, and should not be spelled " 'til".

**to,
at**

Do not use **to** for **at.** CORRECT: *He is at* (not "to") *home this morning. I shall be at* (not "to") *school tomorrow. The child has been sick at* (not "to") *his stomach.*

Do not insert **to** after such words as *been* or *going.* CORRECT: *Where have you been* (not "been to")? *Where is he going* (not "going to")?

In formal English **to,** the sign of the infinitive, should not be allowed to stand for the infinitive. CORRECT: *You may leave if you wish* (not "wish to"). *He writes whenever he has time* (not "time to").

together

Since the word **together** implies the idea of *collecting, coöperating, connecting, comparing,* etc., it is not necessary, as a rule, to use **together** with such words. CORRECT: *Several thousand articles made of aluminum had been collected* (not "collected together") *in the public square. The citizens gladly coöperated* (not "coöperated together") *in collecting the scrap.*

together with, along with

Together with and **along with** are descriptive phrases, and hence do not create a grammatical plural when used with the subject of a verb. Be careful not to use a plural verb after a subject qualified by one of such phrases. CORRECT: *The land, along with the houses on it, was* (not "were") *mortgaged. The Governor, together with his staff, was* (not "were") *present at the ceremonies.* It is often better to have a plural subject than to employ a singular subject with such phrases. THUS: *The Governor and his staff were present* is preferable to *The Governor, together with his staff,* etc.

to my knowledge, to the best of my knowledge

The phrase **to my knowledge** implies *certain knowledge* on the part of the speaker. **To the best of my knowledge** implies *limited or deficient knowledge* on his part. THUS: *I know him well, and he is, to my knowledge, the best carpenter in town. I do not know him well, but he is, to the best of my knowledge and belief, a young man of excellent character.*

tortuous,
torturing

The two words, **tortuous** and **torturing,** are derived from the same Latin word, which means *to twist,* but they have no connection in current usage. **Tortuous** means *twisting, winding;* as, *a tortuous path.* **Torturing** means *putting to torture, causing pain;* as, *a torturing thought, a torturing sensation.* Avoid the mistaken forms "torturous" and "torturesome".

transpire

Do not use **transpire** in the sense of *happen.* **Transpire** means *to come to light, to become known.* THUS: *The news of the battle did not transpire until several weeks after it had been fought.* See **happen.**

tread,
trod

Do not use **trod,** the past tense, for **tread,** the present tense of the verb. CORRECT: *Do not tread on the grass. The horse trod the hay under his feet. Trodden* is the past participle.

treat,
treat of,
treat with

Notice the distinctive uses of these terms. **To treat** means *to present* or *to deal with* a subject. THUS: *He intends to treat that subject in his next lecture.* **To treat of** means *to give a written or spoken exposition of.* THUS: *This book treats of the freedom of the press.* **To treat with** means *to negotiate with.* THUS: *The government is treating with certain countries for a lowering of duties on imports.*

"try and"

"Try and" for *try to* is acceptable in colloquial use; as, "Try and see if you can solve this problem". See **and.**

twenty-one

Note that compound terms such as **twenty-one, thirty-five,** and **eighty-six** are spelled with a hyphen.

twice,
thrice

Do not use the adverbs **twice** and **thrice** as adjectives. CORRECT: *The twofold* (not "twice") *traitor was finally apprehended. He had escaped arrest thrice before.*

two first   See **first two.**

type of   **Type** should always be followed by **of** when used with a noun. CORRECT: *This is a very satisfactory type of machine* (not "type machine"). *He is a fine type of man* (not "type man"). There is no such thing as a "type man" or "type woman", or "type" anything.

ugly   Ugly, in the sense of *unpleasant, dangerous, quarrelsome,* etc., is colloquial in the U.S.; as, "an ugly word", "an ugly wound", "an ugly-tempered person", "an ugly affair".

ulterior,   The words **ulterior** and **underlying** are not
underlying   synonymous or interchangeable. **Ulterior** means *beyond what is seen or admitted, hidden.* It is used in an unfavorable sense; as, *ulterior motives, ulterior purposes.* **Underlying** means *lying beneath, fundamental.* It does not mean *hidden,* and is not used commonly in an unfavorable sense. CORRECT: *The underlying* (not "ulterior") *motivation of the play was that of a conflict of loyalties. The underlying causes of the struggle were economic in nature.*

"unbeknownst to"   A provincialism, meaning *without the knowledge of;* as, "He bought the car unbeknownst to his father".

underhand   **Underhand** is preferable to *underhanded,* though the latter is often heard. (*Underhanded* is the result of association with *left-handed* and *right-handed.*) PREFERABLE: *He was one of the most famous underhand* (not "underhanded") *pitchers in the history of baseball.* Figuratively, the word **underhand**

means *secret, sly, fraudulent.* THUS: *The arrested man was accused of underhand* (not "underhanded") *dealings with the enemy.*

undoubtedly, redoubtably

Do not confuse the spelling and pronunciation of these two words. Notice that **undoubtedly** ends in *-edly,* and that **redoubtably** ends in *-ably.*

uninterested

See **disinterested.**

unique

Since **unique** means *the only one of its kind, without a like or equal,* it is not capable of comparison. Consequently it should not be qualified by such words as *very, most, extremely.* The phrase "quite unique" is acceptable colloquially in the sense of "absolutely without parallel", "altogether singular". Avoid the loose use of **unique** to mean *unusual, rare, odd, interesting,* etc. CORRECT: *Books printed in English before 1500 are very rare* (not "unique"). *This copy of the 1576 edition is unique* (that is, *the only one of its kind*).

United States

Use the article *the* before **United States.** THUS: *the United States of America, the United States flag, the United States of Brazil.* The name **United States** is a collective noun, designating the Federal Union, and is therefore always to be followed by a singular verb. THUS: *The United States was represented at the conference by the Secretary of State.*

universally

Universally means *including or covering all.* Do not add the words "by all" when using it. THUS: *The seizure of the little country was universally condemned* (not "universally condemned by all"). Since the words **universal** and **universally** do not admit of comparison, do not qualify them by such words as *very, so, more.*

unless

The conjunction **unless** should not be confused with the preposition **without**. CORRECT: *He will not attend the meeting unless* (not "without") *he is specially invited*. See **except**.

unmoral,
amoral,
immoral

Unmoral and **amoral** (pronounced ā-mŏr′-al) are synonymous, and mean *nonmoral, not involving morality, outside the realm of moral distinctions and judgments.* The terms are applied, for example, to animals, as having no moral perception. The principles of mathematics are **unmoral** in their nature. **Amoral** is a recently coined word, which has gained a certain standing because it adds to the meaning of **unmoral** the idea that, for certain persons or groups of persons, morality is non-existent, because they do not recognize moral codes. By certain standards of civilization, a savage may be judged **amoral**. **Immoral** means *not moral, contrary to moral law or conscience; specifically, licentious.*

unsanitary

See **insanitary**.

unwieldy

Note the spelling carefully. Do not insert an *l* after the *d*.

unworldly

A frequently misspelled word. Do not omit the *l* before the *d*.

up

Up is a greatly overworked preposition in connection with many words; as, "end up", "sign up", "open up", "pay up". With these, as with many other verbs, **up** should be omitted, as it is unnecessary. **Up** is properly used with verbs when it contributes to or completes their meaning. THUS: *bring up, come up, get up, start up, jump up.* **Up** is acceptable and useful in certain colloquial expressions, such as *bring the accounts up to* *date, an up-to-date record, it's up to you to do it, he's hard up, we're up against it.*

upon,
on

Upon and on are synonymous in such expressions as *upon the table, upon receipt of your letter.* On is preferable as being the shorter of the two.

upwards of

The colloquial term **upwards of** means *more than.* THUS: *There were upwards of a hundred persons in the room.*

usage

See **habit.**

use,
utilize,
employ

Use is the most general of the three words. To utilize means *to make useful, to turn to profitable account;* as *to utilize every means at one's disposal.* To employ means *to use the services of, to devote to a particular purpose;* as, *to employ a person for a job, to employ time and energy in studying.*

used to

The past participle **used,** in the sense of *accustomed,* and the expression **to be used to,** meaning *to be accustomed to,* are frequently employed incorrectly. Used to should never be followed by *could,* as in the illiterate expression, "I used to could do it". The correct form is *I used to be able to do it.* The expressions, "used to was", and "hadn't used to", are also incorrect. CORRECT: *The postman used to bring the letters at nine. I am used to better treatment than this.* In these expressions used is pronounced *yūst.*

The past negative form of **used to** is one of the commonest snags of popular speech. There is no really satisfactory or generally accepted negative form. The forms generally preferred by the best speakers are: *I used not to object to working all day,* and *I did not use* (not "used") *to object.* In questions the constructions generally preferred are: *Didn't* *you use* (not "used") *to live in Cleveland?* A more formal, and more strictly correct, construction is *Used you not to live in Cleveland?* Since the expression **used to** implies the idea of *formerly* or *once,* it is often better to recast the sentence. THUS: *Didn't you formerly* (or *at one time*) *live in Cleveland? Weren't you once friendly with her?*

usually

See **commonly.**

"vacuum"

"Vacuum" as a noun meaning *vacuum cleaner* is wrong, as is also the verb "to vacuum", meaning *to clean with a vacuum cleaner.*

**valuable,
valued,
invaluable**

Do not confuse the meanings of **valuable** and **valued. Valuable** means *of great value or worth,* usually *monetary; as, a valuable painting, valuable property, a valuable arrangement.* **Valued** means *esteemed, held in high regard; as, a valued friend, a valued correspondent, a valued association, highly valued advice.*

Invaluable means *above value, priceless; as, invaluable help, invaluable benefits.*

**venal,
venial**

Venal and **venial** are likely to be confused in spelling and use. The first syllable of each word rhymes with *he.* **Venal** means *capable of being bribed; as, a venal official.* **Venial** means *trivial, excusable, pardonable; as, a venial error, a venial sin.*

venerable

See **ancient.**

venomous

Note that the second vowel in **venomous** is *o,* not *e,* and should be pronounced as *o.*

**veracity,
truth**

The two words are not interchangeable. **Truth** is *that which is true; a true statement, a fact.* **Veracity** means *correctness, truthful-*

ness, honesty. **Veracity** is applied only to persons, or to statements made by them, and has reference to the general quality of truthfulness rather than to the conformity of a particular statement to fact. THUS: *I do not doubt your veracity. I doubt the truth of his account of the incident. The truth* (not "veracity") *of the matter is that we are lost. Tell me the truth* (not "veracity") *about the accident. He has a reputation for veracity* (not "truth").

verbal

See **oral.**

verdict, opinion

Verdict should not be loosely used in the sense of **opinion. Verdict** means *the official decision of a jury,* or *an opinion officially delivered after examination of the facts in the case.* **Opinion** means simply *what a person or a group of persons thinks about something.* THUS: *The board of engineers was asked for its verdict on the condition of the bridge. The jury brought in a verdict of "Not guilty". It was his opinion* (not "verdict") *that the war would be over in six months. It was the opinion* (not "verdict") *of the bystanders that the driver was intoxicated.*

verse

Verse means *any kind of metrical composition.* The thought expressed in **verse** is not necessarily poetic. Jingles and limericks, for example, are verse, but not *poetry.* A **verse,** strictly speaking, is *a single line* of any composition written in verse, but in current usage a *stanza* (that is, one of the recurring units of a poem, consisting of several lines) may also be called a **verse.**

vertebra

Note that **vertebra** is *singular.* The plural is *vertebrae,* of which the last syllable rhymes with *he.*

very

The adverb **very** is greatly overworked. It may frequently be omitted with a consequent improvement and strengthening of style, since emphasis is then supplied by other (and usually more accurate) terms.

Very is used properly to modify a past participle only when the participle is used as an *adjective;* as, *very tired, very upset, very battered, very unbalanced.* Colloquially, however, **very** is commonly used to modify many past participles as such; as, *very pleased, very annoyed, very amused.* From a strictly grammatical point of view, these expressions should be *very highly pleased, very much annoyed, very greatly amused,* etc.

via

Via, a Latin word, means *passing through,* or *by way of,* and should be used only in connection with *travel, shipping routes, mail routes,* etc. It should not be used to mean *through the agency of,* or *by means of.* CORRECT: *They shipped the goods to Dakar via South America. The message reached me through* (not "via") *my cousin. I learned of the accident in* (not "via") *the newspaper.*

virtue,
 virtuosity

Virtue and **virtuosity** are not synonymous. **Virtue** means *moral goodness, merit.* **Virtuosity** means great *technical skill* in the practice of the fine arts, especially in music.

virtually,
 actually

Virtually means *in essence* or *in effect,* but *not* "in fact". **Actually** means *in fact, really.* When your lawyer speaks for you, you are **virtually** speaking yourself, even though you are not **actually** present.

visit

To **visit** means *to dwell with someone temporarily as a guest,* or *to pay a call on someone.* The expression "visit with", meaning *to have a conversation with,* is an unacceptable colloquialism.

viz.

Viz. is the abbreviation of the Latin word *videlicet,* which means, literally, *one may or can see.* The abbreviation is never pronounced, but is spoken as *namely,* or *to wit. Viz.* should always be italicized.

The following sentences illustrate the use of viz.: The first equations give us the values of two unknown quantities, *viz.* the length and the height of the structure. Three authors of the nineteenth century, *viz.* Shelley, Wordsworth, and Godwin, were strongly influenced by Rousseau.

vocation

See **avocation.**

wages

Wages, the plural form of **wage,** was formerly construed as *singular,* and used with a singular verb; as, *the wages of sin is death.* In current usage, **wages** is construed usually as plural. THUS: *His wages have been increased recently.* See **salary.**

"wait on"

The expression "wait on" in the sense of *wait for* is colloquial.

want

Want is used with certain adverbs in many colloquial and local expressions which are not in reputable use. Avoid such localisms as "I want in" (for *I want to come in*), "I want out" (for *I wish to get out*), "I want off" (for *I wish to get off*). Do not use "want of" for *want with.* CORRECT: *What do you want with* (not "of") *so much furniture?* See **desire.**

want, lack, need

Note the distinctive meanings of these words. **Want** means *lack of absolute necessaries, and implies a desire to remedy the deficiency.* **Lack** means a *shortage* or *deficiency* of something. **Need** is *the condition arising from a shortage* or *deficiency.* THUS:

We were often in want of the elementary comforts of life. There is now a lack of rubber. The need for rubber has brought about strict rationing of tires.

was

See **were.**

was,
   is

Use **is,** not **was,** when stating general principles or unchanging facts, even when the principal action of the sentence is represented as in the past. THUS: *Columbus was not the first to believe that the earth is* (not "was") *round. It was a wise man that said that brevity is* (not "was") *the soul of wit. The ancient Egyptians discovered that the volume of a pyramid is* (not "was") *equal to one third of the corresponding prism.*

was believed

Note carefully the time indicated by the infinitive of the verb which follows such constructions as **was believed, was thought.** *He was believed to be ill* means that people thought him ill at the time implied in **was believed.** *He was believed to have been ill* means that people thought that he had been ill at a time previous to that implied in **was believed.** See **seem to have been.**

"way"

The expressions, "way back", "way down yonder", "way behind us", "way out West", etc., are provincialisms which should be avoided except in very informal speech or in jocular remarks.

"ways"

"Ways" is used colloquially for *way,* as in the expression, "a little ways up the hill". Such expressions are, of course, not to be used except in very informal speech.

went

Avoid the childish colloquialisms, "went and took", "went and stole", etc.; as in, "He went and took my knife", "He went and stole my book".

went,
  have gone

Be careful not to use **went** as the past participle of the verb *to go*. **Went** is the past tense; **gone** is the past participle. CORRECT: *We went home early, but we could have gone* (not "went") *earlier. He has finished his business and has gone* (not "went") *home.*

were,
  was,
  is

The subjunctive form **were** is used instead of the indicative forms **was** and **is** with the first and third persons respectively in expressions dealing not with *fact* but with *supposed or conceivable fact,* and with *conditions contrary to fact* or involving *uncertainty or doubt.* The subjunctive form **were** is always used after *as if* and *as though,* and frequently, but not always, after *if* and *though.* The following sentences illustrate common uses of the subjunctive: *If he were* (not "was") *here now, I should be glad to see him. If I were* (not "was") *asked to give my opinion, I should be glad to do so. If this were summer instead of winter, we should be able to manage better. Were I sure I should be needed, I would gladly go. Were he my brother, I could not like him better. I wish I were as old as you. It seems as if you had just arrived. She looks as if she were ready to go. He acts as if he knew me. It seems as though summer would never come. Though he were twice as rich as he is, I should not be impressed.*

Be careful not to use the subjunctive form **were** with *if, whether, though,* and such conjunctions, unless the clause following such a conjunction is *conditional,* or expresses an idea *contrary to fact.* FOR EXAMPLE: *He went to the office to see if his brother was there.* In this sentence the word *if* does not introduce any *doubt* or *condition* into the statement.

The object of his going to the office was simply to find out *whether his brother was there or not*. The same principle applies to the following sentences: *If he is here now, I shall be glad to see him. If a man's income was smaller twenty years ago, the cost of living was likewise lower. If this is clear to you, all is well.*

Do not mix the indicative and the subjunctive moods in the same predicate clause. FOR EXAMPLE, do not say, "If he were well and was still giving lessons in music, I should continue my studies with him". SAY, *If he were well and were still giving,* etc.

what

Since **what** contains within itself the meaning of *that which,* it should never be used as a relative pronoun for *that.* CORRECT: *Everything that* (not "what") *he did displeased me. A man that* (not "what") *knows told me all about it. All that* (not "what") *I have said should be kept secret.*

what is, what are

Whether a singular or a plural verb shall follow **what** depends on whether the speaker is thinking of **what** as a singular or as a plural pronoun. It may be either. Make up your mind clearly, before embarking on the sentence, whether **what** shall be singular or plural, and, having decided, stick by your decision. The following sentences illustrate uses of **what** as singular and as plural: [**what,** singular]—*What was most important was* (not "were") *his promises to help us. What is of the greatest importance to us is* (not "are") *his promises to come to our assistance. What is needed is* (not "are") *a half-dozen chairs for the dining room. What is wanted, and what is absolutely necessary, is* (not "are") *citizens who will take an active interest in public affairs. What causes me the greatest* *concern is* (not "are") *the shortages of raw materials which we shall suffer from next year.* [**What,** plural]—*We are faced with what are* (not "is") *the greatest difficulties of our career. What we call stumbling-blocks are* (not "is") *stepping-stones in disguise. He stayed away from the meeting for what were* (not "was") *doubtless good and sufficient reasons. He showed us some pictures of what are* (not "is") *known as the hedgehog forts. The observatory has photographs of what appear* (not "appears") *to be canals on the planet Mars.*

whatever, whatsoever

Since **whatever** and **whatsoever** mean *all that* or *any that,* do not add *that* to either word, as in "whatever reasons that you may have". CORRECT: *Whatever reasons you may have for not joining us, we shall miss you. Whatsoever* (not "whatsoever that") *he may have done, I shall stand by him.*

when

Do not use a clause beginning with **when** as a definition of a noun; as, "a hurricane is when a very high wind blows". Such usage is as careless as it is senseless. A *hurricane* is a *violent storm,* not "when . . .".

whence

See **hence.**

where

Where-clauses, like *when*-clauses, should not be used in giving the definitions of nouns; as, "A marathon is where people run a long race". See **when.**

Avoid the use of, "see where", in such expressions as "I see where the President has returned".

Do not use the prepositions *at* and *to* with **where,** as in the expression, "Where does he live at now?" "Where are you going to?" CORRECT: *Where does he live? Where is he? Where are you going?* See **at.**

"whereabouts"

"Whereabouts" for **where** is wrong, as in "Whereabouts do you live now?" CORRECT: *Where* (not "whereabouts") *is his new house?*

whether

Avoid the unnecessary expression, "of whether", in referring to questions and problems. CORRECT: *The Prime Minister will take up the question whether* (not "of whether") *the withdrawal of the troops was justifiable or not. We are confronted by the problem whether* (not "of whether") *it is better to rent or to buy a house.* Do not use "as to" before **whether.**

which

The relative pronoun **which** should be used only to refer to a noun or pronoun, or to a noun clause. It should not be used loosely to refer to an *idea* or a *statement,* as in the expression, "He told me to help myself, which I did". Similar misuses of **which** may be noted in the following sentences: "It has been a mild winter, which is fortunate". "He did not come; besides which, he has not answered my letter". Such incorrect expressions may be remedied by recasting the sentences, as follows: *It has, fortunately, been a mild winter. He did not come, and, furthermore, he has not answered my letter.* See **that, who.**

which,
and which,
but which

Do not use **and which** or **but which** unless you have previously used **which.** Do not say, for example, "A fine old house with a large garden, and which I hope to buy, has just been put on the market". CORRECT: *A fine old house, which has a large garden, and which I hope to buy, has just been put on the market. A book on economic reconstruction, which has just been published, and which we hope will interest you, is announced in the enclosed catalogue.* The same rule applies, of course, to the use of **and who** and **but who**, and **whom** and **but whom**.

while

Do not use **while** loosely in the sense of *and*, as in the sentence, "The flower garden is situated on the left, while the vegetable garden is on the right". Avoid also the use of **while** in the sense of *though* whenever **while** might be misunderstood as an adverb expressing *time*. CORRECT: *Though* (not "while") *I did not see him, I expected to hear from him every day. Though* (not "while") *I am at the office every morning, he does not trouble to come.* See **although**.

who,
whom

Who and **whom** are frequently confused by careless speakers and writers. **Who** is used as the *subject of,* or *in the predicate with, a finite verb;* **whom** is used as the *object of a finite verb.* THUS: *The man who brings my vegetables is the man whom you should see.* **Whom** is also used as the *subject of an infinitive.* THUS: *He is a man whom I know to be honest.* Errors in the use of **who** and **whom** are most likely to occur in more complex sentences, especially in those in which parenthetical remarks like *I think* and *I am sure* are inserted. Observe carefully the following sentences: *He is a man who* (not "whom"), *I know, will give satisfaction.* (Notice that in the foregoing sentence **who** is the subject of *will give,* not the object of *I know*). *Give the prize to whom you choose.* (Here **whom** is the object of *choose.*) *Who do they say that I am?* (Here **who** is a nominative in the predicate with *am.*) *Whom do they think me to be?* (**Whom** is here in the objective case as subject of the infinitive *to be.*) *He is a man who, I think, would like you, and whom you would like. Who did you say he was? Who, do you think, will win the* *game? Who* (not "whom") *shall I say called? Whom did you give the prize to? He is a man whom I trust, and who, I am sure, will merit my confidence in him. He is a man whom I think to be worthy of my confidence.* See **that, which.**

wholeheartedly   See **heartily.**

wholly   See **holy.**

**whose,
    who's**

Whose is the possessive of **who.** It should be distinguished from **who's,** the contraction of *who is.* THUS: *Whose is this overcoat? It belongs to the boy who's in the next room.* See **of which.**

**whoever,
    whomever,
    whosoever,
    whomsoever**

The rules for the use of **whoever** and **whomever,** as for **whosoever** and **whomsoever,** are, in general, the same as those for the use of *who* and *whom,* which see. The following special cautions should be noted: **Whoever** (or **whosoever**) should always be used for *the subject of the verb in a clause.* FOR EXAMPLE: *Whoever comes will be welcome. Give the parcel to whoever (whosoever) comes for it.* (In this last sentence, the preposition *to* does not govern the relative pronoun **whoever.** It governs instead the whole relative clause, *whoever comes for it;* and the clause, within itself, requires **whoever** as subject of the verb *comes*). **Whomever** (or **whomsoever**) should be used when the desired relative pronoun is *the object of a verb or of a preposition.* FOR EXAMPLE: *This prize is to be given to whomever you choose. Choose whomsoever you will. He greeted whomever he met on the street.* Observe the following sentences: *This money is for the benefit of whoever needs it. He gave the calendars to whosoever asked for them.*

I shall accept whomsoever you may send. This is for the benefit of whomsoever you choose.

widow

Since the word **widow** applies only to a *woman,* do not use the word *woman* with it, as in the dialectal expression, "She was a poor widow woman".

will

See **shall.**

winters

See **days.**

wire

Wire is used colloquially as a verb meaning *to telegraph,* and as a noun meaning *telegram.* It is not acceptable in this sense in formal usage, though quite acceptable in informal and commercial usage.

wish

See **hope.**

**with,
of**

With is often used incorrectly for **of,** as in the expression, "With Maryland, as with Virginia, the earliest white settlers were English". Correctly such sentences should be written: *Of Maryland, as of Virginia, the first white settlers were English. Of* (not "with") *nasturtiums, as of* (not "with") *petunias, the seeds should not be planted until danger of frost is over.*

without

See **except, unless.**

witness

See **see.**

won't

Informal for *will not.*

**woo,
woos,
wooed**

Note that the spelling of the third person singular in the present tense is **woos,** and that the past tense is spelled **wooed.**

**wood,
woods**

Do not use *a* or *this* with the plural form **woods** (*a dense grove of trees*). CORRECT: *a small wood, this dark wood, these pine woods.*

"worst kind",
  "worst way"

"The worst kind" and "the worst way" are incorrect expressions used to mean *very badly,* or *extremely,* and should be avoided. CORRECT: *The hospital is greatly in need of nurses,* or *needs nurses badly* (not "needs nurses the worst kind"). *She dislikes her new job extremely* (not "the worst way").

worth while
  "worth-while"

The expression **worth while,** when used in the predicate, is properly written as two words. THUS: *It is not worth while to discuss the question.* The colloquial adjective "worth-while" is written with a hyphen; as, "a worth-while job". "Worth-while" is not approved by the best writers.

would

See **should.**

would better,
  would rather

See **had better, had rather.**

"would have"

In expressing a wish, do not use "would have" for *had* or *might have.* CORRECT: *I wish they had* (not "would have") *left earlier. I wish you had* (not "would have") *seen him eat. I wish you might have* (not "would have") *been with us.* See **of.**

"would say"

"Would say" for *wish to say* is a greatly overworked phrase in business correspondence. It should be avoided, both as jargon and as less effective than *I wish to say.*

would seem

See **seem.**

wrench

See **rinse.**

"write-up"

"Write-up" is journalistic cant for a printed account of something. Like other overworked terms, it should be avoided.

"ye" (for **the**)

The use of "ye" for *the,* as in "Ye Olde Oake Tavern", is a silly affectation, meant to convey the idea of antiquity. It results from a misinterpretation of the form *ye* in early printed books in English. The first English printers, having no equivalent in type for the Old English symbol for *th* used in manuscripts, represented the symbol at times by *y,* the printed letter which most nearly resembled it. Hence such forms as *ye* for *the* and *yat* for *that.* Such forms were, however, never pronounced in any way but as *the* and *that.*

year's time, two years' time

Remember that the possessive form **year's** or **years'** should be used in such expressions as *a year's time, two years' time;* and proper distinction should be made between the singular and the plural forms. THUS: *three months' experience, a fortnight's vacation, a month's salary, a day's journey, four weeks' absence.*

you

You, although used in relation to one person, is grammatically *plural,* and must always be followed by a plural verb. Never say "You was". Be careful not to add an *s*-sound to **you** when speaking to more than one person. The form "youse" is unpardonable.

you and I, you and me

You and **I** are the nominative forms, and are used as the subjects of verbs and as nominatives in the predicate. Be careful to use the objective form **me** when the first person singular pronoun is the object of a verb or of a preposition. Errors are particularly likely to arise when the objective of the first person singular is used with **you**. Note the following examples: *He intended the books for you and me* (not "for you and I"). *He left the house in charge of you and me* (not "you and I"). *Between you and me* (not "you and I"), *I think he's mistaken.* Note the following uses of the nominative: *You and I have charge of the children. They are not so tall as you and I* (are). *Neither of them is so tall as you or I.* The same rule applies, of course, to the use of the first person singular with other pronouns.

In certain constructions, the form *you or I* creates an awkward problem with regard to verb form. "You or I am going" is obviously impossible. In such cases, it is better to recast the sentence. THUS: *You are going, or I am. Either you will go or I shall.* See **he.**

Yours sincerely, Yours very truly

Note that no apostrophe is used with the possessive form **yours.** The word **yours** should not be omitted from the phrases **Yours sincerely, Yours truly,** etc., when they are used at the close of letters, as the adverbs *sincerely, truly,* etc., modify the pronoun *yours.* They do not refer to the manner or mood in which the letter is written. **Yours sincerely** means *I am sincerely yours,* not that the letter is written in a sincere manner. The expression "Hastily yours", therefore, is, when interpreted by the strict rules of grammar, not very complimentary to the person to whom the letter is addressed.

yourself

See **myself.**

A Guide to the
Correct Pronunciation of Words
Frequently Mispronounced

A Guide to the
Correct Pronunciation of Words
Frequently Mispronounced

CORRECT PRONUNCIATION requires the proper sounding of the letters and combinations of letters in a word, and the correct placing of the stress or accent in words of more than one syllable (that is, in words of more than one group of letters which can be pronounced as a single sound). In some words not all the letters are sounded, and in such words it is as important to omit these silent letters as it is to give the proper values to the letters that are sounded.

The letters of the alphabet fall into two divisions: *vowels* and *consonants.*

The vowel letters are **a, e, i, o, u,** and in some cases **w** ("double **u**") and **y.** A vowel letter represents a sound made when the voice passes without obstruction through the vocal cavities.

The consonants, which comprise the remaining letters (including **w** and **y** in their non-vowel capacities) represent sounds made when the voice or breath is obstructed by the teeth, lips, tongue, or soft palate.

Consonants form syllables only in combination with vowels, hence the master key to correct pronunciation is the knowledge and use of the proper sound values of the vowels, separately and in combination. As each of the vowels and many of the consonants may be pronounced in several different ways, the following table of marks, symbols, and combinations of letters has been arranged to indicate the proper values of the letters in the lists of words which are given in Part II.

The symbols used in the table and in the lists of words are intended only to serve as a practical guide to the proper pronunciation of ordinary English words, and not as an exhaustive description of the sound of the words.

KEY TO PRONUNCIATION

Vowel Sounds

ā   LONG: as in **ate, fate, mane**

ă   SHORT: as in **at, fat, man**

â   INTERMEDIATE, usually before a terminal r: as in **fare, parent, impair**

a   UNSTRESSED: as in **comma, normal, woman**

ah   (as in **bah**) represents the sound of a in **father, arm, cart**

aw   (as in **saw**) represents the sound of a in **call, tall, gawky**; and the sound of au in **maul, gaudy, fault**

ē   LONG: as in **be, bead, mete**; used also to represent the sound of i in **machine, Mobile**

ĕ   SHORT: as in **bet, bed, met**

ê   INTERMEDIATE, usually before a terminal r: as in **mere, sphere, adhere**

e   UNSTRESSED: as in **dozen, river, silent**

ī   LONG: as in **file, pine, site**; used also to represent the sound of ȳ in **cyanide, dynamo**

ĭ   SHORT: as in **fill, sit, pin**; used also to represent the sound of ў in **abyss, cataclysm**

i   UNSTRESSED: as in **habit, satin, solid**; used also to represent the sound of e in **antedate, betroth**

ō   LONG: as in **dole, note, rote**

ŏ   SHORT: as in **doll, not, rot**

ô   INTERMEDIATE, usually before r: as in **orb, north, retort**

o   UNSTRESSED: as in **actor, together, random**

o͞o   LONG: as in **soon, food, tool**; used also to represent the sound of ū after certain consonants

o͝o   SHORT: as in **good, stood, wool**; used also to represent the sound of u in **full, pull**

oi   (pronounced as aw-ĭ) as in **boil, toil, void** (see footnote, Page 203) ow   as in **how, brow, tower;** used to represent the sound of ou in **hour, flour**

ū   LONG: as in **union, cue, Buick, mule, puny;** ū is pronounced as yū at the beginning of a word and after all consonants except j, r, and frequently after l, and the pronunciation is so indicated in the lists that follow

ŭ   SHORT: as in **cut, buck, pun**

û   INTERMEDIATE, before r: as in **cur, turn, absurd, surly;** used also to represent the sound of e in **fern, were;** and of i in **sir, fir***

u   UNSTRESSED: as in **lettuce, circus;** when the sound is long as well as unstressed, it is indicated as *ū;* when it is short as well as unstressed it is indicated as *ŭ*

ü   French u or German ü: a sound intermediate between ū and ē, with no exact equivalent in English. The *u* in such words as *menu* and *debut,* when pronounced as in French, has this sound, as has the *ü* in such words as *über* (over) when pronounced as in German

CONSONANT SOUNDS

ch   as in **chop, each, rich**

g   as in **get, grow, big**

j   as in **jest, jug, joke;** used to represent the sound of soft g in **engine, giant, gentle**

k   as in **kind, kick, like;** used to represent the sound of hard c in **can, coal;** the sound of hard ch in **christen, ache, echo;** and the sound of q in **unique**

kw   represents the sound of qu in **quarrel, question**

ĸ   represents the German or Scotch ch, as in **Reich, loch;** it approximates the English k, but is produced without letting the k quite stop the current of breath

ɴ   represents the French nasal, as in **bien, bon;** it is produced by prolonging the vowel sound preceding an n without pronouncing the n

*NOTE.   Be careful to distinguish between the sound of oi (as in **oil**) and that represented by ûr (as in **curl, earl, girl**).

ng   as in song, singer, singing; used to represent the sound of n in bank, sink

s   voiceless, as in sit, kiss; used to represent the sound of soft c in ice, ace, ceiling

sh   as in shop, fish; used to represent the sound of the palatalized s in sugar, sure; of the c in spacious, ocean; of the ch in chateau, chivalry; of the si- and ti- in such combinations as -sion and -tion

th   voiceless, as in thick, think, path, threw

TH   voiced, as in this, though, whether, smooth

z   as in zebra, zinc; used to represent the sound of the voiced s in has, raisin, pause

zh   is used to represent the sound of z in azure, and the sound of s in vision, measure

The consonants not included in the foregoing list—b, d, f, h, m, n, p, r, t, v, w, y—have their normal values, as in the following words: bat, date, fat, hat, man, nun, pat, rest, test, vest, west, yet.

CAUTION.   Special care should be taken by persons to whom English is not the native tongue to avoid confusing the sounds of certain English consonants; as, for example, d and t; d and voiced TH; ch and j; r and l; r and w; s and sh; s and z; t and voiceless *th*; v and w.

CAUTIONS AND SUGGESTIONS WITH RESPECT TO PRONUNCIATION

It is possible to mispronounce, in one way or another, almost every word in the English language, and it is therefore impossible to formulate a set of rules which will cover all words and all circumstances. A good dictionary is indispensable and should be consulted regularly. Since pronunciation is largely a matter of imitation, careful attention to the pronunciation of those who speak correctly is likewise indispensable. Repeat until they become familiar the correct pronunciation of words which you have been in the habit of mispronouncing.

Many errors in pronunciation are due to haste and carelessness in speaking. With respect to these the following special cautions should be kept in mind.

1. Do not drop the final g in such words as **calling, going, seeing.**

2. Do not drop the final t in such words as **accept, except, deft, left, kept, swept.**

3. Be careful to give the proper value to consonants in such words as the following:

antarctic	distinctly	predict
arctic	district	risked
asked	effects	strength
breadth	exactness	subject
climactic	fifth	succinct
collect	hold	think
command	hydrant	thousand
compact	insists	told
contract	length	twelfth
depth	monarchical	used
discs	picture	width

4. In the following commonly used words, which are perhaps as consistently mispronounced as any in English, be careful not to omit or slur over a single letter:

accidentally	encomium	itinerary
accurate	factory	laboratory
arithmetic	February	library
awkward	finally	medicine
believe	formerly	medieval
boundary	genealogy	miniature
candidate	generally	occasionally
cantonment	geography	opprobrium
carrying	government	particularly
cemetery	governor	partition
chocolate	grocery	personal
creature	have	plebeian
curiosity	hickory	poem
diamond	history	police
eleven	idea	popular

positively	recognize	slovenliness
preponderance	regular	sophomore
privilege	reservoir	something
probably	sarsaparilla	surprise
pumpkin	Saturday	temperament
quantity	saucy	vacuum
realize	secretary	violet
really	similarly	worldly

5. Do not add letters or syllables in pronouncing a word. The words in the following list are very commonly mispronounced through the addition of an extra vowel or consonant.

across	grievous	remembrance
athlete	hallelujah	sermon
athletics	height	several
attacked	helm	slice
burglar	hindrance	sphinx
column	margin	stupendous
columnist	memorable	tremendous
disastrous	mischievous	troublous
drowned	mountainous	twice
electoral	once	umbrella
elm	overwhelm	unwieldy
farthest	prairie	villain
film	realm	wash

CAUTION. Avoid the habit, common in certain sections, of adding r to words ending in a vowel sound, such as the following: **alpha, awe, comma, draw, fellow, idea, law, paw, raw, yellow.** Do not insert an r into such words as **awful, pawn, yawn.**

6. Do not transpose or misplace letters in pronouncing such words as the following:

aeroplane	hundred	prerogative
anonymous	irrelevant	prescription
brethren	larynx	portrait
bronchial	modern	portray
casualty	performance	superfluous
cavalry	perspiration	tragedy
children	prefer	yacht

SPECIAL CAUTIONS WITH RESPECT TO THE PRONUNCIATION OF VOWELS

Many errors in pronunciation are the result of ignorance of the proper values of the vowels in certain words, particularly of whether the principal vowel in a word is "long" or "short". The following lists of words indicate the proper sound of the key vowel in some frequently mispronounced words.

1. WORDS HAVING ā FOR THE PRINCIPAL VOWEL

abrasive	basal	ignoramus
acorn	basic	implacable
adjacent	bathing	ingratiate
aeriform	bathos	latent
aerodrome	blatant	lathe
aeronautics	brachial	mange
aeroplane	cambric	matrix
aerostat	capon	nape
affidavit	caveat	nasal
afflatus	chafe	naval
algebraic	chaste	navel
alias	chasten	nefarious
alien	chicanery	pathos
alienate	cicada	patriarch
anal	curator	patriot
ancient	complacent	patriotism
angel	dais	patron
anus	data	percale
apex	errata	precarious
aphasia	expatiate	rabies
apricot	expatriate	radiator
aquarium	farrago	radio
aqueous	gala	ratio
armada	gaol	sacred
arraign	gape	stamen
aviator	gauge	status
aviation	glacial	ultimatum
babel	gravamen	vagrant
banal	grimace	vaporish

| varied | vary | wary |
| various | verbatim | wistaria |

2. Words having ă for the Principal Vowel

abstinence	balcony	exclamatory
acetous	baron	facet
acolyte	basil	facile
adage	bass (fish)	fasces
advocacy	beatify	forbade
afferent	cabala	galaxy
affluent	cadaver	gamin
agate	calory	gamut
agile	calumny	garish
alibi	cameo	gather
alimony	caramel	gavel
alkali	carat	gladiator
alpaca	carol	glamor
alum	carom	genealogy
amicable	caryatid	granary
amorous	casual	guarantee
amulet	casualty	hydrangea
analogous	casuistry	laboratory
anathema	catacomb	lariat
anise	catch	lavish
apache	cater-cornered	opacity
aperture	cavern	pageant
apogee	cavil	parent
apparent	cavity	parish
aquatic	chalice	pastel
aqueduct	chamois	paten
aquiline	chaparral	patina
arid	chastise	patrimony
arrant	chastisement	philately
asinine	chastity	plaid
aspirate	clamor	planet
asthma	cravat	plaque
atrophy	davenport	radish
avid	davit	ratiocination
azure	diameter	rational
bade	diastole	ravage

ravel	seraphic	valet
ravening	stamina	valiant
ravish	strategy	valid
renascent	tacit	valor
sacrament	tassel	vapid
sacrilege	vacillate	varicose
salary	vaginal	vaseline

NOTE. The sound of **a** in the following words and in many similar words is considered, in certain sections of the United States (as in Canada and Great Britain), to be intermediate between that of **a** in **man** and of **a** in **mart**:

ask	chaff	last
aunt	chance	laugh
bask	clasp	pass
bath	command	past
calf	demand	path
can't	fast	rasp
cask	gasp	rather
cast	graph	shan't
caste	grass	task

3. WORDS HAVING ē FOR THE PRINCIPAL VOWEL

adherence	cereal	hedonist
adhesion	chameleon	hysteria
aerial	chimera	ingenious
agley	coherence	lemur
albeit	congeries	lenient
allegiance	credence	lesion
ameba	deteriorate	lethal
ameliorate	deviate	pediatrics
amenable	devious	penal
amnesia	equanimity	penalize
ampere	equatorial	precedence
anemia	equine	quietus
apotheosis	equinox	secrete
arboretum	era	secretive
arsenious	facetious	semen
arterial	feline	senile
breviary	funereal	sepia

sequel
sequence
serial
series

serum
specious
spontaneity
spheral

spheroid
subpoena
vehement
vehicle

4. WORDS HAVING ĕ FOR THE PRINCIPAL VOWEL

acetylene
adolescent
allege
amenity
anemone
anesthetic
angelic
antenna
ascetic
austerity
beneficence
bestial
bestiality
bevel
bevy
celery
celibacy
cenotaph
cerebellum
cerebral
cerebrum
cherub
chevalier
chevron
chimerical
clandestine
credulous
crevice

deaf
decade
deluge
denim
desuetude
discretion
envelope
equerry
equipage
equitable
equity
esoteric
felon
ferule
gelid
get
hysterical
illegible
ingenuous
instead
legate
legendary
legible
lenity
lethargy
levee
level
levier

levitation
levity
levy
longevity
maleficent
menace
penalty
penance
petrel
petrol
plebiscite
preface
prejudice
prelate
premise
presentation
regimen
replica
replevin
senate
seraph
sesame
specimen
spherical
steady
tenant
tenet
thresh

5. WORDS HAVING ī or ȳ FOR THE PRINCIPAL VOWEL

acclimate
affiance

aisle
albino

align
annihilate

anodyne
appendicitis
aspirant
asylum
benign
bias
bicycle
biennial
binomial
biography
biology
bipartisan
bipartite
blithe
bronchitis
client
condign
contrariety
defiance
demise
demoniacal

deny
dynamite
dynamo
fiat
finite
hyperbole
hyperthyroid
hypochondriac
hypodermic
hypothesis
ibex
ibis
icon
idyl
indict
iris
iritis
isotherm
item
libido
lichen

long-lived
miasma
nihilist
opine
papyrus
pica
pyrites
satiety
silage
sinecure
sinus
stipend
supine
thyme
tiny
tithe
via
viaduct
viol
viscount
xylophone

Ĝ. Words having ĭ *or* y̆ for the Principal Vowel

aborigines
abyss
acidity
alliterative
antipathy
antiquity
antithesis
asphyxiate
belligerent
beneficiary
bigamy
bigot
bigoted
bilious
billet
bishopric
brigand

chiffonier
chisel
chivalry
christen
chrysalis
cicatrice
cigarette
cinema
crystal
cygnet
cymbal
cynic
cyst
dimeter
dirigible
drivel
filial

financier
frigate
guinea
hypocrisy
hypocrite
hyssop
guitar
idiom
impious
infamous
infamy
infinite
inimical
iridescent
irritate
iterate
lineage

lineal
linear
literal
livelong
municipal
niche
pivot
privilege
privity

privy
pyrrhic
resilient
ribald
rinse
simile
swivel
sycamore
sycophant

trimeter
virulence
visage
visard
viscera
visual
vitreous
vitriol
withy

7. Words having ō for the Principal Vowel

abdomen
adobe
apportion
arboreal
armorial
aroma
begonia
boa
boll
borne
bovine
brogue
cajole
chore
chorus
clothe
clothier
coalesce
cocain
cocoa
cologne

colon
coma
condolence
corporeal
corps
coterie
crochet
croquet
decorum
depot
docent
donor
dory
dosage
dotage
encomium
forebears
forte
global
hoarse
imbroglio

inconsolable
loth
memorial
modish
molar
mourning
omen
onus
oral
oriel
oriole
pictorial
poll
porous
postern
protocol
sloe
sloth
torn
totem
yeoman

8. Words having ŏ for the Principal Vowel

abdominal
abominable
anomalous
anonymous
apostle

apostasy
apostolic
apostrophe
astronomy
automaton

autonomous
bodice
bomb
botany
bother

chirography	doldrums	nostrum
chiropodist	dolomite	ocular
choler	domicile	oligarchy
choleric	dominate	ominous
chronicle	domino	onerous
chronometer	exonerate	orison
codicil	florid	oscillate
collier	florin	osculate
colloquy	forage	ossify
columbine	forehead	pollen
column	globule	polygon
comparable	globular	polytechnic
complaisant	gospel	poniard
composite	grovel	posthumous
compost	holiday	postulate
compromise	holly	posture
comptroller	holocaust	promenade
conative	holograph	rosin
conger	homage	roster
conglomerate	homily	solace
conic	hominy	solder
conjugal	hostage	solecism
consul	impostor	solid
consular	jocular	solitude
deposit	modicum	solstice
diocesan	mollusk	solvent
docile	monetary	stolid
document	nostalgia	volatile

RULE. The sound of *o* in the following words and in words derived from them is, by the best American standards, considered to be intermediate between that of the ŏ in **stop** and the ô in **order**:

boss	horrid	often
coffee	log	on
dog	long	scoff
fog	off	soft
foreign	offal	song
frog	offer	thong
gone	office	throng
hog	offing	wrong

9. (a) WORDS HAVING ū (pronounced as yū) FOR THE PRINCIPAL VOWEL

CAUTION. The mispronunciation of ū after most consonants is one of the commonest errors in spoken English. The correct pronunciation of ū after all consonants except **j**, **r**, and frequently after **l**, is equivalent to yū, as in **union** and **yule**.

ablution	deduce	fugitive
abuse	delude	funeral
abusive	deluge	furious
accumulate	delusion	fusel
acumen	diffusion	fuselage
acute	diminution	fusillade
adduce	dual	future
albumen	ducal	humor
allude	due	illuminate
allure	duel	illusion
allusion	duet	impecunious
aluminum	duke	impugn
antediluvian	duly	impute
assiduity	dune	induce
assume	dupe	infuse
astute	duplicate	innumerable
attune	duplicity	inured
bitumen	durable	legume
bituminous	durance	lubricate
bucolic	duration	lucid
bureau	duress	lucrative
caduceus	dutiable	lucre
cesura	dutiful	ludicrous
collusion	duty	lugubrious
compute	educe	lurid
consume	elucidate	lute
cube	elude	mucilage
cucumber	elusion	mutual
culinary	endurance	nuance
cupidity	endure	nucleus
cupola	enthusiasm	nude
curious	feud	nuisance
cuticle	fuchsia	numerical

numerous	resume	tumid
numismatist	solution	tumor
nutriment	student	tumult
nutrition	studio	tuna
obscure	stupid	tune
pecuniary	sue	tutor
penurious	suit	union
postlude	suitor	unison
prelude	supercilious	usually
prepuce	superintend	usufruct
presume	superior	usurer
puberty	supersede	usurious
pugilist	supine	usurp
puissance	supreme	usurpation
purify	tuba	usury
putrid	tube	utilitarian
reduce	tubercular	utilize
refuse	tuition	utopianism
resolution	tulip	uvula

RULE. The syllable **ew** (except in the words sew, shew, and after **j**, **r**, and **c** when they are preceded by a consonant) is pronounced ū (yū), as in the following words:

dew	gewgaw	pew
dewy	hew	skewer
ewe	lewd	stew
ewer	mew	view
few	new, news	yew

9. (b) WORDS HAVING ū (pronounced as ōō) FOR THE PRINCIPAL VOWEL

CAUTION. When ū follows **j**, **r**, and in most words after **l**, it is pronounced as ōō, as in the following words:

accrue	cerulean	crude
adjudicate	cherubic	cruel
adjure	chute	erudite
agglutinate	clue	flue
blue	conclude	fluid
brochure	conclusion	flute
brute	congruous	frugal

fruit	judicial	rue
garrulity	juice	rule
garrulous	jury	rumor
glue	juvenile	rune
gluten	prudent	seclude
gruel	prune	seclusion
gruesome	prurient	truant
include	recruit	truce
inclusion	rubric	true
jubilee	ruby	truism

10. Words having ŭ for the Principal Vowel

abrupt	cuspidor	puddler
abundant	custom	pumice
accustomed	ducat	punish
adjust	duchy	ranunculus
adult	duct	ruck
adultery	ductile	ruddy
adumbrate	dulcet	ruffian
annunciation	exult	robust
bicuspid	flux	study
bludgeon	fructify	subaltern
budge	fubsy	subtle
budget	fulcrum	succulent
buffet (strike)	function	such
bulge	fustian	suction
bulk	fusty	sulk
bulkhead	gudgeon	sullen
bulky	homunculus	supple
buncombe	hulk	sustenance
bunion	inductive	swum
conductor	insult	tungsten
crust	justice	tunny
crux	lustrous	umpire
cuckold	luxury	uncial
cud	mull	unction
cull	mullion	unctuous
cumin	nuncio	undulate
cupboard	nuptial	unguent
cusp	pronunciation	uxorious

SPECIAL CAUTIONS WITH RESPECT TO THE PRONUNCIATION OF CONSONANTS

The following lists contain frequently mispronounced words grouped with respect to consonants and combinations of consonants. The correct pronunciation is indicated in each case.

1. WORDS HAVING VOICELESS ch (as in church)

anchovy	chariot	chicory
arch	charm	chimpanzee
chair	chasuble	chintz
chalice	chervil	chivy
chamfer	chevy	chore

Note that the following words have the voiceless ch:

archbishop	archenemy	arch-hypocrite
archdeacon	archer	arching
archduke	archery	archness
arched	archfiend	archway

2. WORDS HAVING HARD ch (pronounced as k)

cachinnate	chiropodist	chyme
chalcedony	chiropractor	echo
chalybeate	chlorine	epoch
chameleon	choir	inchoate
chaos	choler	machination
chaotic	chord	schedule
chartulary	chorister	schizoid
chasm	chorus	scholar
chimera	chromium	scholastic
chirography	chyle	scholium

RULE. The syllable **arch** as part of a word is pronounced as **ark** when it ends the word and when it comes before a vowel (except in forms of the noun or verb **arch**, and in **archer, archery**). The following words therefore have the hard **ch**:

anarchist	archaic	archetype
archaeology	archangel	archiepiscopal

archipelago	autarchy	monarchy
architect	matriarch	patriarch
architrave	monarch	patriarchal
archives	monarchical	oligarchy

3. WORDS HAVING FRENCH ch (pronounced as sh)

cache	chanson	chauvinism
cachalot	chapeau	chemise
cachet	chaperon	chenille
cachou	charabanc	chic
chagrin	charade	chicanery
chaise	charivari	chiffon
chalet	charlatan	chiffonier
chamois	charlotte	chivalry
champagne	chartreuse	chute
champaign	chassis	machine
chancre	chateau	moustache
chandelier	chauffeur	schist

4. WORDS HAVING SOFT g (pronounced as j)

agile	gesture	gyroscope
agitate	gibe	gyve
digest	gibbet	hygiene
digit	giblets	imaginary
dirigible	gill (¼ pint)	incorrigible
elegiac	gillyflower	ingeminate
flagellation	gimcrack	legislate
fragile	gin	lunge
gaol	ginger	magic
gelatin	gingivitis	magistrate
gelid	girasol	pageant
gentian	gist	pagination
genteel	gymnasium	panegyric
gerfalcon	gynecology	sagittal
germinate	gypsum	singe
gest	gypsy	tangible
gestation	gyration	vagina
gesticulate	gyroplane	vegetal

5. Words having Hard g (as in go)

agate	giddy	girdle
eager	gig	gizzard
gape	giggle	lager
gear	gild	league
geld	gill (of a fish)	legal
gelding	gillie	regal
gewgaw	gilt	sagacious
geyser	gimlet	tiger
gib	gimp	vagabond
gibbon	gingham	vagary
gibbous	gird	vague

6. Words in which h is Silent

exhaust	heir	honorific
exhibit	herb	hour
exhibition	herbage	hourly
exhilarate	honest	prohibition
exhort	honor	shepherd
exhortation	honorable	vehement
forehead	honorary	vehicle

7. Words in which h is Sounded

habitual	hospitality	humane
herbaceous	host	humanism
herbal	hostage	humanity
herbarium	hostelry	humble
historical	hostler	humid
homily	hotel	humidity
horrible	houri	humiliate
hospitable	huge	inhibition
hospital	human	inhospitable

8. Words in which n before Hard c, Hard ch, k, q, x is usually pronounced as ng

anchor	anxious	canker
anxiety	banquet	conch

concubine	ink	tank
conquer	instinct	sphinx
distinct	minx	uncle
donkey	relinquish	zinc

EXCEPTIONS: conclude, concoct, concomitant, concord, concur, concussion, concrete

9. WORDS HAVING TERMINAL ng

CAUTION.   All words ending in ng are likely to be mispronounced by persons to whom English is not the native tongue. The single nasal sound represented by the letters ng when not followed by another syllable, as in sing, tongue, is one of the most difficult for many persons to make. The one sure way of learning to pronounce the sound correctly is to listen carefully to those who speak English naturally and well, and pronounce it as they do. In producing the sound of terminal ng the back of the tongue touches the soft palate and is held there until the sound is completed. Be careful to avoid the addition of an extra g or k. The following are examples of words ending in ng which are frequently mispronounced.

among	gong	ring
being	hang	seeing
bring	hung	sing
cling	king	smoking
ending	long	song
fang	making	thing
going	nothing	tongue

RULE 1.   Most words of the foregoing class retain the pronunciation of the terminal ng when they are modified by the addition of other syllables; as in bringing, singer, singing.

RULE 2.   When ng is followed by th, the sound of k may or may not be introduced; thus,

> length   (lĕngth or lĕngkth)
> lengthen   (lĕng'-then or lĕngk'-then)
> strength   (strĕngth or strĕngkth)
> strengthen (strĕng'-then or strĕngk'-then)

10. WORDS HAVING MEDIAL **ng** (pronounced as **ngg**)

In the following words the **g** following the **n** is hard, and in pronouncing the sound represented by **ng** an extra **g** is added: **angle** (ăng-g'l), **anguish** (ăng-gwĭsh), **finger** (fĭng-gẽr).

anger	congress	longer
angle	dangle	mangle
anguish	dingle	monger
bangle	finger	mongrel
bungle	languid	single
clangor	languish	spangled
conger	languor	stronger
congregation	linger	tangle

11. WORDS HAVING **n** BEFORE SOFT **g** (nge or ngy)

In the following words the **g** is soft, and is pronounced as **j**:

angel	flange	range
change	grange	singe
cringe	hinge	sponge
danger	mange	springe
dingy	manger	strange

RULE. When words ending in **nge** or **ngy** are modified by the addition of another syllable, the **ng** retains its original sound, as in the following: change, changed, changing; dingy, dingiest; mange, mangy; singe, singeing.

12. WORDS HAVING SILENT **t**

In the following words the **t** is not pronounced:

apostle	fasten	nestle
bristle	glisten	often
bustle	gristle	pestle
castle	hasten	soften
chasten	hostler	thistle
christen	hustle	whistle
epistle	listen	wrestle

13. WORDS IN WHICH **th** OCCURS

The **th** sound is one of the most difficult for persons to whom English is not the native language. It is a single sound, not a combination of **t** and **h** sounds. It is formed by touching with the tongue the backs or points of the upper front teeth, or by putting the tongue between upper and lower teeth, while the breath is forced through. Special care must be taken to avoid pronouncing the **th** sound as **t**, **d**, or **z**. There are two kinds of **th** sounds—the voiceless *th*, as in the words **think, through, thug;** and the voiced TH, as in the words **than, other, whether.** In the lists of words below, the voiceless sound of **th** is represented by *th*, the voiced sound by TH.

(a) Words with Voiceless *th*

arithmetic	quoth	thought
athenaeum	ruthless	thrash
athlete	sheath	thread
author	sloth	threat
authority	smith	three
bath	thank	thresh
beneath	thatch	threw
both	thaw	thrill
breath	theater	throat
broth	theme	throes
cloth	theology	throne
doth	thick	throng
enthusiasm	thicket	throttle
ether	thigh	throw
fifth	thimble	thrush
fourth	thin	thrust
froth	thing	thug
hath	think	thumb
kith	third	thwack
lath	thirsty	thwart
moth	thirteen	thyroid
mouth (*noun*)	thirty	troth
myth	thistle	truth
oath	thong	worth
path	thorn	wrath
pithy	thorough	wroth

RULE. The voiceless *th* (the sound called for in the above list) is always used, according to American practice, under the following conditions:

(1) whenever **th** is used as an ending for nouns:
bir*th*, clo*th*, dea*th*, dep*th*, grow*th*, hear*th*, la*th*, pi*th*, shea*th*, streng*th*, tru*th*, wid*th*, wrea*th*;

(2) whenever **th** is used as an ending for verbs:
do*th*, ha*th*, live*th*, make*th*, sai*th*.

(b) Words with Voiced TH

alтноugh	hiтнer	тнee
anoтнer	laтне	тнeir
baтнe	laтнer	тнem
baтнing	leaтнer	тнere
bequeaтн	liтнe	тнese
boтнer	loaтнe	тнine
breaтнe	moтнer	тнis
broтнer	mouтн (*verb*)	тнiтнer
cloтнes	neiтнer	тноse
cloтнier	oтнer	тноugh
diтнer	poтнer	тнus
eiтнer	raтнer	тну
faтнer	sheaтнe	togeтнer
farтнer	sliтнer	weaтнer
farтнing	smooтн	wheтнer
farтнingale	swarтну	whiтнer
feaтнer	тнan	wiтн
furтнer	тнat	wiтнer
gaтнer	тнe	worтну

RULE 1. **Th** is usually voiced, as in the foregoing words, in verbs or adjectives formed from nouns ending in voiceless *th:*
ba*th*, baтнing; brea*th*, breaтнe; clo*th*, cloтнing; mou*th*, mouтнing; tee*th*, teeтнing; loa*th*, loaтнe; wor*th*, worтну.
Final voiced TH is usually followed by **e:**
baтнe, breaтнe, cloтнe, sheaтнe.

RULE 2. Some nouns ending in voiceless *th* have voiced TH in their plural forms:
mou*th*, mouтнs; tru*th*, truтнs; shea*th*, sheaтнs; clo*th*, clo*th*s or cloтнs.

RULE 3.   Special care should be taken to avoid substituting **d** or **z** for the TH in the article THE and in the pronouns THIS, THESE, THAT, THOSE. Before a word beginning with a vowel or a silent **h**, the article THE is pronounced THē; before a consonant it is pronounced with the **e** unstressed.

RULE 4.   Before a voiceless consonant the voiced TH in WITH usually becomes voiceless: wi*th* fairness, wi*th* sincerity.

RULE 5.   In a few words **th** has the sound of **t**: thyme, phthisical (tĭz′-ĭ-kăl), and in the proper names Esther, Thomas, Thompson. In asthma the **th** is not pronounced at all.

14. WORDS IN WHICH **wh** OCCURS

CAUTION.   Do not omit the **h** sound in pronouncing words spelled with wh. In their original forms such words were spelled **hw**, and the **h** sound should be distinctly voiced. The pronunciation of the **h** serves the practical purpose of distinguishing such words from similar words spelled without the **h**. Note carefully the difference in pronunciation between the following pairs of words.

whale (hwāl)	———	wail (wāl)
what (hwŏt)	———	watt (wŏt)
wheel (hwēl)	———	weal (wēl)
where (hwâr)	———	wear (wâr)
whey (hwā)	———	way (wā)
which (hwĭch)	———	witch (wĭch)
whirled (hwûrld)	———	world (wûrld)
whether (hwĕTH′-er)	———	weather (wĕTH′-er)
while (hwīl)	———	wile (wīl)
whit (hwĭt)	———	wit (wĭt)
white (hwīt)	———	wight (wīt)
whist (hwĭst)	———	wist (wĭst)
whither (hwĬTH′-er)	———	wither (wĬTH′-er)

NOTE that in the pronouns **who, whom, whose,** etc., the **w** is not pronounced at all.

CAUTIONS WITH RESPECT TO CERTAIN COMBINATIONS OF LETTERS

1. WORDS ENDING IN -alogy AND -ology

Avoid confusing the pronunciation of words ending in **-alogy** and of those ending in **-ology**. The following words are the most common in the two groups.

(a) -alogy

analogy (*a*-năl′-*o*-jĭ)   **mineralogy** (mĭn″-er-ăl′-*o*-jĭ)
genealogy (jĕn″-ĭ-ăl′-*o*-jĭ)   **tetralogy** (tĕ-trăl′-*o*-jĭ)

(b) -ology

biology (bī-ŏl′-*o*-jĭ)   **physiology** (fĭz″-ĭ-ŏl′-*o*-jĭ)
geology (jē-ŏl′-*o*-jĭ)   **psychology** (sī-kŏl′-*o*-jĭ)
meteorology (mē″-tĭ-*or*-ŏl′-*o*-jĭ)   **theology** (*th*ē-ŏl′-*o*-jĭ)
philology (fĭ-lŏl′-*o*-jĭ)   **zoology** (zō-ŏl′-*o*-jĭ)*

2. WORDS CONTAINING -ce-, -ci-, -si-, -ti-

Each of these combinations, when followed by the vowels **a, e, o,** usually represents the sound of **sh** or **zh**. The following words illustrate the pronunciation of combinations of this type.

amnesia (ăm-nē′-zhĭ-*a*)   **judiciary** (jōō-dĭsh′-ĭ-ĕr″-ĭ)
ambrosial (ăm-brō′-zhĭ-*al*)   **musician** (myū-zĭsh′-*an*)
coercion (kō-ûr′-shŭn)   **nasturtium** (n*a*-stûr′-shŭm)
contention (kŏn-tĕn′-shŭn)   **nation** (nā′-shŭn)
convulsion (kŏn-vŭl′-shŭn)   **ocean** (ō′-sh*an*)
cretaceous (kr*i*-tā-shŭs)   **oceanic** (ō″-shi-ăn′-ĭk)
delicious (d*i*-lĭsh′-ŭs)   **official** (*o*-fĭsh′-*al*)
efficiency (ĕ-fĭsh′-*en*-sĭ)   **partial** (pahr′-sh*al*)
efficient (ĕ-fĭsh′-*ent*)   **patient** (pā′-sh*ent*)
glacial (glā′-sh*al*)   **tertian** (tûr′-sh*an*)
hosiery (hō′-zher-ĭ)   **tertiary** (tûr′-shĭ-ĕr″-ĭ)

*Note that the first syllable in **zoology** is zō (not zōō).

3. Words having i after l, ll, n

After l, ll, and n the vowel i often does the duty of y and is pronounced as y, as in the words that follow. Avoid pronouncing it in these cases as a separate syllable.

alien (āl'-yen)	espalier (ĕs-păl'-yûr)
alienate (āl'-yen-āt)	familiar (fa-mĭl'-yûr)
auxiliary (awg-zĭl'-ya-rĭ)	Julian (jōōl'-yan)
bilious (bĭl'-yŭs)	million (mĭl'-yŭn)
billiards (bĭl'-yûrdz)	minion (mĭn'-yŭn)
billion (bĭl'-yŭn)	onion (ŭn'-yŭn)
bunion (bŭn'-yŭn)	pavilion (pa-vĭl'-yŭn)
civilian (sĭ-vĭl'-yan)	peculiar (pĭ-kyūl'-yûr)
collier (kŏl'-yûr)	poniard (pŏn'-yûrd)
communion (ko-myūn'-yŭn)	trunnion (trŭn'-yŭn)
companion (kom-păn'-yŭn)	union (yūn'-yŭn)
cotillion (ko-tĭl'-yŭn)	vermilion (vûr-mĭl'-yŭn)

Note also the following: **imbroglio** (ĭm-brōl'-yō), **intaglio** (ĭn-tăl'-yō), **seraglio** (si-răl'-yō).

4. Words containing unstressed e, i, and y

In such words as the following be careful not to give the value of a long vowel to the unstressed or short e, i, or y

beautiful (byū'-ti-fŏŏl)	divorce (di-vōrs')
bountiful (bown'-ti-fŏŏl)	divorcé (di-vōr"-sā')
cigar (si-gahr')	divorcée (di-vōr"-sā')
cigarette (sĭg-a-rĕt')	divulge (di-vŭlj')
delighted (di-lī'-tĕd)	effect (ĕ-fĕkt')
denounce (di-nowns')	effective (ĕ-fĕk'-tĭv)
detain (di-tān')	Italian (ĭ-tăl'-yan)
diploma (di-plō'-ma)	italics (ĭ-tăl'-ĭks)
distill (dĭs-tĭl')	refined (ri-fīnd')
divide (di-vīd')	sincerely (sĭn-sêr'-lĭ)
divine (di-vīn')	truly (trōō'-lĭ)

5. Words ending with -ture

The suffix **-ture** in common words is pronounced **chûr,** as in the following:

creature	future	pasture
culture	literature	posture
furniture	nature	vesture

6. Words containing -ough

The combination -ough may be pronounced in eight different ways in English, and no rule whatever can be given for determining the correct pronunciation in any particular word. The proper sound for each word must be memorized and made familiar by frequent use. Every possible sound of the combination will be found in the nonsensical sentence, "Though the tough cough and hiccough plough Mr. Gough through the hough." The following list contains words illustrating various ways in which the combination is pronounced:

brougham (bro͞om or bro͞o'-um)	rougher (rŭf'-er)
chough (chŭf)	roughhew (rŭf″-hyū′)
clough (klŭf or klow)	slough (slow), *noun,* miry place
doughty (dow'-ti)	slough (slōō), *noun,* tidal flat
hiccough (hĭk'-ŭp)	slough (slŭf), *noun,* cast-off skin
hough (hŏk)	slough (slŭf), *verb,* to cast off
lough (lŏк)	sloughy (slow'-ĭ), *adjective*
nought (nôt)	sloughy (slōō'-ĭ), *adjective*
ought (ôt)	sloughy (slŭf'-ĭ), *adjective*
roughage (rŭf'-ĭj)	sough (suf or sow)
roughen (rŭf'-en)	toughen (tŭf'-en)

Note. The surname **Gough** is pronounced gŏf.

SPECIAL CAUTIONS WITH RESPECT TO ACCENT

1. Words with Primary Accent on First Syllable

absolute	advocacy	assets
absolutely	affluence	brigand
admirable	affluent	cerebral
admiral	aggrandize	cerebrum
admiralty	alias	champion
adulatory	applicable	combatant
advent	approbate	communal
adversary	armistice	communist

comparable
construe
contrary
contrite
controversy
contumacy
contumely
conversant
cornet
cupola
deficit
despicable
desuetude
desultory
detonate
devastate
dirigible
disparate
distaff
equitable
evidently
exquisite
formidable
gondola

guardian
harass
heretic
hospitable
hospital
impious
impotent
inchoate
industry
infamous
infamy
influence
integral
interesting
interim
interlude
intricacy
intricate
inventory
laboratory
lamentable
maintenance
mischievous
necessary

orchestra
pedestal
peony
perjure
plethora
positively
posthumous
preferable
purpose
purposive
quadruplet
quintuplet
reprobate
reputable
requisite
residence
ribald
ribaldry
stigmata
theater
traverse
vehement
vehicle
vicinage

2. WORDS WITH PRIMARY ACCENT ON SECOND SYLLABLE

acetic
acclimate
acclimatize
acumen
address
adjacent
adverse
advice
aggrandizement
albumen
ally
allied
allies
allay

alloy
ancestral
aquatic
ascetic
aspirant
assess
azalea
bitumen
bouquet
canteen
carafe
cartoon
catastrophe
chagrin

cigar
condign
condolence
connivance
consent
curator
demise
device
devise
diastole
direct
discharge
dispirited
diverge

effect
electoral
emetic
entire
epigraphy
episcopal
epitome
excess
exhale
explicit
fanatic
finance
frenetic
fruition
giraffe
gravamen
grimace
guitar

horizon
implicit
incomparable
incorrigible
indisputable
inevitable
inexplicable
inhale
interstices
intuitive
irrefragable
irrefutable
irreparable
irrevocable
italics
municipal
museum
narrator

penates
pituitary
portray
precedence
pyrites
quietus
recall
repetitive
research
resources
robust
romance
rheumatic
satiety
secretive
solicit
splenetic
superfluous

PRONUNCIATION AND MEANING

There are many words spelled alike which are accented or pronounced differently according to meaning. Be careful to distinguish between the two or more possible pronunciations which such words may have. The following lists contain some of the more common of these words.

1. Nouns and verbs of identical spelling, in which the accent falls on the *first* syllable in the noun and on the *second* syllable in the verb:

abstract
addict
affix
annex
attribute
collect
combine
compact
compound

compress
concert
conduct
console
converse
convert
descant
desert
digest

export
import
impress
incense
increase
object
perfume
permit
pervert

prefix	progress	refuse
presage	project	survey
present	premise	suspect
proceeds	rebel	transfer
produce	record	transport

2. Adjectives and verbs of identical spelling, in which the accent falls on the *first* syllable in the adjective and on the *second* in the verb:

absent, frequent, perfect, present, subject, suspect.

3. Note carefully the distinctions in pronunciation in the following pairs of words:

abstract (ăb'-străkt *or* ăb-străkt'), *adjective*
abstract (ăb'-străkt), *verb*

buffet (bŭf'-fĕt), a blow
buffet (bŏŏ-fā'), sideboard

cleanly (klĕn'-lĭ), *adjective*
cleanly (klēn'-lĭ), *adverb*

consummate (kon-sŭm'-ĭt), *adjective*
consummate (kŏn'-sŭ-māt), *verb*

divan (dī'-văn), couch
divan (dĭ-văn'), Turkish council of state

does (dŭz), *verb*
does (dōz), *noun,* plural of **doe**

excuse (ĕks-kyūz'), *verb*
excuse (ĕks-kyūs'), *noun*

gill (jĭl), ¼ pint
gill (gĭl), respiratory organ

hinder (hīn'-der), *adjective*
hinder (hĭn'-der), *verb*

house (hows), *noun*
house (howz), *verb*

instinct (ĭn-stĭngkt′), *adjective*
instinct (ĭn′-stĭngkt), *noun*

inter (ĭn-tûr′), *verb*
inter- (ĭn′-tûr), *prefix*

intimate (ĭn′-tĭ-māt), *verb*
intimate (ĭn′-tĭ-mĭt), *adjective*

invalid (ĭn-văl′-ĭd), *adjective*
invalid (ĭn′-va-lĭd), *noun*

job (jŏb), piece of work
Job (jōb), *proper name*

lead (lĕd), *noun,* a metal
lead (lēd), *verb,* to lead

learned (lûrnd), *verb*
learned (lûr′-nĕd), *adjective*

lower (low′-ûr), *verb,* to frown
lower (lō′-ûr), *adjective, comparative of* **low**; *verb,* to let down

minute (mĭn′-ĭt), *noun*
minute (mĭ-nyūt′ *or* mī-nyūt′), *adjective*

polish (pŏl′-ĭsh), *noun*
Polish (pōl′-ĭsh), *adjective*

prayer (prâr), act of praying
prayer (prā′-ûr), one who prays

precedent (pri-sēd′-ent), *adjective*
precedent (prĕs′-i-dent), *noun*

putting (pŏŏt′-ĭng), *form of verb* to put
putting (pŭt′-ĭng), *form of verb* to putt

read (rēd), *present tense of verb* to read
read (rĕd), *past tense of verb* to read

refuse (ri-fyūz′), *verb*
refuse (rĕf′-yūs), *noun*

separate (sĕp′-a-rāt), *verb*
separate (sĕp′-a-rĭt), *adjective*

slaver   (slăv'-ûr), *verb,* to slobber
slaver   (slāv'-ûr), *noun,* slave ship

tarry   (tahr'-ĭ), *adjective,* of or like **tar**
tarry   (tăr'-ĭ), *verb,* to linger

tear   (têr), *noun*
tear   (târ), *noun or verb*

use   (yūz), *verb*
use   (yūs), *noun*

worsted   (wŏŏs'-tĕd), *noun,* yarn for weaving
worsted   (wûr'-stĕd), *adjective,* defeated

wound   (wōōnd *or* wownd), *noun*
wound   (wownd), *form of verb,* to wind

PAIRS OF WORDS OFTEN CONFUSED IN PRONUNCIATION

Note carefully the differences in spelling and pronunciation in the following pairs of words:

caliber   (kăl'-ĭ-ber), diameter of bullet, or the bore of a gun
caliper   (kăl'-ĭ-per), instrument for determining thickness or diameter of objects

carton   (kahr'-ton), pasteboard box
cartoon   (kahr-tōōn'), pictorial sketch

casualty   (kăz'-yū-al-tĭ), mishap; *plural,* list of killed, wounded, missing in battle
causality   (kawz-ăl'-ĭ-tĭ), relation of cause and effect

Calvary   (kăl'-va-rĭ), the mount of the Crucifixion
cavalry   (kăv'-al-rĭ), horse-soldiers

celery   (sĕl'-er-ĭ), vegetable
salary   (săl'-a-rĭ), fixed payment to employed person

cemetery   (sĕm'-ĭ-tĕr-ĭ), burial-ground
symmetry   (sĭm'-ĭ-trĭ), exact correspondence of parts

censor   (sĕn'-sor), official examiner
censure   (sĕn'-syur), hostile criticism

climactic   (klī-măk′-tĭk), of or pertaining to a climax
climatic   (klī-măt′-ĭk), of or pertaining to the climate

consul   (kŏn′-sŭl), government official
counsel   (kown′-sĕl) advice

dinghy or **dingy**   (dĭng′-gĭ), *noun,* small boat
dingy   (dĭn′-jĭ), *adjective,* drab, smoky

faucet   (faw′-sĕt), fixture for drawing liquid from container
forceps   (fôr′-sĕps), pair of pincers or tongs

finally   (fī′-nal-ĭ), at the end, at last
finely   (fīn′-lĭ), in a fine manner; closely

formally   (fôr′-mal-ĭ), in a formal manner
formerly   (fôr′-mer-lĭ), in time past

gig   (gĭg), light carriage; rowboat
jig   (jĭg), dance

ingenious   (ĭn-jēn′-yŭs), possessed of ingenuity, clever
ingenuous   (ĭn-jĕn′-yu-ŭs), frank

lightening   (līt′-en-ĭng), making less burdensome
lightning   (līt′-nĭng), atmospheric electrical discharge

loose   (lo͞os), *adjective,* unfastened, free
lose   (lo͞oz), *verb,* to suffer loss

minister   (mĭn′-ĭs-ter), one who ministers
minster   (mĭn′-ster), a church

sink   (sĭnk), *verb,* to descend lower and lower; *noun,* a drain
zinc   (zĭnk), *noun,* a metal

specie   (spē′-shē), money in the shape of coin
species   (spē′-shēz), sort, kind, variety

A LIST OF WORDS FREQUENTLY MISPRONOUNCED, SHOWING CORRECT PRONUNCIATION

In the following list of words the proper pronunciation, according to the best American usage, is indicated within the parentheses. In words of several syllables the heaviest stress should be placed on the syllable marked with the principal accent sign ('), and the next heaviest stress should be placed on the syllable marked with the secondary accent sign (").

abdomen (ăb-dō'-měn or ăb'-do-men)
absolute (ăb'-so-lyūt)
absolutely (ăb'-so-lyūt-li)
absorb (ăb-sôrb')
abusive (a-byū'-sǐv)
abysmal (a-bǐz'-mal)
abyss (a-bǐs')
acacia (a-kā'-sha)
accelerate (ăk-sěl'-er-āt)
acceleration (ăk-sěl"-er-ā'-shun)
accelerative (ăk-sěl'-er-ā-tǐv)
acclimate (a-klī'-mit)
acclimation (ăk"-lǐ-mā'-shun)
acclimatization (a-klī"-ma-ti-zā'-shun)
accouchement (a-kōōsh'-mahN)
accouterment (a-kōō'-ter-ment)
accrual (a-krōō'-al)
accumulate (a-kyū'-myū-lāt)
accurate (ăk'-yū-rǐt)
acerbity (a-sûr'-bi-tǐ)
acetic (a-sē'-tǐk)
acetylene (a-sět'-i-lēn)
acoustic (a-kōōs'-tǐk or a-kows'-tǐk)
actual (ăk'-tyū-al)
actuality (ăk"-tyū-ăl'-i-tǐ)
actuary (ăk'-tyū-ěr"-ǐ)

acumen (a-kyū'-měn)
adage (ăd'-ǐj)
adaptation (ăd"-ăp-tā'-shun)
address (a-drěs')
adherence (ăd-hêr'-ěns)
adjectival (ăj"-ěk-tī'-val)
adjective (ăj'-ěk-tǐv)
adjutant (ăj'-ōō-tant)
admirable (ăd'-mǐ-rab'l)
admiralty (ăd'-mǐ-ral-tǐ)
adobe (a-dō'-bǐ)
adorable (a-dōr'-a-b'l)
adult (ă-dŭlt')
adumbrate (ăd-ŭm'-brāt)
adversary (ăd'-vûr-sě"-rǐ)
advertisement (ăd-vûr'-tǐz-ment or ăd"-vûr-tīz'-ment)
advocacy (ăd'-vo-ka-sǐ)
aegis (ē'-jǐs)
aerated (ā'-ûr-āt-ed)
aerial (ā-ēr'-ǐ-al)
aerodrome (ā'-ûr-o-drōm)
aeronautics (ā"-ûr-o-nawt'-ǐks)
aeroplane (ā'-ûr-o-plān)
aesthetic (ěs-thět'-ǐk)
affiance (a-fī'-ans)
afflatus (a-flā'-tŭs)
again (a-gěn' or a-gān')
agate (ăg'-at)

aged (ā'-jĕd)

aggrandizement (a-grăn'-dĭz-ment)

agile (ăj'-ĭl)

agitate (ăj'-i-tāt)

ague (ā'-gyū)

aguish (ā'-gyū-ĭsh)

akimbo (a-kĭm'-bō)

albeit (awl-bē'-ĭt)

albino (ăl-bī'-nō)

albumen (ăl-byū'-mĕn)

alder (awl'-dûr)

alderman (awl'-dûr-man)

alga (ăl'-ga); plural, algae (ăl'-jē)

alias (ā'-lĭ-as)

alibi (ăl'-i-bī)

alien (āl'-yen)

alienate (āl'-yen-āt)

alimony (ăl'-i-mō-nĭ)

alkali (ăl'-ka-lī)

allege (ăl-lĕj')

allegiance (a-lē'-jăns)

allied (a-līd')

allies (a-līz')

alloy (a-loi')

ally (a-lī')

alma mater (ăl'-ma mā'-tûr)

almond (ah'-mŭnd)

almost (awl'-mōst)

alms (ahmz)

aloes (ăl'-ōz)

alpaca (ăl-păk'-a)

already (awl-rĕd'-ĭ)

also (awl'-sō)

altercation (awl"-tûr-kā'-shŭn)

alternate (awl'-tûr-nĭt or ăl'-tûr-nĭt), adjective

alternate (awl'-tûr-nāt or ăl'-tûr-nāt), verb

alternative (awl-tûr'-na-tĭv or ăl-tûr'-na-tĭv)

altruism (ăl'-trōō-ĭzm)

alum (ăl'-um)

aluminium (ăl"-yū-mĭn'-ĭ-ŭm)

aluminum (a-lyū'-mĭ-nŭm)

alumna (a-lŭm'-na); plural, alumnae (a-lŭm'-nē)

alumnus (a-lŭm'-nus); plural, alumni (a-lŭm'-nī)

amalgam (a-măl'-gam)

amalgamate (a-măl'-ga-māt)

amanuensis (a-măn"-yū-ĕn'-sĭs); plural, amanuenses (a-măn"-yū-ĕn'-sēz)

amateur (ăm"-a-tur' or ăm'-a-tyūr")

ambergris (ăm'-bûr-grēs)

ambidextrous (ăm"-bĭ-dĕk'-strŭs)

ambrosia (ăm-brō'-zhia)

ambulance (ăm'-byū-lans)

ameliorate (a-mēl'-yo-rāt)

amen (ā'-mĕn'; singing, ah'-mĕn')

amenable (a-mēn'-a-b'l)

amenity (a-mĕn'-i-tĭ or a-mēn'-i-tĭ)

among (a-mŭng')

ampere (ăm'-pêr)

amphitheater (ăm"-fĭ-thē'-ă-tûr)

analogous (a-năl'-o-gŭs)

analogy (a-năl'-o-jĭ)

analysis (a-năl'-i-sĭs)

ancestral (ăn-sĕs'-tral)

anchovy (ăn-chō'-vĭ or ăn'-chō-vĭ)

ancillary (ăn'-sĭ-lĕr"-ĭ)

anemone (a-nĕm'-ō-nĭ)

anesthesia (ăn"-ĕs-thē'-zhia)

anesthetic (ăn"-ĕs-thĕt'-ĭk)

anesthetist (ăn-ĕs'-thĭ-tĭst)

angel (ān'-jel)

angelic (ăn-jĕl'-ĭk)

angle (ăng'-g'l)

angora (ăng-gō′-ra)
aniline (ăn′-i-lĭn or ăn′-i-lĭn)
anise (ăn′-ĭs)
annex (a-nĕks′), verb
annex (ăn′-ĕks or a-nĕks′), noun
annihilate (a-nī′-i-lāt″)
annuity (a-nyū′-ĭ-tĭ)
anomalous (a-nŏm′-a-lŭs)
anomaly (a-nŏm′-a-lĭ)
anonymity (ăn″-o-nĭm′-i-tĭ)
anonymous (a-nŏn′-i-mŭs)
answer (ăn′-sûr)
antarctic (ănt-ahrk′-tĭk)
antediluvian (ăn″-tĭ-dĭ-lyū′-vi-an)
antenna (ăn-tĕn′-a); plural,
   antennae (ăn-tĕn′-ē)
antipodes (ăn-tĭp′-o-dēz)
apache (a-păch′-i)
apathy (ăp′-a-thĭ)
apiary (ā′-pĭ-ĕr″-ĭ)
apostasy (a-pŏs′-ta-sĭ)
apostle (a-pŏs′-’l)
apotheosis (ăp″-o-thē′-o-sĭs or
   a-pŏth″-i-ō′-sĭs)
apparatus (ăp″-a-rā′-tŭs or
   ăp″-a-răt′-ŭs)
apparent (a-păr′-ent)
appellant (a-pĕl′-ant)
appellee (ăp″-e-lē′)
applicable (ăp′-lĭ-ka-b’l)
appreciation (a-prē″-shĭ-ā′-shŭn)
approval (a-prōōv′-al)
apropos (ăp″-ro-pō′)
aquarium (a-kwār′-ĭ-ŭm)
aquatic (a-kwăt′-ĭk)
archangel (ahrk′-ān′-jel)
archipelago (ahr″-kĭ-pĕl′-a-gō)
architect (ahr′-kĭ-tĕkt)
arctic (ahrk′-tĭk)
arduous (ahr′-dyū-ŭs)
arid (ăr′-ĭd)

armada (ahr-mä′-da or
   ahr-mah′-da)
armistice (ahr′-mi-stĭs)
arraign (a-rān′)
arrant (ăr′-ant)
asbestos (ăs-bĕs′-tos or
   ăz-bĕs′-tos)
asparagus (ăs-păr′-a-gŭs)
asphalt (ăs′-fawlt or ăs′-fălt)
aspirant (ăs-pīr′-ant or ăs′-pi-rant)
aspirate (ăs′-pi-rĭt)
associate (a-sō′-shĭ-āt), verb
associate (a-sō′-shĭ-at), adjective
   and noun
assuage (a-swāj′)
asthma (ăz′-ma or ăs′-ma)
athenaeum (ăth″-i-nē′-ŭm)
athletic (ăth-lĕt′-ĭk)
athwart (a-thwawrt′)
atrophy (ăt′-ro-fĭ)
attacked (a-tăkt′)
attribute (a-trĭb′-yūt), verb
attribute (ăt′-ri-byūt), noun
auburn (aw′-bûrn)
auricle (aw′-ri-k’l)
authoritative (aw-thôr′-i-tā″-tĭv)
autobiography (aw″-to-bī-ŏg′-ra-fĭ)
autogyro (aw″-to-jī′-rō)
automobile (aw″-to-mō′-bēl)
autopsy (aw′-tŏp-sĭ or aw′-tŭp-sĭ)
auxiliary (awg-zĭl′-ya-rĭ)
avenue (ăv′-e-nyū)
aver (a-vûr′)
aviary (ā′-vĭ-ĕr-ĭ)
aviator (ā′-vĭ-ā″-tôr)
avoirdupois (ăv″-er-dū-poiz′)
awry (a-rī′)
aye, ay (ā), aıways
aye, ay (ī), yes
azalea (a-zāl′-ya)
azure (ăzh′-yŭr)

bacillus (ba-sĭl'-ŭs);
  plural, **bacilli** (ba-sĭl'-ī)

bacteria (băk-têr'-i-a); *singular,*
  bacterium (băk-têr'-i-ŭm)

bade (băd)

bailiwick (bāl'-ĭ-wĭk)

balcony (băl'-ko-nĭ)

balk (bawk)

ballet (băl'-ā *or* bă-lā')

ballistics (ba-lĭs'-tĭks)

banal (bā'-nal)

banish (băn'-ĭsh)

banquet (băng'-kwĕt)

baptize (băp-tīz')

barbaric (bahr-băr'-ĭk)

barrage (ba-rahzh')

basalt (ba-sawlt' *or* băs'-awlt)

bas-relief (bah"-ri-lēf' *or*
  bah'-ri-lēf")

bass (bās), musical term

bass (băs), fish

bathe (bāTH), *verb*

battalion (ba-tăl'-yon)

bayou (bī'-o͞o)

bazaar (ba-zahr')

because (bi-kawz')

bedizen (bi-dĭz'-'n *or* bi-dīz'-'n)

behemoth (bi-hē'-mŭth *or*
  bē'-hi-mŏth)

beneficence (bi-nĕf'-i-sĕns)

beneficiary (bĕn"-i-fĭsh'-ĭ-ĕr-ĭ *or*
  bĕn-i-fĭsh'-ûr-ĭ)

benzine (bĕn'-zēn *or* bĕn-zēn')

bequeath (bi-kwēTH')

beret (bĕ-rā' *or* bĕ'-rā)

bestial (bĕst'-yal)

bestiary (bĕs'-tĭ-ĕr-ĭ)

betroth (bi-trôth' *or* bi-trōTH')

bevel (bĕv'-el)

bias (bī'-as)

bicentenary (bī-sĕn'-ti-nĕr"-ĭ
  or bī"-sĕn-tĕn'-a-rĭ)

bifocal (bī-fō'-kal)

billiards (bĭl'-yûrdz)

binocular (bĭn-ŏk'-yū-lar *or*
  bī-nŏk'-yū-lar)

biographical (bī-o-grăf'-ĭ-kal)

biography (bī-ŏg'-ra-fĭ)

biscuit (bĭs'-kĭt)

bisque (bĭsk)

bitumen (bi-tyū'-men)

bivouac (bĭv'-o͝o-ăk *or* bĭv'-wăk}

blackguard (blăg'-ahrd)

blasé (blah-zā')

blaspheme (blăs-fēm')

blasphemy (blăs'-fi-mĭ)

blue (blo͞o)

boa (bō'-a)

boisterous (bois'-ter-ŭs)

boll (bōl)

booth (bo͞oth); *plural,* bo͞oTHs

born (bôrn)

borne (bōrn)

bosom (bo͝oz'-ŭm *or* bo͞oz'-ŭm)

bouillon (bo͞o'-yôN *or* bo͞ol'-yŭn)

boulevard (bo͞o'-le-vahrd *or*
  bo͝ol'-e-vahrd)

bouquet (bo͞o-kā')

bourgeois (bo͝or-zhwah' *or*
  bo͝or'-zhwah)

bourgeoisie (bo͝or"-zhwah"-zē')

bow (bow), to bend or yield

bow (bō), anything bent or curved

bow (bow), forward part of ship

bowdlerize (bowd'-ler-īz)

braggadocio (brăg"-a-dō'-shĭ-ō)

brassière (brăs"-ĭ-âr' *or*
  bra-zêr')

bravado (bra-vah'-dō)

brazier (brā'-zhûr)

breeches   (brĭch'-ĭz)
breviary   (brē'-vĭ-ĕr-ĭ)
bric-a-brac   (brĭk'-a-brăk")
brigand   (brĭg'-and)
bristle   (brĭs'-'l)
broccoli   (brŏk'-o-lĭ)
brochure   (brō-shōōr')
bronchial   (brŏng'-kĭ-al)
brooch   (brōch or brōōch)
brusque   (brŭsk or brōōsk)
buccaneer   (bŭk"-a-nêr')
buffet   (bōō-fā'), sideboard
buffet   (bŭf'-ĕt or bŭf'-ĭt), a blow
bugloss   (byū'-glŏs)
bulk   (bŭlk)
bullion   (bōōl'-yon)
bulrush   (bōōl'-rŭsh)
bulwark   (bōōl'-wûrk)
buncombe   (bŭng'-kŭm)
buoy   (bōō'-ĭ or boi)
buoyant   (bōō'-yant or boi'-ant)
bureaucracy   (byū-rŏk'-ra-sĭ or
   byū-rō'-kra-sĭ)
bustle   (bŭs'-'l)
cacao   (ka-kah'-ō or ka-kā'-ō)
cachalot   (kăsh'-a-lŏt or kăsh'-a-lō)
cache   (kăsh)
cachet   (kă-shā' or kăsh'-ā)
cadet   (ka-dĕt')
caisson   (kā'-sŏn)
caldron   (kawl'-drŭn)
calenture   (kăl'-en-tyūr)
caliph   (kā'-lĭf or kăl'-ĭf)
calisthenics   (kăl"-ĭs-thĕn'-ĭks)
calix   (kā'-lĭks or kăl'-ĭks)
calumny   (kăl'-ŭm-nĭ)
camellia   (ka-mĕl'-ĭ-a)
cameo   (kăm'-ē-ō)
candelabra   (kăn"-dĭ-lah'-bra)
cañon   (kăn'-yŭn)
canon   (kăn'-ŭn)

cantonment   (kăn-tŏn'-ment
   or kăn'-ton-ment)
capitalist   (kăp'-ĭ-tăl-ĭst)
carburetor   (kahr'-byū-rĕt"-ûr)
caries   (kā'-rĭ-ēz)
carillon   (kăr'-ĭ-lŏn or ka-rĭl'-yŭn)
carriage   (kăr'-ĭj)
cartridge   (kahr'-trĭj)
caryatid   (kăr"-ĭ-ăt'-ĭd)
castle   (kăs'-'l)
casuist   (kăzh'-yū-ĭst)
catch   (kăch)
causeway   (kawz'-wā)
caviar   (kăv"-ĭ-ahr' or kah"-vyahr')
ceiling   (sēl'-ĭng)
celery   (sĕl'-er-ĭ)
celestial   (si-lĕs'-chal)
cello   (chĕl'-ō)
cenotaph   (sĕn'-ō-tăf)
centaur   (sĕn'-tawr)
centenary   (sĕn'-ti-nĕr"-ĭ or
   sĕn-tĕn'-a-rĭ)
centrifugal   (sĕn-trĭf'-yū-gal)
ceramics   (sē-răm'-ĭks)
cereal   (sêr'-ē-al)
cerebellum   (sĕr"-ē-bĕl'-ŭm)
cerebral   (sĕr'-ē-bral)
cerebrum   (sĕr'-ē-brŭm)
cerement   (sêr'-ment)
cerulean   (sē-rōō'-lē-an)
chafe   (chāf)
chagrin   (sha-grĭn')
chaise   (shāz)
chalet   (shă-lā' or shăl'-ā)
chalybeate   (ka-lĭb'-i-at)
chameleon   (ka-mē'-lē-ŭn or
   ka-mēl'-yŭn)
chamois   (shăm'-ĭ)
champagne   (shăm-pān')
champaign   (shăm-pān' or
   shăm'-pān)

champion (chăm'-pĭ-ŭn *or*
  chămp'-yŭn)
chancre (shăng'-kûr)
changing (chān'-jĭng)
chanson (shăn'-son)
chaos (kā'-ŏs)
chaotic (kā-ŏt'-ĭk)
chaparral (chăp"-a-răl')
chapeau (shah-pō')
chaperon (shăp'-ûr-ōn)
charabanc (shăr'-a-băng")
charade (sha-rād' *or* sha-r; hd')
charivari (shah-ri-vā'-ri *or*
  sha-rĭv'-a-rē)
charlatan (shahr'-la-tan)
chartreuse (shahr-trûz')
chary (chār'-ĭ)
chasm (kăz'm)
chassis (shăs'-ĭ *or* shăs'-ĭs)
chaste (chāst)
chasten (chās'-'n)
chastise (chăs-tīz')
chastisement (chăs'-tĭz-ment)
chateau (shă-tō')
chauffeur (shō-fûr' *or* shō'-fer)
chauvinism (shō'-vĭn-ĭz'm)
chef (shĕf)
chemise (shi-mēz')
chenille (shi-nēl')
cheroot (she-rōōt')
chevalier (shĕv"-a-lêr')
chic (shēk *or* shĭk)
chicanery (shĭ-kān'-ĕr-ĭ)
chieftain (chēf'-tĭn *or* chēf'-ten)
chiffon (shĭf'-ŏn *or* shĭ-fŏn')
chiffonier (shĭf"-o-nêr')
chimera (kī-mē'-ra *or* kĭ-mē'-ra)
chimerical (kī-mĕr'-i-kal *or*
  kĭ-mĕr'-i-kal)
chimpanzee (chĭm"-păn-zē' *or*
  chĭm-păn'-zē)

chinquapin (chĭng'-ka-pĭn)
chiropodist (kī-rŏp'-o-dĭst)
chiropractor (kī'-rō-prăk"-tôr)
chitterlings (chĭt'-ûr-lĭngs)
chivalrous (shĭv'-al-rŭs)
chlorine (klō'-rēn *or* klō'-rin)
chock-full (chŏk'-fōōl')
chocolate (chŏk'-o-lĭt)
choir (kwīr)
choler (kŏl'-er)
choleric (kŏl'-er-ĭk)
chore (chōr)
chorister (kôr'-ĭs-ter)
chorus (kō'-rŭs)
christen (krĭs'-'n)
chute (shōōt)
cicada (sĭ-kā'-da *or* sĭ-kah'-da)
cicatrice (sĭk'-a-trĭs)
cigar (sĭ-gahr')
cigarette (sĭg'-a-rĕt')
cincture (sĭngk'-chyūr)
cinema (sĭn'-i-ma)
cinematograph (sĭn"-i-măt'-o-grăf)
circuit (sûr'-kĭt)
citation (sī-tā'-shŭn)
citatory (sī'-ta-tō"-rĭ)
citron (sĭt'-rŭn)
clandestine (klăn-dĕs'-tĭn)
clapboard (klăp'-bōrd *or*
  klăb'-ûrd)
clarinet (klăr"-i-nĕt' *or*
  klăr'-i-nĕt)
clematis (klĕm'-a-tĭs)
clew (klōō)
clientele (klī"-en-tĕl')
climactic (klī-măk'-tĭk)
climatic (klī-măt'-ĭk)
clique (klēk)
clothes (klōTHz)
clothier (klōTH'-yûr)
cloths (klôTHz *or* klôths)

clue (kloo)

coalesce (kō″-a-lĕs′)

cocaine (kō-kān′ or kō′-ka-ēn)

coccyx (kŏk′-sĭks)

cocoa (kō′-kō)

codicil (kŏd′-i-sĭl)

coerce (kō-ûrs′)

cognac (kō′-nyăk or kŏn′-yăk)

cognizant (kŏg′-nĭ-zant)

coiffeur (kwah-fûr′)

coiffure (kwah-fyūr′)

coincidently (kō-ĭn′-sĭ-dent-lĭ)

coincidentally (kō-ĭn″-sĭ-dĕn′-tal-ĭ)

colander (kŭl′-an-der or kŏl′-an-der)

colchicum (kŏl′-chĭ-kŭm or kŏl′-kĭ-kŭm)

colleen (kŏl′-ēn or ko-lēn′)

collier (kŏl′-yûr)

collision (ko-lĭzh′-ŭn)

colloquial (ko-lō′-kwĭ-al)

colonel (kûr′-nel)

column (kŏl′-ŭm)

columnist (kŏl′-ŭm-ĭst or kŏl′-ŭm-nĭst)

coma (kō′-ma)

comatose (kŏm′-a-tōs or -tōz; or kō′-ma-tōs or -tōz)

combat (kŏm′-băt or kŭm′-băt or kom-băt′), verb

combat (kŏm′-băt or kŭm′-băt), noun

combatant (kŏm′-ba-tant or kŭm′-ba-tant)

combative (kŏm′-ba-tĭv or kŭm′-ba-tĭv or kom-băt′-ĭv)

combativeness (kom-băt′-ĭv-nĕs or kom-băt′-ĭv-nĭs)

comely (kŭm′-lĭ)

commandant (kom″-an-dahnt′ or kom″-an-dănt′)

commissariat (kŏm″-i-sâr′-ĭ-ăt)

communal (kŏm′-yū-nal or ko-myū′-nal)

communiqué (ko-myū″-ni-kā′ or ko-myū′-ni-kā″)

comparable (kŏm′-pa-ra-b′l)

comparatively (kŏm-pâr′-a-tĭv″-lĭ)

compeer (kŏm-pêr′)

compensate (kŏm′-pĕn-sāt)

complacent (kŏm-plā′-sent)

complaisant (kom-plā′-zant or kŏm′-plā-zănt″)

compliment (kŏm′-pli-mĕnt)

comptroller (kŏn-trōl′-er)

comrade (kŏm′-răd)

concentrate (kŏn′-sen-trāt)

concerto (kŏn-chĕr′-tō)

concord (kŏn′kôrd or kŏng′-kôrd)

concourse (kŏn′-kōrs or kŏng′-kōrs)

concupiscence (kŏn-kyū′-pi-sens)

concurrence (kŏn-kûr′-ens)

concurring (kŏn-kûr′-ĭng)

condign (kŏn-dīn′)

condolence (kŏn-dō′-lens)

conduit (kŏn′-dōō-it or kŏn′-dĭt)

confidant (kŏn″-fi-dahnt′ or kŏn′-fi-dănt″)

confidante (kŏn″-fi-dahnt′ or kŏn′-fi-dănt″)

confident (kŏn′-fi-dent)

confiscatory (kŏn-fĭs′-ka-tō″-rĭ or kŏn′-fĭs-kā″-to-rĭ)

congener (kŏn′-jē-ner)

conger (kŏng′-ger)

congeries (kŏn-jêr′-ĭ-ēz)

congratulatory (kŏn-grăt′-yū-la-tō″-rĭ)

congruent (kŏng′-grōō-ent)

conic (kŏn′-ĭk)

conifer (kō′-nĭ-fer or kŏn′-i-fer)

conjugal (kŏn'-jŏŏ-gal)

conjure (kŏn-jŏŏr' or kŏn'-jer or kŭn'-jer)

connoisseur (kŏn"-i-sûr')

conquer (kŏng'-kûr)

conscientious (kŏn"-shĭ-ĕn'-shŭs)

consommé (kŏn"-so-mā')

consonant (kŏn'-so-nant)

consort (noun: kŏn'-sôrt; verb: kon-sôrt')

constable (kŭn'-sta-b'l or kŏn'-sta-b'l)

constellation (kŏn"-ste-lā'-shŭn)

constitutive (kŏn'-stĭ-tyū"-tĭv or kŏn-stĭt'-yū-tĭv)

construe (kon-strōō' or kŏn'-strōō)

consular (kŏn'-syū-ler)

consultative (kŏn-sŭl'-ta-tĭv)

consummate (adj.: kon-sŭm'-ĭt; verb: kŏn'-su-māt)

contemplate (kŏn'-tĕm-plāt or kŏn-tĕm'-plāt)

contemplative (kŏn-tĕm'-pla-tĭv or kŏn'-tĕm-plā"-tĭv)

content (noun: kŏn'-tĕnt or kon-tĕnt'; verb, adj.: kon-tĕnt')

contest (noun: kŏn'-tĕst; verb: kon-tĕst')

contestant (kon-tĕs'-tant)

contour (kŏn'-tŏŏr or kŏn-tŏŏr')

contralto (kon-trăl'-tō)

contrariety (kŏn"-tra-rī'-e-tĭ)

contrary (kŏn'-trĕr-ĭ)

contribute (kon-trĭb'-yūt)

contrite (kŏn'-trīt or kŏn-trīt')

contrition (kon-trĭsh'-ŭn)

controversy (kŏn'-tro-vûr"-sĭ)

contumely (kŏn'-tyū-mē"-lĭ)

conversant (kŏn'-vûr-sant or kon-vûr'-sant)

convex (kŏn'-vĕks or kŏn-vĕks')

convoy (noun: kŏn'-voi; verb: kŏn-voi')

coquet (kō-kĕt')

coquetry (kō'-ke-trĭ or kō-kĕt'-rĭ)

coquette (kō-kĕt')

cordial (kôr'-jal or kôr'-dyal or kôr'-dĭ-ăl)

corduroy (kôr'-dŭ-roi or kôr"-dŭ-roi')

cornet (kôr'-nĕt or kôr-nĕt')

cornice (kôr'-nĭs)

cornucopia (kôr"-nyū-kō'-pĭ-a)

corollary (kôr'-o-lĕr"-ĭ or ko-rŏl'-a-rĭ)

coronach (kŏr'-o-naк)

corporeal (kôr-pō'-ri-al)

corral (ko-răl' or ko-rahl')

correlate (kŏr'-e-lāt)

corrigenda (kŏr"-ĭ-jĕn'-da)

corrigible (kŏr'-ĭ-ji-b'l)

corrugated (kŏr'-yū-gāt"-ĕd or kŏr'-ŏŏ-gāt"-ĕd)

costume (verb: kŏs-tyūm'; noun: kŏs'-tyūm or kŏs-tyūm')

coterie (kō'-te-rĭ; French, kō"-t'rē')

cotillion (kō-tĭl'-yŭn)

cotillon (kō-tĭl'-yŭn; French, kō"-tē"-yôn')

council (kown'-sĭl)

counsel (kown'-sĕl)

counterfeit (kown'-ter-fĭt)

coup (kōō)

coupé (kōō"-pā')

coupon (kōō'-pŏn)

courier (kŏŏr'-ĭ-er)

courteous (kûr'-tē-ŭs)

courtesan (kôr'-ti-zan or kûr'-ti-zan)

courtesy (kûr'-te-sĭ or kōr-te-sĭ)

courtier (kōr'-tĭ-er or kōrt'-yer)

covenant (kŭv'-ĕ-nănt)

covert (kŭv′-ert)
covey (kŭv′-ĭ)
cousin (kŭz′-’n)
coxswain (kŏk′-s’n or kŏk′-swān)
coyote (kī′-ōt or kī-ō′-tĭ)
cozen (kŭz′-’n)
cravat (kra-văt′)
creature (krē′-chûr)
credence (krē′-dens)
creek (krēk)
cremate (krē′-māt or krē-māt′)
crenate (krē′-nāt)
creole (krē′-ōl)
crescendo (kre-shĕn′-dō or -sĕn′-dō)
crevasse (krĕ-văs′)
crevice (krĕv′-ĭs)
crinoline (krĭn′-o-lĭn or -lēn)
crochet (krō-shā′ or krō′-shā)
crocheted (krō-shād′)
crocheting (krō-shā′-ĭng)
croquet (krō-kā′ or krō′-kā)
croquette (kro-kĕt′)
crotchet (krŏch′-ĕt)
crucial (krōō′-shal)
crux (krŭks)
crystalline (krĭs′-tal-ĭn or -īn)
cuckoo (kŏŏk′-ōō)
cucumber (kyū′-kŭm-ber)
cuisine (kwē-zēn′)
culinary (kyū′-lĭ-nĕr″-ĭ)
cuneiform (kyū-nē′-i-fôrm or kyū′-nē-i-fôrm″)
cupboard (kŭb′-erd)
cupola (kyū′-po-la)
curator (kyū-rā′-ter)
curiosity (kyū″-rĭ-ŏs′-i-tĭ)
currant (kûr′-ant)
current (kûr′-ent)
curriculum (kŭ-rĭk′-yū-lŭm)
currier (kûr′-ĭ-er)

curvet (noun: kûr′-vĕt; verb: kŭr-vĕt′ or kûr′-vĕt)
cyanide (sī′-a-nīd or -nĭd)
cyclamen (sĭk′-la-mĕn or sī′-kla-mĕn)
cygnet (sĭg′-nĕt or sĭg′-nĭt)
cymbal (sĭm′-bal)
cynic (sĭn′-ĭk)
cyst (sĭst)
czar (zahr)
czarina (zah-rē′-na)
dachshund (dahks′-hŏŏnt″ or dăsh′-hŭnd″)
dahlia (dahl′-ya or dăl′-ya or dāl′-ya)
dais (dā′-ĭs or dās)
damning (dăm′-ĭng or dăm′-nĭng)
data (dā′-ta or dah′-ta)
daub (dawb)
dauphin (daw′-fĭn)
davit (dăv′-ĭt or dā′-vĭt)
deaf (dĕf)
debacle (de-bah′-k’l or de-băk′-’l)
debenture (de-bĕn′-chûr)
debouch (de-bōōsh′)
debris (dĕ-brē′ or dĕb′-rē)
debut (dā-byū′ or dĕ-byū′)
debutante (dĕb″-yū-tahnt′)
decade (dĕk′-ād or -ad or de-kād′)
decadence (de-kā′-dens or dĕk′-a-dens)
décolleté (dā-kŏl′-tā)
décor (dā-kôr′)
decorous (dĕk′-o-rŭs or di-kō′-rŭs)
decorum (di-kō′-rŭm)
decoy (di-koi′)
decrease (verb: dē-krēs′; noun: dē′-krēs or dē-krēs′)
defamation (dĕf″-a-mā′-shŭn or dē″-fa-)
deficit (dĕf′-i-sĭt)

defile (dĭ-fīl′)

deformation (dē″-fôr-mā′-shŭn *or* dĕf″-*or*-)

degradation (dĕg″-ra-dā′-shŭn)

deify (dē′-*i*-fī)

deleterious (dĕl″-*i*-tēr′-ĭ-ŭs)

deluge (dĕl′-yūj)

de luxe (dĭ lōōks′ *or* lŭks′; *French*, de lyüx′)

demesne (dĭ-mān′ *or* -mēn′)

demise (dĭ-mīz′)

demitasse (dĕm′-ĭ-tăs″ *or* -tahs″)

democracy (dĭ-mŏk′-ra-sĭ)

demoiselle (dĕm″-wah-zĕl′)

demonetize (dē-mŏn′-*e*-tīz *or* dē-mŭn′-)

demoniac (dĭ-mō′-nĭ-ăk)

demoniacal (dē″-mo-nī′-a-kal)

demonstrable (dĭ-mŏn′-stra-b′l *or* dĕm′-ŭn-)

demurrer (dĭ-mûr′-er)

denim (dĕn′-ĭm)

denouement (dā-nōō′-mawN)

deposition (dĕp″-o-zĭsh′-ŭn *or* dē″-pō-)

depot (dē′-pō *or* dĕp′-ō)

deprecatory (dĕp′-rĕ-ka-tō″-rĭ)

derisive (dĭ-rī′-sĭv)

derisory (dĭ-rī′-so-rĭ)

describe (dĭ-skrīb′)

desert (*verb:* de-zûrt′; *noun:* dĕz′-ert *or* de-zûrt′)

deshabille (dĕz″-a-bēl′)

desiccate (dĕs′-*i*-kāt)

desideratum (dĭ-sĭd″-er-ā′-tŭm)

desperado (dĕs″-pûr-ā′-dō *or* -ah′-dō)

despicable (dĕs′-pĭ-ka-b′l)

dessert (dĭ-zûrt′)

destruction (dĭ-strŭk′-shŭn)

desuetude (dĕs′-wĭ-tyūd *or* dē′-swĭ-tyūd)

desultory (dĕs′-ŭl-tō″-rĭ)

detail (dĭ-tāl′ *or* dē′-tāl)

detonation (dĕt″-o-nā′-shŭn)

detour (dĭ-tōōr′ *or* dē′-tōōr)

deuce (dyūs)

devastate (dĕv′-as-tāt)

develop (dĭ-vĕl′-ŭp)

device (dĭ-vīs′)

dew (dyū)

diabetes (dī″-a-bē′-tēz)

diapason (dī″-a-pā′-zŭn *or* -sŭn)

diaphragm (dī′-a-frăm)

diarrhea (dī″-a-rē′-a)

diastole (dī-ăs′-tō-lē)

dictate (dĭk′-tāt *or* dĭk-tāt′)

dictation (dĭk-tā′-shŭn)

dictator (dĭk-tā′-ter *or* dĭk′-tā-ter)

dietetics (dī″-e-tĕt′-ĭks)

digest (*noun:* dī′-jĕst; *verb:* dĭ-jĕst′ *or* dī-jĕst′)

dilate (dī-lāt′ *or* dĭ-lāt′)

dilatory (dĭl′-a-tō″-rĭ *or* dĭl′-a-tûr-ĭ)

dilemma (dĭ-lĕm′-a *or* dī-lĕm′-a)

dilettante (dĭl″-e-tăn′-tĭ)

diminution (dĭm″-ĭ-nyū′-shŭn)

dinghy (dĭng′-gĭ)

dingy (dĭn′-jĭ)

diocesan (dī-ŏs′-i-san *or* dī-ŏs′-i-zan)

diocese (dī′-o-sēs *or* dī′-o-sĭs)

diphtheria (dĭf-thēr′-ĭ-a)

diploma (dĭ-plō′-ma)

direct (dĭ-rĕkt′ *or* dī-rĕkt′)

direction (dĭ-rĕk′-shŭn *or* dī-rĕk′-shŭn)

directly (dĭ-rĕkt′-lĭ *or* dī-rĕkt′-lĭ)

dirigible (dĭr′-ĭ-jĭ-b′l)

disastrous (dĭ-zăs′-trŭs)
discern (dĭ-zûrn′ *or* dĭ-sûrn′)
discernible (dĭ-zûrn′-ĭ-b'l)
discharge (dĭs-chahrj′)
discreet (dĭs-krēt′)
discrete (dĭs-krēt′ *or* dĭs′-krēt)
disciplinary (dĭs′-ĭ-plĭ-nĕr″-ĭ)
disdain (dĭs-dān′)
dishabille (dĭs″-a-bēl′)
dishevel (dĭ-shĕv′-el)
dispel (dĭs-pĕl′)
disputable (dĭs′-pyū-ta-b'l *or* dĭs-pyūt′-a-b'l)
disputant (dĭs′-pyū-tant)
disputatious (dĭs″-pyū-tā′-shŭs)
disreputable (dĭs-rĕp′-yū-ta-b'l)
dissect (dĭ-sĕkt′)
dissipate (dĭs′-ĭ-pāt)
dissoluble (dĭ-sŏl′-yū-b'l *or* dĭs′-o-lyū-b'l)
distich (dĭs′-tĭk)
distil (dĭs-tĭl′)
distrait (dĭs-trā′; *French,* dēs-trĕ′)
distribute (dĭs-trĭb′-yūt)
divan (dĭ′-văn *or* dĭ-văn′)
diverge (dĭ-vûrj′ *or* di-vûrj′)
divers (dī′-verz)
diverse (dĭ-vûrs′ *or* dī′-vûrs *or* di-vûrs′)
diversion (di-vûr′-shŭn *or* di-vûr′-zhŭn)
diversity (dī-vûr′-si-tĭ *or* di-vûr′-si-tĭ)
divest (dī-vĕst′ *or* di-vĕst′)
divorce (di-vōrs′)
divorcee (di-vōr″-sē′; *French fem.,* di-vōr″-sā′)
doctrinal (dŏk′-trĭ-nal)
does (3rd person of **do,** dŭz; plural of **doe,** dōz)
dolorous (dŏl′-er-ŭs *or* dō′-ler-ŭs)

doggerel (dŏg′-er-el)
domicile (dŏm′-i-sĭl)
donkey (dŏng′-kĭ)
donor (dō′-ner *or* dō′-nôr)
dormitory (dôr′-mĭ-tō″-rĭ)
dose (dōs)
dotage (dōt′-ĭj)
douche (dōōsh)
doughty (dow′-tĭ)
dour (dōōr)
doyen (dwă″-yăɴ′; *English,* dwah′-yen *or* doi′-en)
doze (dōz)
dozen (dŭz′-'n)
draught (drăft)
dromedary (drŏm′-i-dĕr″-ĭ *or* drŭm′-i-dĕr″-ĭ)
dross (drŏs)
drought (drowt)
drouth (drowth)
dual (dyū′-al)
dubiety (dyū-bī′-e-tĭ)
dubious (dyū′-bĭ-ŭs)
ducat (dŭk′-at)
ductile (dŭk′-tĭl)
due (dyū)
duel (dyū′-el)
duet (dyū-ĕt′)
duke (dyūk)
duodecimal (dyū″-o-dĕs′-i-mal)
duodenal (dyū″-o-dē′-nal)
duodenum (dyū″-o-dē′-nŭm)
dupe (dyūp)
duress (dyū′-rĕs)
duty (dyū′-tĭ)
dwarf (dwôrf)
dynamite (dī′-na-mīt)
dynast (dī′-nast *or* dĭn′-ast)
dynasty (dī′-nas-tĭ *or* dĭn′-as-tĭ)
dysentery (dĭs′-en-tĕr″-ĭ)
dyspepsia (dĭs-pĕp′-sha)

easel (ē'-z'l)
eccentric (ĕk-sĕn'-trĭk)
eclair (ā-klâr')
eclat (ā-klah')
eclectic (ĕk-lĕk'-tĭk)
economic (ē"-ko-nŏm'-ĭk *or* ĕk"-o-nŏm'-ĭk)
economical (ē"-ko-nŏm'-i-kal)
economics (ē"-ko-nŏm'-ĭks *or* ĕk"-o-nŏm'-ĭks)
ecstasy (ĕk'-sta-sĭ)
ecumenical (ĕk"-yū-mĕn'-i-kal *or* ē"-kyū-mĕn-i-kal)
eczema (ĕk'-zi-ma *or* ĕk'-si-ma)
edelweiss (ā'-del-vīs)
effervesce (ĕf"-er-vĕs')
efficacious (ĕf"-i-kā'-shŭs)
efficacy (ĕf'-i-ka-sĭ)
effigy (ĕf'-i-jĭ)
ego (ē'-gō *or* ĕg'-ō)
egoism (ē'-gō-ĭz'm *or* ĕg'-ō-ĭz'm)
egotism (ē'-gō-tĭz'm *or* ĕg'-ō-tĭz'm)
egregious (i-grē'-jŭs *or* i-grē'-jĭ-ŭs)
egret (ē'-grĕt *or* ĕg'-rĕt)
eider (ī'-der)
eight (āt)
eighth (āt'th)
electoral (i-lĕk'-ter-al)
electricity (i-lĕk"-trĭs'-i-tĭ *or* ĕl"-ek-trĭs'-i-tĭ)
eleemosynary (ĕl"-i-mŏs'-i-nĕr"-ĭ *or* ĕl"-i-ē-mŏz'-ĭ-nĕr"-ĭ)
elegiac (ĕl"-i-jī'-ăk *or* ĕ-lē'-jĭ-ăk)
elephantiasis (ĕl"-i-făn-tī'-a-sĭs)
elevated (ĕl'-i-vāt"-ĕd)
elite (ā-lēt')
elixir (i-lĭk'-seɾ)
elm (ĕlm)
elocution (ĕl"-o kyū'-shŭn)

elongate (i-lŏng'-gāt *or* ē'-lŏng-gāt)
elucidate (i-lyū'-si-dāt)
elude (i-lyūd')
emaciate (i-mā'-shĭ-āt)
emanate (ĕm'-a-nāt)
emanation (ĕm"-a-nā'-shŭn)
embarrass (ĕm-băr'-as)
embryo (ĕm'-brĭ-ō)
emendation (ē"-mĕn-dā'-shŭn *or* ĕm"-ĕn-dā'-shŭn)
emeritus (i-mĕr'-i-tŭs)
emetic (i-mĕt'-ĭk)
emigrant (ĕm'-i-grănt)
eminent (ĕm'-i-nĕnt)
emissary (ĕm'-i-sĕr"-ĭ)
employe (ĕm-ploi'-ē; *British,* ŏm-ploi'-ā)
employee (ĕm"-ploi-ē' *or* ĕm-ploi'-ē)
empyema (ĕm"-pĭ-ē'-ma)
empyreal (ĕm-pĭr'-i-al *or* ĕm"-pī-rē'-al)
enclave (ĕn'-klāv)
encomium (ĕn-kō'-mĭ-ŭm)
encore (ahng-kōr' *or* ahng'-kōr)
encyclic (ĕn-sĭk'-lĭk)
endemic (ĕn-dĕm'-ĭk)
endive (ĕn'-dīv *or* ĕn'-dĭv *or* ahn'-dīv)
enervate (*verb:* ĕn'-er-vāt; *adjective:* i-nûr'-vāt)
ennui (ahn'-wē)
en route (ahn rōōt')
ensemble (ahn-sŏm'-b'l)
ensign (ĕn'-sīn; naval officer, ĕn'-sĭn)
ensilage (ĕn'-si-lĭj)
entente (ahɴ-tahɴt')
enthusiasm (ĕn-thyū'-zĭ-ăz'm)

entire   (ĕn-tīr')

entourage   (ahn"-tōō-rahzh')

entr'acte   (ahn-trăkt')

entrails   (ĕn'-trālz)

entree   (ahn'-trā)

entrepreneur   (ahn"-trê-prê-nûr')

enumeration   (i-nyū"-mêr-ā'-shŭn)

envelop   (ĕn-vĕl'-ŭp)

envelope   (ĕn'-ve-lōp)

environs   (ĕn-vī'-rŭnz or ĕn'-vi-rŭnz)

epaulet   (ĕp'-o-lĕt)

ephemeral   (ĕ-fĕm'-êr-al)

epilogue   (ĕp'-i-lŏg)

epistle   (i-pĭs'-'l)

epistolary   (i-pĭs'-tō-le-rĭ)

epitome   (i-pĭt'-o-mē)

epoch   (ĕp'-ok or ē'-pŏk)

epochal   (ĕp'-ok-al)

equable   (ĕk'-wa-b'l or ē'-kwa-b'l)

equation   (i-kwā'-zhŭn)

equerry   (ĕk'-wêr-ĭ)

equilibrium   (ē"-kwi-lĭb'-rĭ-ŭm)

equine   (ē'-kwīn)

equinox   (ē'-kwĭ-nŏks or ĕk'-wĭ-nŏks)

equipage   (ĕk'-wi-pĭj)

equipoise   (ē'-kwi-poiz or ĕk'-wi-poiz)

equitable   (ĕk'-wĭ-ta-b'l)

erasure   (i-rā'-zhyŭr)

ere   (âr)

ergo   (ûr'-gō)

err   (ûr)

errata   (i-rā'-ta)

erudite   (ĕr'-ŏŏ-dīt or ĕr'-yū-dīt)

erysipelas   (ĕr"-ĭ-sĭp'-e-las or ĭr"-ĭ-sĭp'-e-las)

escalator   (ĕs'-ka-lā"-têr)

eschew   (ĕs-chōō' or ĕs-chyū')

esophagus   (i-sŏf'-a-gŭs)

esoteric   (ĕs"-o-tĕr'-ĭk)

espionage   (ĕs'-pĭ-o-nij or ĕs"-pĭ-o-nahzh')

estuary   (ĕs'-tyū-ĕr"-ĭ)

et cetera   [etc.]   (ĕt sĕt'-er-a)

etiquette   (ĕt'-ĭ-kĕt or ĕt"-ĭ-kĕt')

eucharist   (yū'-ka-rĭst)

euchre   (yū'-ker)

eunuch   (yū'-nŭk)

eureka   (yū-rē'-ka)

euthanasia   (yū"-tha-nā'-zhĭ-a)

evangelical   (ē"-văn-jĕl'-ĭ-kal or ĕv"-ăn-jĕl'-ĭ-kal)

evidently   (ĕv'-i-dĕnt-lĭ)

evil   (ē'-v'l or ē'-vĭl)

evolution   (ĕv"-o-lyū'-shŭn; British, ē"-vo-lyū'-shŭn)

ewe   (yū)

exaggerate   (ĕg-zăj'-er-āt)

exalt   (ĕg-zawlt')

excellences   (ĕk'-se-lĕn-sĕz)

excellencies   (ĕk'-se-lĕn-sĭz)

exchequer   (ĕks-chĕk'-er or ĕks'-chĕk-er)

excruciate   (ĕks-krōō'-shĭ-āt)

executive   (ĕg-zĕk'-yu-tĭv or ĕk-sĕk'-yū-tĭv)

exemplar   (ĕg-zĕm'-pler or ĕg-zĕm'-plahr)

exeunt   (ĕk'-sē-ŭnt)

exhale   (ĕks-hāl' or ĕg-zāl')

exhaust   (ĕg-zawst')

exhibit   (ĕg-zĭb'-ĭt)

exhilarate   (ĕg-zĭl'-a-rāt)

exhort   (ĕg-zôrt')

exhume   (ĕks-hyūm' or ĕg-zyūm')

exigency   (ĕk'-si-jĕn-sĭ)

exile   (ĕk'-sīl or ĕg'-zīl)

existence   (ĕg-zĭs'-tĕns)

exit   (ĕk'-sĭt or ĕg'-zĭt)

exodus   (ĕk'-so-dŭs)

exorcise (ĕk'-sôr-sīz)

expatiate (ĕks-pā'-shǐ-āt)

experiment (ĕks-pĕr'-i-mĕnt)

expiration (ĕk"-spǐ-rā'-shŭn)

explicable (ĕks'-plǐ-ka-b'l)

exploit (noun: ĕks'-ploit; verb: ĕks-ploit')

explosive (ĕks-plō'-sǐv)

expurgate (ĕks'-per-gāt or ĕks-pûr'-gāt)

exquisite (ĕks'-kwǐ-zǐt)

extant (ĕks'-tant or ĕk-stănt')

extempore (ĕks-tĕm'-pō-re)

extirpate (ĕk'-ster-pāt or ĕks-tûr'-pāt)

extol (ĕks-tŏl' or ĕks-tōl')

extraordinary (ĕks-trôr'-di-nĕr"-ǐ)

exuberance (ĕg-zyū'-ber-ans)

exude (ĕks-yūd' or ĕg-zyūd')

eyas (ī'-as)

eyrie (âr'-ǐ or êr'-ǐ or ī'-rǐ)

fabric (făb'-rǐk)

façade (fa-sahd')

facet (făs'-ĕt)

facetious (fa-sē'-shŭs)

facial (fā'-shal)

facile (făs'-ǐl)

facsimile (făk-sǐm'-i-lē)

fakir (fa-kêr' or fā'-ker)

falcon (fawl'-kun or faw'-kun)

fanatic (fa-năt'-ǐk)

fanfare (făn'-fâr)

fantasia (făn"-ta-zē'-a or făn-tah'-zǐ-a or făn-tā'-zǐ-a)

fasces (făs'-ēz)

fascism (făsh'-ǐz'm or făs'-ǐz'm)

fascist (făsh'-ǐst or făs'-ǐst)

fasten (făs'-'n)

faucet (faw'-sĕt or faw'-sǐt)

fauna (faw'-na)

febrile (fē'-brǐl or fĕb'-rǐl)

fecund (fē'-kŭnd or fĕk'-ŭnd)

feign (fān)

feint (fānt)

feline (fē'-līn)

felon (fĕl'-on)

femur (fē'-mer)

feoff (fĕf or fēf)

feral (fêr'-al)

ferial (fêr'-ǐ-al)

fertile (fûr'-tǐl or fûr'-tīl)

fete (fāt)

fetich (fē'-tǐsh or fĕt'-ǐsh)

fetid (fĕt'-ǐd or fē'-tǐd)

fetish (fē'-tǐsh or fĕt'-ǐsh)

fiancé (fē"-ahn-sā' or fi-ahn'-sā)

fiancée (fē"-ahn-sā')

fiasco (fē-ahs'-kō)

fiat (fī'-ăt)

fiduciary (fǐ-dyū'-shǐ-ĕr"-ǐ)

fiend (fēnd)

fifth (fĭfth)

figure (fĭg'-yūr)

filial (fĭl'-ǐ-al or fĭl'-yal)

film (fĭlm)

finagle (fi-nā'-g'l)

finale (fi-nah'-li)

finance (fǐ-năns' or fī-năns' or fī'-năns)

financier (fĭn"-an-sêr' or fī"-năn-sêr' or fǐ-năn'-sǐ-er)

finis (fī-nǐs)

fiord (fyôrd)

fistula (fĭs'-tyū̆-la)

flaccid (flăk'-sǐd)

flagellate (flăj'-e-lāt)

flageolet (flăj"-o-lĕt')

flagitious (fla-jĭsh'-ŭs)

flagrant (flā'-grant)

florid (flŏr'-ĭd)

florist (flō'-rĭst or flŏr'-ĭst)

foci (fō'-sī)

foetus   (fē'-tŭs)

forage   (fŏr'-ĭj)

forbade   (fŏr-băd')

forbear   (fôr-bâr')

forebear   (fōr'-bâr)

forecast   (*noun:* fōr'-kăst";   *verb:*
    fōr-kăst' *or* fōr'-kăst")

forecastle   (fōk'-s'l; *formally,* fōr'-
    kăs-'l)

forehead   (fŏr'-ĕd)

foreign   (fŏr'-ĭn)

format   (fôr'-mah *or* fôr'-măt)

formative   (fôr'-ma-tĭv)

formidable   (fôr'-mĭ-da-b'l)

forte   (*noun:* fōrt)

forté   (*adverb:* fôr'-tā)

forsythia   (fôr-sĭth'-ĭ-a *or*
    fôr-sī'-thĭ-*a*)

fortnight   (fôrt'-nīt *or* fôrt'-n*i*t)

foyer   (fwah-yā' *or* foi'-ā *or* foi'-*e*r)

fracas   (frā'-k*a*s)

fragile   (frăj'-*i*l)

franchise   (frăn'-chīz)

frappé   (fr*a*-pā')

fricassee   (frĭk"-*a*-sē')

frigate   (frĭg'-ĭt)

frigid   (frĭj'-ĭd)

front   (frŭnt)

frontal   (frŭn'-t*a*l *or* frŏn'-t*a*l)

frontier   (frŭn-têr' *or* frŏn'-têr)

fruition   (frōō-ĭsh'-*ŭ*n)

frustrate   (frŭs'-trāt)

fulcrum   (fŭl'-krŭm)

fulsome   (fŏŏl'-s*ŭ*m *or* fŭl'-s*ŭ*m)

funeral   (fyū-n*e*r-*a*l)

funereal   (fyū-nêr'-*i*-*a*l)

fungi   (fŭn'-jī)

fungus   (fŭng'-gŭs)

funicular   (fyū-nĭk'-yū-l*e*r)

furniture   (fûr'-n*i*-chûr)

furore   (fyū'-rōr)

fusee   (fyū-zē')

fuselage   (fyū'-ze-lĭj *or*
    fyū"-ze-lahzh')

fusillade   (fyū"-zi-lād')

futile   (fyū'-tĭl)

gala   (gā'-la *or* gah'-l*a*)

galaxy   (găl'-*a*k-sĭ)

gallant   (*verb:* ga-lănt';   *adj.* and
    noun: găl'-*a*nt *or* ga-lănt')

gallivant   (găl"-*i*-vănt')

gamin   (găm'-ĭn; *French,* ga-măɴ')

gamut   (găm'-*ŭ*t)

gantlet   (gahnt'-lĕt *or* gănt'-lĕt)

gaol   (jāl)

gape   (gāp *or* găp *or* gahp)

garage   (ga-rahzh')

garrulous   (găr'-yū-lŭs *or*
    găr'-ŏŏ-lŭs)

gaseous   (găs'-*i*-*ŭ*s)

gasometer   (găs-ŏm'-*i*-ter)

gastritis   (găs-trī'-tĭs)

gaucherie   (gō"-sh*e*-rē')

gauge   (gāj)

gauntlet   (gawnt'-lĕt *or* gahnt'-lĕt)

gavel   (găv'-*e*l)

gazetteer   (găz"-*e*-têr')

geisha   (gā'-sh*a*)

geld   (gĕld)

gelid   (jĕl'-ĭd)

gendarme   (zhahn-dahrm' *or*
    zhahn'-dahrm)

genealogy   (jĕn"-*i*-ăl'-*o*-jĭ)

generally   (jĕn'-*e*r-*a*-lĭ)

generic   (j*i*-nĕr'-ĭk)

genie   (jē'-nĭ)

genii   (jē'-nĭ-ī)

genius   (jēn'-yŭs *or* jē'-nĭ-*ŭ*s)

geniuses   (jēn'-yŭs-ĕz)

genre   (zhahɴ'-'r)

genteel   (jĕn-tēl')

gentian   (jĕn'-sh*a*n)

genuine (jĕn'-yū-ĭn)

genus (jē'-nŭs)

gerfalcon (jûr'-fawl-kŭn)

gerrymander (gĕr"-ĭ-măn'-der or jĕr"-ĭ-măn'-der)

gestation (jĕs-tā'-shŭn)

gesticulate (jĕs-tĭk'-yū-lāt)

gesture (jĕs'-tyŭr)

gewgaw (gyū'-gaw)

geyser (gī'-zer or gī'-ser)

ghetto (gĕt'-ō)

ghoul (gōōl)

gibber (jĭb'-er or gĭb'-er)

gibberish (jĭb'-er-ĭsh or gĭb'-er-ĭsh)

gibbet (jĭb'-ĕt)

gibbon (gĭb'-ŭn)

gibe (jīb)

giblet (jĭb'-lĕt)

gill (jĭl), liquid measure

gill (gĭl), organ for breathing

gillyflower (jĭl'-ĭ-flow"-er)

gimcrack (jĭm'-krăk")

gimlet (gĭm'-lĕt)

gin (jĭn)

ginger (jĭn'-jer)

gingivitis (jĭn"-jĭ-vī'-tĭs)

giraffe (ji-rahf')

gist (jĭst)

glacial (glā'-shal)

glacier (glā'-shêr or glăs'-ĭ-êr)

gladiolus (commonly, glăd"-ĭ-ō'-lŭs; technically, gla-dī'-o-lŭs)

glazier (glā'-zher)

glisten (glĭs'-'n)

globular (glŏb'-yū-ler)

gluten (glōō'-ten)

glycerine (glĭs'-er-ĭn or glĭs'-er-ēn)

gnat (năt)

gneiss (nīs)

gnome (nōm)

gnu (nōō or nyū)

goal (gōl)

gondola (gŏn'-do-la)

gooseberry (gōōz'-bĕr-ĭ or gōōs'-bĕr-ĭ)

gorge (gôrj)

gosling (gŏz'-lĭng)

gossamer (gŏs'-a-mer)

gouge (gowj)

goulash (gōō'-lahsh or gōō'-lăsh)

gourd (gōrd; British, gŏŏrd)

gourmand (gŏŏr'-mand; French, gōōr-mahṉ')

government (gŭv'-ern-ment)

gradient (grā'-dĭ-ent)

grammar (grăm'-er)

granary (grăn'-a-rĭ; popularly, grān'-a-rĭ)

grange (grānj)

gratis (grā'-tĭs or grăt'-ĭs)

gratuitous (gra-tyū'-i-tŭs)

gravamen (gra-vā'-mĕn)

grave (grāv)

grease (noun: grēs; verb: grēs or grēz)

greasy (grēs'-ĭ or grēz'-ĭ)

grenadier (grĕn"-a-dêr')

grievous (grēv'-ŭs)

grimace (grĭ-mās')

gristle (grĭs'-'l)

groom (grōōm)

grotesque (gro-tĕsk')

grovel (grŏv'-'l or grŭv'-'l)

guano (gwah'-nō)

guarantee (găr"-an-tē')

guaranty (găr'-an-tĭ)

guardian (gahr'-dĭ-an)

guayule (gwah-yōō'-lā or wī-ōō'-lā)

gubernatorial (gyū"-ber-na-tō'-rĭ-al)

guerdon (gûr'-don)

guerrilla (ge-rĭl'-a)

guidon (gī'-dŭn)

guillotine (gĭl'-o-tēn)

guinea (gĭn'-ĭ)

guise (gīz)

guitar (gi-tahr')

gules (gyūlz)

gunwale (gŭn'-el)

gustatory (gŭs'-ta-tō"-rĭ)

gutta-percha (gŭt'-a-pûr'-cha)

guttural (gŭt'-er-al)

gymnasium (jĭm-nā'-zĭ-ŭm)

gypsum (jĭp'-sŭm)

gypsy (jĭp'-sĭ)

gyrate (jī'-rāt)

gyratory (jī'-ra-tō"-rĭ)

gyroplane (jī'-ro-plān")

gyroscope (jī'-ro-skōp)

gyve (jīv)

habitual (ha-bĭt'-yŭ-al)

habitué (ha-bĭt"-yŭ-ā' or ha-bĭt'-yŭ-ā)

halberd (hăl'-berd)

halcyon (hăl'-sĭ-ŭn)

halfpenny (hā'-pen-ĭ or hāp'-nĭ; American, hahf'-pĕn"-ĭ)

hallelujah (hăl"-e-lōō'-ya)

hallo (ha-lō')

halloo (ha-lōō')

hallucination (ha-lyū"-sĭ-nā'-shŭn)

halo (hā'-lō)

halve (hahv)

halyard (hăl'-yerd)

handkerchief (hăng'-ker-chĭf)

handsome (hăn'-sŭm)

hangar (hăng'-er or hăng'-gahr)

hanger (hăng'-er)

harangue (ha-răng')

harass (hăr'-as or ha-răs')

harbinger (hahr'-bĭn-jer)

harem (hā'-rĕm or hâr'-ĕm)

harlequin (hahr'-le-kwĭn or hahr'-le-kĭn)

hasten (hās'-'n)

hauberk (haw'-bûrk)

haunch (hawnch or hahnch)

haunt (hawnt or hahnt)

hautboy (hō'-boi or ō'-boi)

hauteur (ho-tûr' or o-tûr')

hawser (haw'-zêr or haw'-sêr)

headman (hĕd'-man)

hearth (hahrth)

heather (hĕth-er)

hecatomb (hĕk'-a-tŏm or hĕk'-a-tōōm)

hedonism (hē'-don-ĭz'm)

hegemony (he-jĕm'-o-nĭ or hĕj'-e-mō"-nĭ)

hegira (he-jī'-ra or hĕj'-i-ra)

heifer (hĕf'-er)

height (hīt)

heinous (hā'-nŭs)

heir (âr)

heliotrope (hē'-lĭ-o-trōp)

helium (hē'-lĭ-ŭm)

helm (hĕlm)

helot (hĕl'-ot or hē'-lot)

hemistich (hĕm'-ĭ-stĭk)

hemorrhage (hĕm'-o-rĭj)

heraldic (hĕ-răl'-dĭk)

heraldry (hĕr'-ald-rĭ)

herb (ûrb or hûrb)

herbage (ûr'-bĭj or hûr'-bĭj)

herbarium (hûr-bâr'-ĭ-ŭm)

herculean (hûr-kyū'-li-an or hûr"-kyū-lē'-an)

heresy (hĕr'-e-sĭ)

heroes (hêr'-ōz)

heroine (hĕr'-o-ĭn)

heroism (hĕr'-o-ĭz'm)

heron (hĕr'-ŭn)

heterogeneous (hĕt″-er-o-jē′-ni-ŭs)
heyday (hā′-dā′)
hiatus (hī-ā′-tŭs)
hiccough (hĭk′-ŭp)
hierarchy (hī′-er-ahr″-kĭ)
hieroglyph (hī′-er-o-glĭf″)
hilarious (hĭ-lâr′-ĭ-ŭs or hī-lâr′-ĭ-ŭs)
hilarity (hĭ-lăr′-i-tĭ or hī-lăr′-i-tĭ)
hindrance (hĭn′-drans)
hirsute (hûr′-syūt or hûr-syūt′)
historian (hĭs-tō′-rĭ-an)
holocaust (hŏl′-o-kawst)
homage (hŏm′-ĭj or ŏm′-ĭj)
homely (hōm′-lĭ)
homeopathy (hō″-mi-ŏp′-a-thĭ)
homily (hŏm′-i-lĭ)
homogeneous (hō″-mo-jē′-ni-ŭs)
homogenous (ho-mŏj′-i-nŭs)
homologous (ho-mŏl′-o-gŭs)
homonym (hŏm′-o-nĭm or hō′-mo-nĭm)
honorarium (ŏn″-o-râr′-ĭ-ŭm or hŏn″-o-râr′-ĭ-ŭm)
hoofs (hōōfs)
horizon (ho-rī′-z'n)
hosanna (ho-zăn′-a)
hosiery (hō′-zher-ĭ)
hospitable (hŏs′-pĭ-ta-b'l)
hospital (hŏs′-pĭt-al)
hostage (hŏs′-tĭj)
hostelry (hŏs′-tel-rĭ)
hostile (hŏs′-tĭl)
hostler (hŏs′-ler or ŏs′-ler)
hotel (hō-tĕl′)
houri (hōō′-rĭ or how′-rĭ)
house (hows)
houses (how′-zĕz)
housewife (hows′-wīf″ or hŭz′-ĭf)
housewifery (hows′-wīf″-er-ĭ or hŭz′-ĭf-rĭ)
hovel (hŏv′-el or hŭv′-el)

hover (hŭv′-er or hŏv′-er)
howitzer (how′-ĭt-ser)
humor (hyū′-mer or yū′-mer)
humorist (hyū′-mer-ĭst or yū′-mer-ĭst)
hurricane (hûr′-ĭ-kān or hûr′-ĭ-ken)
hussar (hōō-zahr′)
hussy (hŭz′-ĭ or hŭs′-ĭ)
hustle (hŭs′-'l)
hydrangea (hī-drăn′-ji-a)
hydrant (hī′-drant)
hydrogen (hī′-dro-jen)
hygiene (hī′-jēn or hī′-jĭ-ēn)
hygienic (hī″-jĭ-ĕn′-ĭk or hī-jē′-nĭk)
hygienist (hī′-jĭ-en-ĭst)
hyperbole (hī-pûr′-bo-lē)
hypochondriac (hī″-po-kŏn′-drĭ-ăk)
hypocrisy (hĭ-pŏk′-ri-sĭ)
hypocrite (hĭp′-o-krĭt)
hypothesis (hī-pŏth′-i-sĭs or hĭ-pŏth′-i-sĭs)
ichor (ī′-kôr or ī′-ker)
icon (ī′-kŏn)
idea (ī-dē′-a)
ideal (ī-dē′-al)
ides (īdz)
idiosyncrasy (ĭd″-ĭ-o-sĭng′-kra-sĭ)
idle (ī′-d'l)
idol (ī′-dol)
idyl (ī′-dĭl; *British,* ĭd′-ĭl)
ignominy (ĭg′-no-mĭn-ĭ)
ignoramus (ĭg″-no-rā′-mŭs)
iguana (ĭ-gwah′-na)
illustrate (ĭl′-ŭs-trāt or i-lŭs′-trāt)
illustrative (i-lŭs′-tra-tĭv or ĭl′-ŭs-trā″-tĭv)
imagery (ĭm′-ĭj-rĭ or ĭm′-ĭj-er-ĭ)
imaginary (i-măj′-i-nĕr″-ĭ)
imbroglio (ĭm-brōl′-yō)
immanent (ĭm′-a-nĕnt)
immigrant (ĭm′-i-grănt)

imminent (ĭm'-*i*-nent)

impiety (ĭm-pī'-*e*-tĭ)

impious (ĭm'-pĭ-*ŭs*)

implacable (ĭm-plā'-k*a*-b'l *or* ĭm-plăk'-*a*-b'l)

implement (ĭm'-ple-ment)

implicit (ĭm-plĭs'-ĭt)

import (*noun:* ĭm'-pōrt; *verb:* ĭm-pōrt'; *in contrast to* export, ĭm'-pōrt)

importune (ĭm"-pôr-tyūn' *or* ĭm-pôr'-tyūn)

impostor (ĭm-pŏs'-ter)

imposture (ĭm-pŏs'-tyūr)

impregnate (*verb:* ĭm-prĕg'-nāt; *adjective:* ĭm-prĕg'-n*a*t)

impresario (ĭm"-prā-sah'-rĭ-ō)

improvisation (ĭm"-pro-vī-zā'-shŭn *or* ĭm"-prŏv-ĭ-zā'-shŭn)

impugn (ĭm-pyūn')

inamorata (ĭn-ăm"-*o*-rah'-t*a*)

inane (ĭn-ān')

inanity (ĭn-ăn'-*i*-tĭ)

incendiary (ĭn-sĕn'-dĭ-ĕr-ĭ)

incense (*verb:* ĭn-sĕns'; *noun:* ĭn'-sĕns)

inchoate (ĭn-kō'-ĭt *or* ĭn'-ko-āt)

incidentally (ĭn"-sĭ-dĕn'-t*a*-lĭ)

incinerator (ĭn-sĭn'-er-ā"-ter)

include (ĭn-klo͞od')

inclusive (ĭn-klo͞o'-sĭv)

incognito (ĭn-kŏg'-nĭ-tō)

incomparable (ĭn-kŏm'-p*a*-r*a*-b'l)

incontrovertible (ĭn"-kŏn-tro-vûr'-tĭ-b'l)

incorporeal (ĭn"-kôr-pō'-rĭ-*a*l)

incorrigible (ĭn-kŏr'-ĭ-jĭ-b'l)

increase (*verb:* ĭn-krēs'; *noun:* ĭn'-krēs)

indefatigable (ĭn"-d*i*-făt'-*i*-g*a*-b'l)

indices (ĭn'-d*i*-sēz)

indict (ĭn-dīt')

indictment (ĭn-dīt'-ment)

indigenous (ĭn-dĭj'-*i*-nŭs)

indisputable (ĭn-dĭs'-pyū-t*a*-b'l *or* ĭn"-dĭs-pyūt'-*a*-b'l)

indissoluble (ĭn-dĭs'-*o*-lyū-b'l *or* ĭn-dĭ-sŏl'-yū-b'l)

industry (ĭn'-dŭs-trĭ)

inebriate (ĭn-ē'-brĭ-āt)

inebriety (ĭn"-*i*-brī'-*e*-tĭ)

inertia (ĭn-ûr'-sh*a* *or* ĭn-ûr'-shĭ-*a*)

inevitable (ĭn-ĕv'-*i*-t*a*-b'l)

inexorable (ĭn-ĕk'-s*o*-r*a*-b'l)

inexplicable (ĭn-ĕks'-plĭ-k*a*-b'l)

inextricable (ĭn-ĕks'-trĭ-k*a*-b'l)

infamous (ĭn'-f*a*-mŭs)

infamy (ĭn'-f*a*-mĭ)

infantile (ĭn'-f*a*n-tīl *or* ĭn'-f*a*n-tĭl)

infinite (ĭn'-f*i*-nĭt)

infinitesimal (ĭn"-fĭn-*i*-tĕs'-*i*-m*a*l)

ingenious (ĭn-jēn'-yŭs)

ingénue (ăN"-zhā"-nyü')

ingenuity (ĭn"-je-nyū'-*i*-tĭ)

ingenuous (ĭn-jĕn'-yū-ŭs)

inherent (ĭn-hêr'-ent)

inhospitable (ĭn-hŏs'-pĭ-t*a*-b'l)

initiation (ĭ-nĭsh"-ĭ-ā'-shŭn)

innocuous (ĭ-nŏk'-yū-ŭs)

innumerable (ĭ-nyū'-mer-*a*-b'l *or* ĭn-nyū'-mer-*a*-b'l)

inquiry (ĭn-kwīr'-ĭ *or* ĭn'-kwi-rĭ)

insignia (ĭn-sĭg'-nĭ-*a*)

insular (ĭn'-syū-ler)

insulation (ĭn-syū-lā'-shŭn)

intaglio (ĭn-tăl'-yō *or* ĭn-tah'-lĭ-ō)

integer (ĭn'-t*i*-jer)

integral (ĭn'-t*i*-gr*a*l)

interdict (ĭn'-ter-dĭkt)

interest (ĭn'-ter-ĕst; *British,* ĭn'-trĭst)

interesting (ĭn'-ter-ĕs-tĭng *or* ĭn'-trĭs-tĭng)

interlocutory (ĭn″-ter-lŏk′-yū-tō″-rĭ)

intermezzo (ĭn″-ter-mĕd′-zō)

internecine (ĭn″-ter-nē′-sĭn *or* in″-ter-nē′-sīn)

interpretative (ĭn-tûr′-pre-tā′-tĭv *or* ĭn-tûr′-pre-ta-tĭv)

interstices (ĭn-tûr′-stĭ-sēz)

intestate (ĭn-tĕs′-tāt)

intestinal (ĭn-tĕs′-tĭ-nal *or* ĭn″-tĕs-tī′-nal)

intimate (*adj.:* ĭn′-tĭ-mĭt; *verb:* ĭn′-tĭ-māt)

intrepid (ĭn-trĕp′-ĭd)

intricacy (ĭn′-trĭ-ka-sĭ)

intricate (ĭn′-trĭ-kĭt)

intrigue (*verb:* ĭn-trēg′; *noun:* ĭn-trēg′ *or* ĭn′-trēg)

intuit (ĭn′-tyū-ĭt)

inundate (ĭn′-ŭn-dāt)

invalid (not valid: ĭn-văl′-ĭd; sick: ĭn′-va-lĭd)

inveigh (ĭn-vā′)

inveigle (ĭn-vē′-g′l *or* ĭn-vā′-g′l)

inventory (ĭn′-ven-tō-rĭ)

inviolate (ĭn-vī′-o-lāt)

iodid(e) (ī′-o-dīd *or* ī′-o-dĭd)

iodin(e) (ī′-o-dīn *or* ī′-o-dĭn *or* ī′-o-dēn)

iodoform (ī-ō′-do-fôrm *or* ī-ŏd′-o-fôrm)

ipecac (ĭp′-i-kăk)

irascible (ī-răs′-i-b′l *or* ĭ-răs′-i-b′l)

irate (ī′-rāt *or* ī-rāt′)

iridescence (ĭr″-i-dĕs′-ens)

iris (ī′-rĭs)

iron (ī′-ern)

irony (ī′-ro-nĭ)

irreconcilable (ĭr-rĕk″-on-sīl′-a-b′l *or* ĭr-rĕk′-on-sīl″-a-b′l)

irredentist (ĭr″-i-dĕn′-tĭst)

irrefragable (ĭr-rĕf′-ra-ga-b′l)

irrefutable (ĭr-rĕf′-yū-ta-b′l *or* ĭr-re-fyūt′-a-b′l)

irrelevant (ĭr-rĕl′-i-vant)

irremediable (ĭr″-re-mē′-dĭ-a-b′l)

irreparable (ĭ-rĕp′-a-ra-b′l)

irrevocable (ĭ-rĕv′-o-ka-b′l)

irritable (ĭr′-i-ta-b′l)

isinglass (ī′-zĭng-glăs)

isolate (ī′-so-lāt *or* ĭs′-o-lāt)

isolation (ī″-so-lā′-shŭn *or* ĭs″-o-lā′-shŭn)

isosceles (ī-sŏs′-i-lēz)

issue (ĭsh′-yū *or* ĭsh′-ōō)

isthmus (ĭs′-mŭs *or* ĭsth′-mŭs)

italic (ĭ-tăl′-ĭk)

itch (ĭch)

itinerary (ī-tĭn′-er-ĕr″-ĭ)

jackal (jăk′-awl)

jaguar (jăg′-wahr)

jasmine (jăs′-mĭn *or* jăz′-mĭn)

jaundice (jawn′-dĭs *or* jahn′-dĭs)

jaunt (jawnt *or* jahnt)

javelin (jăv′-lĭn *or* jăv′-e-lĭn)

jejune (ji-jōōn′)

jeopardize (jĕp′-er-dīz)

jewel (jōō′-el *or* jyū′-el)

jewelry (jōō′-el-rĭ *or* jyū′-el-rĭ)

jinrikisha (jĭn-rĭk′-shaw)

jiu-jitsu (jōō-jĭt′-sōō; *Jap.,* jōō′-jĭt″-sōō)

jocose (jo-kōs′)

jocund (jŏk′-ŭnd *or* jō′-kŭnd)

joule (jowl; *commonly,* jōōl)

joust (jŭst *or* jōōst)

jowl (jowl *or* jōl)

jubilation (jōō″-bi-lā′-shŭn)

judiciary (jōō-dĭsh′-ĭ-ĕr″-ĭ)

jugular (jŭg′-yū-ler *or* jōō′-gyū-ler)

junta (jŭn′-ta)

kaiser (kī′-zer)

kaleidoscope (ka-lī′-do-skōp)

kangaroo (kăng″-ga-roō′)

kerosene (kĕr′-o-sēn″ or kĕr″-o-sēn′)

khaki (kah′-kĭ)

khan (kahn or kăn)

khedive (ke-dēv′)

kiln (kĭl or kĭln)

kilometer (kĭl″-o-mē′-ter or kĭl-ŏm′-i-ter)

kimono (kĭ-mō′-nō; popularly, kĭ-mō′-na)

kindergarten (kĭn′-der-gahr″-ten)

kinetic (kĭ-nĕt′-ĭk or kī-nĕt′-ĭk)

kinetoscope (kĭ-nē′-to-skōp or kĭ-nĕt′-o-skōp or kī-nē′-to-skōp or kī-nĕt′-o-skōp)

kiosk (kĭ-ŏsk′)

knowledge (nŏl′-ĕj)

koran (ko-rahn′ or kō′-răn)

laboratory (lăb′-o-ra-tō″-rĭ)

labyrinthine (lăb″-i-rĭn′-thĭn)

lackadaisical (lăk-a-dā′-zĭ-kal)

lager (lah′-ger or law′-ger)

lamentable (lăm′-en-ta-b'l)

language (lăng′-gwĭj)

languid (lăng′-gwĭd)

languish (lăng′-gwĭsh)

languor (lăng′-ger or lăng′-gwêr)

lapel (lă-pĕl′)

larboard (lahr′-bōrd or lahr′-bêrd)

lariat (lăr′-ĭ-at)

laryngeal (la-rĭn′-ji-al or lă″-rĭn-jē′-al)

laryngitis (lăr″-ĭn-jī′-tĭs)

larynx (lăr′-ĭngks)

lascivious (la-sĭv′-ĭ-ŭs)

latent (lā′-tent)

lath (lăth)

lathe (lāTH)

laths (lăTHz or lăths)

laudanum (law′-da-nŭm or lawd′-nŭm)

launch (lawnch or lahnch)

launder (lawn′-der or lahn′-der)

laundry (lawn′-drĭ or lahn′-drĭ)

lecture (lĕk′-chûr)

leeward (lē′-werd; naut., lyū′-erd)

legate (lĕg′-ĭt)

legend (lĕj′-end or lē′-jend)

legendary (lĕj′-en-dĕr″-ĭ)

legerdemain (lĕj″-er-de-mān′)

legged (lĕgd; when combined, -lĕg′-ed)

leghorn (lĕg′-hôrn or lĕg′-êrn)

legislate (lĕj′-ĭs-lāt)

leisure (lē′-zher or lĕzh′-er)

leit-motiv (līt′-mo-tēf″)

lenient (lē′-nĭ-ent or lēn′-yent)

lenity (lĕn′-i-tĭ)

leopard (lĕp′-erd)

lethal (lē′-thal)

lethargy (lĕth′-er-jĭ)

lettuce (lĕt′-us)

levee (lĕv′-ē or lĕ-vē′)

lever (lē′-ver or lĕv′-er)

leverage (lē-ver-ĭj or lĕv′-er-ĭj)

leviathan (le-vī′-a-than)

liaison (lē″-ā″-zôn′; English, li-ā′-zŭn)

libertine (lĭb′-er-tēn or lĭb′-er-tĭn)

library (lī′-brĕr″-ĭ)

libretto (lĭ-brĕt′-ō)

licentiate (lī-sĕn′-shĭ-āt)

lichen (lī′-ken)

licorice (lĭk′-o-rĭs)

lien (lē′-en or lēn)

lieu (lyū)

lieutenant (lyū-tĕn′-ant; British, lĕf-tĕn′-ant, or loō-tĕn′-ant)

lightning (līt′-nĭng)

lilac (lī′-lak)

lineage (lĭn′-i-ĭj)

lineament (lĭn′-i-a-ment)

linear (lĭn'-*i*-er)

lingerie (lăɴ'-zh'rē *or* lahn'-zhe-rē)

lingual (lĭng'-gwal)

linguist (lĭng'-gwĭst)

linotype (lĭn'-*o*-tīp)

liqueur (lĭ-kûr' *or* lĭ-kûr')

liquor (lĭk'-er)

lisle (līl; *French*, lēl)

listen (lĭs'-'n)

litany (lĭt'-*a*-nĭ)

liter (lē'-ter)

literate (lĭt'-er-ĭt)

literati (lĭt"-e-rā'-tī)

literatim (lĭt"-e-rā'-tĭm)

literature (lĭt'-er-a-chûr)

litterateur (lē"-tā"-ra"-tûr' *or* lĭt"-er-a-tûr')

liturgy (lĭt'-er-jĭ)

lived (*past tense of* live: lĭvd; *adjective:* līvd)

livelong (lĭv'-lŏng")

llama (lah'-ma)

loam (lōm *better usage than* lōōm)

loath (lōth)

loathe (lōтн)

locale (lo-kăl')

locative (lŏk'-a-tĭv)

loch (lŏк)

loci (lō'-sī)

loess (lō'-ĕs *or* lûs)

loge (lōzh)

longevity (lŏn-jĕv'-*i*-tĭ)

longitude (lŏn'-jĭ-tyūd)

long-lived (lŏng'-līvd')

lorgnette (lôr"-nyĕt')

lough (lŏк)

lower (frown, low'-er; other meanings, *verb* and *adj.:* lō'-er)

lucid (lyū'-sĭd)

lucrative (lyū'-kra-tĭv)

lucre (lyū'-ker *or* lōō'-ker)

lucubration (lyū"-kyū-brā'-shŭn)

lugubrious (lyū-gyū'-brĭ-ŭs)

luminary (lyū'-mĭ-nĕr"-ĭ)

lupine (lyū'-pĭn)

lure (lyūr)

lurid (lyū'-rĭd)

lute (lyūt)

luxuriant (lŭks-yū'-rĭ-ant)

luxury (lŭk'-shōō-rĭ *or* lŭks'-yū-rĭ)

lyceum (lī-sē'-ŭm)

lymph (lĭmf)

lyre (līr)

lyric (lĭr'-ĭk)

lyrist (līr'-ĭst *or* lĭr'-ĭst)

macabre (ma-kah'-b'r)

macerate (măs'-er-āt)

machine (ma-shēn')

machination (măk"-*i*-nā'-shŭn)

madam (măd'-am)

madame (măd'-am; *French*, ma-dahm')

mademoiselle (măd"-mwa"-zĕl' *or* măd"-e-mo-zĕl'; *colloq.*, măm"-zĕl')

maelstrom (māl'-strom)

magisterial (măj"-ĭs-têr'-ĭ-al)

magistrate (măj'-ĭs-trāt)

magnanimity (măg"-na-nĭm'-*i*-tĭ)

magneto (măg-nē'-tō)

maintenance (mān'-te-nans)

majolica (ma-jŏl'-ĭ-ka *or* ma-yŏl'-ĭ-ka)

malign (ma-līn')

malignant (ma-lĭg'-nant)

malingerer (ma-lĭng'-ger-er)

malkin (maw'-kĭn)

mama (mah'-ma *or* ma-mah')

mamma (mama: mah'-ma *or* ma-mah'; breast: măm'-a)

manage (măn'-ĭj)

manageable (măn'-ĭj-a-b'l)

mandarin (măn'-da-rĭn)

mandate (măn'-dāt or măn'-dĭt)

mandragora (măn-drăg'-o-ra)

manes (mā'-nēz), spirits

maneuver or manoeuvre (ma-noō'-ver or ma-nyū'-ver)

mange (mānj)

manger (mān'-jer)

maniacal (ma-nī'-a-kal)

manifold (măn'-ι-fōld)

mankind (măn"-kīnd')

mannequin (măn'-i-kĭn)

manor (măn'-er)

marchioness (mahr'-shŭn-ĕs)

margarin(e) (mahr'-ja-rēn or mahr'-ga-rēn)

marguerite (mahr"-ge-rēt')

marigold (măr'-ι-gōld)

marital (măr'-ι-tal or ma-rī'-tal)

maritime (măr'-ι-tīm or măr'-ι-tĭm)

marmoset (mahr'-mo-zĕt)

marquee (mahr-kē')

marquess (mahr'-kwĕs or mahr'-kwĭs)

marquis (mahr'-kwĭs; French, mahr"-kē')

marriage (măr'-ĭj)

martial (mahr'-shal)

mask or masque (măsk)

masquerade (măs"-ker-ād')

massacre (măs'-a-ker)

massacred (măs'-a-kerd)

massacring (măs'-a-krĭng)

massage (ma-sahzh')

matériel (ma-têr"-ĭ-ĕl')

matinee (măt"-ι-nā')

matrix (mā'-trĭks or măt'-rĭks)

mature (ma-tyūr')

mausoleum (maw"-so-lē'-ŭm)

mauve (mōv)

mayonnaise (mā"-o-nāz')

measles (mē'-z'lz)

medicinal (me-dĭs'-ι-nal)

medicine (mĕd'-i-sin)

medieval (mē"-dĭ-ē'-val; British, mĕd"-ĭ-ē'-val)

mediocre (mē'-dĭ-ō"-ker, or mē"-dĭ-ō'-ker)

mediocrity (mē"-dĭ-ŏk'-ri-tĭ)

meerschaum (mêr'-shŭm)

meistersinger (mīs'-ter-sĭng"-er or mīs'-ter-zĭng"-er)

mélange (mā-lahɴzh')

melee (mā-lā' or mā'-lā or mĕl'-ā)

meliorate (mēl'-yo-rāt)

memoir (mĕm'-wahr or mĕm'-wôr)

menage (me-nahzh')

menagerie (me-năj'-er-ĭ or me-nazh'-er-ĭ)

menial (mē'-nĭ-al or mēn'-yal)

meningitis (mĕn"-ĭn-jī'-tĭs)

mensuration (mĕn"-shoō-rā'-shŭn)

menthol (mĕn'-thōl or mĕn'-thŏl)

menu (mĕn'-yū or mā'-nyū; French, me-nyü')

meringue (me-răng')

mesa (mā'-sa)

mesalliance (mā"-zăl"-yawɴs' or mā-zăl'-ĭ-ans)

mesdames (mā-dahm')

mesdemoiselles (mād"-mwah"-zĕl')

mesmeric (mĕz-mĕr'-ĭk or mĕs-mĕr'-ĭk)

mesmerism (mĕz'-mer-ĭz'm or mĕs'-mer-ĭz'm)

mesquite (mĕs-kēt' or mĕs'-kēt)

metallurgy (mĕt'-'l-ûr"-jĭ or mĕ-tăl'-er-jĭ)

metamorphosis (mĕt"-a-môr'-fo-sĭs or mĕt"-a-môr-fō'-sĭs)

meteorology (mē"-ti-er-ŏl'-o-jĭ)

metonymy   (me-tŏn'-i-mĭ)

metrist   (mē'-trĭst or mĕt'-rĭst)

mezzanine   (mĕz'-a-nēn or
   mĕz'-a-nĭn)

mezzo   (mĕd'-zō)

miasma   (mī-ăz'-ma or mĭ-ăz'-ma)

microscopist   (mī-krŏs'-ko-pĭst)

midwifery   (mĭd'-wīf''-rĭ or
   mĭd'-wĭf-rĭ)

mien   (mēn)

mignonette   (mĭn''-yŭn-ĕt')

migratory   (mī'-gra-tō''-rĭ)

mikado   (mĭ-kah'-dō)

milch   (mĭlch)

militia   (mi-lĭsh'-a)

millinery   (mĭl'-i-nĕr''-ĭ)

millionaire   (mĭl''-yŭn-âr')

minatory   (mĭn''-a-tō'-rĭ)

mineralogy   (mĭn''-er-ăl'-o-jĭ)

miniature   (mĭn'-ĭ-a-chûr)

minuet   (mĭn''-yū-ĕt' or mĭn'-yū-ĕt)

minute   (noun: mĭn'-ĭt; adjective:
   mĭ-nyūt' or mī-nyūt')

minutiae   (mĭ-nyū'-shĭ-ē or
   mī-nyū'-shĭ-ē)

mirage   (mĭ-rahzh')

misalliance   (mĭs''-a-lī'-ăns)

misanthrope   (mĭs'-an-thrōp or
   mĭz'-an-thrōp)

miscegenation   (mĭs''-i-ji-nā'-shŭn)

miscellaneous   (mĭs''-e-lā'-ni-ŭs)

miscellany   (mĭs'-e-lā''-nĭ or
   mĭs'-e-la''-nĭ)

mischief   (mĭs'-chĭf)

mischievous   (mĭs'-chĭ-vŭs)

misconstrue   (mĭs''-kon-strōō' or
   mĭs-kŏn'-strōō)

mishap   (mĭs-hăp' or mĭs'-hăp)

misogamist   (mĭ-sŏg'-a-mĭst or
   mī-sŏg'-a-mĭst)

misogynist   (mĭ-sŏj'-i-nĭst or
   mī-sŏj'-i-nĭst)

misogyny   (mĭ-sŏj'-i-nĭ or
   mī-sŏj'-i-nĭ)

missile   (mĭs'-il)

mistletoe   (mĭs'-'l-tō or mĭz'-'l-tō)

mnemonics   (ni-mŏn'-ĭks)

mobilization   (mō''-bi-lĭ-zā'-shŭn or
   mō''-bi-lī-zā'-shŭn)

modicum   (mŏd'-ĭ-kŭm)

modiste   (mo-dēst')

moiety   (moi'-e-tĭ)

molecule   (mŏl'-i-kyūl or
   mō'-li-kyūl)

monarchical   (mo-nahr'-kĭ-kal)

monastery   (mŏn'-as-tĕr''-ĭ)

monetary   (mŏn'-i-tĕr''-ĭ or
   mŭn'-i-tĕr''-ĭ)

mongrel   (mŭng'-grel or
   mŏng'-grel)

monkey   (mŭng'-kĭ)

monologist   (mŏn'-o-lôg''-ĭst)

monologue   (mŏn'-o-lôg)

monopolize   (mo-nŏp'-o-līz)

monopoly   (mo-nŏp'-o-lĭ)

monsieur   (me-syû')

moral   (mŏr'-al)

morale   (mo-răl' or mo-rahl')

morass   (mo-răs')

moratorium   (mŏr''-a-tō'-rĭ-ŭm)

mores   (mō'-rēz)

moribund   (mŏr'-i-bŭnd)

moron   (mō'-rŏn)

mortgage   (môr'-gĭj)

mortgagor   (môr''-gi-jôr' or
   môr'-gĭj-er)

mosaic   (mō-zā'-ĭk)

mountainous   (mown'-ti-nŭs)

mow   (to cut: mō; stored hay, etc.:
   mow)

municipal (myū-nǐs'-*i*-p*a*l)

museum (myū-zē'-ŭm)

musicale (myū"-zǐ-kǎl')

muslin (mŭz'-lǐn)

mustache (mŭs-tǎsh' *or* mŭs'-tǎsh)

myrrh (mûr)

mythical (mǐ*th*'-*i*-k*a*l)

nabob (nā'-bŏb)

nadir (nā'-d*er*; *British,* nā'-dêr)

naiad (nā'-ǎd *or* nī'-ǎd)

naive (nah-ēv')

naivete (nah-ēv"-tā')

naked (nā'-kĕd)

nape (nāp; *colloq.,* nǎp)

naphtha (nǎf'-*tha*)

narrate (n*a*-rāt')

nascent (nǎs'-*e*nt *or* nā'-s*e*nt)

nasturtium (n*a*-stûr'-shŭm)

nausea (naw'-shi-*a or* naw'-si-*a*)

nauseous (naw'-shŭs *or* naw'-shǐ-ŭs)

nautch (nawch)

nebula (nĕb'-yū-l*a*)

necessarily (nĕs'-*e*-sĕr"-*i*-lǐ)

necessary (nĕs'-*e*-sĕr"-ǐ)

necessity (n*i*-sĕs'-*i*-tǐ)

necromancy (nĕk'-r*o*-mǎn"-sǐ)

née (nā)

negligee (nĕg"-l*i*-zhā' *or* nĕg'-l*i*-zhā")

negotiable (n*i*-gō'-shǐ-*a*-b'l)

negotiate (n*i*-gō'-shǐ-āt)

negotiation (n*i*-gō"-shǐ-ā'-shŭn)

neither (nē'-THer *or* nī'-THer)

nepenthe (n*i*-pĕn'-*the*)

nephew (nĕf'-yū *or* nĕv'-yū)

nescience (nĕsh'-ǐ-*e*ns *or* nĕsh'-*e*ns)

nestle (nĕs'-'l)

neuralgia (nyū-rǎl'-j*a*)

new (nyū)

newel (nyū'-*e*l)

niche (nǐch)

nicotinism (nǐk'-*o*-tēn-ǐz'm *or* nǐk'-*o*-tǐn-ǐz'm)

nihil (nī'-hǐl)

nihilist (nī'-*i*-lǐst *or* nī'-hi-lǐst)

noisome (noi'-sŭm)

nomad (nō'-mǎd; *Brit.,* nŏm'-ǎd)

nomenclature (nō'-m*e*n-klā"-chûr *or* n*o*-mĕn'-kl*a*-chûr)

nonage (nŏn'-āj *or* nŏn'-ǐj)

nonchalance (nŏn'-sh*a*-l*a*ns)

nonentity (nŏn-ĕn'-t*i*-tǐ)

nonpareil (nŏn"-p*a*-rēl')

nostalgia (nŏs-tǎl'-jǐ-*a*)

nostril (nŏs'-trǐl)

notoriety (nō"-t*o*-rī'-*e*-tǐ)

noxious (nŏk'-shŭs)

nuance (nyū-ahns' *or* nyū'-ahns)

nuisance (nyū'-s*a*ns)

numismatics (nyū"-mǐz-mǎt'-ǐks *or* nyū"-mǐs-mǎt'-ǐks)

numismatist (nyū-mǐz'-m*a*-tǐst *or* nyū-mǐs'-m*a*-tǐst)

nuptial (nŭp'-sh*a*l)

nuthatch (nŭt'-hǎch")

oasis (ō-ā'-sǐs *or* ō'-ā-sǐs)

oaths (ōTHz)

obdurate (ŏb'-dyū-rāt)

obeisance (ō-bā'-s*a*ns *or* ō-bē'-s*a*ns)

obese (*o*-bēs')

obesity (*o*-bēs'-*i*-tǐ *or o*-bĕs'-*i*-tǐ)

obituary (*o*-bǐt'-yū-ĕr"-ǐ)

objurgate (ŏb'-jûr-gāt *or* ŏb-jûr'-gāt)

obligatory (ob-lǐg'-*a*-tō"-rǐ *or* ŏb'-l*i*-g*a*-tō"-rǐ *or* ŏb'-l*i*-gā"-t*o*-rǐ)

oblique (*o*b-lēk')

obloquy (ŏb'-l*o*-kwǐ)

oboe (ō'-bō *or* ō'-boi)

obscenity (ŏb-sĕn'-ĭ-tĭ *or*
  ŏb-sē'-nĭ-tĭ)

obscurantism (ŏb-skyŭr'-an-tĭz'm)

obtuse (ŏb-tyūs')

occasion (o-kā'-zhŭn)

occipital (ŏk-sĭp'-ĭ-tal)

occiput (ŏk'-sĭ-pŭt)

occult (o-kŭlt' *or* ŏk'-ŭlt)

occurrence (o-kûr'-ens)

occurring (o-kûr'-ĭng)

oceanic (ō"-shĭ-ăn'-ĭk)

octavo (ŏk-tā'-vō *or* ŏk-tah'-vō)

octopus (ŏk'-to-pŭs)

ocular (ŏk'-yū-ler)

odoriferous (ō"-der-ĭf'-er-ŭs)

officious (o-fĭsh'-ŭs)

often (ŏf'-en)

ogive (ō'-jīv *or* ō-jīv')

oleomargarine (ō"-li-o-mahr'-ja-rēn
  or ō"-li-o-mahr'-ga-rēn)

oligarchy (ŏl'-ĭ-gahr"-kĭ)

omelet (ŏm'-e-lĕt *or* ŏm'-lĕt)

ominous (ŏm'-i-nŭs)

omniscience (ŏm-nĭsh'-ens; *Brit.*,
  ŏm-nĭs'-ĭ-ens)

onerous (ŏn'-er-ŭs)

onion (ŭn'-yŭn)

only (ōn'-lĭ)

onomatopoeia (ŏn"-o-măt"-o-pē'-ya)

onyx (ŏn'-ĭks *or* ō'-nĭks)

opprobrium (o-prō'-brĭ-ŭm)

oppugn (o-pyūn')

optimist (ŏp'-ti-mĭst)

opulent (ŏp'-yū-lent)

opus (ō'-pŭs; *Brit.*, ŏp'-ŭs)

orangutan (o-răng'-ŏŏ-tăn")

orbital (ôr'-bĭ-tal)

orchestra (ôr'-kĕs-tra)

orchestral (ôr-kĕs'-tral)

orchid (ôr'-kĭd)

ordeal (ôr-dē'-al *or* ôr'-dē-al)

ordure (ôr'-dyŭr)

organization (ôr"-gan-ĭ-zā'-shŭn *or*
  ôr"-gan-ī-zā'-shŭn)

orgies (ôr'-jĭz)

oriole (ō'-rĭ-ōl)

orison (ŏr'-ĭ-zŭn)

orphan (ôr'-fan)

osier (ō'-zher)

osseous (ŏs'-i-ŭs)

ostler (ŏs'-ler)

otiose (ō'-shĭ-ōs)

oust (owst)

oven (ŭv'-en)

overlap (ō"-ver-lăp')

overt (ō'-vûrt)

oviparous (o-vĭp'-a-rŭs)

pace (pās)

paean (pē'-an)

pageant (păj'-ent)

pageantry (păj'-en-trĭ)

pagination (păj"-i-nā'-shŭn)

pagoda (pa-gō'-da)

pajamas (pa-jah'-maz *or*
  pa-jăm'-az)

palanquin (păl"-an-kēn')

palatial (pa-lā'-shal)

paleography (pā"-li-ŏg'-ra-fĭ *or*
  păl'-i-ŏg'-ra-fĭ)

palfrey (pawl'-frĭ)

palsy (pawl'-zĭ)

pamphlet (păm'-flĕt)

panacea (păn"-a-sē'-a)

panache (pa-nahsh')

pancreas (păn'-krē-as *or*
  păng'-krē-as)

panegyric (păn"-e-jĭr'-ĭk)

panegyrist (păn"-e-jĭr'-ĭst *or*
  păn'-e-jĭr"-ĭst)

panegyrize (păn'-e-ji-rīz)

papa (pah'-pah *or* pa-pah')

papier-mâché (pā'-per-ma-shā')

paprika (păp'-rĭ-ka *or* pa-prē'-ka)

papyrus (pa-pī'-rŭs)

parabola (pa-răb'-o-la)

parabolic (păr"-a-bŏl'-ĭk)

parachute (păr'-a-shōōt)

paradisiac (păr"-a-dĭs'-ĭ-ăk)

paraffin (păr'-a-fĭn *or* păr'-a-fēn)

parakeet (păr'-a-kēt)

paralysis (pa-răl'-i-sĭs)

paramour (păr'-a-mōōr)

paraphernalia (păr"-a-fer-nā'-lĭ-a *or* păr"-a-fer-nāl'-ya)

paresis (pa-rē'-sĭs *or* păr'-i-sĭs)

pariah (pa-rī'-a; *in India, properly* pah'-rĭ-a)

parietal (pa-rī'-e-tal)

parliament (pahr'-li-ment)

pari mutuel (păr'-ĭ myū'-tyū-el)

parochial (pa-rō'-kĭ-al)

parole (pa-rōl')

paroquet (păr'-o-kĕt)

parquet (păr-kā' *or* păr-kĕt')

partial (pahr'-shal)

partner (pahrt'-ner)

partridge (pahr'-trĭj)

pasha (pa-shah' *or* pah'-sha *or* păsh'-a)

pasteurized (păs'-ter-īzd *or* păs'-tyŭr-īzd)

pastime (păs'-tīm")

pasty (like paste, pās'-tĭ; a pie, păs'-tĭ *or* pahs'-tĭ *or* pās'-tĭ)

paten (păt'-en)

patent (not hidden, pā'-tent; *other uses,* păt'-ent)

paternoster (pā'-ter-nŏs'-ter *or* păt'-er-nŏs'-ter)

pathos (pā'-thŏs)

patina (păt'-ĭ-na)

patriot (pā'-trĭ-ŭt *or* păt'-rĭ-ŭt)

patron (pā'-trŭn)

patronage (pā'-trŭn-ĭj *or* păt'-rŭn-ĭj)

pecan (pi-kăn' *or* pi-kahn')

peculiar (pi-kyūl'-yer)

pecuniary (pi-kyū'-nĭ-ĕr"-ĭ)

pedagogical (pĕd"-a-gŏj'-ĭ-kal)

pedagogue (pĕd'-a-gŏg)

pedagogy (pĕd'-a-gō"-jĭ *or* pĕd'-a-gŏj"-ĭ *or Brit.,* pĕd'-a-gŏg"-ĭ)

pedestal (pĕd'-es-tal)

pejorative (pē'-jo-rā"-tĭv *or* pĕj'-o-rā"-tĭv *or* pe-jŏr'-a-tĭv)

pellucid (pe-lyū'-sĭd)

penal (pē'-nal)

penalize (pē'-nal-īz)

penalty (pĕn'-al-tĭ)

penates (pe-nā'-tēz)

penchant (pahɴ"-shahɴ' *or* pĕn'-chant)

penguin (pĕn'-gwĭn *or* pĕng'-gwĭn)

peninsula (pen-ĭn'-syū-la)

penitentiary (pĕn"-i-tĕn'-sha-rĭ)

pennyworth (pĕn'-ĭ-wûrth"; *Brit. colloq.,* pĕn'-erth)

penult (pē'-nŭlt *or* pi-nŭlt')

percale (per-kāl')

percolate (pûr'-ko-lāt)

peremptorily (per-ĕmp'-to-ri-lĭ)

peremptory (per-ĕmp'-to-rĭ *or* pĕr'-emp-tō"-rĭ)

perfect (*adjective:* pûr'-fĕkt; *verb:* per-fĕkt' *or* pûr'-fĕkt)

perform (per-fôrm')

perfume (*noun:* pûr'-fyŭm; *verb:* per-fyūm')

peritoneum (pĕr"-ĭ-to-nē'-ŭm)

peritonitis (pĕr"-ĭ-to-nī'-tĭs)

persiflage (pûr'-sĭ-flahzh *or* pĕr"-sĭ-flahzh')

personnel (pûr″-so-nĕl′)

perspiration (pûr″-spi-rā′-shŭn)

pestle (pĕs′-'l or pĕs′-t'l)

petard (pi-tahrd′)

petite (pe-tēt′)

petrel (pĕt′-rel)

petrol (pĕt′-rŏl)

phaeton (fā′-e-t'n)

phalanx (fā′-lăngks or făl′-ăngks)

pharmaceutic (fahr″-ma-syū′-tĭk)

pharmacopoeia (fahr″-ma-ko-pē′-a)

pharyngeal (fa-rĭn′-ji-al or fär″-in-jē′-al)

pharynx (făr′-ĭngks)

phenomenon (fi-nŏm′-i-nŏn)

philately (fi-lăt′-e-lĭ)

philosophical (fĭl″-o-sŏf′-ĭ-kal)

philosophy (fi-lŏs′-o-fĭ)

phlegm (flĕm)

phlegmatic (flĕg-măt′-ĭk)

phoebe (fē′-bē)

phonic (fŏn′-ĭk or fō′-nĭk)

phosphorus (fŏs′-fo-rŭs)

phraseology (frā″-zi-ŏl′-o-jĭ)

phthisic (tĭz′-ĭk)

phthisis (thĭ′-sĭs or fthĭ′-sĭs)

physicist (fĭz′-i-sĭst)

physique (fi-zēk′)

pianist (pĭ-ăn′-ĭst or pē′-a-nĭst)

piano (noun: pĭ-ăn′-ō or pĭ-ah′-nō; adjective: pĭ-ah′-nō)

pianoforte (pĭ-ăn″-o-fōr′-ti or pĭ-ăn′-o-fōrt)

piazza (pĭ-ăz′-a)

pica (pī′-ka)

picayune (pĭk″-a-yōon′ or pĭk″-i-yūn′)

pince-nez (păns′-nā″)

pincers (pĭn′-serz)

pinochle (pē′-nŭk″-'l)

pipit (pĭp′-ĭt)

piquant (pē′-kant)

pique (pēk)

pistachio (pĭs-tah′-shĭ-ō or pĭs-tā′-shĭ-ō)

pituitary (pĭ-tyū′-ĭ-tĕr″-ĭ)

placable (plā′-ka-b'l or plăk′-a-b'l)

placard (noun: plăk′-ahrd; verb: pla-kahrd′ or plăk′-ahrd)

placate (plā′-kāt or plăk′-āt)

plagiarism (plā′-jĭ-a-rĭz'm or plā′-ja-rĭz'm)

plaid (plăd; Scot. plād)

plait (plāt or plēt)

planet (plăn′-ĕt)

plantain (plăn′-tĭn)

plaque (plăk or plahk)

platen (plăt′-'n)

platinotype (plăt′-i-no-tīp″)

plaza (plah′-za or plăz′-a; Spanish, plah′-tha)

plebeian (pli-bē′-yan)

plebiscite (plĕb′-ĭ-sīt or plĕb′-ĭ-sĭt or plē′-bĭ-sīt)

plenary (plē′-na-rĭ or plĕn′-a-rĭ)

plenipotentiary (plĕn″-ĭ-pō-tĕn′-shĭ-ĕr″-ĭ or plĕn″-ĭ-pō-tĕn′-sha-rĭ)

plethora (plĕth′-o-ra)

pleurisy (plōor′-ĭ-sĭ)

plover (plŭv′-er or plō′-ver)

pneumatic (nyū-măt′-ĭk)

pneumonia (nyū-mō′-nĭ-a)

poem (pō′-ĕm or pō′-ĭm)

poignant (poin′-yant or poin′-ant)

poinsettia (poin-sĕt′-ĭ-a)

polemic (pō-lĕm′-ĭk)

pomander (pō′-măn-der or po-măn′-der)

pomegranate (pŏm′-grăn″-ĭt or pom-grăn′-ĭt or pŭm-grăn″-ĭt or pŭm-grăn′-ĭt)

pommel (pŭm′-el or pŏm′-el)

poniard (pŏn'-yerd)

pontifical (pŏn-tĭf'-ĭ-kal)

pontoon (pŏn-tōon')

poor (pŏor)

porcelain (pōr'-se-lĭn or pōrs'-lĭn)

porpoise (pôr'-pus)

portiere (pōr'-tyâr or pōr-tĭ-âr')

portmanteau (pōrt-măn'-tō)

portrait (pōr'-trāt or pōr'-trĭt)

positively (pŏz'-i-tĭv-lĭ)

posse (pŏs'-e)

possess (po-zĕs')

postern (pōs'-têrn)

posthumous (pŏs'-chū-mŭs)

post-mortem (pōst"-môr'-tem)

postulant (pŏs'-chū-lant)

postulate (noun: pŏs'-chū-lat; verb: pŏs'-chū-lāt)

potpourri (pō"-pōō"-rē' or pŏt"-pŏor'-ĭ)

poultice (pōl'-tĭs)

poultry (pōl'-trĭ)

poverty (pŏv'-er-tĭ)

prairie (prâr'-ĭ)

precedence (prē-sēd'-ens)

precedency (prē-sēd'-en-sĭ)

precedents (prĕs'-e-dents)

precinct (prē'-sĭngkt)

preciosity (prĕsh"-ĭ-ŏs'-i-tĭ)

predecessor (prĕd"-e-sĕs'-er or prĕd'-e-sĕs"-er)

predilection (prē"-dĭ-lĕk'-shun or prĕd"-ĭ-lĕk'-shun)

preface (prĕf'-ĭs)

preferable (prĕf'-er-a-b'l)

prefix (verb: pre-fĭks'; noun: prē'-fĭks)

prelate (prĕl'-ĭt)

prelude (prĕl'-yūd or prē'-lyūd)

premature (prē"-ma-tvūr' or prē'-ma-tyūr)

premier (adjective: prē'-mĭ-er or prĕm'-yer; noun: prē'-mĭ-er or pre-mēr')

premiere (prê-myâr')

premise (noun: prĕm'-ĭs; verb: pre-mīz')

prepuce (prē'-pyūs)

prerogative (pre-rŏg'-a-tĭv)

presage (noun: prĕs'-ĭj; verb: pre-sāj')

prescience (prē'-shĭ-ens or prĕsh'-ĭ-ens)

preside (pre-zīd')

president (prĕz'-i-dent)

prestige (prĕs-tēzh' or prĕs'-tĭj)

presumptuous (pre-zŭm'-chū-ŭs)

pretext (prē'-tĕkst)

prettily (prĭt'-i-lĭ)

pretty (prĭt'-ĭ)

pretzel (prĕt'-sel)

prevalence (prĕv'-a-lens)

prima donna (prē'-ma dŏn'-a)

primer (prīm'-er), that which primes

primer (prĭm'-er), book

pristine (prĭs'-tēn or prĭs'-tĭn)

privacy (prī'-va-sĭ or prĭv'-a-sĭ)

privet (prĭv'-ĕt or prĭv'-ĭt)

privilege (prĭv'-i-lĭj)

privy (prĭv'-ĭ)

probity (prŏb'-i-tĭ or prō'-bi-tĭ)

proboscis (pro-bŏs'-ĭs)

procedure (pro-sē'-dyūr)

proceed (pro-sēd')

proceeds (verb: pro-sēdz'; noun: prō'-sēdz)

process (prŏs'-ĕs or prō'-sĕs)

produce (verb: pro-dyūs'; noun: prŏd'-yūs)

proem (prō'-ĕm)

profile (prō'-fīl or prō'-fēl)

program (prō'-grăm)

progress (*noun:* prŏg'-rĕs *or* prō'-grĕs; *verb:* pro-grĕs')

project (*verb:* pro-jĕkt'; *noun:* prŏj'-ĕkt)

projectile (pro-jĕk'-tĭl)

proletarian (prō"-le-târ'-ĭ-an)

proletariat (prō"-le-târ'-ĭ-at)

prolix (pro-lĭks' *or* prō'-lĭks)

prolocutor (pro-lŏk'-yu-têr)

promenade (prŏm"-e-nahd' *or* prŏm"-e-nād')

promise (prŏm'-ĭs)

promulgate (pro-mŭl'-gāt *or* prŏm'-ŭl-gāt)

pronunciation (pro-nŭn"-sĭ-ā'-shun *or* pro-nŭn"-shĭ-ā'-shun)

propaganda (prŏp"-a-găn'-da)

prophecy (prŏf'-e-sĭ)

prophecies (prŏf'-e-sĭz)

prophesies (prŏf'-e-sīz)

prophesy (prŏf'-e-sī)

propitiate (pro-pĭsh'-ĭ-āt)

pro rata (prō rā'-ta *or* prō rah'-ta)

prosaic (pro-zā'-ĭk)

proselyte (prŏs'-e-līt)

prosody (prŏs'-o-dĭ)

protégé (prō"-te-zhā')

proteid (prō'-te-ĭd)

protein (prō'-te-ĭn *or* prō'-tēn)

protest (*verb:* pro-tĕst'; *noun:* prō'-tĕst)

protocol (prō'-to-kŏl)

proviso (pro-vī'-zō)

provost (prŏv'-ŭst; *milit.,* pro-vō')

pseudonym (syū'-do-nĭm *or* psyū'-do-nĭm)

psychiatric (sī"-kĭ-ăt'-rĭk *or* psī"-kĭ-ăt'-rĭk)

psychiatry (sī-kī'-a-trĭ *or* psī-kī'-a-trĭ)

ptarmigan (tahr'-mĭ-gan)

ptomaine (tō'-mān *or* tō-mān')

pueblo (pwĕb'-lō)

puerile (pyū'-er-ĭl)

pugilist (pyū'-jĭ-lĭst)

puissance (pyū'-ĭ-sans *or* pyū-ĭs'-ans *or* pwĭs'-ans)

pulmonary (pŭl'-mo-nĕr-ĭ)

pulmotor (pŭl'-mō-ter *or* poŏl'-mō-ter)

pulsate (pŭl'-sāt *or* pŭl-sāt')

pumice (pŭm'-ĭs)

pumpkin (pŭmp'-kĭn; *commonly,* pŭng'-kĭn)

pungent (pŭn'-jent)

punitive (pyū'-ni-tĭv)

purlieu (pûr'-lyū)

purport (*verb:* pûr-pōrt' *or* pûr'-pōrt; *noun:* pûr'-pōrt)

pursue (pûr-syū')

pursuivant (pûr'-swĭ-vant)

purulent (pyū'-roō-lent *or* pyūr'-yū-lent)

pusillanimous (pyū"-sĭ-lăn'-i-mŭs)

put (poŏt)

putt (pŭt)

puttee (pŭt'-ĭ; *commonly,* pŭt-tē')

pyorrhea (pī"'-o-rē'-a)

pyramid (pĭr'-a-mĭd)

pyriform (pĭr'-ĭ-fôrm)

pyrites (pī-rī'-tēz *or* pĭ-rī'-tēz *or* pī'-rīts)

pyrrhic (pĭr'-ĭk)

pyx (pĭks)

quadrille (kwah-drĭl')

quaff (kwahf)

quagmire (kwăg'-mīr *or* kwahg'-mīr)

quahaug (kwaw'-hŏg *or* kwa-hŏg')
qualm (kwahm *or* kwawm)
quandary (kwŏn'-da-rĭ *or* kwŏn-dār'-ĭ)
quarantine (kwôr'-an-tēn *or* kwôr"-an-tēn')
quaternary (kwa-tûr'-na-rĭ)
quaternion (kwa-tûr'-nĭ-un)
quatrain (kwŏt'-rān)
quay (kē)
querulous (kwĕr'-yū-lŭs *or* kwĕr'-ŏŏ-lŭs)
question (kwĕs'-chŭn)
questionnaire (kwĕs"-chŭn-âr')
queue (kyū)
quiescent (kwī-ĕs'-ent)
quietus (kwī-ē'-tŭs)
quinin (kwĭn'-ĭn)
quinine (kwī'-nīn *or* kwĭ-nēn' *or* kwĭn'-ēn)
quinquereme (kwĭn'-kwe-rēm)
quixotic (kwĭks-ŏt'-ĭk)
quoin (koin *or* kwoin)
quoit (kwoit *or* koit)
quorum (kwō'-rŭm)
quotient (kwō'-shent)
rabbi (răb'-ī *or* răb'-ĭ)
rabies (rā'-bĭ-ēz *or* rā'-bēz)
raccoon (ră-kōōn')
raconteur (răk"-ŏn-tûr')
radiate (rā'-dĭ-āt)
radiator (rā'-dĭ-ā"-ter)
radii (rā'-dĭ-ī)
radio (rā'-dĭ-ō)
radish (răd'-ĭsh)
raffia (răf'-ĭ-a)
raillery (rāl'-er-ĭ *or* răl'-er-ĭ)
raja (rah'-ja)
rampage (răm'-pāj *or* răm-pāj')
ranchero (răn-chā'-rō)
rancid (răn'-sĭd)

rancor (răng'-ker)
range (rānj)
ranger (rān'-jer)
ransack (răn'-săk)
rapier (rā'-pĭ-er)
rapine (răp'-ĭn)
rapport (ră-pōrt')
rarefied (râr'-e-fīd)
raspberry (răz'-bĕr"-ĭ)
ratafia (răt'-a-fē'-a)
rather (rahтн'-er)
ratio (rā'-shō)
ratiocination (răsh"-ĭ-ŏs-ĭ-nā'-shŭn)
ration (rā'-shŭn *or* răsh'-ŭn)
rational (răsh'-ŭn-al)
rattan (ră-tăn')
really (rē'-al-ĭ)
rebel (*verb:* re-bĕl'; *noun, adjective:* rĕb'-el)
recalcitrant (re-kăl'-sĭ-trant)
recall (*verb:* re-kawl'; *noun:* re-kawl' *or* rē'-kawl)
recapitulate (rē'-ka-pĭt'-yū-lāt)
receipt (re-sēt)
recess (re-sĕs' *or* rē'-sĕs)
recipe (rĕs'-i-pē)
recluse (*adjective:* re-klōōs'; *noun:* re-klōōs' *or* rĕk'-lōōs)
recognizance (re-kŏg'-nĭ-zans; *in Law commonly,* re-kon'-ĭ-zans)
recognize (rĕk'-og-nīz)
recollect (rĕk"-o-lĕkt')
recondite (rĕk'-un-dīt *or* re-kŏn'-dīt)
reconnaissance (re-kŏn'-i-sans)
reconnoiter (rĕk"-o-noi'-ter)
record (*verb:* re-kôrd'; *noun:* rĕk'-ôrd)
recoup (re-kōōp')
recruit (re-krōōt')
recurrence (re-kûr'-ens)

recurring   (re-kûr'-ĭng)

recusant   (rĕk'-yū-zant or
re-kyū'-zant)

redolent   (rĕd'-o-lent)

refectory   (re-fĕk'-to-rĭ)

referable   (rĕf'-er-a-b'l)

referee   (rĕf"-er-ē')

referred   (re-fûrd')

reflex   (noun and adjective: rē'-flĕks;
verb: re-flĕks')

regicide   (rĕj'-i-sīd)

regime   (rā-zhēm')

regiment   (noun: rĕj'-i-ment; verb:
rĕj'-i-mĕnt)

regular   (rĕg'-yū-ler)

relay   (noun and adjective: re-lā' or
rē'-lā; verb: re-lā')

reliques   (rĕl'-ĭks or re-lēks')

remediable   (re-mē'-dĭ-a-b'l)

remembrance   (re-mĕm'-brans)

remonstrate   (re-mŏn'-strāt)

renaissance   (rĕn"-e-sahns' or
re-nā'-sans)

renascence   (re-năs'-ens)

renege   (re-nēg'; popularly, re-nĭg')

renew   (re-nyū')

renewal   (re-nyū'-al)

renown   (re-nown')

reparable   (rĕp'-a-ra-b'l)

repartee   (rĕp"-er-tē')

repay   (re-pā')

repertoire   (rĕp'-er-twahr or
rĕp'-er-twawr)

repetition   (rĕp"-e-tĭsh'-ŭn)

repetitious   (rĕp"-e-tĭsh'-ŭs)

replica   (rĕp'-lĭ-ka)

reputable   (rĕp'-yū-ta-b'l)

requiem   (rē'-kwĭ-em or rĕk'-wĭ-em)

reredos   (rēr'-dŏs)

research   (re-sûrch' or rē'-sûrch)

resemble   (re-zĕm'-b'l)

reservist   (re-zûr'-vĭst)

reservoir   (rĕz'-er-vwôr or
rĕz'-er-vwahr)

residuum   (re-zĭd'-yū-ŭm)

resiliency   (re-zĭl'-ĭ-en-sĭ)

resin   (rĕz'-ĭn)

resolution   (rĕz"-o-lyū'-shŭn)

resolve   (re-zŏlv')

resources   (re-sōr'-sĕz or rē'-sōr-sĕz)

respirable   (re-spīr'-a-b'l or
rĕs'-pi-ra-b'l)

respite   (rĕs'-pĭt)

restaurant   (rĕs'-to-rant)

resume   (re-zyūm')

résumé   (rā"-zyū-mā')

retina   (rĕt'-ĭ-na)

retinue   (rĕt'-ĭ-nyū)

retro-   (rĕt'-rō; in physiological
terms usually, rē'-trō-)

retroactive   (rĕt"-rō-ăkt'-ĭv)

retrospect   (rĕt'-rō-spĕkt or
rē'-trō-spĕkt)

reveille   (re-vāl'-yĭ; in U.S. service,
rĕv'-e-lē" or rĕv'-e-lē')

revelation   (rĕv"-e-lā'-shŭn)

revenue   (rĕv'-e-nyū)

reverberation   (re-vûr"-ber-ā'-shŭn)

revocable   (rĕv'-o-ka-b'l)

revolt   (re-vōlt' or re-vŏlt')

rhapsodic   (răp-sŏd'-ĭk)

rhomb   (rŏmb or rŏm)

ribald   (rĭb'-ald)

riband   (rĭb'-and)

ribband   (rĭb'-bănd")

ricochet   (rĭk"-o-shā')

righteous   (rī'-chŭs)

rinse   (rĭns)

riposte   (re-pōst')

rise   (rīz)

risible   (rĭz'-i-b'l)

risqué   (rēs"-kā')

robot (rō'-bot *or* rŏb'-ŏt)
robust (ro-bŭst')
rococo (ro-kō'-kō *or* rō"-ko-kō')
roily (roil'-ĭ)
role (rōl)
romance (ro-măns' *or* rō'-măns)
roof (rōōf)
roofs (rōōfs)
root (rōōt)
rosin (rŏz'-ĭn)
roster (rŏs'-ter *or* rōs'-ter)
rostrum (rŏs'-trŭm)
rotate (rō'-tāt *or* rō-tāt')
rotatory (rō'-ta-tō"-rĭ *or*
    ro-tā'-to-rĭ)
rotogravure (rō"-to-gra-vyūr' *or*
    rō"-to-grā'-vyūr)
roué (rōō-ā')
rouge (rōōzh)
rout (rowt)
route (rōōt *or commonly*, rowt)
routine (rōō-tēn')
rowel (row'-el)
rutabaga (rōō"-ta-bā'-ga)
sabotage (săb"-o-tahzh' *or*
    săb'-o-tĭj)
saboteur (săb"-o-tûr')
sacerdotal (săs"-er-dō'-tal)
sachem (sā'-chem)
sachet (să-shā' *or* săsh'-ā)
sacrament (săk'-ra-ment)
sacrifice (*noun:* săk'-ri-fīs *or* săk'-ri-
    fīz; *verb:* săk'-ri-fīz *or* săk'-ri-fīs)
sacrificial (săk"-ri-fĭsh'-al)
sacrilege (săk'-ri-lĕj *or* săk-ri-lĭj)
sacrilegious (săk"-ri-lē'-jŭs *or*
    săk"-ri-lĭ'-jŭs)
sacrosanct (săk'-ro-săngkt)
safety (sāf'-tĭ)
saga (sah'-ga *or* sā'-ga)
sagittal (săj'-ĭ-tal)

sahib (sah'-ĭb)
said (sĕd)
salaam (sa-lahm')
salary (săl'-a-rĭ)
salient (sā'-lĭ-ent)
saline (sā'-līn)
saliva (sa-lī'-va)
salivary (săl'-i-vĕr"-ĭ)
salmon (săm'-ŭn)
salon (sah"-lôN')
saltire (săl'-têr)
salutary (săl'-yū-tĕr"-ĭ)
salutatory (sa-lyū'-ta-tō"-rĭ)
salute (sa-lyūt')
salvage (săl'-vĭj)
salve (sahv *or* săv)
salver (săl'-ver)
sandwich (sănd'-wĭch *or* sănd'-wĭj)
sanguinary (săng'-gwĭ-nĕr"-ĭ)
sanguine (săng'-gwĭn)
sapience (sā'-pĭ-ens)
sapphire (săf'-īr)
sarcophagi (sahr-kŏf'-a-jī)
sarsaparilla (sahr"-sa-pa-rĭl'-a)
satellite (săt'-e-līt)
satiate (sā'-shĭ-āt)
satiety (sa-tī'-e-tĭ)
satire (săt'-īr)
satyr (săt'-er *or* sā'-ter)
saucy (sôs'-ĭ)
sauerkraut (sowr'-krowt")
savant (sa-vahN' *or* săv'-ant)
says (sĕz)
scapula (skăp'-yū-la)
scarab (skăr'-ab)
scathe (skāтн)
scene (sēn)
scenario (se-nah'-rĭ-ō *or* se-nâr'-ĭ-ō
    or she-nah'-rĭ-ō)
schedule (skĕd'-yūl)
schism (sĭz'm)

schist (shĭst)

sciatic (sī-ăt′-ĭk)

scimitar (sĭm′-i-ter)

scintillate (sĭn′-ti-lāt)

sciolist (sī′-o-lĭst)

scion (sī′-ŭn)

scissors (sĭz′-erz)

scone (skōn or skŏn)

scourge (skûrj)

scythe (sīTH)

seamstress (sĕm′-strĕs or
sĕm′-strĭs)

seance (sā-ahNS′ or sā′-ahns)

secant (sē′-kant)

secretary (sĕk′-re-tĕr″-ĭ)

secretive (se-krē′-tĭv)

sedan (se-dăn′)

segregate (sĕg′-re-gāt)

seine (sān or sēn)

seismic (sīz′-mĭk or sīs′-mĭk)

seismograph (sīz′-mo-grăf or
sīs′-mo-grăf)

semester (se-mĕs′-ter)

senate (sĕn′-ĭt)

seneschal (sĕn′-e-shal)

senile (sē′-nīl or sē′-nĭl)

senility (se-nĭl′-i-tĭ)

sentient (sĕn′-shent or sĕn′-shĭ-ent)

sepal (sē′-pal or sĕp′-al)

sequester (se-kwĕs′-ter)

sequin (sē′-kwĭn or sĕk′-ĭn)

seraglio (se-răl′-yō or sĕ-rahl′-yō)

sergeant (sahr′-jent)

series (sêr′-ēz or sêr′-ĭz)

serious (sêr′-i-ŭs)

sesame (sĕs′-a-mē)

sew (sō)

sewage (syū′-ĭj)

sewerage (syū′-er-ĭj)

sheik (shēk or shāk)

shekel (shĕk′-el)

shellac (she-lăk′ or shĕl′-ăk)

shew (shō)

shillalah (shĭ-lā′-la or shĭ-lā′-lē)

short-lived (shôrt′-līvd′ or
shôrt′-lĭvd′)

shove (shŭv)

shovel (shŭv′l)

sibylline (sĭb′-ĭ-līn or sĭb′-ĭ-lĭn)

sidereal (sī-dêr′-e-al)

sieve (sĭv)

silhouette (sĭl″-ōō-ĕt′)

simile (sĭm′-ĭ-lē)

simony (sĭm′-o-nĭ or sī′-mo-nĭ)

simultaneous (sī″-mŭl˳tā′-ne-ŭs or
sĭm″-ŭl-tā′-ne-ŭs)

since (sĭns)

sinecure (sī′-ne-kyūr or sĭn′-e-kyūr)

singe (sĭnj)

sinister (sĭn′-ĭs-ter)

sirrah (sĭr′-a)

sirup (sĭr′-ŭp)

ski (skē)

sleazy (slā′-zĭ or slē′-zĭ)

sleek (slēk)

sleight (slīt)

sloth (slōth or slôth)

slough (mud, slow; swamp or inlet,
slōō; cast skin, slŭf)

sloven (slŭv′-en)

sluice (slōōs)

sobriquet (sō′-brĭ-kā)

soccer (sŏk′-er)

sociology (sō″-sĭ-ŏl′-o-jĭ or
sō″-shĭ-ŏl′-o-jĭ)

soften (sŏf′-en)

sojourn (noun: sō′-jûrn or sō-jûrn′
or sŏj′-ûrn; verb: sō-jûrn′ or sō′-
jûrn or sŏj′-ûrn)

solace (sŏl′-is)

solder (sŏd′-er)

soldier (sōl′-jer)

solecism (sŏl'-e-sĭz'm)

solemn (sŏl'-em)

solo (sō'-lō)

solstice (sŏl'-stĭs)

sombrero (sŏm-brā'-rō)

sonorous (so-nō'-rŭs or sŏn'-o-rŭs)

soot (soŏt or sōot)

sophism (sŏf'-ĭz'm)

sophist (sŏf'-ĭst)

sophomore (sŏf'-o-mōr)

soufflé (soō"-flā' or soō'-flā)

sough (sŭf or sow)

southerly (sŭтн'-er-lĭ)

sovereign (sŏv'-er-ĭn or sŏv'-rĭn or
   sŭv'-rĭn)

sovereignty (sŏv'-er-in-tĭ or
   sŏv'-rĭn-tĭ or sŭv'-rĭn-tĭ)

soviet (sō"-vĭ-ĕt' or sō'-vĭ-ĕt)

spa (spah)

specialty (spĕsh'-al-tĭ)

specie (spē'-shĭ)

species (spē'-shĭz; plural usually,
   spē'-shēz)

spectacular (spĕk-tăk'-yŭ-ler)

spermaceti (spûr"-ma-sē'-tĭ or
   spûr"-ma-sĕt'-ĭ)

sphinx (sfĭngks)

spinach (spĭn'-ĭch or spĭn'-ĭj)

spinet (spĭn'-ĕt or spĭn'-ĭt or
   spĭ-nĕt')

spiritual (spĭr'-ĭ-chū-al)

sponge (spŭnj)

spontaneity (spŏn"-ta-nē'-ĭ-tĭ)

springe (sprĭnj)

squalor (skwahl'-er or skwā'-ler)

squamous (skwā'-mŭs)

squirrel (skwûr'-el or skwĭr'-el)

stabilize (stā'-bĭ-līz or stăb'-ĭ-līz)

staccato (sta-kah'-tō)

stalactite (sta-lăk'-tīt or stăl'-ak-tīt)

stalagmite (sta-lăg'-mīt or
   stăl'-ag-mīt)

stalwart (stahl'-wert)

stamen (stā'-men)

stamina (stăm'-ĭ-na)

stanchion (stăn'-shŭn)

starboard (stahr'-bōrd or
   stahr'-berd)

static (stăt'-ĭk)

status (stā'-tŭs)

steelyard (stēl'-yahrd; colloquially,
   stĭl'-yerd)

stein (stīn)

stereopticon (stĕr"-e-ŏp'-tĭ-kon or
   stêr"-e-ŏp'-tĭ-kon)

stereotype (stĕr'-e-o-tīp" or
   stêr'-e-o-tīp")

stevedore (stē'-ve-dōr")

stimuli (stĭm'-yŭ-lī)

stimulus (stĭm'-yŭ-lŭs)

stipend (stī'-pĕnd)

stirrup (stĭr'-ŭp or stûr'-ŭp)

stogie (stō'-gĭ)

stoic (stō'-ĭk)

stomach (stŭm'-ak)

stranger (strān'-jer)

stratum (strā'-tŭm or străt'-ŭm)

strictly (strĭkt'-lĭ)

strophe (strō'-fe)

strychnine (strĭk'-nĭn or strĭk'-nīn)

student (styū'-dent)

studio (styū'-dĭ-ō)

suave (swahv or swăv)

subaltern (sŭb-awl'-tern; in Logic,
   sŭb'-al-tern)

subpoena (sŭb-pē'-na or sŭ-pē'-na)

subsidence (sŭb-sīd'-ens or
   sŭb'-sĭ-dens)

subtile (sŭb'-tĭl or sŭt'l)

subtle (sŭt'l)

subtly (sŭt'-lĭ)

succinct (sŭk-sĭngkt′)
suede (swād)
suffice (su-fīs′ or su-fīz′)
suggest (sŭg-jĕst′ or su-jĕst′)
suite (swēt)
sultan (sŭl′-tan or sōōl-tahn′)
sumac (shōō′-măk or syū′-măk)
superfluous (syū-pûr′-flōō-ŭs)
supposititious (sŭ-pŏz″-ĭ-tĭsh′-ŭs)
suppress (sŭ-prĕs′)
supremacy (sū-prĕm′-a-sĭ)
surcease (sûr-sēs′)
surmise (verb: sûr-mīz′; noun: sûr-mīz′ or sûr′-mīz)
surprise (sûr-prīz′)
surveillance (sûr-vāl′-ans or sûr-vāl′-yans)
suture (syū′-chûr)
svelte (svĕlt)
swastika (swăs′-tĭ-ka or swahs′-tĭ-ka)
swath (swahth)
swathe (swāтн)
sword (sōrd)
sycophant (sĭk′-o-fant)
syncope (sĭng′-ko-pē)
synod (sĭn′-ŭd)
synonymous (sĭ-nŏn′-ĭ-mŭs)
syringe (sĭr′-ĭnj)
systole (sĭs′-to-lē)
tabu (ta-bōō′)
talisman (tăl′-ĭs-man or tăl′-ĭz-man)
tanager (tăn′-a-jer)
tangible (tăn′-ji-b'l)
tarantula (ta-răn′-chū-la)
tarpaulin (tahr-paw′-lĭn)
tassel (tăs'l)
tattoo (tă-tōō′)
taut (tawt)
taxidermist (tăk′-sĭ-dûr″-mĭst)

teat (tēt)
tedious (tē′-dĭ-ŭs or tēd′-yŭs or tē′-jŭs)
televisor (tĕl′-e-vī″-zer)
temperament (tĕm′-per-a-ment)
temporarily (tĕm′-po-rĕr″-ĭ-lĭ)
tenable (tĕn′-a-b'l or tē′-na-b'l)
tenet (tĕn′-et or tē′-net)
tercentenary (tûr-sĕn′-te-nĕr″-ĭ or tûr″-sĕn-tĕn′-a-rĭ)
tertian (tûr′-shan)
tertiary (tûr′-shĭ-ĕr″-ĭ or tûr′-sha-rĭ)
theater (thē′-a-ter)
thistle (thĭs′l)
threepence (thrĭp′-ens or thrĕp′-ens)
threnody (thrĕn′-o-dĭ)
threshold (thrĕsh′-ōld or thrĕsh′-hōld)
throes (thrōz)
throstle (thrŏs'l)
thug (thŭg)
thyme (tīm)
thyroid (thī′-roid)
tiara (tĭ-âr′-a or te-ah′-ra)
timbre (tĭm′-ber; Fr., tăɴ′-br′)
tirade (tī′-rād or tĭ-rād′)
tissue (tĭsh′-yū or tĭsh′-ōō)
tocsin (tŏk′-sĭn)
tomato (to-mā′-tō or to-mah′-tō)
took (tŏŏk)
topographic (tŏp″-o-grăf′-ĭk)
topography (to-pŏg′-ra-fĭ)
toreador (tŏr′-e-a-dôr″ or tŏr″-e-a-dôr′)
tornado (tôr-nā′-dō)
tortoise (tôr′-tŭs or tôr′-tĭs)
tortuous (tôr′-chū-ŭs)
torture (tôr′-chûr)
totalitarian (tō-tăl″-ĭ-târ′-ĭ-an)

totalizator   (tō″-tăl-ĭ-zā′-ter)

toucan   (tōō-kahn′ or tōō′-kan)

toupee   (tōō-pē′)

tournament   (tōŏr′-na-ment or
tûr′-na-ment)

tourniquet   (tōŏr′-ni-kĕt)

tout   (towt)

trait   (trāt)

transferable   (trăns-fûr′-a-b'l)

transference   (trăns-fûr′-ens or
trăns′-fêr-ens)

trapeze   (tra-pēz′)

traversing   (trăv′-er-sĭng)

treacle   (trēk'l)

treatise   (trē′-tĭs or trē′-tĭz)

trefoil   (trē′-foil)

trepan   (tre-păn′)

trestle   (trĕs'l)

tribunal   (trī-byū′-nal or
trĭ-byū′-nal)

tribune   (trĭb′-yūn)

tripartite   (trī-pahr′-tīt or
trĭp′-er-tīt)

triptych   (trĭp′-tĭk)

trochee   (trō′-kē)

trombone   (trŏm′-bōn or
trŏm-bōn′)

trophy   (trō′-fĭ)

troth   (trŏth or trōth)

trough   (trôf)

trow   (trō)

truculent   (trŭk′-yū-lent or
trōō′-kyū-lent)

tryst   (trĭst or trīst)

tulle   (tōōl)

turbulence   (tûr′-byū-lens)

turgid   (tûr′-jĭd)

turpentine   (tûr′-pen-tīn)

turquoise   (tûr′-koiz or tûr′-kwoiz)

turret   (tûr′-ĕt or tûr′-ĭt)

tutti-frutti   (tōō′-tĭ-frōō′-tĭ)

twopenny   (tŭp′-en-ĭ)

uhlan   (ōō′-lahn or yū′-lan)

ukase   (yū-kās′ or yū′-kās)

ukulele   (yū″-kyū-lā′-le)

ultimatum   (ŭl″-ti-mā′-tŭm)

umbrella   (ŭm-brĕl′-a)

unanimity   (yū″-na-nĭm′-i-tĭ)

unanimous   (yū-năn′-i-mŭs)

unprecedented   (ŭn-prĕs′-e-dĕn″-tĕd)

untoward   (ŭn-tō′-erd or ŭn-tōrd′)

ureter   (yū-rē′-ter)

urethra   (yū-rē′-thra)

ursine   (ûr′-sīn or ûr′-sĭn)

usage   (yūs′-ĭj or yūz′-ĭj)

usufruct   (yū′-zyū-frŭkt)

usurious   (yū-zhōŏr′-ĭ-ŭs)

usurp   (yū-zûrp′)

uxorious   (ŭks-ō′-rĭ-ŭs)

vacate   (vā′-kāt)

vacation   (vā-kā′-shŭn)

vaccinate   (văk′-si-nāt)

vaccine   (văk′-sēn or văk′-sĭn)

vacillation   (văs″-i-lā′-shŭn)

vacuum   (văk′-yū-ŭm)

vagary   (va-gâr′-ĭ or va-gā′-rĭ)

vagina   (va-jī′-na)

vaginal   (văj′-i-nal or va-jī′-nal)

vagrant   (vā′-grant)

valet   (văl′-ĕt or văl′-ā)

valise   (va-lēs′)

vase   (vās or vāz)

vaudeville   (vōd′-vĭl or vō′-de-vĭl)

vegetable   (vĕj′-e-ta-b'l)

vehement   (vē′-e-ment or
vē′-he-ment)

vehicle   (vē′-i-k'l or vē′-hi-k'l)

vehicular   (ve-hĭk′-yu-ler)

vengeance   (vĕn′-jans)

venue   (vĕn′-yū)

verbatim   (vûr-bā′-tĭm)

vernacular   (vûr-năk′-yū-ler)

version (vûr'-shŭn; *or commonly,* vûr'-zhŭn)

vertebra (vûr'-te-bra)

vertigo (vûr'-tĭ-gō)

via (vī'-a)

viands (vī-andz)

viceroy (vīs'-roi)

vicinity (vi-sĭn'-i-tĭ)

victuals (vĭt'lz)

victualer (vĭt'l'-er *or* vĭt'-ler)

vignette (vĭn-yĕt')

viking (vī'-kĭng)

vilify (vĭl'-i-fī)

villain (vĭl'-in)

viola (ve-ō'-la *or* vī-ō'-la)

violin (vī'-o-lĭn" *or* vī"-o-lĭn')

violoncello (vē"-o-lŏn-chĕl'-ō *or* vī"'-o-lŏn-sĕl'-ō)

virile (vĭr'-ĭl *or* vī'-rĭl)

virulent (vĭr'-yū-lent *or* vĭr'-ōō-lent)

viscera (vĭs'-er-a)

viscid (vĭs'-ĭd)

viscount (vī'-kount")

viscous (vĭs'-kŭs)

visor (vĭz'-er *or* vīz'-er)

vitals (vī'-talz)

vitamin (vī'-ta-mĭn *or* vĭt'-a-mĭn)

viticulture (vĭt'-ĭ-kŭl"-chûr *or* vī'-tĭ-kŭl"-chûr)

vituperation (vī-tyū"-per-ā'-shŭn)

viviparous (vī-vĭp'-a-rŭs)

waft (wahft)

wainscoting (wān'-skŭt-ĭng *or* wān'-skŏt-ĭng)

wash (wahsh)

wassail (wahs'l *or* wahs'-āl)

watch (wahch)

water (waw'-ter *or* wah'-ter)

whale (hwāl)

wheel (hwēl)

where (hwâr)

whether (hwĕтн'-er)

which (hwĭch)

while (hwīl)

whistle (hwĭs'l)

window (wĭn'-dō)

wistaria (wĭs-tā'-rĭ-a)

with (wĭтн)

withe (wĭ*th* *or* wĭтн *or* wīтн)

wizen (wĭz'n)

women (wĭm'-en)

wont (wŭnt)

won't (wōnt), will not

worsted (wûrst'-ed), defeated

worsted (wŏŏs'-tĕd), yarn

wort (wûrt)

wrestle (rĕs'l)

wroth (rô*th* *or* rō*th*)

xylophone (zī'-lo-fōn *or* zĭl'-o-fōn)

yea (yā)

yeast (yēst)

yeoman (yō'-man)

zebra (zē'-bra)

zenith (zē'-nĭ*th* *or* zĕn'-ĭ*th*)

zephyr (zĕf'-er)

zeugma (zyūg'-ma)

zinnia (zĭn'-ĭ-a)

zoological (zō"-o-lŏj'-ĭ-kal)

zoologist (zō-ŏl'-o-jĭst)

zoology (zō-ŏl'-o-jĭ)

zwieback (tsvē'-bahk *or* tswē'-bahk; *commonly,* swī'-băk *or* zwī'-băk)

A Guide to the
Correct Spelling of Words
Frequently Misspelled

A Guide to the
Correct Spelling of Words
Frequently Misspelled

IT IS NOT POSSIBLE to make a simple set of hard and fast rules for English spelling. No good speller ever spells by rules, however, and almost every rule has its exceptions. It is more important, and much easier, to remember how a word is written, how it looks on the page, than to remember which rule governs its spelling. The only way to learn to spell correctly is to read carefully, to notice the correct spelling of words, to study the proper order and arrangement of the letters that form the words, and to impress the correct image of the word on the mind.

RULES, AIDS, AND CAUTIONS IN SPELLING

Write out several times the spelling of each unfamiliar word, and keep a list of all new words, as well as of words you are inclined to misspell. Notice carefully the similarities in related words—**dispensable, dispensary, dispensation; audible, audience, audition, audit, auditorium**—as well as the differences in such related words as **stratagem, strategic, strategy.** Study carefully words in which only one of several consonants is doubled, as in **disappoint, disappear, dissipate, harass, recommend;** and likewise words in which more than one consonant is doubled, such as **accommodate, assassinate, embarrass, possession.**

The rules for spelling refer chiefly to the parts of words and to the arrangement and combination of such parts as *syllables, roots, prefixes* and *suffixes.*

A syllable is a letter or group of letters which can be pronounced as a single sound. Thus, the word **straighten** has two syllables: **straight en;** the word **inhabit** has three syllables: **in hab it.**

A prefix is a letter or group of letters combined or united with the beginning of a word or root of a word to modify its meaning. In the word **prefigure,** the syllable **pre** is the prefix, and **figure** is the root, or main part of the word. In the word **recopy,** the syllable **re** is the prefix, and **copy** is the root.

A suffix is an element consisting of one or more syllables added to the end of a word or to the root of a word to change or modify its meaning, as **ly** in **eagerly, ed** in **mended, ish** in **feverish,** and **ness** in **greenness.**

SPECIAL RULES REGARDING THE ORDER OR THE COMBINATION OF LETTERS IN WORDS

1. WORDS CONTAINING ei OR ie.

To most words of this nature the familiar old jingle applies:

> I before E
> Except after C,
> Or when sounded as A,
> As in *neighbor* or *weigh*.

Another convenient aid to the memory is the word **Celia.** If **c** precedes the combination, **e** follows the **c,** as in **Celia;** if **l** or any other consonant precedes the combination, **i** usually follows that consonant, as in **Celia.** The following lists contain some of the more common words with this combination of letters:

(a) **ie** (*pronounced as* ē)

achieve	grieve	retrieve
believe	niece	shield
brief	piece	shriek
chief	pier	siege
field	pierce	thief
fiend	relieve	wield
fierce	reprieve	yield

(b) **ei** (*pronounced as* ē)

ceiling, conceive, deceive, perceive, receive

(c) **ei** (*pronounced as* ā)

feint	obeisance	sleigh
freight	reign	veil
inveigh	rein	weigh
neighbor	skein	weight

EXCEPTIONS to (a), (b), and (c): **either, fancier, financier, fiery, foreign, friend, glacier, glazier, heifer, height, inveigle, leisure, mischief, mischievous, seize, sieve, sovereign, view, weird.**

2. VERBS ENDING IN **ceed, cede,** AND **sede.**

Only three common verbs end in *ceed:* **exceed, proceed, succeed.** (Note the spelling of the noun **procedure.**)

One word only ends in *sede:* **supersede.**

Other words of the group end in *cede:* **accede, concede, intercede, precede, recede.**

SPECIAL RULES AND CAUTIONS WITH REGARD TO PREFIXES

When a prefix ends with the same letter with which the root to which it is to be united begins, be careful to retain both letters in spelling the word: **connect, correlate, dissimilar, misshapen, innocuous.** The following lists call attention to some common words likely to be misspelled through carelessness with regard to prefixes and initial syllables.

1. WORDS BEGINNING WITH **a** PRECEDING A SINGLE CONSONANT:

abandon	adequate	align
abominate	adopt	aloof
abortion	adore	aluminum
abound	adorn	amaze
abrasive	adult	ameliorate
abundant	adulterate	amenable
abuse	afraid	amend
acute	agree	amenity
adapt	alacrity	amiss
adept	alert	among

amount	apartment	aroma
amuse	apology	arose
anatomy	apostle	arouse
anoint	arena	atomic
another	arise	atone

2. WORDS BEGINNING WITH a PRECEDING TWO OR MORE CONSO-
   NANTS:

abbreviate	affluent	annual
accede	afford	annul
accelerate	affright	annunciation
accent	affront	apparent
accept	aggravate	appeal
access	aggregate	appear
accident	aggression	appease
acclaim	aggrieve	appellation
acclimate	allay	appendix
accommodate	allege	apperceive
accompany	allegory	appertain
accomplish	allergy	appetite
accord	alleviate	applaud
account	alley	apply
accredit	alliance	appoint
accrue	alligator	apportion
accumulate	alliteration	appraise
accurate	allocation	appreciate
accuse	allot	apprehend
accustom	allow	approach
addicted	alloy	appropriate
addition	allure	approve
address	allusive	approximate
adduce	ally	arrange
affable	ammonia	array
affair	annals	arrest
affect	anneal	arrive
affiliate	annex	arrogant
affinity	annihilate	assail
affirm	annotate	assassin
affix	announce	assay
afflict	annoy	assemble

assent	associate	attention
assert	assort	attest
assess	assume	attire
asset	assure	attitude
assiduous	attach	attract
assign	attack	attribute
assimilate	attain	attrition
assist	attend	attune

3. WORDS BEGINNING WITH THE PREFIXES co-, col-, com-, con-, cor-:

co-operate	command	communicate
co-ordinate	commemorate	communism
collaborate	commence	commute
collapse	commend	connect
collateral	commensurable	connive
collation	comment	connote
colleague	commerce	connubial
collect	commiserate	correct
college	commissary	correlate
collegiate	commission	correspond
collide	commit	corroborate
collision	committee	corrode
collocation	commodious	corrosive
colloquial	commodity	corrugated
collusion	common	corrupt

4. NOTE CAREFULLY THE FOLLOWING WORDS IN WHICH THE s OF THE PREFIX dis- IS NOT REPEATED:

disable	disannul	disarray
disabuse	disappear	disassemble
disaffected	disappoint	disassociate
disagree	disapprove	disaster
disallow	disarm	disavow

5. IN THE FOLLOWING WORDS BEGINNING WITH THE PREFIX dis-, THE ROOT BEGINS WITH s, AND THE s IS THEREFORE DOUBLED IN THE SPELLING:

dissatisfy	dissemble	dissension
dissect	disseminate	dissent

dissertation	dissimulate	dissolve
disservice	dissipate	dissonance
dissever	dissociate	dissuade
dissidence	dissoluble	dissuasion
dissimilar	dissolute	dissyllable

6. WORDS BEGINNING WITH e PRECEDING A SINGLE CONSONANT:

eclectic	emancipate	episcopal
eclipse	emendation	episode
economics	emerald	epistle
edible	emerge	epitaph
edify	emetic	epitome
edition	emigrate	epoch
editorial	eminent	eradicate
educate	emissary	erase
egotism	emotion	erect
egregious	emulate	erode
elaborate	enable	erosion
electric	enact	erotic
elegant	enema	erupt
elegy	enemy	etiquette
element	energy	evade
elevate	enervate	evaluate
eligible	enormous	evangelist
eliminate	enounce	evaporate
elocution	enumerate	evasion
eloquence	enunciate	event
elucidate	epicure	evict
emaciate	epidemic	evident
emanate	epigram	evolution

7. IN THE FOLLOWING LIST, OBSERVE THAT EACH OF THE PREFIXES
   OR INITIAL SYLLABLES, ec-, ef-, el-, er-, es-, ENDS WITH THE
   SAME CONSONANT WITH WHICH THE ROOT TO WHICH IT IS
   ATTACHED BEGINS, AND THAT THE CONSONANT IS THEREFORE
   DOUBLED:

eccentric	effect	effervesce
ecclesiastic	effectually	effete
efface	effeminate	efficacy

efficient	effusion	erratic
effigy	ellipse	erroneous
effloresce	elliptical	error
effluence	ennoble	essay
effort	errand	essence
effulgent	errant	essential

8. WORDS BEGINNING WITH in- FOLLOWED BY A VOWEL:

inability	inaugurate	inexpiable
inaccessible	inauspicious	inexplicable
inaccurate	inebriate	inexpressible
inactive	ineffable	inextinguishable
inadequate	ineffaceable	inextricable
inadmissible	ineffectual	inimical
inadvertence	inefficient	inimitable
inadvisable	inelegant	iniquity
inalienable	ineligible	initial
inalterable	inequality	initiate
inane	ineradicable	inoculate
inanimate	inertia	inoffensive
inanition	inestimable	inoperable
inapplicable	inevitable	inopportune
inappropriate	inexact	inordinate
inaptitude	inexhaustible	inorganic
inarticulate	inexorable	inundate
inattentive	inexpensive	inure
inaudible	inexperience	inutile

9. IN THE FOLLOWING WORDS THE PREFIX in- PRECEDES A ROOT WHICH BEGINS WITH n, AND THE n IS THEREFORE DOUBLED:

innate	innocuous	innuendo
innervate	innominate	innumerable
innocence	innovate	innutritious

RULE. The same principle applies to the following words, in which the last letter of the prefix and the first letter of the root are the same, hence the spellings: interrogate, interregnum, interrupt, misshapen, misspell, misspend, misstate, misstep, pre-eminent, pre-empt, pre-existence, re-enlist, re-engage, re-enter, etc.

SPECIAL RULES AND CAUTIONS WITH REGARD TO SUFFIXES

1. (a) Words of one syllable ending in a single consonant which follows a single vowel double the final consonant before a suffix beginning with a vowel:

clan, clannish; fit, fitted; fun, funny; sad, sadden; sit, sitting; tap, tapped.

(b) The final consonant is *not* doubled before a suffix beginning with a consonant:

fit, fitful; sad, sadness.

2. Words ending in two or more consonants usually remain unchanged when a suffix is added:

call, called; cold, coldness; cost, costing; revolt, revolting.

3. (a) Words of more than one syllable, ending in a single consonant preceded by a single vowel, if accented on the last syllable usually double the final consonant before a suffix beginning with a vowel:

commit, committing; excel, excelled; occur, occurrence; regret, regrettable, regretted, regretting.

EXCEPTIONS: chagrin, chagrined; transfer, transferable, transference.

(b) When, in adding a suffix, the accent is shifted to a preceding syllable, the foregoing rule does *not* apply:

combat, combatant, combative; infer, inference.

EXCEPTION: excel, excellence, excellent.

(c) The final consonant is *not* doubled before a suffix beginning with a consonant:

regret, regretful; unfit, unfitness.

4. Words of more than one syllable, ending in a single consonant preceded by a single vowel, if *not* accented on the last syllable, usually

do *not* double the final consonant before a suffix beginning with a vowel:

> benefit, benefited, benefiting; bigot, bigoted; despot, despotic; kidnap, kidnaped, kidnaper, kidnaping; quarrel, quarreled, quarreling; redden, reddened; rivet, riveted; worship, worshiper, worshiping.

EXCEPTIONS: Certain words which have two syllables almost equally accented do not follow this rule:

> dewlap, dewlapped; handicap, handicapped, handicapping; humbug, humbugged; outfit, outfitter; sandbag, sandbagged.

5. Words ending in a consonant preceded by two vowels do not double the final consonant before a suffix beginning with a vowel:

> boor, boorish; meet, meeting; repeat, repeatable; shout, shouted; counterfeit, counterfeiter.

6. Words ending in silent e usually drop the e before a suffix beginning with a vowel:

> live, living; love, lovable; note, noted; ague, aguish; stone, stony; compare, comparable; inflate, inflated, inflating; refute, refutation; abridge, abridging.

EXCEPTIONS: To retain the proper sound of the consonant, and to avoid confusing the eye, words ending in ce and ge, and a few other words, do not drop the silent e before a suffix beginning with certain vowels, as in the following cases:

> courage, courageous; peace, peaceable; notice, noticeable; mile, mileage; hoe, hoeing; shoe, shoeing; dye, dyeing; singe, singeing; tinge, tingeing. (The word mortgagor is an exception to this general exception.)

RULE. Words ending in ee and oo add suffixes without change:

> see, seeing; oversee, overseer; flee, fleeing; glee, gleeful; woo, wooed, wooing.

7. Words ending in silent e preceded by one or more consonants usually retain the e before a suffix beginning with a consonant:

> late, lateness; peace, peaceful; shame, shameless; taste, tasteless; vague, vaguely (here gu is equivalent to g); vile, vilely; revenge, revengeful.

EXCEPTIONS: argue, argument; true, truly; due, duly.

NOTE. In American usage, the final e is usually dropped before the suffix -ment when it is preceded by dg:

abridge, abridgment; acknowledge, acknowledgment; judge, judgment; lodge, lodgment.

8. (a) Final y following one or more consonants changes to i before the addition of letters other than i:

beauty, beautiful; busy, business; justify, justified, justifies; pretty, prettily; fly, flier. EXCEPTION: busyness (the state of being busy).

(b) When the addition begins with i, the y remains unchanged:

fly, flying; busy, busying.

(c) A verb ending in y preceded by a consonant forms its present third person singular by dropping the y and adding ies; and its past third person singular by dropping the y and adding ied:

cry, cries, cried; defy, defies, defied; supply, supplies, supplied.

9. Some verbs which end in ie change ie to y before the termination ing:

die, dying; lie, lying; vie, vying; tie, tying (or tieing).

10. Words ending in c add k before an additional syllable beginning with e, i, or y:

bivouac, bivouacked; frolic, frolicking; panic, panicky; picnic, picnicking; mimic, mimicked; traffic, trafficking.

11. Words ending in l do not drop the l before the addition of ly:

comical, comically; cool, coolly; evil, evilly; local, locally; poetical, poetically.

12. Words ending in n do not drop the n before adding the suffix ness:

clean, cleanness; even, evenness; green, greenness.

13. Combinations with **ful.** The second l of the word **full** is dropped when the word is used as a suffix:

beautiful, cupful, resourceful, successful, thoughtful.

IMPORTANT WORDS FREQUENTLY MISSPELLED, GROUPED ACCORDING TO ENDING

1. WORDS ENDING IN -able

abominable
acceptable
adjustable
admirable
adorable
advisable
agreeable
allowable
amenable
applicable
available
avoidable
bearable
believable
blamable
breakable
changeable
charitable
comfortable
commendable
comparable
conceivable
culpable
debatable
dependable
describable
desirable
despicable
detachable
detestable

eatable
endurable
excitable
excusable
explicable
fashionable
favorable
forgettable
forgivable
formidable
habitable
hospitable
imaginable
impassable
improbable
incurable
indefinable
indispensable
ineffable
inestimable
inevitable
inexorable
inextricable
inflammable
innumerable
inscrutable
inseparable
insufferable
insupportable
interminable

intolerable
inviolable
irrefragable
justifiable
laudable
laughable
liable
likable
lovable
manageable
marriageable
movable
noticeable
objectionable
palatable
peaceable
perishable
portable
potable
practicable
preferable
presentable
presumable
profitable
punishable
questionable
receivable
recognizable
reconcilable
redeemable

regrettable	tenable	unmistakable
remediable	tillable	unspeakable
serviceable	traceable	unthinkable
sizable	tractable	unutterable
sociable	transferable	usable
suitable	treasonable	valuable
surmountable	unbeatable	vulnerable
syllable	unconquerable	wearable
teachable	unconscionable	workable

2. WORDS ENDING IN -ible

accessible	edible	negligible
admissible	eligible	ostensible
audible	exhaustible	perceptible
collapsible	expressible	perfectible
combustible	extensible	permissible
compatible	fallible	plausible
contemptible	feasible	possible
convertible	flexible	reducible
credible	forcible	reprehensible
deducible	horrible	responsible
deductible	incorrigible	sensible
defensible	indelible	susceptible
destructible	intelligible	tangible
digestible	invincible	terrible
discernible	irresistible	transmissible
divisible	legible	visible

3. WORDS ENDING IN -ance

abeyance	annoyance	elegance
abundance	appearance	endurance
acceptance	arrogance	exuberance
accordance	assurance	grievance
acquaintance	balance	guidance
admittance	brilliance	instance
allegiance	connivance	insurance
alliance	contrivance	irrelevance
allowance	defiance	maintenance
ambulance	distance	nuisance

obeisance	reliance	significance
observance	remembrance	substance
perseverance	remittance	sustenance
predominance	repentance	temperance
radiance	resistance	tolerance
relevance	resonance	vengeance

4. WORDS ENDING IN -ence

absence	dependence	obedience
abhorrence	difference	occurrence
abstinence	diffidence	patience
adherence	dissidence	precedence
audience	eminence	preference
beneficence	essence	presence
cadence	evidence	prevalence
circumference	excellence	prudence
coherence	existence	recurrence
coincidence	impertinence	reference
competence	impudence	reminiscence
concurrence	incidence	residence
conference	indolence	resilience
confidence	inference	reticence
conscience	influence	reverence
consistence	incandescence	sentence
convenience	innocence	silence
correspondence	insistence	subsistence
credence	interference	transference
deference	magnificence	violence

5. WORDS ENDING IN -ar

altar	collar	jugular
angular	consular	liar
beggar	corpuscular	lobar
binocular	dollar	lunar
burglar	familiar	molar
calendar	grammar	molecular
caterpillar	hangar	muscular
cellar	insular	nebular
circular	jocular	nectar

ocular
oracular
particular
peculiar
peninsular
pillar
polar
poplar
popular

rectangular
regular
scholar
secular
similar
singular
solar
spectacular
stellar

sugar
tabular
tubercular
tubular
vehicular
vernacular
vicar
vinegar
vulgar

6. Words ending in -er

adviser
alter
announcer
banister
barrister
believer
boarder
border
boulder
caterer
colander
cylinder
condenser
debater
defender

developer
diameter
disaster
eager
examiner
haberdasher
idolater
juggler
laborer
lavender
lecturer
manufacturer
messenger
miner
minister

minster
murder
observer
parishioner
partner
passenger
plotter
poster
premier
provider
reciter
soldier
telegrapher
traveler
upholsterer

7. Words ending in -or

administrator
anchor
auditor
author
aviator
bachelor
behavior
benefactor
camphor
cantor
captor

castor
censor
chancellor
collector
commentator
competitor
compressor
conqueror
contributor
councilor
counselor

creator
creditor
debtor
demeanor
dictator
director
distributor
editor
educator
elevator
equator

escalator
executor
factor
furor
gladiator
governor
guarantor
harbor
humor
impostor
incinerator
indicator
inferior
inquisitor
inspector
instigator
insulator
inventor
investigator

investor
janitor
legislator
licensor
lubricator
manipulator
manor
minor
mortgagor
motor
narrator
neighbor
odor
orator
pallor
pastor
precentor
predecessor
prior

protector
radiator
reflector
sailor
sculptor
sector
senator
separator
solicitor
suitor
superior
supervisor
surveyor
survivor
tenor
traitor
ventilator
visitor
warrior

8. WORDS ENDING IN -eous

courageous
courteous
cretaceous
erroneous
extraneous
gaseous
gorgeous

herbaceous
heterogeneous
hideous
homogeneous
igneous
instantaneous
miscellaneous

nauseous
outrageous
plenteous
righteous
simultaneous
spontaneous
umbrageous

9. WORDS ENDING IN -ious

abstemious
ambitious
anxious
atrocious
audacious
auspicious
ceremonious
conscientious
conscious

contagious
copious
curious
delicious
delirious
disputatious
dubious
efficacious
egregious

envious
facetious
fastidious
ferocious
fictitious
fractious
furious
glorious
gracious

illustrious
infectious
ingenious
injurious
judicious
lascivious
loquacious
luscious
luxurious
malicious
mysterious
noxious
obnoxious

obvious
odious
officious
ostentatious
pernicious
precarious
precious
pretentious
pugnacious
rapacious
religious
sacrilegious
salacious

spacious
specious
spurious
supercilious
superstitious
suspicious
tenacious
various
vicarious
vicious
victorious
vivacious
voracious

10. WORDS ENDING IN **-ous**

amorous
analogous
anomalous
anonymous
blasphemous
boisterous
callous
carnivorous
circuitous
covetous
credulous
desirous
dexterous
disastrous
fabulous
famous
garrulous
generous

gratuitous
grievous
hazardous
heinous
jealous
ludicrous
luminous
marvelous
miraculous
mischievous
momentous
monotonous
monstrous
mountainous
omnivorous
poisonous
preposterous
ravenous

ridiculous
rigorous
scrupulous
solicitous
stupendous
sulphurous
synonymous
traitorous
treacherous
tremendous
tremulous
valorous
venomous
vigorous
villainous
vinous
viscous
wondrous

11. WORDS ENDING IN **-uous**

ambiguous
arduous
assiduous
conspicuous
contemptuous

contiguous
fatuous
impetuous
incestuous
incongruous

ingenuous
innocuous
perspicuous
presumptuous
promiscuous

sinuous	sumptuous	tumultuous
spirituous	tempestuous	unctuous
strenuous	tenuous	vacuous
superfluous	tortuous	virtuous

12. Words ending in -ise

advertise	devise	incise
advise	disguise	manuprise
apprise	emprise	merchandise
arise	enfranchise	premise
chastise	enterprise	reprise
circumcise	excise	revise
comprise	exercise	rise
compromise	exorcise	supervise
demise	franchise	surmise
despise	improvise	surprise

13. Words ending in -ize

aggrandize	criticize	humanize
agonize	crystallize	immortalize
analyze	demoralize	italicize
anatomize	deputize	jeopardize
anglicize	dogmatize	legalize
apologize	economize	liberalize
apostrophize	emphasize	localize
apprize	energize	magnetize
authorize	epitomize	manumize
bacterize	equalize	memorialize
baptize	eulogize	mercerize
brutalize	evangelize	mesmerize
canonize	extemporize	metamorphize
catechize	familiarize	methodize
catholicize	fertilize	minimize
cauterize	fossilize	modernize
centralize	fraternize	monopolize
characterize	galvanize	moralize
Christianize	generalize	nationalize
civilize	gormandize	naturalize
classicize	harmonize	neutralize
colonize	hellenize	organize

ostracize
oxidize
parenthesize
particularize
pasteurize
patronize
philosophize
plagiarize
polarize
professionalize
protestantize
pulverize
realize
recognize

reorganize
revolutionize
satirize
scandalize
scrutinize
signalize
solemnize
soliloquize
specialize
spiritualize
standardize
stigmatize
subsidize
summarize

syllogize
symbolize
sympathize
tantalize
temporize
tranquilize
tyrannize
utilize
vaporize
visualize
vitalize
vocalize
vulcanize
vulgarize

14. Words ending in -sion

abrasion
adhesion
admission
allusion
apprehension
aspersion
circumcision
cohesion
collision
collusion
commission
comprehension
concussion
condescension
confession
confusion
contusion
conversion
convulsion
corrosion
decision
declension
dimension
discussion

dispersion
dissension
dissuasion
diversion
division
effusion
elision
elusion
emission
emulsion
envision
erosion
evasion
excursion
expulsion
extension
fusion
illusion
immersion
incision
inclusion
incursion
invasion
inversion

mission
occasion
omission
percussion
permission
persuasion
perversion
precision
preclusion
pretension
profusion
propulsion
provision
remission
reversion
revision
suasion
submersion
submission
suffusion
suspension
tension
version
vision

15. Words ending in -tion

ablution
abortion
accusation
action
affection
apposition
assertion
assimilation
association
attention
attribution
attrition
collation
collection
combination
combustion
commotion
compensation
compilation
completion
compunction
conception
condition
confirmation
conservation
constitution
construction
contention
contortion
contraption
contravention
contrition
convention
conversation
conviction
creation
cultivation
defection
degradation

deletion
deliberation
depredation
deprivation
derivation
description
desertion
destitution
detection
detention
differentiation
digestion
dilapidation
dilation
dilution
dispensation
dissolution
distention
distinction
distortion
distraction
elation
emigration
emotion
evacuation
evaluation
eviction
exhibition
expectation
extinction
faction
fascination
fiction
fraction
friction
function
ignition
immigration
inclination

infection
infiltration
inflation
inhibition
initiation
insertion
inspection
inspiration
instigation
institution
intention
intervention
junction
location
lotion
mention
motivation
narration
negation
negotiation
nomination
notation
notion
nutrition
oblation
obligation
opposition
palliation
perfection
perforation
perspiration
pollution
precaution
premonition
preparation
preservation
prevention
promotion
proportion

proposition	repletion	selection
ration	reputation	separation
recreation	resolution	situation
reforestation	restitution	solution
registration	resurrection	unction
relaxation	retention	vacation
reparation	rotation	valuation
repatriation	salvation	vegetation
repetition	sedition	vindication

PLURALS

1. The plural of most nouns is formed by adding s to the singular:

   hat, hats; acrobat, acrobats; banana, bananas.

2. Nouns of which the singular ends in s, **ch, x,** or **z** usually add **es** to form the plural:

   mass, masses; patch, patches; tax, taxes; buzz, buzzes.

3. Nouns ending in **y** preceded by a consonant form the plural by changing **y** to **i** and adding **es:**

   fly, flies; city, cities; community, communities.

4. Nouns ending in **y** preceded by a vowel form the plural by adding **s:**

   chimney, chimneys; foray, forays; money, moneys.

5. Nouns ending in **o** preceded by a vowel add **s** to form the plural:

   folio, folios; cameo, cameos; radio, radios; rodeo, rodeos.

6. Some nouns ending in **o** preceded by a consonant add **es** to form the plural, as in the case of the following commonly used words:

buffaloes	embargoes
calicoes	frescoes (or **frescos**)
cargoes	heroes
dominoes (the game)	jingoes
echoes	mosquitoes

mottoes (or mottos)	tomatoes
mulattoes	tornadoes
Negroes	torpedoes
potatoes	volcanoes

Others, including most musical terms which end in **o**, add **s** to form the plural:

banjos	mementos (or mementoes)
bolos	octavos
cantos	pianos
contraltos	quartos
dynamos	silos
Eskimos	solos
gigolos	sopranos
halos (or haloes)	zeros

7. Most nouns ending in **f** change the **f** to **v** and add **es** to form the plural:

half, halves; scarf, scarves (or scarfs); self, selves; sheaf, sheaves; thief, thieves; wolf, wolves.

EXCEPTIONS:

beliefs, chiefs, dwarfs, griefs, handkerchiefs, hoofs, mischiefs, roofs, staffs.

8. Proper names usually add **s** to form the plural, unless they end in **ch, s, x,** or **z,** in which case they add **es:**

the Kellys, the six Marys, the Finleys, the Harrises, the Foxes, the Heinzes.

9. Letters, figures, symbols, and words *used as such* form their plurals by adding the apostrophe and **s** (**'s**):

three m's; two 2's; if's and and's.

10. Certain commonly used words of foreign origin retain their foreign plural forms. The following is a list of some of the more important of these words, with their plurals:

agendum—agenda	analysis—analyses
alumna—alumnae	axis—axes
alumnus—alumni	bacterium—bacteria

basis—bases
chassis—chassis
crisis—crises
datum—data
erratum—errata
focus—foci
locus—loci
hypothesis—hypotheses

larva—larvae
parenthesis—parentheses
phenomenon—phenomena
radius—radii
stratum—strata
tableau—tableaux
thesis—theses

Some words of foreign origin may either retain their foreign plurals or form their plurals by adding s or es:

apparatus — apparatus or apparatuses
appendix — appendices or appendixes
bureau — bureaus or bureaux
cherub — cherubim or cherubs
criterion — criteria or criterions
formula — formulae or formulas
genus — genera or genuses
index — indices or indexes
memorandum — memorandums or memoranda
seraph — seraphim or seraphs

11. The plural of a compound noun is usually formed by adding s to the principal word of the combination:

fathers-in-law; hangers-on; passers-by; by-standers; solicitors general; attorneys general (or attorney generals); major generals; Knights Templar (in Freemasonry; otherwise Knights Templars).

Note. Sometimes both parts of the compound word take the plural form:

manservant, menservants; woman-servant, women-servants.

SPECIAL RULES AND CAUTIONS WITH REGARD TO PLURALS

1. Certain nouns retain the Old English plural ending en:

brother — brethren or brothers; child — children; man — men; woman — women; ox — oxen.

2. Some nouns have a plural form identical with the singular:

bison, deer, grouse, moose, series, sheep, species.

RULE. The plural form of **cannon, shot, shell, fish, fowl,** and some other words is identical with that of the singular when the words are used in a collective sense. The plural form in **s** is used to denote individuals. THUS: *the cannon were mounted; two new cannons; a lake full of fish; two little fishes.*

3. Certain peculiar plural forms should be noted:

louse—lice, mouse—mice, foot—feet, tooth—teeth, goose—geese.

4. Certain nouns have plural forms but are singular in meaning:

news, means, mumps, measles, economics, physics, mathematics, series, species.

NOTE. **Athletics** is usually treated as a plural. **Wages** was formerly considered a singular noun, but is more commonly regarded as a plural at the present time.

5. Words ending in **ful.** Note that the plural is formed by adding **s** to the *end* of the word only:

cupfuls, handfuls, basketfuls, housefuls.

POSSESSIVES

1. The possessive form of the singular ends with **s** preceded by an apostrophe ('s):

boy's, James's, Brahms's symphonies, Dickens's novels, Keats's poems. (The additional **s** in such words as **James's** and **Brahms's** is pronounced as **es**.)

EXCEPTIONS. With certain proper names in which the letter **s** is prominent, the possessive case is denoted by adding only an apostrophe after the name:

Achilles' heel; Euripides' tragedies; Ulysses' wanderings; Moses' laws; in Jesus' name. Note also the expression, **for conscience' sake.**

2. The possessive plural of nouns ending in s or es has an apostrophe after the s:

the boys' skates, the Harrises' house, the sailors' yarns.

3. Nouns which do not have a plural form ending in s or es add an apostrophe and s to form the possessive plural:

children's, men's, alumni's, cherubim's.

4. In such expressions as anyone else, everybody else, the possessive is formed by adding the apostrophe and s to the word else:

anyone else's house, no one else's.

5. When a group of words is used to express a single idea, the possessive form is given only to the last word of the expression:

the mayor of Detroit's plan; the king of England's portrait; King George VI's family; Doubleday, Doran's spring list; the Prince of Wales's title; Alfred the Great's victory; Prince Henry the Navigator's scheme; my brother-in-law's car.

6. The possessive of pronouns is written without the apostrophe:

hers, his, yours, theirs, ours, its.

COMPOUND WORDS

Compound words and expressions fall into three groups: those written as separate words (book review), those written with a hyphen (book-learned), and those written as one word (bookkeeper). It is impossible to make a simple set of rules governing the spelling of compound words because the practice of writers and dictionaries is not consistent or settled, and because those compounds which are most commonly written in any one way cannot be identified by any single or certain sign. Careful attention to the practice of good writers and frequent consultation of a good dictionary are the only sure methods of avoiding errors in the spelling of compound words. The following rules and cautions will be helpful:

1. The tendency at present is to *avoid* the use of the hyphen in forming compounds, and, where confusion is not likely to result, to write the expression as one word. This is particularly true of compound words of frequent use:

> antiseptic, bipartisan, demigod, extraordinary, midshipman, nonconformist, overrun, prearrange, semiannual, supernatural, tricolor.

2. Use the hyphen in writing such compound forms as the following:

> father-in-law, great-grandson, great-great-grandmother.

3. Hyphenate two or more words which are combined into one descriptive expression *preceding* a noun:

> all-out warfare, long-awaited reform, so-called reformer, up-to-date ideas, matter-of-fact attitude, cast-iron rules, six-cylinder engine, three-by-five cards, three-mile zone, narrow-minded critics, secondhand books, holier-than-thou manner.

NOTE. When such combinations as the foregoing *follow* the noun they should not be connected with hyphens:

> his ideas were up to date; the reform was long awaited.

4. The hyphen is not used with adverbs:

> a fairly played game, a sharply worded retort, a well run race.

5. Compound words of recent coinage, or coined for special purposes, and most compound expressions not yet in general use, are written with a hyphen:

> anti-Nipponese, European-process cocoa, nutrition-minded, priority-control board, poet-composer.

A LIST OF COMPOUND WORDS WRITTEN WITH
A HYPHEN

The following list contains specimens of almost every kind of compound word which employs the hyphen:

ante-bellum	birth-rate	brand-new
anti-Semitism	boarding-house	brother-in-law

brother-officer
business-like
by-product
child-study
coal-black
copy-book
cross-examine
dog-tired
eight-tenths
ex-Senator
extra-dangerous
fellow-citizen
fellow-man
football-player
grain-dealer
half-baked
half-dozen
half-truth
hocus-pocus
home-made
kick-off
knife-edge
know-nothing
let-up

mail-box
man-of-war
measuring-rod
mid-year
near-mahogany
non-Catholic
old-fashioned
one-hundredth
over-anxious
over-study
pan-German
pay-off
pay-roll
pocket-knife
post-Biblical
post-tidal
pre-existence
printing-house
profit-sharing
property-owner
quarter-mile
self-made
self-respect
semi-independent

sense-perception
shop-soiled
show-window
stand-by
story-teller
stumbling-block
sub-basement
super-righteous
ten-cent (piece)
ten-strike
title-page
tongue-tied
twenty-fifth
twenty-five
ultra-ambitious
un-American
under-exposed
walking-stick
wave-length
well-being
well-doer
vice-president
woman-like
working-man

A LIST OF COMPOUND WORDS WRITTEN WITHOUT A HYPHEN

The following list contains specimens of frequently used compound words which are written as one word:

airplane
airship
airtight
already
although
altogether
always
antechamber
anticlimax

anybody
anyhow
anyone
anything
baseball
basketball
battleship
bedroom
beeswax

beforehand
biennial
bimonthly
birthday
blackmail
blueprint
bookkeeper
bookmaker
boyhood

bygones
candlepower
cardboard
childlike
classmate
copyright
craftsman
crowbar
daylight
dooryard
downfall
downright
downstairs
dressmaker
everybody
everyone
everything
everywhere
extraordinary
extraterritorial
fellowship
fireside
flashlight
football
footlights
fourfold
gatekeeper
godfather
godsend
grandfather
greyhound
gunpowder
handbook
handiwork
handwriting
headquarters
heartbeat
herein
hereinafter
heretofore
herewith

herself
himself
homelike
horsepower
hothouse
householder
however
inasmuch
indoors
infrared
interstate
intramural
itself
ladylike
landowner
lawgiver
lawsuit
letterhead
lifesaver
lifetime
lighthouse
linesman
lockout
locksmith
lookout
manhole
metalwork
midnight
moonlight
moreover
motorman
musicianship
myself
nevertheless
newborn
newsboy
newspaper
nobody
nonaggression
nonbelligerent
noncombatant

noncommissioned
nonentity
nonessential
nonresident
nonsense
northeast
notwithstanding
nowadays
offshore
offside
oneself
ourselves
outdo
outdoors
outgoing
outset
outside
overflow
overwork
playfellow
playwright
postgraduate
posthumous
postmaster
prehistoric
proofreader
railroad
riverside
roundabout
salesman
schoolgirl
schoolroom
selfsame
semicentennial
sheepskin
shipbuilding
shirtwaist
shoemaker
sidewalk
somebody
somehow

someone	timekeeper	whatever
something	together	whenever
sometime	trademark	wherein
somewhere	tradesman	wherever
spendthrift	tricycle	wherewithal
staircase	typewrite	whichever
steamboat	ultramarine	whomever
stockholder	undemocratic	whomsoever
subcellar	undergraduate	whosesoever
superhuman	underground	whosoever
tableware	upright	windfall
taxicab	upstairs	windpipe
taxpayer	upstart	withstand
themselves	warlike	woodwork
thereabouts	watercolor	workaday
thereafter	watershed	workday
threadbare	weekday	workman

SPECIAL RULES AND CAUTIONS REGARDING THE USE OF THE HYPHEN

The use of the hyphen in dividing whole units in compound words and expressions has been illustrated in the foregoing section. The following rules and cautions apply to the employment of the hyphen within single words:

1. A hyphen should be used to separate a prefix from the root of a word when the eye or the brain of the reader might be deceived by the appearance of the word if written solidly. Thus:

co-warden (to avoid the division coward-en)
co-worker (to avoid the division cow-orker)
re-cover (to cover again) as distinguished from recover (to win back)
re-creation (creating anew) as distinguished from recreation (refreshment)
re-formation (shaping anew) as distinguished from reformation (act of reforming).

This rule applies particularly to words in which the last letter of a prefix is the same as the first letter of a root:

anti-imperialistic, co-operation, co-ordinate, re-enter.

Note. Certain words of this kind are frequently written thus:

coöperation, coördinate, reënter.

2. Be careful *not* to divide at the end of a line a word of one syllable, no matter how long the word may be. If there is not sufficient space to include the whole word on the line, carry it over to the next line. The following are examples of words of one syllable which may, therefore, not be divided by a hyphen at the end of a line:

length, passed, streamed, stretched, straight, through.

3. Be careful not to separate a syllable of one or two letters from the rest of a word by dividing the word between two lines. If there is not sufficient space at the end of a line to include the whole of such words as the following, carry over the whole word to the next line:

able, any, duty, evil, forces, idly, July, obey.

4. Aid the reader's eye and brain in dividing words with a hyphen, and be careful not to mislead him into misconstruing or mispronouncing a single syllable which is separated from the rest of the word. Notice in the sample words that follow the proper method of separating syllables with respect to the position and combination of consonants:

bat-ter, com-pre-hen-sion, com-pres-sion, con-trol, cyl-in-der, dis-patch-ing, func-tion, fur-ni-ture, gam-ble, man-a-ger, man-nish, pho-tog-ra-pher, phy-si-cian, pro-nounced, sil-ver, sit-u-a-tion, straight-ened, suf-fer, tak-ing.

Caution. Remember that each of the endings, **-cian, -sion, -tion,** is a separate syllable, pronounced **shun,** and should never be divided.

A LIST OF WORDS FREQUENTLY MISSPELLED, SHOWING CORRECT SPELLING

The following is a list of words very commonly misspelled. In every case only the correct spelling is given. As you read over each word, notice what vowel is used in an unaccented syllable; whether a consonant is single or doubled; and whether there are letters which are not pronounced. In cases where two or more words are so similar in spelling that they might be confused, a brief definition is given in parentheses after each.

abdomen
abdominal
absorb
absurd
academy
academic
accentual
accept (to receive)
   except (*prep.*, omitting; *verb*,
     to omit)
access (admittance)
   excess (greater amount)
accessory
accidentally
accommodate
accompanying
accomplish
accoutrements
accumulate
accurately
accustomed
acetic (of vinegar)
   ascetic (abstinent)
acoustics
acquitted
acre
acreage
across

acumen
adaptation (adjustment)
   adoption (taking by choice)
additionally
address
adjacent
adjust
adoption (*see* adaptation)
adversary
advice (*noun*)
advise (*verb*)
affect (*verb*, to influence)
   effect (*verb*, to accomplish;
     noun, result produced)
aggravated
aghast
aisle (passageway)
   isle (island)
alabaster
albumen
alias
alimentary (pertaining to nutrition)
   elementary (pertaining to elements)
all (the whole of)
   awl (instrument for piercing holes)

alleviate

alley (narrow passage)
 ally (associate)

allotted

allude (to refer)
 elude (to escape)

allusion (reference)
 elusion (act of eluding)
 illusion (deceptive appearance)

ally (see alley)

already

altar (of a church)

alter (to change)

altogether

amateur

amount

amphitheater (or amphitheatre)

analysis

analytic

analyze

ancestral

angel (spiritual being)

angle (space between two meeting lines)

aniline

annual (yearly)
 annular (ring-shaped)

annuity

annular (see annual)

anointed

anonymity

antiquary

anxiety

apartment

apiece

apology

apparent

appreciate

apprise (to inform)

apprize (to appraise)

appropriate

aquatic

arbitrament

arbitrary

arctic

arguing

argument

arise

arising

aristocrat

arithmetic

around

arouse

arraign (to accuse)

arrange (to put in order)

arrangement

arranging

arrival

arriving

article

artisan

artistically

ascend

ascent (rising)
 assent (agreement)

ascetic (see acetic)

assassin

assent (see ascent)

associate

athletics

atrocity

attack

attacked

attar

auger (tool for boring holes)

augur (noun, one who predicts; verb, to predict)

auxiliary

avoirdupois

awkward

baccalaureate

bachelor

bare (uncovered)
 bear (to carry)
bared
barely
baring (uncovering)
 barring (excluding)
 bearing (carrying)
barred (excluded)
beggar
believe
benefited
benefiting
berth (sleeping-place)
 birth (being born)
besiege
bestial
biased
bifocal
bigoted
birth (*see* berth)
bivouac
bivouacked
boarder (one who boards)
border (boundary)
born (brought into existence)
borne (carried)
boundary
bourgeois
breadth (width)
breath (*noun*)
breathe (*verb*)
breviary
bridal (wedding)
bridle (head-gear of horse)
bruit (to spread rumor)
brute (unthinking)
bulletin
bullion
buoy
buoyant
buoyed

bureau
bureaucracy
burglar
burst
cacophony
cafeteria
caisson
calendar
calibre (*or* caliber)
calumny
camellia
camouflage
canapé (appetizer)
 canopy (covering)
candidate
cannon (artillery)
canon (law, rule)
canopy (*see* canapé)
cantaloupe
canvas (cloth)
canvass (to solicit, examine, *etc.*)
capital (city)
capitol (state house)
carouse
carriage
casserole
casualty
catalogue
cataract
catarrh
category
caucus
cavalry (horse-soldiers)
ceiling
cemetery
censor (to examine)
censure (to criticize)
census
chagrined
champagne
change

changing
chaperon
characteristic
chassis
chauffeur
chimneys
chitterling
chord (combination of tones)
  cord (string, rope)
cigarette
cinch
cinnamon
cite (to refer to)
  sight (vision)
  site (position)
clematis
clerestory
climactic (pertaining to a climax)
climate
climatic (pertaining to the climate)
coarse (unrefined)
  course (progress, direction)
cocoa
coconut
colander
collaborate
colonel
color
column
comically
competent
complement (full quantity)
compliment (polite expression)
complexion
conceive
confidant (one to whom secrets are confided)
confidante (*feminine*)
confident (trustful)

confidentially
confidently
connoisseur
consensus
construe
consul (government official)
  council (group of advisers)
  counsel (advice, *or* an adviser)
consummate
controlling
coolly
coral (hornlike secretion of certain sea animals)
  corral (enclosure for animals)
cord (*see* chord)
corduroy
corollary
corps (group of persons)
  corpse (a dead body)
corral (*see* coral)
correlate
corroborate
costume (dress)
  custom (usage)
council (*see* consul)
  counsel (*see* consul)
councilor (member of a council)
  counselor (an adviser)
counterfeit
course (*see* coarse)
courtesy
curiosity
currant (raisin)
current (*adjective*, circulating; *noun*, stream)
custom (*see* costume)
dahlia
daily
dairy (place for milk)
  diary (daily record)
debris

debut
deceased (dead)
  diseased (afflicted with disease)
deceive
decent (fitting)
  descent (act of descending)
  dissent (disagreement)
defendant
defer
deficit
definite
deity (a god)
  diet (food, or a public assembly)
dependent
descendant
descent (*see* decent)
desiccate
despair
desperate
detached
develop
developed
developing
development
device
dewy
diary (*see* dairy)
die (*verb,* to cease to exist; *noun,*
  1. small cube used in gaming;
  2. tool)
  dye (color)
diet (*see* deity)
different
dilapidated
dilemma
dined (took dinner)
dinned (made a loud noise)
diphtheria
disappear
disappoint
disastrous

discipline
disciplinary
discriminate
diseased (*see* deceased)
dishabille
dishevel
disparage
dispensary
dissatisfied
dissent (*see* decent)
dissipate
divide
divine
docile
dormitories
dote
dual (double)
duel (combat between two)
duly
duress
dwarfs
dye (*see* die)
dyeing (coloring)
dying (ceasing to live)
echoes
eclectic
ecstasy
edifice
educate
effect (*see* affect)
eighth
electricity
electoral
eleemosynary
elementary (*see* alimentary)
elicit (to draw out)
  illicit (unlawful)
eliminate
elude (*see* allude)
elusion (*see* allusion)
embark

embarrass
embarrassed
embarrassing
emigrant (one who migrates from a country)
emigrate (to migrate from)
eminent (outstanding)
  immanent (indwelling, inherent)
  imminent (impending, threatening)
emphatically
emulate
enervate
enthusiasm
entirely
envelop (*verb*)
envelope (*noun*)
equipped
evenness
everybody
exaggerate
exalt
exceed
excellent
excerpt
excess (*see* access)
excise
exhaust
exhilarate
expatiate
extirpate
extraordinary
extrovert (*or* extravert)
facilities
fascinate
faze
felon
fiery
finagle
finally

financier
flea (insect)
flee (to run away)
focussing
forebode
forehead
foreign
foresee
forfeit
formally (in a formal manner)
formerly (in time past)
forth (forward)
fourth (4th)
foyer
fracas
frantic
frantically
fraternities
freeze (to harden into ice)
frieze (ornamented band)
frolicsome
fuchsia
fulfill
fulsome
furor (fury)
furore (a "rage")
further
futile
gage (pledge, security)
  gauge (measure)
gaiety (*or* gayety)
gaily (*or* gayly)
galaxy
gambling (gaming for money)
gamboling (frolicking)
gaol (jail)
  goal (destination)
gas
gases
gauge (*see* gage)
genealogy

gerrymander
gesture
gibe
giblets
gnaw
goddess
government
grammar
grandeur
granite
greenery
greenness
gruesome
guarantee
guaranty
harangue
harass
height
helm
herculean
hinder
hippopotamus (*plural,* hippopota-
   muses)
holey (having holes)
holly (tree)
holy (sacred)
   wholly (entirely)
hoof (*plural,* hoofs)
horehound
hues
human
humane
hundred
hyacinth
hygiene
hypocrisy
hypocrite
ice cream
iced tea
idiosyncrasy
illicit (*see* elicit)

illusion (*see* allusion)
imagery
imaginary
immanent (*see* eminent)
immigrant (one who migrates into
   a country)
immigrate (to migrate into)
imminent (*see* eminent)
impetuosity
impromptu
incendiary
incidentally
inflammatory
ingratiate
innuendo
inoculate
instinct
intellectual
intersperse
introvert
inveigh
inveigle
iridescent
iris
irrelevant
isle (*see* aisle)
its (*possessive of* it)
it's (*contraction of* it is)
jeopardy
jest
laboratory
labyrinth
laid (*past tense of* lay)
laity
languor
larynx
later
lateral
latter (*opposed to* former)
lavender
lead (metal)

led (guided)
legitimate
leisure
length
lens
lessen (to make less)
lesson (instruction)
lethargy
liaison
library
lightening (*verb,* "lightening a burden")
lightning (*noun*)
likelihood
likely
lily
linotype
literal (according to the letter; not exaggerated)
littoral (pertaining to the shore)
literature
littoral (*see* literal)
livelihood
liveliness
loath (*adjective,* reluctant)
loathe (*verb,* to regard with disgust)
loathsome
loneliness
loose (*adjective,* not tight)
lose (*verb,* to suffer loss)
lye (strong alkaline solution)
maintain
maintenance
maneuvers
mange
mangy
mantel (shelf)
mantle (garment)
manual
marriage

marshal (*verb,* to gather; *noun,* an official)
martial (military)
material (pertaining to matter)
matériel (supplies, equipment)
mauve
meant
medicinal
medicine
mediocre
mediocrity
melancholy
melon
merchandise
metal (substance)
mettle (spirit, courage)
metallurgist
mettle (*see* metal)
mid-air
millennium
mimic
mimicking
miner (one who mines)
minor (smaller)
minister (one who serves)
minster (church)
moratorium
move
murmur
muscle (bodily organ producing motion)
mussel (bivalve mollusk)
naive
naphtha
naturally
nausea
naval (pertaining to ships)
navel (depression in middle of abdomen)
necessity
negotiate

nickel
nineteen
ninety
ninth
notoriety
nucleus
occurred
occurring
ocher (or ochre) (red or yellow pigment)
okra (vegetable)
oneself
opinionated
opportunity
optimist
orient (verb)
overrun
pageant
paid (past tense of pay)
pamphlet
papoose
parallel
paralleled
paralysis
paralyze
parishioner
parliament
partner
passed (went by)
past (pertaining to a former time)
pastime
patent
pavilion
perceive
perennial
perform
perhaps
permanganate
personal (private)
personnel (body of persons engaged in some service)

pharmaceutical
phosphorus
phraseology
physician
physiology
pigeon
plagiarism
plain (adjective, clear; noun, level area)
plane (adjective, smooth; verb, to make smooth; noun, a tool)
playwright
poignant
pomegranate
pore (verb, to read intently; noun, small opening)
pour (to cause to flow)
portable (capable of being carried)
potable (drinkable)
portion (share)
potion (draft of medicine)
practical
prairie
precede
precinct
prejudice
prepense
pretense
prevalent
primitive
principal (adjective, noun, chief)
principle (noun, rule of action)
privilege
probably
proboscis
procedure
proceed
profit (gain)
prophet (seer)
propaganda
prophecy (noun)

prophesy (*verb*)
prophet (*see* **profit**)
prove
psychiatry
psychology
ptarmigan
pulmotor
pumpkin
putrefy
qualify
quantity
quay (*pronounced as* "key")
queue (*pronounced as* "cue")
rain (fall of water)
   reign (rule)
   rein (part of harness)
rap (to strike)
   wrap (to cover up)
rarefied
rarity
really
receipt
receive
recipe
recipient
recluse
recollect
recommend
referred
regretting
reign (*see* **rain**)
rein (*see* **rain**)
relief
relieve
rely
rendezvous
renown
reprimand
requiem
reredos
reservoir

resin
respectfully (with respect)
respectively (as relating to each)
restaurant
rhetoric
rheumatism
rhinoceros
rhyme
rhythm
rime (*another form of* **rhyme**; white frost)
rite (ceremony)
ruffian
sabotage
said (*past tense of* **say**)
sandwich
sapphire
sarsaparilla
satellites
scalpel
scenery
schedule
science
seismograph
seize
selvage
sentiment
separate
serf (land-slave)
   surf (foam of sea)
sergeant
severally (separately)
severely (strictly)
sheriff
shone (did shine)
shown (exhibited)
shriek
siege
sieve
sight (*see* **cite**)
silhouette

sincerity

sinecure

singe (to scorch)

site (*see* cite)

skiing

sociological

solicit

soliloquy

soothe

sophomore

sovereign

spatial

specialty

speech

spontaneity

squab

squabble

staccato

stair (set of steps)

stare (to gaze)

stake (stout stick)

steak (piece of meat)

stare (*see* stair)

stationary (not in motion)

stationery (writing materials)

statistics

statue (sculptured figure)

stature (height)

statute (law)

steak (*see* stake)

steal (*verb*)

steel (form of iron)

steely

stiletto

stimulus

straight (not crooked)

strait (narrow)

strictly

stricture

stupefy

subterranean

subtlety

succeed

succinct

succotash

succumb

suffrage

suit (clothes)

suite (*pronounced* swēt; set of rooms, furniture, etc.)

superintendent

supersede

suppress

surplice (ecclesiastical vestment)

surplus (excess, overplus)

swob

sycophant

syllable

symmetry

symptom

synonym

tamale

tariff

temperament

temperature

tessellated

their (*possessive pronoun*, "their hands")

there (*adverb*, opposed to here)

therefor (for that, for it)

therefore (because of that)

thinness

thorough

thousandths

threw (*verb*)

through (*preposition*, "through the gate")

till

tobacco

tonsillitis

tortoise

track (path, course)

tract (pamphlet; area, region)
trafficking
tragedy
traipse
tranquil
tranquillity
treasurer
turkeys
tyrannically
tyranny
ukulele
umbrella
undoubtedly
until
unwieldy
usually
varieties
vaudeville
ventilate
verbatim
vernacular
vice (wickedness)
 vise (appliance for holding things)
vilify
villain
violoncello
viscount
vise (see vice)

vitamin
wander (to ramble)
 wonder (to marvel)
waive (to give up)
wave (of the sea)
weather (state of atmosphere)
 wether (castrated ram)
 whether (*conjunction;* "whether or not")
weird
whither (*adverb;* "Whither are you going?")
 wither (*verb,* to dry)
wholly (*see* holy)
widgeon
wield
wintry
withal
withhold
wobble
woeful
wonder (*see* wander)
wooed (*past tense of* woo)
wrack
wrap (*see* rap)
yacht
yea
yeoman
yield

PART IV

A Guide to the
Correct Pronunciation and
Spelling of Proper Names

NOTE. In the following lists only the English pronunciation of a foreign name is given if it is more commonly used than the foreign pronunciation. The following abbreviations should be noted: *Am.* (American), *Am. Sp.* (American Spanish), *Br.* (British), *Dut.* (Dutch), *Eng.* (English), *Fr.* (French), *Ger.* (German), *Hun.* (Hungarian), *It.* (Italian), *Pol.* (Polish), *Port.* (Portuguese), *Rus.* (Russian), *Sp.* (Spanish).

I. NAMES OF PERSONS

Aaron (âr'-ŭn)

Aeschylus (ĕs'-kĭ-lŭs *or* ēs'-kĭ-lŭs)

Aesop (ē'-sop)

Agassiz (ăg'-*a*-se)

Agatha (ăg'-*a*-tha)

Aldrich (awl'-drĭch)

Aloysius (ăl″-*o*-ĭs'-ĭ-ŭs *or* ăl″-*o*-ĭsh'-ŭs)

Ampere (*Fr.*, ahN″-pâr')

Amundsen (ah'-mŭn-s*e*n)

Aquinas (*a*-kwī'-n*a*s)

Archimedes (ahr″-kĭ-mē'-dēz)

Aristides (ăr″-ĭs-tī'-dēz)

Aristophanes (ăr″-ĭs-tŏf'-*a*-nēz)

Attila (ăt'-ĭ-l*a*)

Auchinleck (aw'-kĭn-lĕk)

Bach (*Ger.*, bahк)

Balzac (*Fr.*, băl'-zăk)

Barnard (bahr'-n*a*rd)

Baruch (b*a*-rook')

Basil (băz'-ĭl)

Baudelaire (*Fr.*, bo″-d'lâr')

Bayard (*Fr.* bah″-yahr')

Beatrice (bē'-*a*-trĭs)

Beatty (*Br.*, bē'-tĭ; *Am.*, bā'-tĭ)

Beauchamp (bē'-cham)

Beethoven (bā'-tō-v*e*n)

Benjamin (bĕn'-j*a*-mĭn)

Berenice (bĕr″-*e*-nī'-se)

Bernard (bûr'-nahrd *or* bûr-nahrd')

317

Bertillon (Fr., bĕr″-tē-yôN′)

Besant (bĕz′-ant or be-zănt′)

Boccaccio (It., bok-kaht′-cho)

Bolivar (Eng., bŏl′-ĭ-ver; Sp., bō-
lē′-vahr)

Botticelli (It., bŏt″-te-chĕl′-le)

Brontë (brŏn′-tĭ)

Brougham (brōōm or brōō′-ŭm)

Buccleugh (bŭk-klōō′)

Buchan (bŭk′-an)

Buchanan (bŭ-kăn′-an)

Cabell (kăb′-el)

Cabot (kăb′-ŭt)

Caesar (sē′-zer)

Cagliostro (It., kahl-yôs′-tro)

Calhoun (kăl-hōōn′)

Caligula (ka-lĭg′-yŭ-la)

Cambyses (kăm-bī′-sēz)

Camoëns (kăm′-o-ĕns; Port., de
Camões, dĕ kah-moiNsh′)

Campbell (kăm′-b'l)

Carew (ka-rōō′ or kā′-rĭ)

Carnegie (kahr-nā′-gĭ)

Cato (kā′-tō)

Catullus (ka-tŭl′-ŭs)

Cavell (kăv′-el)

Cecil (Br., sĕs′-il; Am., sē′-sil)

Cedric (sĕd′-rĭk or sē′-drĭk)

Cellini (It., chĕl-lē′-ne)

Cervantes (Sp., thĕr-vahn′-tās;
Eng., sêr-văn′-tēz)

Cézanne (Fr., sā″-zahn′)

Charlemagne (shahr′-le-man)

Charlotte (shahr′-lŏt)

Chateaubriand (Fr., shah″-tō″-brē″-
ahN′)

Chekhov (Rus., chĕ′-kof)

Cheops (kē′-ŏps)

Cherubini (It., kā″-rōō-bē′-ne)

Chiang Kai-shek (Chinese, jahng′
kī′-shĕk′)

Chopin (Fr., sho-păN′)

Clough (klŭf)

Cockburn (kō′-bûrn)

Comte (Fr., kôNt)

Condé (Fr., kôN″-dā′)

Condorcet (Fr., kôN″-dôr″-sĕ′)

Corneille (Fr., kôr″-nā′-y′)

Corot (Fr., ko-rō′)

Correggio (It., kor-rĕd′-jo)

Cortes or Cortez (Sp., kôr-tâs′;
Eng., kôr′-tĕz)

Cowper (kōō′-per)

Crabbe (krăb)

Curie (kü″-rē′)

Cyril (sĭr′-ĭl)

Cyrus (sī′-rŭs)

Daguerre (da″-gâr′)

Dalhousie (dăl-hōō′-zĭ)

Dana (dā′-na)

Dante Alighieri (Eng., dăn′-tĕ;
It., dahn′-tā ah″-lē-gyâ′-rē)

Darius (da-rī′-ŭs)

Daudet (Fr., do″-dĕ′)

Deborah (dĕb′-o-ra)

Debussy (dê-bü″-sē′)

Decatur (de-kā′-têr)

de Gaulle (dĕ gōl′)

Deland (de-lănd′)

Delilah (de-lī′-la)

Democritus (de-mŏk′-rĭ-tŭs)

Demosthenes (de-mŏs′-the-nēz)

Descartes (Fr., dā″-kahrt′)

De Valera (dā va-lā′-rah)

Diderot (Fr., dēd″-rō′)

Diogenes (dī-ŏj′-e-nēz)

Disraeli (dĭz-rā′-lĭ)

Dolores (do-lō′-rĕs)

Domitian (do-mĭsh′-ĭ-an or
do-mĭsh′-an)

Donizetti (It., dō″-ne-dzĕt′-te)

Donne (dŭn)

Doré (*Fr.*, do″-rā′)
Dostoevski (*Rus.*, dôs″-tŏ-yĕf′-sk*e*)
Doughty (dō′-tĭ)
Dumas (*Fr.*, dü″-mah′)
Duse (*It.*, dōo′-zā)
Eisenhower (ī-zen-how″-er)
Elihu (ĕl′-ĭ-hyū *or* e-lī′-hyū)
Elisha (e-lī′-sh*a*)
Elzevir (ĕl′-ze-vêr)
Emile (*Fr.*, *a*-mēl′)
Enoch (ē′-nŭk)
Epictetus (ĕp″-ĭk-tē′-tŭs)
Epicurus (ĕp″-*i*-kyū′-rŭs)
Esau (ē′-saw)
Euclid (yū′-klĭd)
Euripides (yu-rĭp′-*i*-dēz)
Ezekiel (e-zē′-kĭ-el *or* e-zēk′-yel)
Fahrenheit (făr′-en-hīt *or* fahr′-en-hīt)
Farquhar (fahr′-kwêr *or* fahr′-kêr)
Faure (*Fr.*, fōr)
Fenelon (*Fr.*, fā″-n′-lôɴ′)
Fernandez (*Sp.*, fĕr-năn′-dĕ*th*)
Ferrara (*It.*, fĕr-rah′-rah)
Flaubert (*Fr.*, flō″-bâr′)
Foch (*Fr.*, fosh)
Freneau (frē-nō′)
Freud (*Ger.*, froid)
Froebel (*Ger.*, frû′-bel)
Froissart (*Fr.*, frwah″-sahr′)
Froude (frōod)
Galileo (găl″-*i*-lē′-ō)
Gamaliel (g*a*-mā′-l*i*-ĕl)
Garand (găr′-*a*nd)
Garibaldi (*It.*, gah″-re-bahl′-de)
Gascoigne (găs-koin′)
Gauss (*Ger.*, gows)
Gauguin (*Fr.*, go″-găɴ′)
Gautier (*Fr.*, go″-tyā′)
Genevieve (jĕn″-*i*-vēv′)
Genghis Khan (jĕn′-gĭz kahn′)

Geoffrey (jĕf′-rĭ)
Gerry (gĕr′-ĭ)
Giles (jīlz)
Giorgione (*It.*, jor-jō′-nā)
Giotto (*It.*, jŏt′-tō)
Giovanni (*It.*, jō-vahn′-n*e*)
Giraud (zhē-rō′)
Gluck (*Ger.*, glŏok)
Godiva (go-dī′-v*a*)
Goethals (gō′-*th*alz)
Goethe (*Ger.*, gû′-t*a*)
Gough (gŏf)
Gounod (*Fr.*, gōo″-nō′)
Guise (*Fr.*, gēz)
Guitry (*Fr.*, gē-trē′)
Guizot (*Fr.*, gē″-zō′)
Haile Selassie (hī′-l*e* s*e*-lăs′-*e*)
Hakluyt (hăk′-lōot)
Haydn (*Ger.*, hī′-d′n)
Hegel (*Ger.*, hā′-gel)
Heine (*Ger.*, hī′-n*e*)
Helena (hĕl′-e-n*a*)
Herod (hĕr′-ŭd)
Herodotus (he-rŏd′-*o*-tŭs)
Hesiod (hē′-sĭ-od)
Hippocrates (hĭ-pŏk′-r*a*-tēz)
Hohenzollern (*Ger.*, hō″-*e*n-tsŏl′-êrn)
Holinshed (hŏl′-ĭnz-hĕd)
Horthy (*Hun.*, hôr′-t*e*)
Houghton (hō′-tŭn *or* how′-tŭn)
Houston (hyūs′-tŭn; *in New York City,* hows′-tŭn)
Inge (ĭng)
Isaiah (ī-zā′-y*a* *or* ī-zī′-*a*)
Iscariot (ĭs-kăr′-*i*-ot)
Ivan (*Rus.*, ē′-vahn; *Eng.*, ī′-v*a*n)
Japheth (jā′-fĕ*th*)
Jean (*Fr.*, zhahn; *Eng.*, jēn)
Joab (jō′-ăb)
Joan (jōn)

Job (jŏb)
Joffre (*Fr.*, zhŏfr')
Joralemon (jo-răl'-*i*-mŭn)
José (*Sp.*, hō-sā')
Joubert (*Fr.*, zhōo"-bâr')
Jowett (jō'-ĕt *or* jow'-ĕt)
Juarez (*Am. Sp.*, hwah'-rās)
Jules (*Fr.*, zhül)
Kamehameha (*Hawaiian*, kah-mā"-ha-mā'-ha)
Kearney (kahr'-nĭ)
Keats (kēts)
Keble (kē'-b'l)
Kemal Atatürk (kĕ-mahl' ah"-tah-türk')
Kosciusko (kŏs"-ĭ-ŭs'-kō)
Kossuth (*Hun.*, kŭsh'-ōot; *Eng.*, kŏs'-ōō*th*)
Kotzebue (*Ger.*, kot'-se-bōo)
Krupp (*Ger.*, krōop)
Kublai Khan (kōo'-blī kahn')
La Bruyère (*Fr.*, lah brü"-yâr')
La Rochefoucauld (*Fr.*, lah rôsh"-fōo-kō')
La Vallière (*Fr.*, lah vahl"-yâr')
Leah (lē'-*a*)
Leibnitz (*Ger.*, Leibniz; līp'-nĭts)
Leigh (lē)
Leighton (lā'-tŭn)
Lenin (lĕn'-ĭn)
Leonard (lĕn'-êrd)
Le Sage (*Fr.*, lê sahzh')
Levi (lē'-vī)
Lewes (lyū'-*es*)
Litvinoff (lĭt-vē'-nof)
Llewellyn (lōo-ĕl'-ĭn)
Louis Philippe (*Fr.*, lōo"-ē' fē"-lēp')
Lyly (lĭl'-ĭ)
Macaulay (m*a*-kaw'-lĭ)

Machiavelli (*It.*, mah"-kyah-vĕl'-*le*; *Eng.*, măk"-ĭ-*a*-vĕl'-ĭ)
Maeterlinck (mā'-ter-lĭngk)
Magellan (m*a*-jĕl'-*an*)
Mahomet (m*a*-hŏm'-ĕt)
Malthus (măl'-*thŭs*)
Marat (*Fr.*, mah"-rah')
Marquette (*Fr.*, mahr"-kĕt')
Marryat (măr'-*i*-*a*t)
Massenet (*Fr.*, mahs'-nĕ')
Mather (măth'-*e*r)
Maupassant (*Fr.*, mo"-pah"-sahɴ')
Mayer (mī'-*e*r)
Medici (*It.*, mĕd'-*e*-chē)
Melanchthon (m*i*-lăngk'-th*an*)
Melchisedec (mĕl"-kĭz'-*i*-dĕk)
Mercator (mûr-kā'-t*e*r)
Mercier (*Fr.*, mĕr"-syā')
Meyer (mī'-*e*r)
Meynell (mĕn'-*e*l)
Michael (mī'-k*e*l)
Michelangelo (mī'-k*e*l-ăn'-j*e*-lō)
Michelet (*Fr.*, mēsh"-lĕ')
Millais (mĭ-lā')
Millet (*Fr.*, mē"-lĕ')
Milne (mĭln)
Miltiades (mĭl-tī'-*a*-dēz)
Mirabeau (*Fr.*, mē"-r*a*-bō')
Mithridates (mĭ*th*"-rĭ-dā'-tēz)
Molière (*Fr.*, mo"-lyâr')
Montessori (mŏn"-tĕs-sō'-r*e*)
Montgomery (mŭnt-gŭm'-*e*r-ĭ)
Mozart (*Ger.*, mō'-tsahrt; *Eng.*, mō"-zahrt')
Murillo (*Sp.*, mōo-rēl'-yō)
Musset (*Fr.*, mü"-sĕ')
Naaman (nā'-*a*-m*a*n)
Naomi (nā-ō'-mĭ)
Napier (nā'-pyer)
Nazimova (*Rus.*, nah-zē'-mo-vaɴ)

Nehemiah (nē"-hi-mī'-*a*)
Ney (nā)
Nietzsche (nē'-ch*e*)
Nigel (nī'-jĕl)
Nobel (*Swedish*, no-bĕl')
Ovid (ŏv'-ĭd)
Paderewski (*Pol.*, pah"-dĕ-rĕf'-sk*e*)
Paganini (*It.*, pah"-gah-nē'-n*e*)
Pasteur (*Fr.*, pahs"-tûr')
Pater (pā'-ter)
Pavlova (*Rus.*, pahv'-lō-vah)
Pepys (pēps *or* pĕps *or* pĕp'-ĭs)
Pericles (pĕr'-ĭ-klēz)
Pestalozzi (*It.*, pĕs"-ta-lŏt'-s*e*)
Pétain (*Fr.*, pā"-tăn')
Petrarch (pē'-trahrk)
Pierre (*Fr.*, pyâr)
Pilate (pī'-lat)
Pinchot (pĭn'-shō)
Pinero (pĭ-nĕr'-ō)
Pizarro (*Sp.*, pē-*th*ahr'-ō; *Eng.*, pĭ-zahr'-rō)
Plantagenet (plăn-tăj'-*e*-nĕt)
Plautus (plaw'-tŭs)
Pliny (plĭn'-ĭ)
Plotinus (plo-tī'-nŭs)
Poincaré (*Fr.*, pwăn"-kah"-rā')
Polk (pōk)
Polycrates (po-lĭk'-ra-tēz)
Ponce de León (*Sp.*, pōn'-*th*ā dā lā-ōn')
Porsena (pôr'-se-na)
Potiphar (pŏt'-ĭ-fahr)
Poussin (*Fr.*, pōō"-săn')
Powhatan (pow"-ha-tăn')
Powys (pō'-ĭs)
Praxiteles (prăks-ĭt'-*e*-lēz)
Protagoras (pro-tăg'-*o*-ra*s*)
Proust (*Fr.*, prōōst)
Ptolemy (tŏl'-*e*-mĭ)
Puccini (*It.*, pōōt-chē'-n*e*)

Pulitzer (pyū'-lĭt-ser)
Pythagoras (pĭ-*th*ăg'-*o*-ra*s*)
Quiller-Couch (kwĭl'-er-kōōch')
Rachmaninov (*Rus.*, rahk-mah'-ne-nof)
Racine (*Fr.*, ra-sēn')
Rameses (răm'-*e*-sēz)
Raphael (răf'-*a*-el)
Réaumur (*Fr.*, rā"-o-mür')
Renan (*Fr.*, ra-nahn')
René (*Fr.*, ra-nā')
Reuter (*Ger.*, roi'-ter)
Richelieu (*Fr.*, rē'-shê"-lyû"; *Eng.*, rēsh'-ê-lōō")
Robespierre (*Fr.*, ro"-bĕs"-pyâr')
Rochambeau (*Fr.*, ro"-shahn"-bō')
Rodin (*Fr.*, ro"-dăn')
Rodriguez (*Sp.*, ro-drē'-gās)
Roebling (rōb'-lĭng)
Roentgen (*Ger.*, rûnt'-gĕn)
Rommel (rŭm'-*e*l)
Roosevelt (rō'-za-vĕlt)
Rossetti (ro-sĕt'-*e*)
Rossini (ros-sē'-n*e*)
Rousseau (rōō"-sō')
Ruyter (*Dut.*, roi'-ter *or* rī'-ter)
Saint-Saëns (*Fr.*, săn"-sahns')
Salome (sa-lō'-m*e*)
Sappho (săf'-ō)
Savonarola (săv"-o-na-rō'-la)
Schley (slī)
Schopenhauer (*Ger.*, shō'-pĕn-how"-er)
Schuyler (skī'-ler)
Scipio (sĭp'-ĭ-ō)
Seneca (sĕn'-*e*-ka)
Seymour (sē'-mōr)
Sheila (shē'-la)
Shostakovitch (shŏs-ta-kō'-vĭch)
Sigismund (sĭj'-ĭs-mŭnd)
Sobieski (*Pol.*, so-byĕs'-kĭ)

Socrates (sŏk'-ra-tēz)
Sophia (so-fī'-a)
Sophocles (sŏf'-o-klēz)
Sothern (sŭᴛʜ'-ern)
Sousa (soō'-sa)
Spee (spā)
Stalin (stah'-lēn)
Steuben (Ger., shtoi'-bĕn; Eng.,
    styū'-ben)
Strauss (Ger., shtrows;
    Eng., strows)
Synge (sĭng)
Tacitus (tăs'-i-tŭs)
Tamerlane (tăm"-er-lān')
Tecumseh (te-kŭm'-se)
Tertullian (tûr-tŭl'-i-an)
Tetrazzini (It., tĕ"-traht-sē'-ne)
Thales (thā'-lēz)
Themistocles (the-mĭs'-to-klēz)
Thoreau (thō'-rō)
Thucydides (thyū-sĭd'-ĭ-dēz)
Timoshenko (tĭm-ō-shĕng'-kŏ)
Tirpitz (Ger., tĭr'-pĭts)
Titian (tĭsh'-an)
Torricelli (It., tôr"-re-chĕl'-le)
Trollope (trŏl'-ŭp)
Tchaikovsky (Rus., chī-kôf'-ske)
Tudor (tyū'-der)
Turgenev (Rus., toŏr-gĕn'-yĕf)
Uhland (Ger., oō'-lahnt)
Ursula (ûr'-syū-la)
Vanbrugh (văn'-bru)
Van Dyck (văn dīk')

Van Eyck (văn īk')
Van Gogh (văn gôᴋ)
Van Rensselaer (văn rĕn'-sĭ-ler)
Vasari (It., vah-zah'-re)
Vaughan (vawn)
Vega (Sp., vā'-gah)
Velasquez (Sp., vā-lahs'-kāth)
Villa (Am. Sp., vē'-yah)
Villon (Fr., vē"-yôɴ')
Vinci (It., vĭn'-che)
Wagner (Ger., vahg'-ner;
    Eng., wăg'-ner)
Warwick (wawr'-ĭk)
Watteau (Fr., vah"-tō')
Weber (Ger., vā'-ber;
    Eng., wĕb'-er)
Wilhelmina (wĭl"-hĕl-mē'-na)
Winant (wī'-nant)
Wolcott (woŏl'-kot)
Wolseley (woŏlz'-lĭ)
Wolsey (woŏl'-zĭ)
Wycherley (wĭch'-er-lĭ)
Wyclif (wĭk'-lĭf)
Xantippe (zăn-tĭp'-ĭ)
Xavier (zăv'-ĭ-er or zā'-vĭ-er)
Xenocrates (ze-nŏk'-ra-tēz)
Xenophanes (ze-nŏf'-a-nēz)
Xenophon (zĕn'-o-fŏn)
Xerxes (zûrk'-sēz)
Yeats (yāts)
Yonge (yŭng)
Zoroaster (zō"-ro-ăs'-ter)
Zuloaga (Sp., thoō"-lo-ah'-gah)

II. NAMES OF PLACES

Abukir (ah"-boō-kêr')
Abydos (a-bī'-dŏs)
Addis Ababa (ahd'-ĭs ah'-ba-ba)
Aegean (e-jē'-an)

Aetna or Etna (ĕt'-na)
Afghanistan (ăf-găn'-ĭs-tăn)
Aisne (ān)
Alameda (ăl"-a-mā'-da)

Albuquerque (ăl″-byū-kûr′-ke)
Aleutian *Islands* (a-lyū′-shan)
Amiens (*Fr.*, ah″-myăɴ′;
 Eng., ăm′-ĭ-enz)
Anaconda (ăn″-a-kŏn′-da)
Andes (ăn′-dēz)
Anjou (*Fr.*, ahɴ″-zhōo′;
 Eng., ăn′-jōo)
Ankara (ahng′-ka-ra)
Annapolis (a-năp′-o-lĭs)
Antietam (ăn-tē′-tam)
Antigua (ăn-tē′-gwah *or* ăn-tē′-ga)
Antilles (*Fr.*, ahɴ″-tēl′;
 Eng., ăn-tĭl′-ēz)
Apennines (ăp′-e-nīnz)
Appalachian (ăp″-a-lăch′-ĭ-an *or*
 ăp″-a-lāch′-ĭ-an)
Appomattox (ăp″-o-măt′-ŭks)
Arequipa (ah″-rā-kē′-pah)
Arezzo (ah-rĕt′-so)
Argyll (ahr-gīl′)
Arkansas (*State,* ahr′-kan-saw;
 River, ahr′-kan-saw *or*
 ahr-kăn′-zas)
Armagh (ahr-mah′)
Armentières (ahr″-mahɴ″-tyâr′)
Aroostook (a-rōos′-tŏok)
Assisi (ahs-sē′-ze)
Asuncion (ah-sōon″-syōn′)
Athens (*Greece,* ăth′-ĕnz;
 N.Y., ā′-thĕnz)
Ausable (aw-sā′-b'l)
Avon (ā′-vŭn)
Azores (a-zōrz′)
Azov (ah′-zof)
Baden (bah′-den)
Bahamas (ba-hā′-maz *or*
 ba-hah′-maz)
Bahia (ba-ē′-a)
Baku (bah-kōo′)
Balaklava (băl-a-klah′-va)

Balearic (băl′-e-ăr′-ĭk)
Balkan (bawl′-kan)
Baluchistan (ba-lōo′-chĭ-stahn′
 or ba-lōo′-kĭ-stăn)
Banff (bămf)
Bangor (băng′-gôr)
Barents (bah′-rĕnts)
Barbados (bahr-bā′-dōz)
Barre, *Vt.* (băr′-ĭ)
Bataan (ba-tahn′)
Baton Rouge (băt′-un rōozh″)
Batum (bah-tōom′)
Bayeux (*Fr.*, bah″-yû′;
 Eng., bā-yōo′)
Bayonne (*France,* bah″-yôn″;
 N.J., bā″-yōn′)
Bayreuth (bī″-roit′)
Beirut (bā′-rōot *or* bā-rōot′)
Belize (be-lēz′)
Bengal (bĕn-gawl′)
Benghazi (bĕn-gah′-ze)
Bering (bêr′-ĭng *or* bâr′-ĭng)
Berkeley (*Eng.,* bahrk′-lĭ;
 Am., bûrk′-lĭ)
Berkshire (*England,* bahrk′-shĭr;
 Mass., bûrk′-shĭr)
Berlin (*Germany,* bĕr-lēn′ *or*
 bûr-lĭn′; *U.S.A.,* bûr′-lĭn)
Bermuda (bûr-myū′-da)
Berwick (*Scotland,* bĕr′-ĭk;
 U.S.A., bûr′-wĭk)
Biarritz (byah″-rēts′)
Billerica, *Mass.* (bĭl′-rĭk″-er)
Bizerte (bē″-zĕrt′)
Blenheim (blĕn′-im)
Boeotia (bē-ō′-shĭ-a)
Bogotá (bō″-gō″-tah′)
Boise, *Idaho* (boi′-sĭ)
Bologna (bo-lō′-nyah)
Bonneville *Dam, Ore.* (bŏn″-ĭ-vĭl)
Bosporus (bŏs′-po-rŭs)

Boulogne (*Fr.*, bōō″-lôn'-y'; *Eng.*, bu-loin')

Bowie, *Md.* (bŏŏ'-ĭ)

Bremen (brā'-men)

Breslau (brĕs'-low)

Bretagne (*Fr.*, brĕ-tahn'-y'; *Eng.*, brĭt'-a-nĭ)

Bruges (*Fr.*, brōōzh; *Eng.*, brōō'-jĭz)

Bryn Mawr (brĭn mahr')

Buena Vista (bwā'-nah vēs'-tah)

Buenos Aires (*Am. Sp.*, bwā'-nōs ĭ'-rās; *Eng.*, bō'-nos âr'-ez)

Butte, *Mont.* (byūt)

Cairo (*Egypt,* kī'-rō; *Ill.*, kā'-rō)

Calais (kăl'-ā *or* kăl'-ĭs)

Calgary (kăl'-ga-rĭ)

Calydon (kăl'-ĭ-dŏn)

Campagna (kahm-pahn'-yah)

Canaan (kā'-nan)

Canajoharie (kăn″-a-jo-hăr'-ĭ)

Canandaigua (kăn″-an-dā'-gwa)

Canarsie (ka-nahr'-si)

Cannes (kahn)

Cantigny (kahN-tē″-nyē')

Capernaum (ka-pûr'-nĭ-ŭm)

Cap Gris Nez (kahp grē nā')

Caracas (kah-rah'-kahs)

Caribbean (kăr″-ĭ-bē'-an *or* ka-rĭb'-e-an)

Carolina (kăr″-o-lī'-na)

Carpathian (kahr-pā'-thi-an)

Casablanca (kah″-sah-blăng'-kah)

Ca-ite (kah-vē'-tā)

Cayenne (kī'-ĕn' *or* kā-ĕn')

Cayuga (ka-yōō'-ga)

Celebes (sĕl'-ē-bēz *or* sĕ-lē'-bēz)

Ceylon (se-lŏn')

Chalcedon (kăl'-se-don *or* kăl-sē'-don)

Chaldea (kăl-dē'-a)

Chalons (shah″-lôN')

Chamonix (shah″-mo″-nē')

Chapultepec (chah-pōōl″-tā-pĕk')

Chartres (shahrtr')

Chateau-Thierry (shah″-tō″-tyĕ″-rē')

Chautauqua (sha-taw'-kwa)

Cherbourg (shĕr″-bōŏr')

Chersonese (kûr'-so-nēz)

Cheshire (chĕsh'-er)

Cheyenne (shī-ĕn')

Chicago (shĭ-kaw'-gō *or* shĭ-kah'-gō)

Chichester (chĭch'-ĕs-ter)

Chihuahua (che-wah'-wah)

Chillicothe (chĭl″-i-kŏth'-i)

Chillon (*Fr.*, shē″-yôN'; *Eng.*, shĭl'-on *or* shĭ-lŏn')

Chimborazo (*Am. Sp.*, chēm″-bo-rah'-sō; *Eng.*, chĭm″-bo-rah'-zō)

Chiswick (chĭz'-ĭk)

Chocorua (cho-kôr'-ŏŏ-a)

Cienfuegos (syĕn-fwā'-gōs)

Cincinnati (sĭn-sĭ-năt'-ĭ)

Circassia (sûr-kăsh'-ĭ-a *or* sûr-kăsh'-a)

Cologne (ko-lōn')

Colombia (ko-lŏm'-bē-a)

Colón (ko-lōn')

Colorado (kŏl″-o-rah'-dō *or* kŏl″-o-răd'-ō)

Compiègne (kôN″-pyĕn'-y')

Concepcion (kon-sĕp'-syōn')

Connaught (kŏn'-awt)

Connecticut (ko-nĕt'-ĭ-kŭt)

Copenhagen (kō″-p'n-hā'-gen)

Corregidor (kôr-rā'-gĭ-dôr)

Coventry (kŏv'-en-trĭ *or* kŭv'-en-trĭ)

Cracow (krā'-kō)

Crimea (krī-mē'-a *or* krĭ-mē'-a)

Cristobal (krĭs-tō'-bal)

Croatia (kro-ā'-shǐ-*a* or kro-ā'-sh*a*)

Culebra (kōō-lā'-brah)

Curaçao (*Am. Sp.*, kōō"-rah-sah'-ō; *Eng.*, kyū"-r*a*-sō')

Cuyahoga (kī"-*a*-hō'-g*a*)

Cuzco (kōōs'-kō)

Czechoslovakia (chěk"-*o*-slo-vah'-kǐ-*a*)

Dahomey (dah-hō'-mē)

Dairen (dī'-rěn')

Dakar (d*a*-kahr')

Darien (dā"-rǐ-ěn'; *U.S.A.*, dā'-rǐ-ěn)

Deccan (děk'-*a*n)

Delhi (děl'-ǐ)

Delphi (děl'-fī)

Des Moines (dā moin')

Detroit (de-troit')

Dijon (dē"-zhôn')

Djibouti *or* **Jibuti** (jē"-bōō"-tē')

Dnieper (nē'-p*er*)

Dniester (nē'-st*er*)

Dordogne (dôr"-dōn'-y')

Drogheda (drŏ'-ᴋē"-d*a*)

Dubuque (dŏŏ-byūk')

Duluth (dŏŏ-lōō*th*')

Dulwich (dŭl'-ǐj)

Dumbarton (dŭm-bahr'-t*o*n)

Dumfries (dŭm-frēz')

Dunedin (dŭn-ē'-dǐn)

Dunfermline (dŭn-fěrm'-lǐn)

Dunkirk (*Eng.*, dŭn'-kûrk; *Fr.*, Dunkerque, dûɴ"-kěrk')

Dunsinane (dŭn'-sǐ-nān or dŭn-sǐn'-*a*n)

Duquesne (dŏŏ-kān')

Durazzo (dŏŏ-raht'-sō)

Durham (dûr'-*a*m)

Dusseldorf (düs'-*e*l-dôrf)

Ecuador (ěk'-w*a*-dôr")

Edinburgh (ěd'-ǐn-bŭ-rŭ)

Eire (âr'-*e*)

Eisenach (ī'-zen-ahᴋ)

Elgin (*Scotland*, ěl'-gǐn; *Ill.*, ěl'-jǐn)

Epirus (*e*-pī'-rŭs)

Eritrea (ěr"-ǐ-trā'-*a*)

Escanaba (ěs"-k*a*-naw'-b*a*)

Ethiopia (ē"-*th*ǐ-ō'-pǐ-*a*)

Eupen (oi'-pěn)

Euphrates (yŭ-frā'-tēz)

Euxine (yūk'-sǐn)

Falkland (fawk'-l*a*nd)

Falmouth (fǎl'-m*ŭth*)

Fayal (fī-ahl')

Fujiyama (fōō'-je-yah'-m*a*)

Friesland (frēz'-l*a*nd)

Galápagos (gah-lah'-pah-gōs)

Ganges (gǎn'-jēz)

Gatun (gah-tōōn')

Gaza (gā'-z*a*)

Genoa (jěn'-*o*-*a*)

Gethsemane (gě*th*-sěm'-*a*-n*e*)

Ghent (gěnt)

Gibraltar (jǐ-brawl'-t*er*)

Glasgow (glǎs'-gō or glǎs'-kō)

Gloucester (glŏs'-t*er*)

Guadalajara (gwah"-ᴛʜah-lah-hah'-rah)

Guadalcanal (gwah"-ᴛʜahl-kah-nahl')

Guadeloupe (gwah"-d*e*-lōōp' or gaw"-d*e*-lōōp')

Guam (gwahm)

Guantanamo (gwahn-tah'-nah-mō)

Guatemala (gwah"-t*e*-mah'-lah)

Guayaquil (gwī"-ah-kēl')

Guernsey (gûrn'-zǐ)

Guiana (g*e*-ah'-n*a*)

Guinea (gǐn'-ǐ)

Haifa (hī'-f*a*)

Haiti (hā'-tǐ)

Haverhill (hā'-ver-ĭl)
Havre (*Fr.*, Le Havre, lû ah'-vr';
  Eng., hah'-ver)
Hawaii (hah-wī'-ē)
Hebrides (hĕb'-rĭ-dēz)
Helena, *Mont.* (hĕl'-e-na)
Helsinki (hĕl-zĭn'-kĭ)
Hilo (hē'-lō)
Himalaya (hĭ-mah'-la-ya)
Hoboken (hō'-bō-ken)
Holyoke (hōl'-yōk)
Honolulu (hō'-no-lōō'-lōō)
Houston (hyūs'-tŭn; *in*
  N.Y., hows'-tŭn)
Illinois (ĭl"-ĭ-noi')
Iowa (ī'-o-wa)
Iquique (e-kē'-kā)
Iran (e-rahn')
Iraq (e-rahk')
Istanbul (e-stahn-bōōl')
Jena (yā'-nah)
Joliet (jō'-lĭ-ĕt)
Karelia (ka-rē'-lĭ-a)
Kenya (kē'-nyah)
Keokuk (kē'-o-kŭk)
Kharkov (khar'-kŏf)
Khartum (kahr-tōōm')
Kiev (kē'-yĕf)
Kilauea (kē"-low-ā'-a)
Kissimee (kĭ-sĭm'-i)
Krakatao (krah"-kah-tah'-ō)
Kyoto (kyō'-tō)
La Jolla (la hoi'-a)
La Junta (la hŏŏn'-ta)
La Paz (lah pahs')
Laredo (la-rā'-dō)
Lausanne (lo-zăn')
Leinster (lĕn'-ster *or* lĭn'-ster)
Leipzig (*Ger.*, līp'-tsĭĸ;
  Eng., līp'-sĭk)

Leominster (*England*, lĕm'-ster;
  Mass., lĕm'-in-ster)
Libya (lĭb'-ĭ-a)
Liége (*Fr.*, lyâzh; *Eng.*, le-ĕzh' *or*
  le-āzh')
Lille *or* Lisle (lēl)
Lima (*Peru*, lē'-mah; *Ohio*, lī'-ma)
Limoges (li-mōzh')
Loire (lwahr)
London (lŭn'-dŭn)
Los Angeles (los ăngʼ-gel-ĕs)
Louisville (lōō'-i-vil)
Louvain (lōō"-văɴ')
Luzon (lōō-zŏn')
Macao (ma-kah'-o)
Madras (ma-drahs')
Madrid (ma-drĭd')
Mafeking (măf'-e-kĭng)
Maggiore (mahd-jō'-re)
Mainz (mīnts)
Majorca (ma-jôr'-ka)
Malay (ma-lā' *or* mā'-lā)
Malden (mawl'-den)
Malta (mawl'-ta)
Mamaroneck (ma-măr'-o-nĕk)
Manchukuo (*Eng.*, mahn'-chōō'-
  kwō')
Maracaibo (mah"-rah-kī'-bō *or*
  măr"-a-kī'-bō)
Mareth Line (mah'-rĕth līn)
Marmara *or* Marmora (mahr'-ma-
  ra)
Marquesas (mahr-kā'-sahs)
Marseille *or* Marseilles (*Fr.*,
  mahr"-sĕ'-y'; *Eng.*, mahr-sālz')
Martinique (mahr"-tĭ-nēk')
Massaua (mahs-sah'-wah)
Mauch Chunk (mawk' chungk')
Mauna Loa (mow'-nah lō'-ah)
Mauritius (maw-rĭsh'-ī-ŭs *or*
  maw-rĭsh'-ŭs)

Meaux (mō)

Medina (mā-dē'-nah)

Megara (mĕg'-a-ra)

Mesa Verde (mā'-sah vâr'-dā)

Metuchen, *N.J.* (me-tŭch'-en)

Meuse (*Fr.*, mûz; *Eng.*, mūz)

Miami (mī-ăm'-ĭ)

Michigan (mĭsh'-ĭ-gan)

Milan (mĭ-lăn' *or* mĭl'-an)

Mindanao (mĭn-dah-nah'-ō)

Miquelon (*Fr.*, mē"-k'-lôn'; *Eng.*, mĭk'-ĕ-lŏn)

Missouri (mĭ-zŏŏr'-ĭ *or* mĭ-sŏŏr'-ĭ)

Mobile (*city*, mō-bēl'; *bay and river*, mō'-bēl)

Modena (mô-dā'-nah)

Mojave (mo-hah'-vā)

Moluccas (mo-lŭk'-az)

Monaco (mŏn'-a-kō)

Monastir (mŏn"-as-tĭr')

Monongahela (mo-nŏng"-ga-hē'-la)

Mons (môns)

Montevideo (*Am. Sp.*, mōn"-tā-vē-thā'-ō; *Eng.*, mŏn"-te-vĭd'-e-ō)

Montpelier, *Vt.* (mŏnt-pēl'-yer)

Montpellier, *France* (môn"-pĕl"-yā')

Mont-Saint-Michel (môn"-săn"-mē"-shĕl')

Montserrat (mŏnt"-sĕ-răt')

Moray (mûr'-ĭ)

Moscow (mŏs'-kō)

Mosul (mō-sŏŏl')

Mozambique (mō"-zam-bēk')

Munich (myū'-nĭk)

Murmansk (mŏŏr-mahnsk')

Mysore (mī-sōr')

Mytilene (mĭt"-ĭ-lē'-nē)

Nagasaki (nah"-gah-sah'-kē)

Nahant (na-hănt')

Namur (nah-mür')

Nancy (*Fr.*, nahn"-sē'; *Eng.*, năn'-sĭ)

Nantes (*Fr.*, nahnt; *Eng.*, nănts)

Natal (na-tahl')

Natick (nā'-tĭk)

Nevada (ne-văd'-a *or* ne-vah'-da)

Newfoundland (nyū-fŭnd-lănd' *or* nyū'-fŭnd-lănd")

New Orleans (nyū ôr'-le-anz)

Nicaragua (nĭk"-a-rah'-gwah)

Nice (nēs)

Niger (nī'-jer)

Nigeria (nī-jêr'-ĭ-a)

Nîmes *or* **Nismes** (nēm)

Nineveh (nĭn'-e-vĕ)

Norwich (*England*, nôr'-ĭj *or* nôr'-ĭch; *U.S.A.*, nôr'-wĭch *or* nôr'-ĭch)

Oahu (ō-ah'-hŏŏ)

Oaxaca (wah-hah'-kah)

Oceania (ō"-she-ăn'-ĭ-a *or* ō"-she-ā'-nĭ-a)

Oise (wahz)

Okhotsk (*Rus.*, ō-ĸôtsk'; *Eng.*, ō-kŏtsk')

Oklahoma (ō"-kla-hō'-ma)

Oman (o-mahn')

Oneida (ō-nī'-da)

Onondaga (ŏn"-on-daw'-ga)

Orleans (*Fr.*, ôr"-lā"-ahn'; *Eng.*, ôr-lēnz')

Osceola (ŏs"-ĭ-ō'-la)

Ossining (ŏs'-ĭ-nĭng)

Otaheite (ō"-ta-hē'-te)

Ottawa (ŏt'-a-wa)

Ottumwa (ŏ-tŭm'-wa)

Ouachita (wahsh'-ĭ-taw)

Ouse (ōōz)

Ovid, *N.Y.* (ō'-vĭd)

Papeete (pah"-pā-ā'-tā)

Paraguay (păr'-a-gwā *or* pah"-rah-gwī')

Paramaribo (păr″-*a*-măr′-ĭ-bō)
Passaic (p*a*-sā′-ĭk)
Pass Christian, *Miss.*,
  (păs krĭs-tĭ-ăn′)
Patiala (pŭt-ĭ-ah′-l*a*)
Pavia (pah-vē′-ah)
Peiping (bā′-pĭng′)
Pelée (p*a*-lā′)
Pelion (pē′-lĭ-*o*n)
Penzance (pĕn-zăns′)
Peru (pē-rōō′)
Philippi (fĭ-lĭp′-ī)
Philippine (fĭl′-ĭ-pēn)
Phoenix (fē′-nĭks)
Pisa (*It.*, pē′-sah; *Eng.*, pē′-z*a*)
Poitiers (pwah″-tyā′)
Popocatepetl (p*o*-pō″-kah-tā′-pĕt′l)
Port Said (pōrt sah-ēd′ *or* sād)
Potomac (p*o*-tō′-m*a*k)
Poughkeepsie (p*o*-kĭp′-sĭ)
Prague (prāg)
Prairie du Chien (prā′-rĭ dŏo shēn′)
Presque Isle (prĕsk ēl′)
Provence (pr*o*-vahns′)
Puebla (pwā′-blah)
Pueblo (pwĕb′-lō)
Puerto Rico (pwĕr′-tō rē′-kō)
Punjab (pŭn-jahb′)
Quebec (*Fr.*, kā″-bĕk′; *Eng.*, kwĭ-
  bĕk′)
Queretaro (kā-rā′-tah-rō)
Quito (kē′-tō)
Rabaul (rah′-bowl)
Racine (r*a*-sēn′)
Rainier (rā-nêr′)
Raleigh (raw′-lĭ)
Reading (rĕd′-ĭng)
Reims *or* Rheims (*Fr.*, răns; *Eng.*,
  rēmz)
Rensselaer (rĕn′-sĭ-l*e*r)
Reykjavik (rā′-ky*a*-vēk″)

Riga (rē′-g*a*)
Rio de Janeiro (rē′-ō dā zh*a*-nā′-rō)
Rio Grande (rē′-ō grahn′-dā)
Ripon (rĭp′-ŏn)
Riviera (r*e*-vyâ′-rah)
Rouen (rōō″-ahn′)
Ruhr (rōōr)
Saar (zahr)
Saguenay (săg″-*a*-nā′)
Saigon (sī-gŏn′)
Saint Cloud (*France,* săn″ klōō′;
  Minn., sänt klowd′)
St. Croix (sent kroi′)
Saint-Cyr (săn″-sēr′)
St. Denis (săn″ d*a*″-nē′)
Saint-Germain (săn″-zhĕr″-măn′)
St. Helena (sent h*e*-lē′-n*a*)
St. Louis, *Mo.* (sänt lōō′-ĭs)
Saint-Mihiel (săn″-mē″-yĕl′)
St. Pierre (săn″ pyâr′)
Saint-Quentin (săn″-kahn″-tăn′)
Sakhalin (sah″-kah″-lēn′)
Salisbury (sawlz′-ber-ĭ)
Salonika (sah″-lo-nē′-kah)
Samarkand (săm″-*e*r-kănd′)
Samoa (sah-mō′-ah)
Sandusky (s*a*n-dŭs′-kĭ)
San Jacinto *River, Tex.* (săn j*a*-sĭn′-
  tō)
San Joaquin *River, Calif.* (săn wah-
  kēn′)
San José (săn h*o*-sā′ *or* ho-zā′)
San Juan (săn hwahn′)
San Luis Potosi (sahn lōo-ēs′ pō″-
  to-sē′)
Santa Fe (săn′-t*a* fā′)
Santiago (sahn″-t*e*-ah′-gō)
Sarajevo (sah″-rah-yĕ′-vo)
Sault Sainte Marie (sōō′ sänt m*a*-
  rē′)
Schenectady (sk*e*-nĕk′-t*a*-dĭ)

Schoharie   (sko-hăr′-ĭ)

Schuylkill   (skōōl′-kĭl)

Scilly *Isles*   (sĭl′-ĭ)

Scituate   (sĭch′-ŏŏ-āt)

Seattle   (se-ăt′-′l)

Sevastopol   (*Rus.*,   syĕ″-vahs-tô′-pol-y′;   *Eng.*,   se-văs′-to-pol;   *formerly*   se-băs′-to-pol)

Sèvres   (sâ′-vr′)

Shamokin, *Pa.*   (sha-mō′-kin)

Shenandoah   (shĕn″-an-dō′-a)

Shiloh   (shī′-lō)

Sinai   (sī-nī *or* sī′-nā-ī)

Skaneateles, *N.Y.*   (*locally,* skĭn″-ĭ-ăt′-lĕs)

Slough, *England*   (slow)

Smolensk   (smŏ-lyĕnsk′)

Sodom   (sŏd′-om)

Sofia   (*Eng.*, so-fē′-a)

Soissons   (swah″-sôN′)

Somaliland   (so-mah′-lĭ-lănd)

Somme   (sôm)

Spokane   (spo-kăn′)

Spuyten Duyvil   (spī′-ten dī′-v′l)

Staten *Island*   (stăt′-en)

Steuben   (*U.S.A.*, styū′-ben)

Stavanger   (stah′-vahn-gûr)

Suez   (sōō-ĕz′ *or* sōō′-ĕz)

Sumatra   (sŏŏ-mah′-tra)

Surabaya   (sōō″-rah-bah′-yah)

Susquehanna   (sŭs″-kwe-hăn′-a)

Suwanee   (sŏŏ-wah′-nĭ *or* swah-nē′)

Swaziland   (swah′-zi-lănd″)

Syracuse   (sĭr′-a-kyūs *or* sĭr″-a-kyūs′)

Tahiti   (tah-hē′-tĭ *or* tah′-ē-tĭ)

Tampico   (tahm-pē′-kō)

Tanganyika   (tăn″-găn-yē′-ka)

Tangier   (tăn-jêr′)

Tegucigalpa   (tā-gōō″-se-gahl′-pah)

Teheran   (tĕ-h′rahn′ *or* tē-e-rahn′)

Tehuantepec   (tā-wahn″-tā-pĕk′)

Terre Haute, *Ind.*   (tĕr′-i hōt′)

Tetuan   (tĕ-twahn′)

Thailand   (tah′-i-lănd)

Thames   (*England,*   tĕmz;   *Conn.*,   thămz *or* tāmz)

Thermopylae   (*th*ûr-mŏp′-ĭ-lē)

Tibet   (tĭ-bĕt′ *or* tĭb′-ĕt)

Ticonderoga   (tī-kŏn″-der-ō′-ga)

Tientsin   (tĭn′-tsĭn′)

Tijuana *or* Tía Juana   (te-hwah′-nah *or* tē′-a hwah′-nah)

Tintagel   (tĭn-tăj′-el)

Tirol *or* Tyrol   (*Ger.*, te-rōl′;   *Eng.*,   tĭr′-ŏl)

Titicaca   (tē″-te-kah′-kah *or* tĭt″-ĭ-kah′-kah)

Torquay   (tôr-kē′)

Toulouse   (tōō″-lōōz′)

Tours   (tōōr)

Trafalgar   (*Sp.*, trăf″-al-gahr′;   *Eng.*,   tra-făl′-ger)

Transvaal   (trăns-vawl′)

Trieste   (*It.*, tre-ĕs′-tā;   *Eng.*, trĭ-ĕst′)

Tucson   (tōō-sŏn′)

Tunisia   (tyū-nĭsh′-ĭ-a;   -nĭsh′-a)

Turin   (tyū′-rĭn *or* tyū-rĭn′)

Tutuila   (tōō″-tōō-ē′-lah)

Ukraine   (yū′-krān *or* yū-krān′)

Uruguay   (*Am. Sp.*, ōō″-rōō-gwī′;   *Eng.*, yū′-rōō-gwā)

Valparaiso   (*Chile,* vahl″-pah-rah-ē′-sō;   *Eng.*, văl″-pa-rī′-sō;   *Indiana,* văl″-pa-rā′-zō)

Venezuela   (*Am. Sp.*, vā″-nā-swā′-lah;   *Eng.*, vĕn″-e-zwē′-la)

Veracruz, *form.* Vera Cruz   (*Am. Sp.*, vā′-rah-krōōs′;   *Eng.*, vĕr′-a-krōōz′)

Cape Verde   (kāp vûrd′)

Vermont   (vûr-mŏnt′)

Versailles (*Fr.*, vĕr″-sah′-y′; *Eng.*, vûr-sälz′)

Vichy (*Fr.*, vē″-shē′; *Eng.*, vĭsh′-ĭ)

Vincennes (*Fr.*, văN″-sĕn′; *Eng.*, vĭn-sĕnz′)

Vladivostok (vlah″-dĭ-vŏs-tôk′)

Vosges (vōzh)

Waban, *Mass.* (waw′-ban)

Wabash (waw′-băsh)

Waikiki (wah′-ē-kē″-kē)

Wasatch (waw′-săch *or* waw-săch′)

Waukegan (waw-kē′-gan)

Waukesha (waw′-ki-shaw)

Weimar (vī′-mahr)

Wellesley (wĕlz′-lĭ)

Westminster (wĕst′-mĭn″-ster)

Wichita (wĭch′-ĭ-taw)

Wilkes-Barre (wĭlks′-băr-ĭ)

Willamette (wĭl-ăm′-et)

Woburn, *Mass.* (wō′-bŭrn)

Woolwich (wŏŏl′-ĭj *or* wŏŏl′-ĭch)

Worcester (wŏŏs′-ter)

Wyoming (wī-ō′-mĭng *or* wī′-o-mĭng)

Xenia (zē′-ni-a)

Yokohama (yō″-kō-hah′-mah)

Yosemite (yo-sĕm′-i-te)

Ypres (ē′-pr′)

Ypsilanti (ĭp″-sĭ-lăn′-tĭ)

Yucatan (yōō″-kah-tahn′)

Zuyder Zee (*Dut.*, zoi′-der zā; *Eng.*, zī′-der zē)

III. NAMES FROM LITERATURE

NOTE. Names of authors are included in the list headed "Names of Persons."

Adonais (ăd″-o-nā′-ĭs)

Adonis (a-dō′-nĭs)

Aeneas (ē-nē′-as)

Aeneid (ē-nē′-ĭd)

Agonistes (ăg″-o-nĭs′-tēz)

Ali Baba (ah′-lē bah′-bah)

(L′) Allegro (lah-lā′-grō)

Amphitrite (ăm″-fĭ-trī′-tē)

Amphitryon (ăm-fĭt′-rĭ-ŏn)

Anacreon (a-năk′-re-ŏn)

Ananias (ăn″-a-nī′-as)

Androcles (ăn′-dro-klēz)

Andromache (ăn-drŏm′-a-kē)

Andromeda (ăn-drŏm′-e-da)

Antigone (ăn-tĭg′-o-ne)

Aphrodite (ăf″-ro-dī′-te)

Apis (ā′-pĭs)

Apocalypse (a-pŏk′-a-lĭps)

Apocrypha (a-pŏk′-rĭ-fa)

Areopagitica (ăr″-e-ŏp″-a-jĭt′-ĭ-ka *or* ăr″-e-ŏp″-a-gĭt′-ĭ-ka)

Ares (ā′-rēz)

Armageddon (ahr″-ma-gĕd′-dŏn)

(D′) Artagnan (dahr″-tah″-nyahN′)

Astarte (ăs-tahr′-tē)

Astyanax (ăs-tī′-a-năks)

Ate (ā′-tē)

Atreus (ā′-trōōs *or* ā′-trĭ-ŭs)

Atrides (a-trī′-dēz)

Atropos (ăt′-ro-pŏs)

Aucassin (ō″-kah″-săN′)

Augean (aw-jē′-an)

Baal (bā′-al)

Bacchus (băk′-ŭs)

Balaam (bā′-lam)

Banquo (băng′-kwō *or* băng′-kō)

Bassanio (bahs-sahn'-ĭ-ō)

Beëlzebub (be-ĕl'-ze-bŭb)

Belial (bē'-lĭ-al or bĕl'-yal)

Bellerophon (bĕ-lĕr'-o-fŏn)

Beowulf (bā'-ō-wŏolf)

Bergerac (bâr"-zha"-rahk')

Blefuscu (ble-fŭs'-kyū)

Boaz or Booz (bō'-ăz or bō'-ŏz)

Bohème (bō"-ĕm')

Boötes (bō-ō'-tēz)

Boreas (bō'-rĭ-as)

Briareus (brī-ā'-rĭ-ŭs)

Briseis (brī-sē'-ĭs)

Brobdingnag (brŏb'-dĭng-năg)

Bucephalus (byū-sĕf'-a-lŭs)

Busiris (byū-sī'-rĭs)

Calliope (ka-lī'-o-pē)

Calypso (ka-lĭp'-sō)

Candide (kahɴ"-dēd')

Cassiopeia (kăs"-i-o-pē'-ya)

Cenci (chĕn'-chē)

Centaur (sĕn'-tawr)

Cerberus (sûr'-be-rŭs)

Ceres (sē'-rēz)

Charon (kā'-rŏn)

Charybdis (ka-rĭb'-dĭs)

Chloe (klō'-e)

Cid (sĭd)

Cimmerian (si-mē'-rĭ-an)

Circe (sûr'-sē)

Cleopatra (klē"-o-pā'-tra)

Clio (klī'-ō)

Coriolanus (kō"-rĭ-ō-lā'-nŭs)

Corydon (kôr'-i-dŏn)

Cressida (krĕs'-i-da)

Cyclades (sĭk'-la-dēz)

Cyclops (sī'-klŏps)

Cymbeline (sĭm'-be-lēn or sĭm'-be-līn)

Cynthia (sĭn'-thĭ-a)

Cytherea (sĭth"-e-rē'-a)

Daedalus (dĕd'-a-lŭs or dē'-da-lŭs)

Damocles (dăm'-o-klēz)

Danaë (dā'-na-ē)

Daphne (dăf'-nĭ)

Decameron (de-kăm'-er-ŏn)

Delilah (de-lī'-lah)

Demeter (de-mē'-ter)

Desdemona (dĕs-de-mō'-na)

Deucalion (dyū-kā'-lĭ-on)

Deuteronomy (dyū"-ter-ŏn'-o-mĭ)

Dido (dī'-dō)

Diomedes (dī"-o-mē'-dēz)

Dionysius (dī"-o-nĭsh'-i-ŭs)

Dionysos (dī"-o-nī'-sos)

Dives (dī'-vēz)

Don Quixote (Sp., dōn kē-hō'-tā; Eng., dŏn kwĭks'-ōt)

Dunsinane (dŭn'-si-nān or dŭn-sĭn'-an)

Ecclesiastes (ĕ-klē"-zĭ-ăs'-tēz)

Egeus (e-jē'-ŭs)

Elia (ē'-li-a)

Elizabethan (e-lĭz"-a-bē'-than or e-lĭz"-a-bĕth'-an)

Elysian (e-lĭz'-i-an or e-lĭzh'-an)

Elysium (e-lĭz'-i-um or e-lĭzh'-i-um)

Endymion (ĕn-dĭm'-i-ŏn)

Erato (ĕr'-a-tō)

Erebus (ĕr'-e-bŭs)

Eros (ē'-rŏs)

Euphues (yōo'-fyū-ēz)

Euryanthe (yōo"-rĭ-ăn'-the)

Eurydice (yōo-rĭd'-i-sē)

Euterpe (yōo-tûr'-pe)

Eyre (âr)

Falstaff (fawl'-stăf)

Faust (fowst)

Fidelio (fē-dā'-lĭ-ō)

Forsyth (fôr-sīth')

Galatea (găl"-a-tē'-a)

Ganymede (găn'-ĭ-mēd)
Gawain (gah'-wān)
Giaour (jowr)
Gil Blas (zhēl' blahs')
Gioconda (jō-kŏn'-da)
Goliath (gō-lī'-*ath*)
Golgotha (gŏl'-go-*tha*)
Götterdämmerung (gût"-er-děm'-
 er-ŏong)
Gyges (gī'-jēz)
Hades (hā'-dēz)
Haidée (hā"-dē' *or* hī"-dē')
Haroun-al-Raschid (hah-rōōn'
 -ahl-rah'-shēd)
Hecate (hěk'-*a*-tē *or* hěk'-at)
Hecuba (hěk'-yŏŏ-b*a*)
Helicon (hěl'-*i*-kŏn)
Heptameron (hěp-tăm'-*er*-ŏn)
Heptateuch (hěp'-t*a*-tyŭk")
Heraclea (hěr"-*a*-klē'-*a*)
Heracles (hěr'-*a*-klēz)
Hercules (hûr'-kyŭ-lēz)
Hiawatha (hī"-*a*-wah'-*tha or*
 hē"-*a*-wah'-*tha*)
Hippolytus (hĭ-pŏl'-*i*-tŭs)
Homeric (ho-měr'-ĭk)
Hyperion (hī-pē'-ri-ŏn)
Iago (ē-ah'-gō)
Icarus (ĭk'-*a*-rŭs)
Ichabod (ĭk'-*a*-bŏd)
Igraine (ĭ-grān')
Io (ī'-ō)
Ionic (ī-ŏn'-ĭk)
Iphigenia (ĭf"-*i*-ji-nī'-*a*)
Iseult (ĭ-sōōlt')
Isis (ī'-sĭs)
Isolde (ĭ-sōld')
Ixion (ĭks-ī'-ŏn)
Jaques (jāks *or* jā'-kwēz)
Jehoshaphat (je-hŏsh'-*a*-făt)

Jekyll (jē'-k*i*l)
Juliet (jōōl'-yet *or* jōō'-li-et)
Khayyám (kī"-yahm')
Koran (kō-rahn' *or* kō'-ran)
Lachesis (lăk'-*i*-sĭs)
Laertes (lā-ûr'-tēz)
Laocoön (lā-ŏk'-o-ŏn)
Laodamia (lā-ŏd"-*a*-mī'-*a*)
Laputa (l*a*-pyū'-t*a*)
Lares (lā'-rēz)
Les Misérables (lā mē"-zā"-
 rah'-b'l)
Lethe (lē'-thē)
Leviticus (le-vĭt'-*i*-kŭs)
Loki (lō'-kĭ)
Lorelei (lō'-r*a*-lī)
Lothario (lō-thā'-ri-ō)
Lycidas (lĭs'-*i*-dăs)
Mahabharata (mah"-hah-bah'-
 r*a*-t*a*)
Medea (me-dē'-*a*)
Medusa (me-dyū'-s*a*)
Mélisande (mā"-lĭ"-zahnd')
Menelaus (měn"-*i*-lā'-ŭs)
Mephistopheles (měf"-ĭs-tŏf'-*i*-lēz)
Minotaur (mĭn'-o-tawr)
Mnemosyne (nē-mŏs'-*i*-nē)
Moloch (mō'-lŏk)
Morpheus (môr'-fyūs *or*
 môr'-f*i*-ŭs)
Munchausen (mŭn-chaw'-zěn)
 (*Ger.*, Münchhausen, münĸ'-
 how"-zěn)
Myrmidon (mûr'-m*i*-dŏn)
Nausicaa (naw-sĭk'-*i*-a *or*
 now-sĭk'-*i*-a)
Neoptolemus (nē"-ŏp-tŏl'-*i*-mŭs)
Nereid (nē'-ri-ĭd)
Nereus (nē'-rōōs *or* nē'-ri-ŭs)
Nibelung (nē-b*a*-lōōng)

Nibelungenlied (nē'-ba-lōŏng"-ĕn-lēt")

Nike (nī'-kē)

Niobe (nī'-o-bĕ)

Oceanus (ō-sē'-a-nŭs)

Odysseus (ō-dĭs'-syūs or ō-dĭs'-i-ŭs)

Odyssey (ŏd'-i-sĭ)

Oedipus (ē'-dĭ-pŭs or ĕd'-ĭ-pŭs)

Oeneus (ē'-nyūs)

Oenone (ē-nō'-ne)

Ophir (ō'-fer)

Orpheus (ôr'-fyūs or ôr'-fi-ŭs)

Osiris (ō-sī'-rĭs)

Ossian (ŏsh'-an)

Ouida (wē'-da)

Panope (păn'-o-pĭ)

Pantagruel (păn-tăg'-rōō-ĕl)

Panurge (păn-ûrj')

Parthenope (pahr-thĕn'-o-pē)

Pasiphae (pa-sĭf'-a-ē)

Patroclus (pa-trō'-klŭs)

Pegasus (pĕg'-a-sŭs)

Peleus (pē'-lyūs or pē'-li-ŭs)

Pelion (pē'-li-ŏn)

Pelleas (pĕl"-ā"-ahs')

Pelops (pē'-lŏps)

Penates (pe-nā'-tēz)

Penelope (pe-nĕl'-o-pe)

Pentateuch (pĕn'-ta-tyūk")

Penthesilea (pĕn"-thĕs-ĭ-lē'-a)

Perdita (pûr'-di-ta)

Persephone (pûr-sĕf'-o-nē)

Perseus (pûr'-syūs or pûr'-si-ŭs)

Phaedra (fē'-dra)

Phaethon (fā'-i-thŏn)

Pharaoh (fā'-rō or fâ'-rō)

Philemon (fī-lē'-mon)

Philoctetes (fĭl"-ŏk-tē'-tēz)

Philomela (fĭl"-o-mē'-la)

Phlegethon (flĕg'-i-thŏn or flĕj'-i-thŏn)

Phoebus (fē'-bŭs)

Pierian (pī-ē'-rĭ-an)

Pindaric (pĭn-dăr'-ĭk)

Polydamas (pŏl"-i-dā'-mas)

Polynices (pŏl"-i-nī'-sēz)

Polyphemus (pŏl"-i-fē'-mŭs)

Polyxena (po-lĭks'-i-na)

Porthos (Fr., pōr"-tōs'; Eng., pōr'-thŏs)

Portia (pōr'-sha or pōr'-shi-a)

Poseidon (po-sī'-dŏn)

Priapus (prī-ā'-pŭs)

Procne (prŏk'-ne)

Procrustes (pro-krŭs'-tēz)

Prometheus (pro-mē'-thyūs or pro-mē'-thi-ŭs)

Proserpina (pro-sûr'-pĭ-na)

Proserpine (pro-sûr'-pĭ-nē or prŏs'-er-pīn)

Protesilaus (pro-tĕs"-i-lā'-ŭs)

Proteus (prō'-tyūs or prō'-ti-ŭs)

Psyche (sī'-ke)

Pyramus (pĭr'-a-mŭs)

Pyrrha (pĭr'-a)

Quo Vadis (kwō vah'-dĭs or kwō vā'-dĭs)

Romola (rŏm'-o-la)

Romulus (rŏm'-yū-lŭs)

Rubáiyát (rōō-bī"-yaht' or rōō-bī'-yaht)

Sapphira (sa-fī'-ra)

Sappho (săf'-ō)

Scheherazade (she-hā"-rā-zah'-de)

Scylla (sĭl'-a)

Semele (sĕm'-i-lē)

Sibyl (sĭb'-ĭl)

Siegfried (Ger., zēk'-frēt; Eng., sēg'-frēd)

Sisyphus (sĭs'-*i*-fŭs)
Siva (shē'-v*a* or sē'-v*a*)
Stygian (stĭj'-ĭ-*a*n)
Styx (stĭks)
Symplegades (sĭm-plĕg'-*a*-dēz)
Tannhauser (tahn'-hoi″-zer)
Tartarus (tahr'-t*a*-rŭs)
Telemachus (t*e*-lĕm'-*a*-kŭs)
Tereus (tē'-rōōs or tē'-ri-ŭs)
Terpsichore (tûrp-sĭk'-*o*-rē)
Tethys (tē'-*th*ĭs)
Teucer (tyū'-ser)
Teufelsdrockh (toi'-fĕlz-drûk″)
Thaïs (*Fr.*, tah'-ēs; *Eng.*, *th*ā'-ĭs)
Thersites (*th*ûr-sī'-tēz)
Theseus (*th*ē'-syūs or *th*ē'-si-ŭs)
Thetis (*th*ē'-tĭs)
Thisbe (*th*ĭz'-bē)
Thyestes (*th*ī-ĕs'-tēz)
Thyrsis (*th*ûr'-sĭs)
Tisiphone (tĭ-sĭf'-*o*-nē)

Titania (t*i*-tā'-n*i*-*a* or
  t*i*-tah'-n*i*-*a*)
Tithonus (t*i*-*th*ō'-nŭs)
Triptolemus (trĭp-tŏl'-*i*-mŭs)
Trovatore (*It.*, trō″-vah-tō'-rā)
Tybalt (tĭb'-*a*lt)
Typhoeus (tī-fō'-yūs)
Uriah (yōō-rī'-*a*)
Uriel (yōō'-rĭ-ĕl)
Viola (vī'-*o*-l*a* or vī-ō'-l*a*)
(Die) Walküre (dē vahl-kür'-*e*)
Xanadu (zăn'-*a*-dōō)
Ygdrasil (ĭg'-dr*a*-sĭl)
Yorick (yôr'-ĭk)
Yseulte (ē″-sûlt')
Zarathustra (zah″-r*a*-*th*ōōs'-tr*a*)
Zephyrus (zĕf'-ĭ-rŭs)
Zeus (zyūs)
Zoë (zō'-*i*)
Zuleika (zōō-lā'-kah or
  zōō-lī'-kah)

IV. MISCELLANEOUS NAMES

Algonquin (ăl-gŏng'-kĭn)
Amherst (ăm'-erst)
Apache (*a*-păch'-*i*)
Arab (ăr'-*a*b)
Aramaic (ăr″-*a*-mā'-ĭk)
Arapahoe (*a*-răp'-*a*-hō)
Areopagus (ā″-ri-ŏp'-*a*-gŭs or
  ăr″-*i*-ŏp'-*a*-gŭs)
Aries (ā'-rĭ-ēz)
Aryan (ăr'-ĭ-*a*n or ahr'-y*a*n)
Ave Maria (ah'-vā mah-rē'-ah)
Baptist (băp'-tĭst)
Bastille (băs-tēl')
Bedouin (bĕd'-ōō-ĭn or bĕd'-ōō-ēn)
Boche (bōsh)
Bodleian (bŏd-lē'-*a*n or bŏd'-li-*a*n)

Boer (bōōr or bōr)
Bohea (bō-hē')
Bolshevik (bŏl'-shē-vĭk or
  bōl'-shē-vĭk)
Bowdoin (bō'-d'n)
Braille (brāl)
Byzantine (b*i*-zăn'-tĭn or
  bĭz'-*a*n-tĭn)
Cambrian (kăm'-bri-*a*n)
Capricorn (kăp″-rĭ-kôrn')
Capuchin (kăp'-yū-chĭn or
  kăp″-yū-shēn')
Caucasian (kaw-kā'-shan or
  kaw-kā'-zh*a*n or kaw-kăsh'-*a*n
  or kaw-kăzh'-*a*n)
Celtic (sĕl'-tĭk or kĕl'-tĭk)

Chippewa (chĭp'-ĭ-waw)
Chisholm (chĭz'-am)
Christendom (krĭs'-'n-dŭm)
Colosseum (kŏl"-ŏ-sē'-ŭm)
Comanche (ko-mắn'-chi)
Croat (krō'-ăt)
Croatian (krō-ā'-shan)
Czech (chĕk)
Damascene (dăm"-a-sēn')
Eiffel (ā"-fĕl')
Epicurean (ĕp"-ĭ-kyū-rē'-an)
Faneuil *Hall* (făn'-'l or făn'-yĕl or fŭn'-'l)
Fascisti (fah-shēs'-tĭ)
February (fĕb'-rŏŏ-ĕ-rĭ)
Fenian (fē'-ni-an)
Gael (gāl)
Gaelic (gāl'-ĭk)
Gallic (găl'-ĭk)
Gentile (jĕn'-tīl)
Gnostic (nŏs'-tĭk)
Gotham (gŏth'-am or gō'-tham)
Gothic (gŏth'-ĭk)
Hawaiian (hah-wī'-yan)
Hebraism (hē'-bra-ĭzm)
Hellene (hĕl-lēn')
Hellenic (hĕ-lĕn'-ĭk)
Huguenot (hyū'-ga-nŏt)
Iroquois (ĭr"-o-kwoi')
Islam (ĭs'-lahm or ĭz'-lahm)
Israel (ĭz'-ri-ĕl)
Italian (i-tăl'-yan)
Jacobean (jăk"-o-bē'-an)
Jacobin (jăk'-o-bĭn)
Jacobite (jăk'-o-bīt)
Jesuit (jĕz'-yŏŏ-ĭt)
Kafir (kăf'-er)
Kanaka (ka-nah'-ka or ka-năk'-a)
Magdalen (măg'-da-lĭn)
Magdalen(e) *College* (mawd'·lĭn)

Magdalene (măg"-da-lēn or măg"-da-lē'-nē)
Magi (mā'-jī)
Magog (mā'-gŏg)
Magyar (*Hun.*, mŏd'-yŏr; *Eng.*, măg'-yahr or măj'-yahr)
Maori (mah'-o-ri or mow'-rĭ)
Marseillaise (*Fr.*, mahr"-sĕ"-yāz'; *Eng.*, mahr"-sĕ-lāz')
Maya (mah'-ya)
Messiah (mĕ-sī'-a)
Messianic (mĕs"-i-ăn'-ĭk)
Messrs. (mĕs'-erz or mĕs'-yerz)
Michaelmas (mĭk'-el-mas)
Miserere (mĭz"-a-rē'-re or mĭz"-a-rā'-re)
Mohican (mo-hē'-kan)
Navajo (năv'-a-hō)
Nirvana (nĭr-vah'-na)
Notre Dame (nō"-tr' dahm')
Osage (ō-sāj' or ō'-sāj)
Pall Mall (păl măl')
Philistine (fi-lĭs'-tĭn or fĭl'-is-tĭn)
Pisces (pĭs'-ēz)
Pompeian (pŏm-pā'-yan or pŏm-pē'-yan)
Protean (prō'-te-an or prō-tē'-an)
Provençal (prō"-vahn"-sahl')
Punic (pyū'-nĭk)
Romany (rŏm'-a-nĭ)
Sagittarius (săj"-i-tā'-ri-ŭs)
Saturn (săt'-ûrn)
Seidlitz (sĕd'-lĭtz)
Semite (sĕm'-īt)
Semitic (si-mĭt'-ĭk)
Septuagint (sĕp'-tyū-a-jĭnt)
Shangri-la (shahng'-grĭ-lah")
Shoshone (sho-shō'-ni)
Sinn Fein (shēn fān')
Sioux (sōō)
Sirius (sĭr'-ĭ-ŭs)

Sorbonne (sôr″-bŏn′)
Soult (sōōlt)
Stoic (stō′-ĭk)
Tatar (tah′-ter)
Tibetan (tĭ-bĕt′-an *or* tĭb′-ĕt-an)

Tophet (tō′-fĕt)
Tremont (tri-mŏnt′)
Uranus (yōō′-ra-nŭs)
Wednesday (wĕnz′-di)
Wilhelmina (wĭl″-hĕl-mē′-na)

PART V

A Guide to the Pronunciation and Meaning of Familiar Foreign Words and Phrases

NOTE. Many foreign words, particularly such French words as *amateur, encore, ensemble,* and others, have been so thoroughly absorbed into English that they are included in the lists of English words, as is customary in standard dictionaries, and are therefore not repeated here. The pronunciation indicated for the words given below is that most commonly used in English, rather than the exact foreign pronunciation. Similarly, the meanings given here are not necessarily the most literal translations, but do indicate the exact sense in which the foreign word or expression is used in English conversation and writing.

ad infinitum   (*Lat.,* ăd ĭn″-fĭ-nī′-tŭm)

Without limit.

ad interim   (*Lat.,* ăd ĭn′-te-rĭm)

For the interval.

ad valorem   (*Lat.,* ăd va-lō′-rĕm)

Referring to taxes: *In proportion to invoiced value of goods.*

agenda   (*Lat.,* a-jĕn′-da)

Memoranda of items to be considered at a meeting.

agent provocateur
(*Fr.,* ah″-zhahN′ prō″-vo″-kah″-tûr′)

A person employed to detect suspected offenders by associating with them and enticing them to commit illegal acts.

aide-de-camp
(*Fr.,* ād′-de-kahN′ *or* ād′-de-kămp″)

An officer attached to a general to carry orders, etc., for him.

337

à la carte (*Fr.*, ah la kahrt′)

By the bill of fare; dishes with a stated price for each (contrasted with **table d'hôte**).

à la mode (*Fr.*, ah″ la mōd′)

In the fashion; fashionable.

a posteriori (*Lat.*, ā″ pōs-tē″-rĭ-ō′-rī)

From effect to cause, from facts to generalizations, inductively (applied to reasoning). Contrasted with **a priori.**

a priori (*Lat.*, ā″ prī-ō′-rī)

From cause to effect, deductively (applied to reasoning). By extension the phrase is also used to mean *presumptively, to the best of one's knowledge.*

argot (*Fr.*, ahr′-gō *or* ahr′-got)

Jargon, slang (of a group, especially of thieves).

atelier (*Fr.*, ăt′-el-yā)

Workshop, studio.

attaché (*Fr.*, ăt″-a-shā′ *or* a-tăsh′-ā)

One attached to a suite or staff, as of an ambassador.

aubade (*Fr.*, o-bahd′)

A morning concert or serenade.

au courant (*Fr.*, ō″ kōō″-rahɴ′)

Up to date, well informed.

auld lang syne (*Scot.*, awld lăng sīn)

"The good old times."

au naturel (*Fr.*, ō″ nah″-tyü-rĕl′)

In natural form; (cooked) in the simplest way.

aviso (*Sp.*, a-vī′-zō)

Notification; dispatch-boat.

belles-lettres (*Fr.*, bĕl″-lĕt′-r′)

Writings or studies of a purely literary sort.

bête noire (*Fr.*, bāt″ nwahr′)

A person or thing that one specially dislikes.

bijou (*Fr.*, bē′-zhōō″)

Jewel; exquisite trinket.

billet doux (*Fr.*, bĭl′-ā dōō′)

A love letter.

bona fide (*Lat.*, bō′-na fī′-de)

Genuine, sincere.

bon mot (*Fr.,* bôn" mō')	A witty remark.
bon vivant (*Fr.,* bôn" vē"-vahn')	A lover of good living.
carpe diem (*Lat.,* kahr'-pe dī'-em)	Literally, seize the day. Enjoy the present moment.
caveat (*Lat.,* kā'-vi-ăt)	Literally, let him beware. A warning or caution.
chaise longue (*Fr.,* shāz" lông')	Literally, long chair. An elongated seat or couch.
chargé d'affaires (*Fr.,* shahr"-zhā' da-fâr')	A deputy or temporary substitute for an ambassador; a lesser diplomatic official.
charlotte russe (*Fr.,* shahr'-lot rōōs')	A dessert of cake with a whipped-cream or custard filling.
chef d'oeuvre (*Fr.,* shĕ" dû-vr')	A masterpiece.
coup de grâce (*Fr.,* kōō" de grahs')	A merciful blow; a death blow; the finishing stroke.
coup d'état (*Fr.,* kōō" dā-tah')	A violent or illegal change in the government of a country; hence, any unexpected stroke of policy.
cul de sac (*Fr.,* kŏol' de săk')	A blind alley; a passage with only one outlet.
de jure (*Lat.,* dē jōō'-re)	By right; by a lawful title.
de trop (*Fr.,* de trō')	Not wanted; in the way.
diseur (*Fr.,* dē"-zûr')	A professional reciter.
diseuse (*Fr.,* dē"-zûs')	Feminine of **diseur.**
dolce far niente (*It.,* dol'-chā fahr nyĕn'-tā)	Literally, pleasant to do nothing. Pleasant idleness.
élan (*Fr.,* ā"-lahn')	Vivacity; urge for action.
élan vital (*Fr.,* ā"-lahn' vē"-tahl')	Vital force; the inner creative principle in organisms.

embonpoint (*Fr.*, ahn″-bôn″-pwăn′)

Plumpness, stoutness.

entente cordiale
(*Fr.*, ahn″-tahɴt′ kôr″-dyahl′)

Cordial understanding between two countries.

entremets (*Fr.*, ahn′-tre-mā)

Literally, between dishes. Side dishes; dainties, sweets.

ersatz (*Ger.*, ĕr-zahts′)

Substitute.

esprit de corps (*Fr.*, ĕs″-prē′ de kôr′)

Loyalty to the interests of a group to which one belongs.

exeunt omnes (*Lat.*, ĕks′-e-ŭnt ŏm′-nēz)

Literally, all go out. Stage direction: all leave the stage.

ex officio (*Lat.*, ĕks o-fĭsh′-ĭ-ō)

By virtue of or because of one's office.

faux pas (*Fr.*, fō″ pah′)

A false step; especially, a compromising act, or offense against social conventions.

fleur-de-lis
(*Fr.*, flûr″-de-lē′ *or* flûr″-de-lēs′)

Literally, flower of the lily. The iris; the conventionalized iris on the royal arms of France.

genius loci (*Lat.*, jē′-nĭ-us lō′-sī)

The attendant spirit of a place; hence, the associations, etc., of that place.

habeas corpus (*Lat.*, hā′-bi-as kôr′-pŭs)

Literally, (that) you may have the body. A writ requiring a person to be brought before a court or judge.

hors de combat (*Fr.*, ôr″ de kôn″-bah′)

Out of the fight; disabled.

hors d'oeuvres (*Fr.*, ôr″ dû′-vr′)

A relish or appetizer served usually before a meal.

ibidem (*Lat.*, ĭ-bī′-dĕm; *abbr.*, "**ibid.**")

In the same place.

idée fixe (*Fr.*, ē″-dā′ fēks′)

A fixed idea; an idea that dominates the entire mind.

idem (*Lat.*, ī′-dĕm; *abbr.*, "**id.**")

The same; the same word; (in) the same author.

id est (*Lat.*, ĭd ĕst; *abbr.*, "**i.e.**")

That is.

imprimatur (*Lat.*, ĭm″-prĭ-mä′-ter)

Literally, let it be printed. Official license to print or publish a book.

joie de vivre (*Fr.*, zhwah′ de vē′-vr′)

Keen enjoyment of life.

laissez faire (*Fr.*, lĕ-sā fâr′)

Letting events take their own course.

mandamus (*Lat.*, măn-dā′-mŭs)

Literally, we command. A higher court's writ conveying orders to a lower court; any court order issued to enforce performance of a public duty.

mise en scène (*Fr.*, mē″-zahN sân′)

The scenery and properties used in presenting a play; the surroundings of an event.

mot juste (*Fr.*, mō zhüst)

The exactly right word.

nisi (*Lat.*, nī′-sī)

Literally, unless; if not. A court decree valid *unless* cause is shown for rescinding it before a given time.

noblesse oblige
(*Fr.*, nō″-blĕs′ ō″-blēzh′)

Nobility obligates; privilege of high rank or birth entails responsibility.

nocturne (*Fr.*, nŏk′-tûrn)

A dreamy musical composition; in painting, a night scene.

non sequitur (*Lat.*, nŏn sĕk′-wĭ-ter)

Literally, it does not follow. A conclusion or inference that does not follow from a previous statement from which it is supposed to be inferred.

nuncio (*It.*, nŭn′-shĭ-ō)

The Pope's permanent official representative at a foreign seat of government.

outré (*Fr.*, ōō″-trā′)

Eccentric; extravagant.

pace (*Lat.*, pā'-sĭ)

By the leave of; used in expressing polite disagreement, as, "*pace* Dr. Wilson."

par excellence (*Fr.*, pahr ĕk'-se-lahns)

Pre-eminently, outstandingly.

parfait (*Fr.*, pahr-fā')

A frozen dessert of whipped cream, eggs, sirup, etc.

pari passu (*Lat.*, păr'-ĭ păs'-ōō)

With equal pace; simultaneously and equally.

parvenu (*Fr.*, pahr'-ve-nyū)

A person who has risen from obscurity, usually by the acquisition of wealth; an upstart.

passé (*Fr.*, pă-sā')

Past; past one's prime; behind the times, outmoded.

pâté de foie gras
(*Fr.*, pah"-tā' de fwah" grah')

A paste of fattened goose liver.

patois (*Fr.*, păt'-wah)

Dialect; provincial speech.

pièce de résistance
(*Fr.*, pyĕs" de rā"-zēs"-tahℕs')

The most important dish of a meal; hence, the most important item of a collection.

pied-à-terre (*Fr.*, pyā"-dah-târ')

A temporary lodging.

prima facie (*Lat.*, prī'-ma fā'-shĭ-ē)

At first considering, before there has been time for inquiry or examination.

pro tempore
(*Lat.*, prō tĕm'-po-re)

For the time being; temporarily. (*Abbr.* "**pro tem.**")

qui vive (*Fr.*, kē vēv')

The French sentry's challenge (compare the English, "Who goes there?"). "On the *qui vive*" means *on the alert.*

quod erat demonstrandum
(*Lat.*, kwōd ĕr'-ăt dĕm"-ŏn-străn'-dŭm; *abbr.*, "**Q.E.D.**")

Literally, which was the thing to be demonstrated. A formula appended at the end of a proof in geometry.

raison d'être ⟨*Fr.*, rā″-zôN′ dâ′-tr′)

The cause or justification of a thing's existence.

requiescat in pace
  (*Lat.*, rĕk″-wĭ-ĕs′-kăt ĭn pā′-sĭ)

May he (or she) rest in peace.

sang-froid (*Fr.*, sahN″-frwah′)

Literally, cold blood. Coolness in danger or difficulty.

savoir faire (*Fr.*, să″-vwahr′ fâr′)

The ability to do or say the right thing readily and gracefully.

scherzo (*It.*, skĕr′-tsō)

A gay movement of a sonata, symphony, etc.

sine die (*Lat.*, sī-ne dī′-ē)

In parliamentary procedure, without appointing a day to assemble again.

sine qua non (*Lat.*, sī′-ne kwä nŏn′)

Literally, without which not. An indispensable condition or qualification.

sotto voce (*It.*, sŏt′-ō vō′-chä)

Under the breath; in an undertone.

status quo (*Lat.*, stā′-tŭs kwō)

The state of affairs as it has been and is.

table d'hôte (*Fr.*, tah′-b'l dōt′)

Literally, table of the landlord. A meal at a restaurant or hotel provided at a fixed price (the opposite of **à la carte**).

tête-à-tête (*Fr.*, tāt-*a*-tāt′)

Literally, head to head. A private or confidential conversation.

tutoyer (*Fr.*, tyü″-twah″-yā′)

From *Fr.*, *tu*, thou. To speak familiarly to a person.

vice versa (*Lat.*, vī′-se vûr′-sa)

The other way round.

videlicet (*Lat.*, vĭ-dĕl′-ĭ-sĕt;
  abbr., "**viz.**", *usually read "namely"*)

Literally, one may or can see. To wit; that is to say; namely.

visa (*Fr.*, vē′-za)
 [or **visé** (*Fr.*, vē′-zā)]

An endorsement on a passport showing approval by the proper authority.

viva (*It.*, vē′-vah)

Long live ———! Long life to him!

viva voce (*Lat.*, vī′-va vō′-se)

By word of mouth; orally.

Wanderjahr (*Ger.*, vahn′-der-yahr″)

Year of wandering; period of travel of a student or artisan during apprenticeship.

Wanderlust
 (*Ger.*, vahn′-der-lōōst)

A strong longing for wandering or travel.

Weltanschauung
 (*Ger.*, vĕlt′-ahn′-show″-ōong)

A philosophy that seeks to give an explanation of the purpose of the world as a whole.

Weltansicht (*Ger.*, vĕlt′-ahn″-zĭkt)

A view or apprehension of the universe as a whole.

Weltpolitik (*Ger.*, vĕlt′-po-lĭ-tēk′)

Literally, world politics or policy. International politics.

Weltschmerz (*Ger.*, vĕlt′-shmĕrts″)

Sadness resulting from a pessimistic view of the world and life.

Zeitgeist (*Ger.*, tsīt′-gīst″)

The spirit of the time; the general trend of thought and feeling in a period of time.